Methodological Issues in Applied Social Psychology

SOCIAL PSYCHOLOGICAL APPLICATIONS TO SOCIAL ISSUES

Published under the auspices of the
Society for the Psychological Study of Social Issues

A Continuation Order Plan is available for this series. A continuation order will bring delivery of each new volume immediately upon publication. Volumes are billed only upon actual shipment. For further information please contact the publisher.

Methodological Issues in Applied Social Psychology

Edited by
Fred B. Bryant, John Edwards, R. Scott Tindale, Emil J. Posavac, Linda Heath, Eaaron Henderson, and Yolanda Suarez-Balcazar

Loyola University of Chicago
Chicago, Illinois

A project of the faculty and students
in the Applied Social Psychology Graduate Program
at Loyola University of Chicago
published under the auspices of the
Society for the Psychological Study of Social Issues

Plenum Press • New York and London

Library of Congress Cataloging-in-Publication Data

Methodological issues in applied social psychology / edited by Fred B.
Bryant ... [et al.].
     p.   cm. -- (Social psychological applications to social issues
; v. 2)
     "A project of the faculty and students in the Applied Social
Psychology Graduate Program at Loyola University of Chicago
published under the auspices of the Society for the Psychological
Study of Social Issues."
   Includes bibliographical references and index.
   ISBN 0-306-44173-X
   1. Social psychology--Methodology.   I. Bryant, Fred Boyd, 1952-
   II. Society for the Psychological Study of Social Issues.
III. Series.
   [DNLM: 1. Psychology, Social--methods.   HM 251 M592]
HM251.M4533   1992
302'.01--dc20
DNLM/DLC
for Library of Congress   92-21626
                                                              CIP

ISBN 0-306-44173-X

© 1992 Plenum Press, New York
A Division of Plenum Publishing Corporation
233 Spring Street, New York, N.Y. 10013

Printed in the United States of America

Editorial Advisory Board

Contributors

Fabricio E. Balcazar, University of Illinois at Chicago/UAP, Chicago, Illinois 60608

Peter M. Bentler, Department of Psychology, University of California, Los Angeles, California 90024

Leonard Bickman, Department of Psychology and Human Development, Vanderbilt University, Nashville, Tennessee 37203

Anita DeLongis, Department of Psychology, University of British Columbia, Vancouver, British Columbia V6T 1Z4 Canada

Stephen B. Fawcett, Department of Human Development, University of Kansas, Lawrence, Kansas 66045

Michelle Fine, CUNY Graduate School and University Center, New York, New York 10036

Kenneth J. Hemphill, Department of Psychology, University of British Columbia, Vancouver, British Columbia V6T 1Z4 Canada

Sara Kiesler, Department of Social and Decision Sciences, Carnegie Mellon University, Pittsburgh, Pennsylvania 15213

Darrin R. Lehman, Department of Psychology, University of British Columbia, Vancouver, British Columbia V6T 1Z4 Canada

Melvin M. Mark, Department of Psychology, Pennsylvania State University, University Park, Pennsylvania 16802

Jack McKillip, Department of Psychology, Southern Illinois University at Carbondale, Carbondale, Illinois 62901

Richard E. Olmstead, Department of Psychology, University of California, Los Angeles, California 90024

Emil J. Posavac, Department of Psychology, Loyola University of Chicago, Chicago, Illinois 60626

Lawrence J. Sanna, Department of Psychology, Pennsylvania State University, University Park, Pennsylvania 16802

R. Lance Shotland, Department of Psychology, Pennsylvania State University, University Park, Pennsylvania 16802

Joan E. Sieber, Department of Psychology, California State University, Hayward, California 94542

James L. Sorensen, Langley Porter Psychiatric Institute, University of California, San Francisco, California 94110

Lee Sproull, School of Management, Boston University, Boston, Massachusetts 02215

Yolanda Suarez-Balcazar, Department of Psychology, Loyola University of Chicago, Chicago, Illinois 60626

R. Scott Tindale, Department of Psychology, Loyola University of Chicago, Chicago, Illinois 60626

Virginia Vanderslice, Praxis Associates, Philadelphia, Pennsylvania 19119

David A. Vollrath, Division of Business and Economics, Indiana University at South Bend, South Bend, Indiana 46634

John Walsh, Department of Sociology, University of Illinois at Chicago, Chicago, Illinois 60680

Paul M. Wortman, Department of Psychology, State University of New York at Stony Brook, Stony Brook, New York 11794

Paul R. Yarnold, Division of General Internal Medicine, Northwestern University Medical School, Chicago, Illinois 60611

Preface

Many authors have argued that applying social psychology to the solution of real-world problems builds better theories. Observers have claimed, for example, that applied social psychology reveals more accurate principles of human behavior because its data are based on people in real-life circumstances (Helmreich, 1975; Saxe & Fine, 1980), provides an opportunity to assess the ecological validity of generalizations derived from laboratory research (Ellsworth, 1977; Leventhal, 1980), and discloses important gaps in existing theories (Fisher, 1982; Mayo & LaFrance, 1980). Undoubtedly, many concrete examples can be mustered in support of these claims.

But it also can be argued that applying social psychology to social issues and problems builds better research methods. Special methodological problems arise and new perspectives on old methodological problems emerge when researchers leave the laboratory and tackle social problems in real-world settings. Along the way, we not only improve existing research techniques but also develop new research tools, all of which enhance our ability to obtain valid results and thereby to understand and solve socially relevant problems. Indeed, Campbell and Stanley's (1966) seminal work on validity in research design grew out of the application of social science in field settings. In this spirit, the principal aim of this volume is to present examples of methodological advances being made as researchers apply social psychology in real-life settings.

Many methodological problems encountered in applied social psychological research have never before arisen in basic social psychological research. This is because of differences in objectives, settings, and research populations between the two fields. For example, applied research typically requires the establishment of clear, accepted operational definitions of dependent variables—a need that often dictates the assessment of multiple real-world behaviors, as opposed to laboratory analogues or simulations. This has led to the development of novel research techniques, such as structured diary methods, through which ongoing behaviors can be assessed over time in real-world settings (see Chapter 5, this volume, by DeLongis, Hemphill, & Lehman).

In addition, applied social psychologists often have a greater need than do basic social psychologists to determine the latency and duration of treatment effects in actual application, so as to maximize the policy relevance of results and to facilitate cost-benefit analysis. This has led to the refinement of research procedures, such as time series analysis, which can be used to study groups in real-life settings over long periods (see Chapter 6 by Mark, Sanna, & Shotland). Furthermore, in applied social research there is a greater need than in basic social research to explore variations in the ways treatments are implemented across sites and to discover unintended side effects that interventions may produce. This has led to the creation of techniques for using qualitative data reliably in empirical investigations (see Chapter 10 by Fine & Vanderslice).

Perhaps the thorniest methodological problem encountered in applied social research is the need to draw unequivocal inferences about cause and effect in field settings. The frequent inability to rely on randomized experimental designs in applied research has led to a heightened awareness of specific threats to valid inference and has spawned a host of creative strategies for reducing the plausibility of these threats (e.g., Cook & Campbell, 1979). It has also generated a variety of quasi-experimental research designs, such as the control construct design, that had been unavailable before (see Chapter 8 by McKillip).

This greater use of nonexperimental designs has also led to the refinement of existing analytic procedures, such as structural equations modeling, that are capable of detecting cause-and-effect relationships in longitudinal data (see Chapter 7 by Olmstead & Bentler). In addition, researchers have creatively applied to quasi-experimental data such techniques as meta-analysis that were previously used only with randomized studies, and have improved these procedures in the process (see Chapter 4 by Wortman). Other applied researchers have developed innovative statistical techniques for analyzing data from nontraditional research methods, such as "N-of-1" designs, that had previously lacked statistical conclusion validity (see Chapter 9 by Yarnold).

Because applied social research often takes place in established organizational settings, it frequently requires a wider range of research skills than does traditional basic research. Applied researchers, for example, have had to learn how to plan and negotiate research arrangements in real-world settings, so as to obtain required resources (see Chapter 1 by Bickman); how to define research problems and solutions in ways that incorporate the views and priorities of multiple stakeholders (see Chapter 2 by Suarez-Balcazar, Balcazar, & Fawcett and Chapter 10 by Fine & Vanderslice); and how to communicate research results effectively to those who can use them (see Chapter 13 by Posavac). Applied social psychologists have also confronted a morass of ethical dilemmas unique to the study of human behavior outside the laboratory, and the insights gained have enabled them to devise research procedures that are both ethical and valid in the real world (see Chapter 3 by Sieber & Sorensen).

Still other instances of methodological innovation in applied social psychology involve new methods that have sprung from advances in technology. A crucial catalyst in many of these cases has been the increased capability and availability of computers, which have made possible such new research techniques as computer-simulated "thought experiments" (see Chapter 11 by Tindale & Vollrath) and electronic field studies (see Chapter 12 by Kiesler, Walsh, & Sproull). One can only wonder what marvelous methodological inventions will evolve as this technology continues to develop.

The specific methodologies addressed in this volume range from commonly used procedures such as meta-analysis, time series designs, and structural equations modeling to less traditional approaches such as structured diary methods, control construct designs, and N-of-1 analyses. We have chosen these particular methodologies not because of their prevalence in the field, but rather because they represent the tremendous diversity of approaches to data collection that characterizes applied social psychology. Numerous other methods (e.g., experience-sampling procedures, panel designs, focus groups, large-scale surveys, and a wealth of quasi-experimental designs) could have been included but for space limitations.

Research methods are tools for building knowledge, and knowledge is a tool for solving problems. Thus, research methods are ultimately problem-solving tools. As with other types of human implements, current methods have evolved from earlier methods and have been shaped by the forces of contemporary need, creative ingenuity, and technological expertise (see Clark, 1974; Larsen, 1961). This evolution entails endless trial and error, through which modern research tools are gradually refined by repeated field testing, much like the process of natural selection (see Basalla, 1988; Gilfillan, 1970).

Methodological advances in applied social psychology are driven by the need to solve meaningful practical problems. Tools that function well on the drawing board or in the controlled confines of the laboratory often fail to operate under rigorous real-world conditions, and when existing tools are inadequate, the ingenious artisan either modifies them to suit current needs or fashions new tools to accomplish the task.

This book presents examples of methodological advances being made as researchers turn from basic to more applied work. The authors of these chapters focus on what they have learned about a particular research method by using it to study problems in real-world settings. Drawing on actual cases of research application, they discuss the specific problems they encountered, the potential solutions they considered, and the methodological lessons they learned through hard-won experience.

These methodological applications encompass a wide variety of different content areas. Within the domain of *health and medicine,* for example, methodological lessons are presented from research on drug treatment and health care programs (see Chapter 3 by Sieber & Sorensen), on the assessment of medical technology (see Chapter 4 by Wortman), on stress and coping (see Chapter 5 by DeLongis et al.), and on media campaigns for health promotion (see Chapter 8 by McKillip). Within the field of *community psychology,* methodological insights are presented from research on environmental obstacles to people with physical disabilities (see Chapter 2 by Suarez-Balcazar et al.), on the lives of "street people" (see Chapter 3 by Sieber & Sorensen), and on the impact of community action groups (see Chapter 6 by Mark et al.). Within the realm of *education,* methodological lessons are presented from research on school desegregation and minority achievement (see Chapter 4 by Wortman) and on the restructuring of schools and school systems (see Chapter 10 by Fine & Vanderslice). Within the area of *criminal justice,* methodological insights are presented from research on homicides and mass media violence (see Chapter 6 by Mark et al.) and on jury decision making (see Chapter 11 by Tindale & Vollrath). Within the domain of *interpersonal relations,* methodological lessons are presented from research on friendship development (see Chapter 7 by Olmstead & Bentler) and on the sharing of discretionary information in business organizations (see Chapter 12 by Kiesler et al.).

Although these applications have often yielded different methodological lessons, this variation is more a consequence of using different research methods than of studying different social problems. Methodological problems and solutions, like basic psychological processes, cross the boundaries of different content areas. Through cross-fertilization, lessons learned by researchers in one social-problem area may be used by researchers to avoid methodological problems in other areas.

Considered together, the chapters in this volume also cover many, if not all, aspects of the research process. The topics range from resource planning and problem identification to research design, data collection, analysis, and, finally, communication of results. In this sense, the volume represents a microcosm of the research process in applied social psychology.

The faculty and students of Loyola University's Applied Social Psychology Program are pleased to have the opportunity to work with the Society for the Psychological Study of Social Issues (SPSSI) and with Plenum Publishing Corporation in preparing this second volume in a series on social psychological processes and social issues. We hope that this book on methodological issues in applied social psychology will be useful to students and researchers in social psychology, by showing how the application of social psychology to social problems improves research methodology.

References

Basalla, G. (1988). *The evolution of technology.* New York: Cambridge University Press.

Campbell, D. T., & Stanley, J. C. (1966). *Experimental and quasi-experimental designs for research.* Chicago: Rand McNally.

Clark, R. W. (1974). *The scientific breakthrough: The impact of modern invention.* London: Nelson.

Cook, T. D., & Campbell, D. T. (1979). *Quasi-experimentation: Design and analysis issues for field settings.* Chicago: Rand McNally.

Ellsworth, P. C. (1977). From abstract ideas to concrete instances: Some guidelines for choosing natural research settings. *American Psychologist, 32,* 604–615.

Fisher, R. J. (1982). *Social psychology: An applied approach.* New York: St. Martin's Press.

Gilfillan, S. C. (1970). *The sociology of invention.* Cambridge, MA: MIT Press.

Helmreich, R. L. (1975). Applied social psychology: The unfulfilled promise. *Personality and Social Psychology Bulletin, 1,* 548–560.

Larsen, E. (1961). *A history of invention.* New York: Roy.

Leventhal, H. (1980). Applied social psychological research: The salvation of substantive social psychological theory. In R. F. Kidd & M. J. Saks (Eds.), *Advances in applied social psychology* (Vol. 1, pp. 190–193). Hillsdale, NJ: Erlbaum.

Mayo, C., & LaFrance, M. (1980). Toward an applicable social psychology. In R. F. Kidd & M. J. Saks (Eds.), *Advances in applied social psychology* (Vol. 1, pp. 81–96). Hillsdale, NJ: Erlbaum.

Saxe, L., & Fine, M. (1980). Reorienting social psychology toward application: A methodological analysis. In L. Bickman (Ed.), *Applied social psychology annual* (Vol. 1, pp. 71–91). Beverly Hills, CA: Sage.

Acknowledgments

This volume on methodological advances that stem from the application of social psychology is the product of the combined efforts of several organizations and of many individuals. It is the second in a planned series on applications of social psychological processes to social issues, and it involves the collaboration of SPSSI, Plenum Press, and Loyola University of Chicago's graduate program in applied social psychology.

We wish to thank the officers and publication committee of SPSSI for giving us the opportunity to edit this series and for their work and support in bringing to fruition the present collection of chapters. We would also like to thank the editorial and production staffs of Plenum Press, especially Eliot Werner, for their help in this project.

We extend our gratitude for their contributions in creating this book to the students in our graduate program who actively participated in researching possible topics and in writing reviews of initial drafts: Denise Archambault, Jill Carmody, Debbie Dilworth, Suzanne Farrell, Joseph Filkins, Marie MacKay, David Njus, Maureen O'Brien, Liz Sanders, Susan Sheffey, Christine Smith, Ed Torpy, Jerry Vasilias, and Kyle Weeks.

We gratefully acknowledge the 26 members of our Editorial Advisory Board for their advice and support in this particular project and for their constructive reviews of chapter drafts. We are especially grateful to Sharon Brehm, Marilynn Brewer, James H. Davis, Christine Dunkel-Schetter, Ronald Fisher, Sara Kiesler, Barbara Loken, Geoffrey Maruyama, Joseph McGrath, Stuart Oskamp, Amado Padilla, Michael Pallak, Daniel Perlman, Linda Perloff, Dennis Rosenbaum, Michael Saks, and Tom Tyler. We are also indebted to our colleagues Leonard Bickman, Al DeWolfe, Joe Durlak, Maryse Richards, and Judith Wittner for their helpful feedback on this project and on initial drafts of several of these chapters.

Finally, and most important, we thank the 25 authors for their efforts. Their hard work and creativity provide fresh insights into the research methods of applied social psychology and better enable us to use these valuable tools effectively.

FRED B. BRYANT
JOHN EDWARDS
R. SCOTT TINDALE
EMIL J. POSAVAC
LINDA HEATH
EAARON HENDERSON
YOLANDA SUAREZ-BALCAZAR

Contents

3. Ethical Issues in Community-Based Research and Intervention 43

Joan E. Sieber and James L. Sorensen

4. Lessons from the Meta-Analysis of Quasi-Experiments 65

Paul M. Wortman

9. Statistical Analysis for Single-Case Designs

Paul R. Yarnold

10. Qualitative Activist Research: Reflections on Methods and Politics

Michelle Fine and Virginia Vanderslice

11. "Thought Experiments" and Applied Social Psychology 219

R. Scott Tindale and David A. Vollrath

12. Computer Networks in Field Research 239

Sara Kiesler, John Walsh, and Lee Sproull

13. Communicating Applied Social Psychology to Users: A Challenge and an Art 269

Emil J. Posavac

1

Resource Planning for Applied Research

Leonard Bickman

Most books on research methods do not discuss the resources needed to conduct the research, nor is this topic usually covered in courses on research. However, applied research requires consideration of the realistic constraints on the research process. This chapter is intended to assist the researcher in dealing with the constraints imposed by limited resources common in almost all research. Before making final decisions about the specific design to use and the type of data collection procedures to employ, the investigator must take into account the resources available and the constraints on these resources. Planning and care in implementing the research can be as important as the research questions asked. This chapter will describe how to consider resource questions before making final design and data collection decisions. In particular, this chapter will consider the following resources:

- *Data*. What are the sources of information needed and how will they be obtained?
- *Time*. How much time is required to conduct the entire research project and its elements?
- *Personnel*. How many researchers are needed and what are their skills?
- *Money*. How much money is needed to plan and implement the research and in what categories

It should be noted that this chapter, because of space limitations, cannot deal with the critical issue of where and how to obtain resources to conduct applied

Leonard Bickman • Department of Psychology and Human Development, Vanderbilt University, Nashville, Tennessee 37203.
Methodological Issues in Applied Psychology, edited by Bryant et al. Plenum Press, New York, 1992.

research. The reader is directed to other sources, such as Baron's chapter in *The Compleat Academic* (1987), or the *APA Guide to Research Support* (Herring, 1987).

Data as a Resource

The most important resource for any research project is the data used to answer the research question. Data for research can be obtained primarily in two ways: from original data collected by the investigator and from already-existing data. First the issues of primary data collection, and then secondary data analysis, will be discussed.

Primary Data Collection

This section addresses five major issues in planning for primary data collection: site selection, authorization, the data collection process, accessibility, and other support needed.

Site Selection

Applied and basic research differ on a number of dimensions, but probably the most salient difference is the location of the research (Bickman, 1981). In most cases, basic research will take place in a site that is controlled by the investigator, usually a psychological laboratory or a college classroom. Applied research can occur in diverse settings. Sometimes the site is specified by the research question, as when the researcher is asked to assess the functioning of a specific program. In other cases, the investigator has the option of choosing among one or more sites.

The selection of appropriate sites is of utmost importance to the success of the project. For example, Grady and Wallston (1988) devote a chapter in their book on health research to a description of health care settings. They point out that health care settings differ in terms of whether they are concerned with sickness or wellness, and if the former, whether they focus on acute care, chronic care, or rehabilitation. The choice of setting will determine the types of individuals or patients studied and the events to observe. The setting will have a clear impact on the research not only in defining the population studied, but also in formulating the research question addressed, the research design implemented, the measures used, and the inferences that can be drawn from the study. For example, if we were studying the correlation of age with certain sicknesses, we would come to different conclusions if we studied the elderly in Golden Age

Clubs rather than in nursing homes. The latter will have sicker and less independent individuals. Choosing settings can also determine whether there are enough research participants available. Thus, a researcher would usually not want to select a health club to implement a smoking cessation program because most of the members of the club probably do not smoke.

Another example of an emphasis on settings is provided by Jorgensen's (1989) text on participant observation. Jorgensen characterizes settings as differing on visibility and openness. A visible setting is one that is available to the public. Some of these settings, such as universities and hospitals, may be visible enough to be listed in the phone directory. Other visible settings may be less public, but accessible, and include areas that involve drugs or prostitution that police know about. Invisible settings are hidden and concealed from outsiders. These settings include both legal and illegal activities. In most organizations, there are groups of individuals whose activities are kept secret from nonmembers and, in some cases, even from members. A setting's openness will depend upon the degree of negotiation that is required for access, but visibility and openness are not the same. A university is a visible institution, but the deliberations in the provost's office concerning faculty salaries are not open to the faculty, let alone the general public. Highly visible settings may also contain less visible activities. For example, public parks are often a location for illicit sexual activities.

A distinction between "front stage" and "backstage" made by Goffman (1959) also helps distinguish settings. Front stage activities are available to anyone, while backstage entrance is limited. Thus, the courtroom in a trial is the front stage activity that is open to anyone who can obtain a seat. Entrance to the judge's chamber is more limited, presence during lawyer–client conferences is even more restricted, and presence as an observer during jury deliberations is impossible. The researcher needs to assess the openness of the setting before taking the next step: seeking authorization for the research.

Authorization

Even totally open and visible settings usually require some degree of authorization for data collection. Public space may not be as totally available to the researcher as it may seem. For example, it is a good idea to notify the authorities if the research team is going to be present in a public setting for some time. While the researcher's presence is certainly not illegal and should not require permission to conduct observations or interviews, residents of the area may become suspicious and call the police. For example, in a study I directed, interviews were conducted in a rural area. The interviewers, being unfamiliar with the area (which lacked street signs), drove through the same stretch of road repeatedly looking for particular houses. Residents, not accustomed to seeing "strange" cars, called the sheriff. The interviewers were stopped and taken to the sheriff's station for questioning. Calls were made to the university to verify the interviewers' legitimacy. A simple letter or call to each local law enforcement office would have prevented this problem.

If the setting is a closed one, the researcher will be required to obtain the permission of the individuals who control or believe they control access. (Chapter 3, this volume, by Sieber and Sorensen discusses the ethical considerations of seeking cooperation from these "gatekeepers.") If there are a number of sites that are eligible for participation, and they are within one organization, then it behooves the researcher to explore the independence of these sites from the parent organization. In planning a study of bystander reactions to staged shoplifting (Bickman & Rosenbaum, 1977; Bickman, 1984), I had to obtain the cooperation of the supermarket in which the crime was to be staged. I had the choice of contacting the headquarters of the company or approaching each supermarket manager for permission to conduct the study. If I approached the main office first and were refused permission, then the project could not be implemented. However, if one local manager refused, then another one could be approached. In this case, I first approached a local manager who informed me that he could not participate without headquarters' approval. The manager, however, was persuaded to provide a supporting letter to accompany my request for permission. A personal visit to the head of security helped obtain the necessary cooperation.

Not only does the planner need to know at which level of the organization to negotiate, but also which individuals to approach. Again, this will take some intelligence gathering. Personal contacts help since authorities are usually more likely to meet and be cooperative if the researcher is recommended by someone they know and trust. Thus, the investigator should search for some connection to the organization. If the planner is at a university, then it is possible that someone on the board of trustees is an officer of the organization. If so, contact with the university's development office is advisable. Is the organization part of the federal bureaucracy? If so, then contact with a congressional office might help. The idea is to obtain advance recommendations from credible sources and hence to avoid approaching an organization cold.

Permission from a central authority does not necessarily imply cooperation from the sites needed for data collection. Nowhere is this more evident than in state–county working relationships. Often central approval will be required just to approach local sites. However, the investigator should not erroneously believe that central approval guarantees cooperation from those lower down on the organization's hierarchy. This belief can lead the investigator into behaving in an insensitive manner. Those at the upper levels of an organization tend to believe they have more power than they actually wield. A wise investigator will put a great deal of effort into obtaining cooperation at the local level. At this level are the individuals who feel they control that environment and with whom the investigator will be interacting during the data collection phase. The persons in this environment will not only include management, but the workers and their representatives (e.g., unions). Keeping them informed of the purpose and progress of the study, and what is happening to and in *their* environment, should be a high priority.

Some closed organizations have procedures that must be followed if they are going to issue permission to conduct research in their setting. Confidentiality is usually a significant issue with any organization. Will participants be identified or identifiable? How will the data be protected from unauthorized access? Will competitors learn something about the organization from this research that will put it at a disadvantage? Will individuals in the organization be put in any jeopardy by the project? These issues need to be resolved before approaching an organization for permission.

Organizations that have experience with research usually have standard procedures that they follow with researchers. For example, school systems typically have standard forms to complete and deadlines by which these forms must be submitted. These organizations understand the importance of research and are accustomed to dealing with investigators. In contrast, other organizations may not be familiar with applied research. Most for-profit corporations fall in this category. In dealing with these groups, the investigator will first have to convince the authorities that research, in general, is a good idea and that their organization will gain something from their participation. Most importantly, the organization has to be convinced that they will not be taking a significant risk in participating. The planner must be prepared to present a strong case as to why a non-research-oriented organization should want to involve themselves in a research project.

Finally, any agreement between the researcher and the organization should be in writing. This may be an informal letter addressed to the organization's project liaison officer (there should be one) for the research. The letter should describe the procedures that will take place and indicate the dates that the investigator will be on site. The agreement should be detailed and include how the organization will cooperate with the research. This written agreement may avoid misunderstandings that are based on past in-person or telephone discussions (i.e., "I thought you meant . . .").

Data Collection Process

Gaining access for primary data collection is just the start of the planning process. Careful attention then needs to be paid to the details of the study. These include recruiting the participants and the logistics required at the site.

Participants. The primary purpose of obtaining access to a site is to be able to collect data from or about people. The researcher should *not* assume that having access insures that the target subjects will agree to participate in the study.

Moreover, skepticism is warranted in accepting the assurances from management concerning others' willingness to participate in a study. For example, in an evaluation of a nutrition program for the elderly (Bickman, 1985), cooperation was obtained from the federal agency that funded the program and from each local project manager to implement and evaluate a program. The local managers furnished the number of elderly in their sites and estimated the percentage of elderly that they thought would participate in the study. Random assignment of sites to treatment and control conditions proceeded based on these estimates. During the recruitment phase of the data collection, it was clear that the study would fall far short of the required number of subjects. The design of the study was jeopardized when new sites had to be recruited to increase the sample size.

In a review of 30 randomized studies on drug abuse Dennis (1990) found that 54% seriously underestimated the client flow by an average of 37%. Realistic and accurate participant estimates are necessary to allocate resources and to ensure sufficient statistical power. This latter point has often been ignored in the past, as research by Lipsey et al. (1985) found that 90% of the 122 evaluation studies they reviewed had insufficient statistical power to detect small effect sizes. Sixty percent of the studies would not reliably find a medium effect if it was present. Rossi (1990) expressed similar concerns about the low power of psychological research in his review of 221 articles published in three psychological journals. He concluded that low power contributes to the abundance of Type II errors and the difficulties many investigators experience in replicating others' work. Many funding agencies are now insisting that power analyses be conducted when submitting grant proposals. Moreover, these power analyses should be supported by evidence that the number of cases used in these analyses are valid estimates.

Planners can try to avoid shortfalls in the number of cases or subjects needed by conducting a small pilot study (Boruch & Wothke, 1985). In a pilot, the researcher can verify enrollment and attendance data as well as willingness to participate. Thus, an investigator who wishes to collect data from students in a college classroom is well advised not only to learn the number of students enrolled in the course, but how many, on the average, show up for class. In some cases this may be less than half of those enrolled. To estimate the percentage that would be willing to participate, it is advisable to ask potential subjects if they would take part in a study similar to the one planned. Alternatively, the investigator may be able to gauge the participation rate from the experiences of other researchers.

In cases where potential subjects enter into some program or institution, it will be important to verify the actual subject flow (e.g., number per week). For example, if the study requires participation of subjects who are receiving psychotherapy, then it is critical to know how many *new* patients enter the program each week. This will establish the maximum number of subjects that could participate in the study. By estimating the volunteer rate, the planner can judge the total amount of time needed to conduct the study. If that total time proves too long, the planner will know that additional sites need to be recruited. Related to the number of participants is the assurance that the project will be able to implement the planned-for research design. Randomized designs are especially vulnerable to implementation problems. It is easy to promise that there will be no new taxes, that the check is in the mail, and that a randomized experiment will be conducted. It is often difficult to deliver on these promises. In an applied setting, the investigator should obtain agreement from authorities *in writing* that they will cooperate in the conduct of the study. This agreement must be detailed, procedurally oriented, and must clearly specify the responsibilities of the researcher and those who control the setting.

Logistics. The ability to implement the research depends on the ability of the investigator to carry out the planned data collection procedures. A written plan for data collection is critical to success, but it does not guarantee effective implementation. A pilot or "walk-through" of the procedure is necessary to determine if it is feasible. In this procedure, the investigator needs to consider the following:

Accessibility. There are a large number of seemingly unimportant details that can damage a research project if they are ignored. Will the research participants have the means to travel to the site? Is there sufficient public transportation? If not, will the investigator arrange for transportation? If the study is going to use an organization's space for data collection, will the investigator need a key? Is there anyone else who may use the space? Who controls scheduling and room assignment? Have they been notified? When using someone else's space, it is important to make certain that the investigator is able to control it during the time it is promised. For example, a researcher about to collect posttest data in a classroom should ensure that he or she will not be asked to vacate the space before data collection is completed.

Other Support. Are the light and sound sufficient for the study? If the study requires the use of electrical equipment, will there be sufficient electrical outlets? Will the equipment reach the outlets, or should extension cords be brought? Do the participants need food or drink? How will these be provided? Are there restroom facilities available? Are the surroundings quiet enough to conduct the study? Can modifications be made in the environment necessary to conduct the study? Is the environment safe? Are there enough chairs, pencils, space, forms, and assistants available to collect the data? If the data collectors are in the field, do they have proper identification? Are the appropriate persons in the home organization aware of the study and the identity of the data collectors? Are those persons prepared to vouch for the legitimacy of the research? Is there sufficient space not only to collect the data, but to house the research team, assemble the data collection instruments, and analyze and store the data. Space is a precious commodity in many institutions. Do not assume that the research project will have sufficient space. Obtain a commitment from those who control space in the planning phase and *before* a grant proposal is submitted.

Secondary Data Analysis

Another approach to conducting applied research is to use already-existing data. This method has the advantage of lower costs and time savings, but it may also entail managing a large amount of flawed and/or inappropriate data. In some cases, these data will exist in a format that is designed for research purposes. There are a number of secondary data sources developed by university consortia federal sources such as the Bureau of the Census and commercial data such as *Inform,* a data base of 550 business journals. In other studies, the data will exist as administrative records that were *not* designed to answer research questions. This section deals primarily with using a record system for secondary data analysis. More information about secondary research can be obtained from Stewarts (1984).

In the planning process, the investigator must have confidence that the records contain the information that is required for the study. Assurances from authorities are helpful, but a direct examination of a representative sample of records should be conducted. Sampling records will not only provide the researcher with an indication of the content of the records, but also of their quality. It is frequently the case that clinical or administrative records are not suitable for research purposes. First, the records may be stored in a way that makes them inaccessible for research purposes. For example, there may not be a central collection point for all records, thus increasing the costs of collecting data. Second, if the records are computerized, this may be of tremendous advantage to the investigator, but not all the information that was collected on paper may be transferred to the computer data base. The investigator needs to confirm the availability and content of records needed for the research.

The planner must also have some confidence in the quality of the records. Are the records complete? Why were the data originally collected? The data base may serve some hidden political purpose that could induce systematic distortions. What procedures are used to deal with missing data? Do the computerized records bear a close resemblance to the original records? Are some data items periodically updated or purged from the computer file? How were the data collected and entered, and by whom? To have a good idea of quality, the planner should interview the data collectors, observe the data entry process, and compare written records to the computerized version. Conducting an analysis of administrative records only seems easy if it is not done carefully.

To gain access to a record system, the investigator also must demonstrate how the confidentiality of the records will be protected. If the records contain client names, then there is a significant risk associated with providing those records to a researcher. If individual names are not necessary, the organization may be willing, often at a cost, to provide sanitized records with personally identifying information removed. In cases where the names are not important to the researcher, but it is important to link individuals to the data base or to data collected later, then a computerized linking file should be established that the providing organization can use to link names with researcher-established identification numbers.

Time as a Resource

Time takes on two important dimensions in planning applied research— *calendar* and *clock* time. *Calendar* time is the total amount of time that is available for the project. Calendar time varies across projects. It may be a semester for a course-related research project, 3 years for an externally funded research grant, or 2 weeks for a research contract. The calendar time can substantially affect the scope of a research project.

Time and the Research Question

The calendar time allowed in a study should be related to the research questions (see Kelly & McGrath, 1988, for an extended discussion of how time relates to the research question). Is the phenomenon under study something that lasts a long period of time, or does it only exist for a brief period? Does the phenomenon under study occur in cycles? Is the time allocated to data collection sufficient?

The first consideration of time is to examine its relationship to the phenomenon that is being studied. For example, if the event to be studied occurs infrequently and for a short period of time, and if it is somewhat unpredictable, then a long period of calendar time may be needed to capture enough occurrences of this event. If the study deals with physical aggression on the streets, for example, and if the investigator wants to study this phenomenon by observing it, then clearly a long period of observation would be needed. In fact, the nature of this infrequent and unpredictable event would probably rule against using observation as a data collection technique. Other time-dependent phenomena may take a long period of time to unfold and manifest themselves. Thus, a drug treatment program that takes a lengthy period for the effects of the treatment to materialize would require a long period of study if the investigator wanted to document an impact. If the phenomenon is cyclical in nature, then the researcher should plan the length of the data collection period to include the various cycles to obtain an accurate representation of the phenomenon. If the project is an evaluation of a program, then the evaluator may need to wait for the program to stabilize before collecting data. Until this initial stage is completed, the program may be highly variable in its operation. Calendar time needs to be allocated in the research for this aspect of program development. All these points argue that in planning an applied research project the investigator must have some familiarity with the phenomenon under study. The researcher may fail to implement a good study if the relationship between time and the subject studied are not considered.

Time and Data Collection

The second way in which time should be considered is in terms of the actual or real *clock time* needed to accomplish some task. The event that is being studied might exist infrequently and only for a short period of time. Thus, we might need a long period of calendar time devoted to the project, but only a short period of clock time for data collection. As will be noted in subsequent parts of this chapter, estimating time is related to many other estimates made during the planning of research. Once having established the time estimates, the investigator needs to estimate how long it will take for actual data collection. In computing this estimate, the researcher should consider questions of recruitment, access, and cooperation. For example, if a study is being conducted in a hospital setting using patients, the planner should determine the criteria for inclusion in the study, calculate how many patients would meet those criteria, and estimate the percentage of the patients that would volunteer to participate in the study. An estimate of attrition or dropout from the study is also needed. If high attrition is predicted, then more time is needed for data collection to have sufficient statistical power. Thus, in computing time, the investigator should have an accurate and comprehensive picture of the environment in which the study will be conducted.

Time Budget

In planning to use any resource, the researcher should create a budget that describes how the resource will be allocated. Both calendar and clock time need to be budgeted. To budget calendar time, the duration of the entire project must be known. In applied research, the duration typically is set at the start of the project and the investigator then tailors the research to fit the length of time available. There may be little flexibility in total calendar time on some projects.

The report may be needed for a legislative decision or the contract may specify a product at a certain time.

Funded research projects usually operate on a calendar basis; that is, the project will be funded for a specific amount of time. This sets the upper limit of the time budget. The investigator then plans what he or she believes can be accomplished within that period of time. Students will usually operate with semester or quarter deadlines. Again the project will need to be tailored to the amount of time available. The exceptions for students are theses and dissertations that typically have no fixed deadlines. Regardless, the work often expands to fit the time available. Researchers must be able to specify project scope and approach to fit a limited time frame. A mistake many researchers make in estimating the time budget is to underestimate the time needed, which often results in the late delivery of their products.

The second time budget refers to clock time. How much actual time will it take to develop a questionnaire or to interview all the participants? It is important to decide what unit of time will be used in the budget. That is, what is the smallest unit of analysis of the research process that will be useful in calculating how much time it will take to complete the research project? To answer this question, we now turn to the concept of tasks.

Tasks and Time

To "task out" a research project, the planner is required to list all the significant activities (tasks) that must be performed to complete the project. The tasks in a project budget are similar to the expense categories needed in planning a personal financial budget. The financial budget is calculated on various categories such as rent, utilities, food, and so on. When listing all of these expense items, an implicit decision is made concerning the level of refinement that will be used. For example, under the food budget, it is rare for a family to categorize their food budget into vegetables, meat, fruit, and milk products. On the other hand, a family might decide to divide the food budget into eating in restaurants versus the purchasing of food for home consumption. In a similar vein, the investigator needs to decide what categories will be used to plan the research.

Table 1 shows an example of an abbreviated task outline for a research project. It shows the major tasks preceded by an action verb. These major tasks are usually divided into finer subtasks. The degree of refinement depends on how carefully the investigator needs to budget. When the estimates need to be very precise, tasks should be divided more finely. For experienced investigators, the very refined process might not be necessary.

To construct a time budget, the investigator needs to list all the tasks that

Table 1. Major Tasks of a Typical Research Project

Task 1	Conduct literature review and develop conceptual framework
Task 2	Develop instruments
Task 3	Construct sample frame and select sample
Task 4	Collect data
Task 5	Analyze data
Task 6	Write report

need to be accomplished during the research project. Typically these can be grouped into a number of major categories, as shown in Table 1. The first category usually encompasses conceptual development. This includes literature reviews and thinking and talking about the problem to be investigated. Time needs to be allocated for consulting with experts in areas where investigators need additional advice. The literature reviews could be categorized into a number of steps ranging from computerized searches to writing a summary of the findings. Investigators might also want to include in this category the conduction of meta-analytic reviews that involve the quantitative integration of empirical studies. Books by Rosenthal (1984) and Cooper (1989) provide details about this process.

The second phase found in most projects is instrument development and refinement. Regardless of whether the investigator plans to do intensive face-to-face interviewing, self-administered questionnaires, or observation, time needs to be allocated to search for, adapt, or develop relevant instruments used to collect data. Time also needs to be allocated for pilot testing the instruments. In pilot testing, preliminary drafts of instruments are used in the field with persons similar to the participants in the study. Some purposes of pilot testing are to ascertain the length of time needed to administer the instrument, to check on ease of administration, to practice coding of information, and to determine if there are ambiguities in the way respondents interpret the instrument. Pilot testing should never be left out of any project. Typically, there will be "new" flaws that were not noted by members of the research team in previous applications of the instrument. Respondents often interpret instruments differently than researchers. Moreover, widespread use of an instrument does not insure that participants in your research project will interpret the instrument in the same way.

If the data collection approach involves extracting information from administrative records, pilot testing must take a different form. The researcher should pilot test the training planned for data extractors and the data-coding process. Checks should be included for accuracy and consistency across coders.

When external validity or generalizability is a major concern, the researcher will need to plan especially carefully the construction of the sample. The sampling procedure describes the potential subjects and how they will be selected to participate in the study. This procedure may be very complex, depending upon the type of sampling plan adopted. Henry (1990) provides the new investigator with an excellent description of sampling methods.

The next phase of research is usually the data collection. Data collection can include many techniques. For example, the study may involve reviewing previous records (see Stewart, 1984). The investigator needs to determine how long it will take to gain access to those records, as well as how long it will take to extract the data from the records and whether information the investigator assumes is on those records is there. Records kept for administrative purposes often do not match research needs. Careful sampling and inspection of those records in planning the project are necessary steps to avoid the embarrassment of inability to complete the project because of lack of data. In planning research, assumptions about data need to be recognized, questioned, and then carefully checked.

If the researcher is planning to conduct a survey, the procedure for estimating the length of time needed for this process could be extensive. Fowler (1988) describes the steps needed in conducting a survey. These include developing the instrument, recruiting and training interviewers, sampling, and the actual data collection. Telephone interviews require some special techniques that are described in detail by Lavrakas (1987). This chapter cannot go into depth about these and other data collection methods other than to indicate that time estimates need to be attached to each task associated with data collection.

The next phase usually associated with any research project is data analysis. Whether the investigator is using qualitative or quantitative methods, time must be allocated for the analysis of data. Analysis not only includes statistical testing using a computer, but also the preparation of the data for computer analysis. Steps included in this process are cleaning of the data—that is, making certain that the responses are readable and are not ambiguous to data entry personnel—physically entering the data, and checking for the internal consistency of the data. For example, if a subject said "no" in response to a question about whether he eats meals out of the home, there should be no answers recorded for that subject about the types of restaurants that he frequents. Other procedures typically included in quantitative analysis are the production of descriptive statistics, that is, frequencies, means, standard deviations, and measures of skewness. More complex studies may require conducting inferential statistical tests. Analytical procedures for qualitative data collection procedures need to be tailored for the specific project. The reader is referred to books by Jorgensen (1989), Denzin (1989), Fetterman (1989), and Schwandt and Halpern (1988) for further guidance.

Finally, time needs to be allocated for communicating the results. (Posavac's chapter in this volume details the "art" of communicating about applied social research with users.) Applied research projects typically require a final report.

This report is usually a lengthy, detailed analysis. Since most people do not read the entire report, it is critical to include a two- or three-page executive summary that succinctly and clearly summarizes the main findings. In applied research projects, the lay audience is typically not concerned with statistical tests, methodology, or literature reviews. These individuals typically just want to know what was found. However, the quality of the findings cannot be interpreted without an understanding of the methodology and analysis. The executive summary should focus on the findings and present these as the highlights of the study. No matter how much effort and innovation went into data collection, the procedures are of interest primarily to other researchers and not to typical sponsors of applied research. The best the researcher can hope to accomplish with the latter audience is to educate them about the limitations of the findings based on specific methods used.

The investigator should allocate time not just for producing a report, but also for verbally communicating this information to sponsors. Verbal communications may include briefings as well as testimony to legislative bodies. Moreover, if the investigator desires to have the results of the study utilized, it is likely that time needs to be allocated to work with the sponsor and other organizations in interpreting and applying the findings of the study. This last utilization-oriented perspective is often not included in planning a time budget.

Once the researcher has described all the tasks and subtasks, the next part of the planning process is to estimate how long it will take to complete each task. This is a difficult process unless there are previous data upon which to base these estimates. One way to approach this problem is to reduce each task to its smallest unit. For example, in the data collection phase, an estimate of the total amount of interviewing time is needed. The simplest way to estimate this total is to simply calculate how long each interview should take. Pilot data are critical to developing accurate estimates. If pilot interviews took an average of 2 hours each to complete, and if the study calls for 100 interviews, then simple arithmetic indicates that 200 hours need to be allocated for this task. However, does this estimate include everything important? Is travel time included? Are callbacks to respondents who are not home part of this estimate? Is the time required for editing the data and coding open-ended responses included? Another example is data entry time. It is relatively easy to compute how many keystrokes a data entry person can complete in an hour and then simply divide this by the number of keystrokes needed for the entire project. This computation is a rough estimate because data from complex instruments will take longer to enter than data from less complex instruments. Pilot testing for data entry is very useful if this task is going to be a major time user and, therefore, financial expense of the project.

Whatever estimate the investigator derives, it is likely to be just that—an estimate—and there will be a margin of error associated with it. Whether the estimate is too conservative or liberal will depend in part on the context in which the planning needs to occur. For example, if the researcher is planning to compete for a research contract, then an underestimate may occur because competition may place pressure on the planner to underestimate the costs of conducting the research. On the other hand, inexperienced individuals operating under no particular time pressure (e.g., graduate students) may overestimate time required for conducting a research project. As a rule of thumb, underestimates are more likely and more costly than overestimates. If the research sponsor can afford the time and the money, it would be safe to add an extra 10–15% to any estimate. Clearly, this addition indicates a lack of certainty and precision. However, do not despair; even with many years of experience, highly paid planners in defense firms overrun their contracts frequently.

The clock-time budget simply indicates how long it will take to complete each task. What this budget does not tell you is the sequencing and the real calendar time needed for conducting the research. Calendar time can be calculated from the above estimates, but the investigator will need to make certain other assumptions. For example, if the study uses interviewers to collect data and 200 hours of interviewing time are required, the length of calendar time needed for this will depend on a number of factors. Most clearly, the number of interviewers will be a critical factor. One interviewer will take a minimum of 200 hours to complete that task, while 200 interviewers can do it in 1 hour. Thus, we need to specify the staffing levels and research team skills for the project. This is the next kind of budget that needs to be developed.

Personnel

Skills Budget

Once the investigator has described the tasks that need to be accomplished, the second step is to decide what kinds of people are needed to conduct those tasks. What characteristics are needed for a trained observer or an interviewer? What are the requirements for a supervisor? What skills does a data analyst need? Who will be able to manage the project and write the reports? These questions need to be considered in planning a research project. To assist the investigator in answering these questions, a skills matrix should be completed. The skills matrix shown in Table 2 describes the requisite skills needed for the tasks and attaches names or positions of the research team to each cluster of skills. Typically, a single individual does not possess all the requisite skills, so a team will need to be developed for the research project. In that case, the labels are simply economist, statistician, and so on.

In addition to specific research tasks, management of the project needs to be considered. Someone will have to manage the various parts of the project to

Table 2. Skills Matrix

Person	Research design	Case studies	Sampling	Institutional development	Cost analysis	Statistics	Education
Director	X	X		X	X		X
Statistician	X		X		X	X	
Economist				X	X	X	
Research assistant							
Research assistant			X	X	X	X	X

make sure that they are working together and that the schedule is being met. To return to the example about the number of interviewers, it is not reasonable, unless the individuals are geographically dispersed, to use 200 interviewers for 1 hour each simply because of the excessive amount of time that would be needed to supervise and train that many interviewers. The first consideration is how many individuals can be recruited, supervised, and trained to carry out certain tasks. Second, how finely can tasks be categorized so that more individuals can accomplish them? For example, it is sensible to use multiple interviewers but not to use multiple data analysts. One person might be best working full time to conduct the data analysis. On the other hand, one person working full time doing all the interviews would not be recommended. Consideration of time available, skills, supervision, training, and burnout are all relevant in computing the next table: the number of hours per person to be allocated for each task.

Person Loading

Once the tasks are specified and the amount of time required to complete each task is estimated, it is necessary to assign these tasks to individuals. The assignment plan is described by a person-loading table (see Table 3). This table shows a more refined categorization of the tasks needed to develop instruments. The left-hand side of the table lists the tasks developed for the project. The top of the table lists all the individuals, or categories of individuals, who will be needed to accomplish these tasks. The example shows that specifying data needs will be conducted by the project director for 10 hours and require 20 hours of secretarial support. Locating existing instruments will be done by the research assistants working a total of 40 hours each. The interviews will be conducted by the research assistants, with 10 hours of supervision by the project director, for a total of fifty hours. The statistician will be involved in three tasks: specifying data needs (10 hours), analyzing interviews (15 hours), and conducting the analysis (30 hours). This table allows the investigator to know if (1) the right mix

Table 3. Person-Loading Chart

			Personnel hours			
	Director	Research Assistant	Economist	Statistician	Secretary	Research Assistant
Task 2. Develop instruments						
2.1 Specify data needs	10	—	5	10	20	—
2.2 Review existing instruments	—	—				—
2.21 Locate instruments	—	40			10	40
2.22 Evaluate instruments	20	20			5	20
2.3 Construct inst.-need matrix	20	20				20
2.4 Develop new instruments						
2.41 Develop interviews	20	20			30	30
2.42 Conduct interviews	10	40				40
2.43 Analyze interviews	10	40		15		40
2.44 Construct scales	20	50			30	50
2.45 Field test instruments	10	40				40
2.46 Conduct analysis	10	60		30	20	60
Total (hours)	130	330	5	55	115	340

of skills will be present in the research team to accomplish the tasks, and (2) if the amount of time allocated to each individual to conduct those tasks is reasonable. Both of these, the skills and the time, will be necessary in developing the next planning tool.

Gantt Chart

We need to return to real, or calendar, time at some point in the planning process. The project will be conducted under real-time constraints. Thus, the tasking chart needs to be superimposed on a calendar. The allocation of calendar time to each task and subtask is shown in Figure 1. This is called a Gantt chart. The chart simply shows the tasks on the left-hand side and months on the top of the chart. Each bar shows the length of calendar time allocated for the completion of specific subtasks. This does not mean that if a bar takes up 1 month that the task will actually take a whole month of clock time to complete. The task might only take 15 hours, but needs to be spread over a full month.

The Gantt chart shows not only how long each task takes, but also the relationship in calendar time between tasks. While inexact, the chart can show the precedence of research tasks. A more detailed and exact procedure is to produce a PERT chart showing the dependency relationships between tasks.

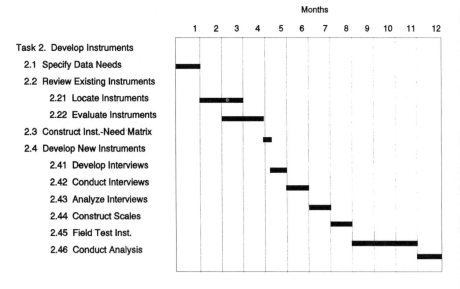

Figure 1. Gantt Chart.

These charts are typically not needed for the types of research projects used in social sciences.

One of the key relationships and assumptions made in producing a plan is that individuals will not work more than 40 hours a week. Thus, the person-loading chart needs to be checked against the Gantt chart to make sure that the task can be completed by those individuals assigned to it within the period specified in the Gantt chart. This task is more complex than it seems, since individuals will typically be assigned to multiple tasks within a specified time. It is important to calculate, for each individual involved in the project, how much actual calendar time he or she will be working on all the tasks to which he or she is assigned. Individuals should not be allocated to more tasks or time than can be spent. (Very reasonably priced computer programs that can run on microcomputers are available to help the planner to these calculations and draw the appropriate charts.) At this point in the planning process, the investigator should have a very clear estimate of the time budget. The time budget and person-loading chart are both needed to produce a financial budget—the next step in the planning process.

Financial Resources

Usually the biggest part of any research budget is personnel—research staff. Social science research, especially applied social science, is very labor intensive. Moreover, the labor of some individuals can be very costly. To produce a budget based on predicted costs, the investigator needs to follow a few simple steps.

Based on the person-loading chart, the investigator can simply compute total personnel costs for the project by multiplying the hours allocated to each individual by their hourly cost. The investigator should compute personnel costs by each task. In addition, if the project crosses different years, then the planner will need to provide for salary increases in the estimate. Hourly cost typically includes salary and fringe benefits. If the investigator needs to break down costs by month, this procedure will allow that as well. Table 4 illustrates personnel

Table 4. Personnel Costs

	Director	Economist	Statistician	Secretary	Research assistant I	Research assistant II
Total (hours)	130	5	55	115	330	340
Hourly rates	$40	$40	$40	$8	$10	$11
Total costs	$5,200	$200	$2,200	$920	$3,300	$3,740
Total personnel costs $15,560						

Table 5. Other Direct Costs

	Travel	Telephone	Postage	Duplication	Supplies	Computer
Task 2. Develop instruments						
2.1 Specify data needs						
2.2 Review existing instruments						
2.21 Locate instruments		100	25	10		
2.22 Evaluate instruments						
2.3 Construct inst.-need matrix						
2.4 Develop new instruments						
2.41 Develop interviews						
2.42 Conduct interviews	200 miles × .26 = $52	25		100 copies × .05 = $50		
2.43 Analyze interviews						150
2.44 Construct scales						
2.45 Field test instruments	200 miles × .26 = $52	10		2000 copies × .05 = $1000		
2.46 Conduct analysis					50	200
	$104	$135	$25	$160	$50	$350

Total other direct costs $824
Total personnel costs $15,560
Total direct costs $16,384
Overhead (50% of direct costs) $8,192
Total costs $24,576

costs for each task. The figures used in this table are for illustrative purposes only, and are not meant to be current salaries for these individuals. Budgets for contracts usually follow this procedure. For grant applications from academic institutions, these calculations will not be necessary. However they are highly recommended to be able to adequately plan and monitor a project.

Table 5 illustrates how other items need to be allocated to the budget to include such cost items as computer time, supplies, duplication, postage, telephone, and travel. In computing how much needs to be allocated in each one of these areas, the same type of analysis used for personnel should be applied. For example, for the duplication costs, the investigator should consider how many pages will be duplicated and the cost of each page. Thus, if the study includes a 10-page questionnaire to be distributed to 200 individuals, then 2,000 pages at $.05 each should be allocated for this task, for a total of $100. The investigator might want to include some additional funds for extra copies and for errors in duplication. The same type of calculation can be used to produce cost estimates for reports. Five reports may be needed with an estimate of 100 pages each and 20 copies of each report. This costs a total of $500 for duplication. If the report includes covers and binding, these expenses would need to be added to the cost.

Travel costs can be estimated in a similar fashion. If travel is going to be by air to a specific location, then a travel agent can provide the cost of each trip. Given the complex fare structures available, the investigator might want to use an average cost or, to be on the safe side, the maximum regular airfare. If the research team is going to visit a number of places across the country that cannot be specified until the project is funded, then a scenario needs to be developed. Such a scenario could include computing average fares to 10 or 12 likely places to visit. In computing the budget then, one simply takes the average of these 10 places, and multiplies it by the number of visits and number of persons making visits to compute the airfare. The use of a personal car is typically reimbursed at a fixed rate per mile. To estimate meals and lodging, calculate the average cost of meals and hotel, in that particular city, at a cost per day. However, some contracts may specify a per diem or the maximum amount that can be spent on food and lodging per day.

The investigator needs to examine the tasks to determine if there are any special costs associated with the project. For example, if there is going to be a telephone survey conducted, then this part of the budget becomes critical to compute accurately. If a mailed questionnaire is the method, then postage for initial mailings, return mail, follow-up reminders, and other correspondence must be computed. Similarly, if there is going to be a great deal of mainframe computer time expended, then the investigator needs to accurately estimate the amount of computer time needed to conduct the analysis. Help can usually be obtained from the computer center at a university in calculating these figures.

After computing personnel and other costs, institutions usually have an indirect or overhead cost added to the direct expenses of the project. This is the cost associated with conducting research that cannot be allocated to each specific project. It typically includes costs for space, utilities, maintenance, as well as those associated with the university's or firm's management and accounting systems related to grants and contracts. Indirect costs will vary from institution to institution and should be included as part of the budget. For-profit firms also will add a profit percentage to a contract.

In calculating a budget, the distinction between academic and nonacademic settings should be kept in mind. Researchers in academic institutions are not accustomed to calculating personnel budgets as described. Instead, an estimate is made about how many people would be needed or what percentage of time a faculty member is willing to devote to a project, and that is included as part of the budget. This often is a workable solution because the faculty time is fairly flexible. Thus, when the workload of one project is underestimated the faculty member may just work harder or longer on that project and not spend as much time on other activities. However, to have an accurate estimate of personnel time required for a project, the procedure described above is recommended.

After the budget has been calculated, the investigator may be faced with a total cost that is not reasonable for the project either because the sponsor does not have those funds available or because the bidding for the project is very competitive. If this occurs, the investigator has a number of alternatives available, the most reasonable of which is to eliminate or reduce the scope of some tasks. For example, instead of interviewing 200 persons, interview 100. Alternatively, keep the number of persons interviewed the same but cut back on the length of each interview to reduce costs. There is, of course, a limit as to how far the project can be cut back. For example, a series of tasks that grossly underestimate the amount of time required will not be evaluated favorably by knowledgeable reviewers. The underestimate will simply indicate to the reviewers that the investigator does not have the capability to conduct the research because he or she was not very realistic about the amount of time or resources required. Another alternative to reducing the size of the budget is to use less expensive staff. The trade-off is that a more expensive staff is usually more experienced, and should be able to accomplish a task in less time. Using less experienced staff, however, should result in an increase in the amount of time allocated to conduct that task. The investigator might also want to look for more efficient methods of conducting the research. For example, the use of matrix sampling, where individuals receive different parts of questionnaires, may reduce costs. If a randomized design is possible, it may be feasible, but often very risky, to collect only posttest data and eliminate all pretest data collection. The investigator needs to use ingenuity to try to devise not only a valid, reliable and sensitive project, but one that is efficient as well.

The financial budget, as well as the time budget, should force the investigator to realize the trade-offs that are involved in applied research. Should the investigator use a longer instrument, at a higher cost, or collect less data from more subjects? Should the subscales on an instrument be longer, and thus more reliable, or should more domains be covered, with each domain composed of fewer items and thus less reliable? Should an emphasis be placed on representative sampling as opposed to a purposive sampling procedure? Should the researcher use multiple data collection techniques, such as observation and interviewing, or should the research plan include only one technique with more data collected by that procedure? These and other questions are ones that any research planner faces. However, when under strict time and cost limitations, the saliency of these alternatives is very high.

Monitoring Project Implementation

Finally, the investigator should be sure to include in the planning phase methods by which the project can be kept on schedule. Budgetary responsibility requires at least monthly accounting of the expenses. The detailed Gantt chart can be very helpful in determining whether the project is slipping behind schedule. It is often the case that what is implemented in the field does not follow what was planned. The purpose of the planning is not to force a rigid structure on the field operations, but to anticipate difficulties. Unless some standard is developed and applied, the investigator cannot be sure that the project is tracking correctly.

The use of these planning tools as management tools can help the researcher obtain the goal of a competently conducted project. Research management is not a task that is usually taught in graduate programs, but one that is learned on the job. This chapter discusses techniques intended to assist the investigator both in planning and in managing a research project.

References

Baron, R. A. (1987). Research grants: A practical guide. In M. P. Zanna & J. M. Darley (Eds.), *The compleat academic* (pp. 152–169). New York: Random House.

Bickman, L. (1981). Some distinctions between basic and applied approaches. In L. Bickman (Ed.), *Applied social psychology annual* (Vol. 2, pp. 23–44). Beverly Hills, CA: Sage.

Bickman, L. (1984). Bystander intervention in crimes: Theory, research, and applications. In J. Karylowski, J. Redowsky, E. Staub, & D. Bar-Tal (Eds.), *Development and maintenance of prosocial behavior: International perspectives.* New York: Plenum.

Bickman, L. (1985). Randomized field experiments in education: Implementations lessons. In R. Boruch (Ed.), *Randomized field experimentation* (pp. 39–53). New Directions for Program Evaluation, no. 28. San Francisco, CA: Jossey-Bass.

Bickman, L., & Rosenbaum, D. (1977). Crime reporting as a function of bystander encouragement, surveillance, and credibility. *Journal of Personality and Social Psychology, 35,* 577–586.

Boruch, R. F., & Wothke, W. (Eds.). (1985). *Randomization and field experimentation.* New Directions in Program Evaluation Series, no. 28. San Francisco, CA: Jossey-Bass.

Cooper, H. M. (1989). *Integrating research: A guide for literature reviews* (2nd ed.). Newbury Park, CA: Sage.

Dennis, M. L. (1990). Assessing the validity of randomized field experiments: An example from drug treatment research. *Evaluation Review, 14,* 347–373.

Denzin, N. K. (1989). *Interpretive interactionism.* Newbury Park, CA: Sage.

Fetterman, D. M. (1989). *Ethnography: Step by step.* Newbury Park, CA: Sage.

Fowler, F. J., Jr. (1988). *Survey research methods.* Newbury Park, CA: Sage.

Goffman, E. (1959). *The presentation of self in everyday life.* Garden City, NY: Doubleday.

Grady, K. E., & Wallston, B. S. (1988). *Research in health case settings.* Newbury Park, CA: Sage.

Henry, G. T. (1990). *Practical sampling.* Newbury Park, CA: Sage.

Herring, K. L. (Ed.). (1987). *APA guide to research support* (3rd ed.). Washington, DC: American Psychological Association.

Jorgensen, D. L. (1989). *Participant observation: A methodology for human studies.* Newbury Park, CA: Sage.

Kelly, J. R., & McGrath, J. E. (1988). *On time and method.* Newbury Park, CA: Sage.

Lavrakas, P. J. (1987). *Telephone survey methods: Sampling, selection, and supervision.* Newbury Park, CA: Sage.

Lipsey, M. W., Crosse, S., Dunkle, J., Pollard, J., & Stobart, G. (1985). Evaluation: The art and sorry state of the science. *New Directions in Program Evaluation, 22,* 7–28.

Rosenthal, R. (1984). *Meta-analytic procedures for social research.* Beverly Hills, CA: Sage.

Rossi, J. S. (1990). Statistical power of psychological research: What have we gained in 20 years? *Journal of Consulting and Clinical Psychology, 58,* 646–656.

Schwandt, T. A., & Halpern, E. S. (1988). *Linking auditing and meta-evaluation: Enhancing quality in applied research.* Newbury Park, CA: Sage.

Stewart, D. W. (1984). *Secondary research: Information sources and methods.* Beverly Hills, CA: Sage.

2

Problem Identification in Social Intervention Research

Yolanda Suarez-Balcazar, Fabricio E. Balcazar, and Stephen B. Fawcett

> Applied research is carried out with practical applications in mind . . . it differs from basic research in that it seeks to show the means to reduce an abstract idea to a useful purpose.
>
> National Science Foundation (1966, p. 15)

Society faces complex and ever-growing social problems that call for appropriate and effective social interventions. Although it is not in the hands of social scientists to "save the world," social responsibility has long been a part of the value system of psychology (Lewin, 1948; Miller, 1969), its relevant organizations (e.g., Society for the Psychological Study of Social Issues), and its subdisciplines (e.g., the Division of Community Research and Action).

This chapter provides an overview of relevant methodological considerations for the problem selection phase in the context of an *intervention-research paradigm* (Fawcett et al., in press; Rothman, 1980). This approach represents a departure from traditional social psychology approaches to problem identification (e.g., Deutsch & Hornstein, 1975; Oskamp, 1984) because the process is

Yolanda Suarez-Balcazar • Department of Psychology, Loyola University of Chicago, Chicago, Illinois 60626.   **Fabricio E. Balcazar** • University of Illinois at Chicago/UAP, Chicago, Illinois 60608.   **Stephen B. Fawcett** • Department of Human Development, University of Kansas, Lawrence, Kansas 66045.

Methodological Issues in Applied Psychology, edited by Bryant et al. Plenum Press, New York, 1992.

designed to set the ground for developing interventions and to involve participants in the various phases of the process. The intervention-research paradigm
also emphasizes the natural context in which individuals operate as the appropriate context for conducting the research and development process. This approach
is consistent with both action research (Lewin, 1948) and applied behavior analysis paradigms (Baer, Wolf, & Risley, 1968, 1987).

Applied social scientists not only try to understand and explain the world,
they attempt to design interventions to solve social problems (Baer et al., 1968,
1987; Hornstein, 1975; Kidd & Saks, 1980; Weick, 1984). However, many
efforts to address specific social problems have traditionally been left to human
service providers such as social workers and other practitioners who deliver
services to people in need of them. Because research has been separated from
practice, social science has been removed from its place at the forefront of social
intervention.

A fundamental difference between social scientists and human service providers is that scientists have the primary function of "comprehending the world"
by producing knowledge that permits them and others to understand aspects of
the world better. By contrast, practitioners have the function of "changing the
world," that is, producing material effects that permit clients, organizations, or
communities to attain their desired outcomes (Rothman, 1980). By combining
these two approaches into an intervention-research paradigm, social scientists
can add knowledge and scientific understanding about the world while attempting to solve its problems (Balcazar, Suarez-Balcazar, & Fawcett, in press;
Fawcett et al., in press; Rothman & Thomas, in press).

Rothman's (1980) intervention-research paradigm was formulated in an
effort to convert the research and development approach (R & D) from industrial
product development into an R & D model for human services. One rationale for
this was that human service practitioners have not enjoyed the fruits of scientific
research to the same degree that industry has benefited from research in the
physical sciences. The emphasis in an R & D process is on development, field
testing, and diffusion of prescriptive formulations for human service practitioners
rather than hypothesis testing in the traditional sense of the term. In this paradigm, theory is arrived at inductively from the accumulation of practical and
applied knowledge contributed by repeated attempts to solve specific social
problems.

The first section of this chapter reviews some important considerations
regarding problem definition in the context of an intervention-research paradigm.
The second section reviews three phases of the problem identification and analysis process: (1) gaining entry into the setting, (2) specifying the problem, and
(3) analyzing the problem. A case study is included at the end to illustrate
the various phases of the process.

Conceptual Framework

Defining what constitutes a "social problem" has been a topic of theoretical discussion and research for many years. Seidman and Rappaport (1986) provided a useful review of the issue in the context of community research and action. They consider problems to be bound by the time, place, and specific context in which people that define such problems operate. They argued that "problems are a function of the implicit assumptions of our culture, which both limit potential solutions and predetermine who and what are seen as problems" (p. 2).

Fawcett (1990) proposed a definition of a social problem in terms of a "discrepancy between an *actual* and an *ideal* level of behavior and related community condition that is labeled by the people experiencing it as important" (p. 67). This definition offers two advantages. First, it allows people experiencing a given condition to identify a potential problem. Second, implicit goals for action may be formulated by asking people to think in terms of ideal conditions. As such, if the ideal for an advocacy group of people with disabilities is to have all public buildings accessible to wheelchairs in a given community (i.e., appropriate ramps, elevators, and bathrooms) and only about 50% of the buildings meet those conditions of accessibility, then the discrepancy may be considered a problem. The group could set the goal of making all public buildings accessible and start an advocacy campaign. Issues become problems when they happen to be of importance to a community of interest and people's level of satisfaction with the issue is perceived as low. Edwards (1990) reviewed some important questions in defining social problems regarding who defines the problem and what values predominate when attempting to identify and solve a problem. We attempt to answer these questions in this chapter.

Overall, the definition and analysis of social problems is influenced by the culture and values of observers, on the one hand, and participants' perceptions and actual experiences with the problem, on the other. This implies that problems may be defined differently by those who actually experience them and by those who simply perceive or observe them. Notice that psychologists and other social scientists are usually observers, yet society looks at them for definitions of most social problems. This practice may perpetuate what Ryan (1971) pointedly identified as "blaming victims for their own predicament." An approach to overcome that practice comes from the consumer involvement movement (Crewe & Zola, 1983), which attempts to reduce the biases by involving clients, patients, or consumers in the process of defining their own problems and participating in the design of solutions.

The process of problem identification in intervention research should take into consideration the following principles: (1) avoiding victim blaming, (2) involving participants in the problem identification process, and (3) examining the environmental context in which the problem occurs. The following is a brief discussion of these principles.

Avoiding Victim Blaming. The trap of victim blaming occurs when researchers attempt to solve social problems—even with the best intentions—without regard for the fundamental conditions that produce and maintain them. In short, it is the absence of contextual features in the analysis of problems that makes it easy for researchers and service providers to fall into this trap. Ryan (1971) cites the example of a housing authority program in a major city designed to teach welfare mothers how to prevent child lead poisoning in their public units. Agency staff assumed that these mothers did not do a good job in protecting their children, while failing to consider other solutions to the problem. A contextual approach to this problem could have simply focused on removing lead paint from the buildings and repainting the apartments with lead-free paint. Yet, the professionals in this situation were more inclined to see "something wrong" with the welfare mothers than to recognize the "wrong" in the buildings.

Victim blaming has also been maintained by what Seidman and Rappaport (1986) identified as American society's strong reliance on individualism. This is a tendency "to find individuals responsible for their own problems, despite the antecedent and contextual, social, and political factors" (p. 4). Intervention researchers can avoid victim blaming by attempting to identify systemic social and environmental factors connected with the problem situation.

Involving Participants. Consumer involvement is a critical principle in applied intervention research because it suggests that participants become collaborators and partners in the research process (Fawcett, 1990; Kelly, 1986). This type of relationship increases the chances of developing appropriate interventions that are more likely to be maintained by the individuals involved (Chavis, Stuckey, & Wadersman, 1983).

A consumer involvement approach to social research allows participants to provide input about the severity of the problem, to discuss the environmental and social conditions that affect the problem, and to take an active role in producing the desired change. By emphasizing consumer involvement, applied research programs are more likely to be accepted and to "fit" local values and needs (Warwick & Kelman, 1976). Programs are more likely to be perceived as coming from the community and not from outsiders when consumers are actively involved. Another argument in support of this approach is that for interventions to be accepted and maintained by a community or interest group, participants must share a sense of "ownership" of the intervention (Fawcett, Mathews, & Fletcher, 1980; Jaccard, Turrisi, & Wan, 1990).

Despite the apparent benefits of involving participants as partners in the problem identification process, the practice is far from common. Two obstacles are the time required in building a relationship with participants and that some participants might lack the skills necessary to make their involvement meaningful. In the latter case, consumers may benefit from training in specific relevant skills. Thus, the philosophy of the consumer involvement movement asserts that because consumers are the best judges of their own interests, they should have the larger voice in determining what services are provided (DeJong, 1979).

Examining Environmental Context. Problems do not occur in a vacuum. Events and individuals are intrinsically connected with complex and changing environments. Such environments include past events as part of the history of the setting, individuals involved, and current events. Kantor (1959), from a behavioral analysis perspective, emphasized the importance of conducting contextual analyses in order to identify current and previous events that are affecting a given behavior. According to Kantor, behaviors are multicaused and multidetermined, which represents a departure from the traditional Skinnerian stimulus–response–consequence paradigm. A problem behavior, then, would be the result of multiple antecedent events (including past history) and multiple consequent events that interact and change in a particular time and space. Strategies to identify these variables are discussed later in this chapter.

Problem Identification and Analysis

Investigators come under the influence of a problem area in different ways, including personal interest, experience with the issue, and being influenced by another colleague's work in the area. Regardless of how one is influenced in selecting an area of applied social research, specific research questions are best selected on the basis of a review of the literature (Bailey, 1977).

This section outlines issues and tactics in the problem identification process, adapted from Balcazar et al. (in press), Fawcett (1990), and Fawcett et al. (in press). Three phases are discussed here: (1) gaining entry into the setting, (2) specifying the problem, and (3) analyzing the problem.

Gaining Entry into the Setting

Establishing a collaborative relationship with potential participants and gaining access to their settings (e.g., schools, institutions, or community agencies) is an important initial step. One strategy that researchers have used to gain entry is to develop relationships with people from the setting (e.g., Suarez de

Balcazar, Fawcett, & Balcazar, 1988). Such contact persons can then introduce researchers to key individuals or "gatekeepers" who might control the access to the setting or to other key community members.

The purpose of this phase is to become familiar with the setting and the people involved—their goals, activities, and functions—to gain their trust, and to establish your own credibility among community members. Researchers should be able to respect the cause community members pursue and the values they share. By serving as a consultant or facilitator, a researcher can develop rapport with group members. Intervention research emphasizes a collaborative relationship with potential participants rather than an expert relationship (Hornstein, 1975).

From an ethnographic perspective, anthropologists such as Agar (1980) recommended several strategies for entering a community: (1) arrange casual observations of the setting (e.g., walk through the neighborhood and go to local stores and other places where people meet); (2) make gradual approximations to the target community or individuals (e.g., initiate informal conversations with people met in stores, bars, parks, etc.); and (3) maintain a continued presence in the setting for a period of time (e.g., become a regular client in a local store, park, or bar). Sometimes an established professional from the community (e.g., a doctor, nurse, teacher, or the director of a local social service agency) might be able to introduce the researcher to other key community members. Those professionals are frequently eager to enlist help from other professionals when their intentions are consistent with community needs or interests.

Having the "right" attitude in relating with members of a potential research site is a critical factor. This implies demonstrating a genuine concern for the people and a humble and unpretentious attitude. A collaborative research process requires researchers to show community members a desire to learn from their experience. The research process is as much an opportunity to learn, as it is an opportunity to teach. The researcher's expertise becomes valuable when combined with local people's personal experiences with the problem at hand.

One obstacle that researchers commonly face in gaining entry into settings or communities is their lack of identification with its members. Ethnic and cultural differences may be a barrier to a collaborative research process since participants may feel misunderstood by researchers. Ethnically diverse research teams will be more accepted into a given community to facilitate a reciprocal identity between participants and researchers (Balcazar et al., in press).

Specifying the Problem

The specification of the problem should rely on participants' experiences, values, goals, and expectations (Kelly, 1986). Identifying the problem requires extensive input and feedback from those who experience the problem. Attention to participants' values and norms will help ensure sensitivity to cultural issues, perhaps increasing later participation and acceptance of the intervention (Warwick & Kelman, 1976).

Social psychologists have traditionally used survey research to identify problems. Strategies include reviewing census and archival data, analyzing descriptive demographic trends, and assessing people's changes in attitudes and feelings (Edwards, Tindale, Health, & Posavac, 1990; Hornstein, 1975). In addition, social researchers also use interviews and standardized surveys, scales, and various sociometric measures to assess individuals' perceptions of problematic behaviors, events, and/or situations (Mason & Bramble, 1989).

In an intervention-research paradigm, direct observations of the problem behavior(s) in their naturalistic context are also strongly recommended. This process includes gathering information about the frequency, duration, and/or topography of the behavior or target event. Direct observations require a specific operational definition of the behavior of interest, which specifies how the behavior or event will be measured and a specific description of the situation(s) in which the behavior or event occurs (Goldfried & D'Zurilla, 1969). An operational definition should answer questions such as: What is the problem? How is it going to be measured? How can you tell the problem is improving or worsening?

The extent of the detail of the definition depends on the complexity of the behavior or situation under study. For example, in the case study described in the next section of this chapter, the problem situation of inappropriate parking in handicapped parking spaces was defined as:

> A designated handicapped parking space was used inappropriately when a vehicle that did not display a legal identification was stopped (not moving for at least 5 seconds) in the designated space. Types of legal identification are a license plate with the words "Disabled Veteran," or a blue window tag with the white wheelchair symbol. (Suarez de Balcazar, Fawcett, & Balcazar, 1988, p. 292)

Within an applied intervention-research model, researchers can address or identify problems at the individual, group, or community levels. At the *individual level,* the focus is on helping individuals with behavioral deficits or excesses to acquire new behaviors, or change current behaviors. The individual helps identify the problem, describes its dimensions, and notes environmental features that contribute to the problem. A number of examples are included in the self-management literature (e.g., Baer, 1984).

At the *group level* the focus is on groups or individuals within groups (Glenwick & Jason, 1980). Such groups of individuals may share a common experience or goal, such as having a physical disability or advocating against drunk driving. Some examples include studies conducted with community-based agencies (Balcazar, Seekins, Fawcett, & Hopkins, 1990; Briscoe, Hoffman, & Bailey, 1975; Seekins, Mathews, & Fawcett, 1984).

At the *community level* (e.g., Geller, Bruff, & Nimmer, 1985; Loken, Swim, & Mittelmark, 1990) the focus is on populations that share a common concern and that may identify a problem which involves several parties and institutions. Examples include citizen groups, parent councils, or neighborhood associations that may act unilaterally or as part of a coalition. At this level, groups of individuals or coalitions may work together toward a common goal. For instance, a local community health advocacy organization may assist professionals in identifying public health needs in the community. On the other hand, community interventions may be designed to impact on general problems of a geographical population, such as encouraging safety belt use (Geller et al., 1985), reducing highway speeding (Van Houten & Nau, 1981), and enhancing pedestrian safety (Van Houten, 1988).

Overall, regardless of the level of the intervention, researchers may benefit from developing collaborative relationships with potential participants as they help specify the problem and assist in the development of the assessment strategies. Furthermore, collaborative intervention programs are more likely to be accepted if those directly affected by the problem are involved in the choice of program goals (Jaccard et al., 1990; Wolf, 1978).

Analyzing the Problem

Although subjective assessment of attitudes, values, beliefs, and expectations might provide useful information, the primary source of data in the problem identification phase of intervention research is direct observations of the specific problem in the context in which it occurs. Such observations allow for a functional analysis of antecedent and consequent environmental variables that maintain identified problems (Bailey, 1977).

A functional analysis of the problem yields information about the conditions under which the problem occurs, and the environmental conditions and consequences maintaining the problem. Conducting a functional analysis of the problem includes:

1. *Identifying conditions that affect the onset of the problem: Antecedent events.* Goldfried and D'Zurilla (1969) suggest using naturalistic observations and self-recording to gather information about the conditions under which the problem occurs. Some key questions that may help identify such conditions include: When did the problem first occur? What event came before and after early occurrences of the problem? Who is most affected by the problem? How are they affected? Identify-

ing a cause–effect relationship is not always possible or as important as identifying predisposing variables antecedent to the problem.

2. *Identifying conditions that maintain the problem: Consequent events.* Strategies to identify the conditions that are maintaining a problem include direct observations, interviews, and examining policies, regulations, or enforcement practices. Some relevant questions that researchers may ask include: What events typically follow the problem event? Who benefits from leaving the problem as it is? What broader contextual features such as policies, regulations, or enforcement practices contribute to the maintenance of the problem? What current social, economic, and environmental factors affect the level of the problem? How do people's attitudes and beliefs help maintain the problem? Answers to these questions will help identify and clarify the conditions that maintain the problem.

Conclusion

The focus of the problem identification phase in an intervention-research paradigm is to specify the problem event or behavior and functionally analyze contextual variables in which the problem occurs. This process should be conducted jointly with potential participants, while avoiding victim-blaming assumptions about the nature of the problem. Identifying antecedent and consequent events allows researchers to develop a comprehensive intervention that attempts to alter those antecedents and/or consequences in order to change problem behaviors. A functional analysis can reveal that a given problem is due to the presence of inappropriate antecedent and/or consequent events or due to the absence of appropriate antecedent events and/or consequences. Notice that the focus of the analysis is on the contextual or environmental conditions that surround a particular problem behavior or event. This is a departure from traditional assessment strategies which are primarily focused on the evaluation of individual personality characteristics.

Case Study: Inappropriate Use of Handicapped-Parking Spaces

Problem Identification and Analysis

At the time this study was conducted, the authors were affiliated with The Research and Training Center on Independent Living (RTC/IL) at the University of Kansas, funded by a grant from the National Institute on Disability Rehabilitation Research (NIDRR). The purpose of this center was to develop effective technologies to facilitate independent living for people with physical disabilities.

One of the main tasks of the RTC/IL staff was to prepare and conduct a needs assessment survey of people with disabilities receiving services from Independent Living Centers (ILCs) across the nation. The assessment and agenda setting methodology developed for this purpose was called the *concerns report method,* which is a systematic strategy to assist disadvantaged populations identify community strengths and problems as they perceive them and generate ideas for community improvement (Fawcett, Seekins, Whang, Muiu, & Suarez de Balcazar, 1982; Fawcett et al., 1988).

The main steps in the method were as follows:

1. A working group was selected, which consisted of a representative group of consumers who selected items for the survey. Items were selected from an index of community issues relevant to the population of interest. The working group used a menu of concerns from which they selected or adapted approximately 35 items for a concerns survey. The menu had been developed and pilot tested with various groups of people with disabilities (Suarez de Balcazar, Bradford, & Fawcett, 1988) and low-income families (Schriner & Fawcett, 1988). Interviews with people with disabilities and experts in the field, as well as an extensive literature review, were used to generate items for areas like employment, education, health, accessibility, transportation, advocacy, and community services.

2. A needs assessment survey was prepared. Each item was evaluated on two dimensions: respondents opinions about the importance of the item and their satisfaction with the current status of the item. In one application with a group of people with disabilities an item read:

	How important is it to you that . . .	How satisfied are you that . . .
Handicapped-parking spaces in commercial lots are respected by residents.	not very 1 2 3 4 5	not very 1 2 3 4 5

3. The survey was administrated to consumers of each local community through service agencies. Once the questionnaires were returned, responses were analyzed to identify the mean percentage of satisfaction and importance for each item. A problem typically reflects an item rated as very important but with low satisfaction, whereas a community strength would be an item with high ratings of importance and satisfaction. Then, a list of the top five to ten strengths and potential problems was prepared.

4. Once data were analyzed, a public meeting or focus group discussion

with community members was conducted. The results of the survey were presented to interested community members who were invited to discuss the dimensions of identified problems and strengths and to generate ideas for improvement. Finally, a policy report that summarized the main strengths and problems, the dimensions of the problems as perceived by the people who experienced them, and a list of suggestions for improvement was prepared for distribution. These reports are usually disseminated to interested parties like agency administrators, decision makers, advocacy organizations, and self-help groups.

The concerns report method presents a departure from most traditional needs assessment and agenda-setting methodologies. Potential consumers are involved throughout the entire process, from designing the survey to discussing the results. The following section illustrates the problem identification phase in the process of conducting intervention research on the issue of enforcement of handicapped parking ordinances.

Gaining Entry into the Setting

A local application of the concerns report method in a midwestern university town of about 50,000 inhabitants indicated handicapped parking among the top 10 problems identified by people with disabilities in this community. The first author consulted with an advocacy group of individuals who wanted to take action on some of the issues identified in the needs assessment. They invited the researcher to discuss possible action strategies to address the problem of violations of the local handicapped-parking ordinance. The first author attended several meetings while getting to know the group and the type of accessibility problems that members were facing. The researcher played the role of participant observer and consultant.

Specifying the Problem

Lack of enforcement of handicapped-parking ordinances was identified as a problem in different needs assessment survey applications conducted in 12 states involving over 18,000 people with disabilities (Suarez de Balcazar, Bradford, & Fawcett, 1988). Some of the dimensions of the handicapped-parking problem discussed during the public forum included: inappropriate use of handicapped-parking spaces by nondisabled drivers, absence of upright parking signs in many sites, lack of appropriate marking of the spaces, and lack of enforcement of parking ordinances.

A literature review in the areas of accessibility and handicapped parking was conducted. This review revealed that very few studies had actually analyzed the function of handicapped-parking signs (e.g., Jason & Jung, 1984). It was found that signs alone may not be sufficient to maintain behavior changes (e.g., Jason & Liotta 1982; Van Houten & Nau, 1981; Winett, 1978), while aversive consequences—such as police enforcement—have been more effective in promoting compliance with a variety of state and local laws (e.g., Geller, Winett, & Everett, 1982; Schnelle, Kirchner, Casey, Uselton, & McNees, 1977).

In addition to the concerns report method, other strategies were also used to further specify and understand the level of the problem. First, visual inspections of several parking lots in the community were conducted using a checklist based on federal standards (Department of Housing and Urban Development, 1980). Second, direct observations of selected parking spaces were conducted at different hours of the day to collect a preliminary estimate of the frequency of inappropriate parking. Third, several group members and the researcher conducted interviews with business managers, people with disabilities, local officials, and occasional violators to discuss their views about the problem.

These strategies yielded some useful information: the locations of parking lots where parking violations occurred frequently, the lack of police enforcement, and business owners lack of commitment to make their parking lots accessible. Several managers of supermarkets and department stores indicated their willingness to address the issue and cooperate with the consumer organization. Finally, it was also found that about 60% of people with disabilities in the community either drove a car, or had someone drive them to stores at least twice a week.

Analyzing the Problem

A functional analysis of the problem yielded the following information:

1. *Conditions that affected the onset of the problem: Antecedent events.* Considering data collected through direct observation, interviews, the literature review, and the public forum, we concluded that the problem was most critical in parking spaces demarcated only with ground signs. These spaces were frequently hard for drivers to see for several reasons: faded paint, dirt, oil drops, and water. During the winter months snow would cover the markers on the ground. Coincidentally, many consumers indicated that winter was also the time when they preferred to have the most access because of the cold temperatures and hazardous conditions on the ground.

Second, it was found that police officers could not enforce the handicapped-parking ordinance in the absence of an upright metal sign. The reason was that every time a violator came to court, he or she would argue that the marker was not clearly visible.

Third, direct observations during pilot evaluations of the problem indicated that nearly twice as many violations occurred during the late afternoon and evening hours, and on cool or rainy days, as during morning hours and on sunny days. Using the operational definition provided earlier in this paper, pilot observations indicated that parking violations occurred an average of 20% of the time in the spaces observed, rising as high as 70% during the early evening hours.

Fourth, several business managers indicated that they were not aware of the specifications for appropriate posting of handicapped parking spaces, where to order such signs, or how much they would cost (Suarez-Balcazar & Fawcett, 1990).

2. *Conditions that maintained the problem: Consequent events.* The city had an ordinance that specified a $25 fine for illegal parking in a handicapped-parking space. Unfortunately, the ordinance was rarely enforced. The absence of appropriate consequences, such as fines for people parked illegally, seemed to be a critical variable. A sense of impunity or perhaps irrelevancy about this particular law was pervasive. The most frequent remarks made by potential violators of the parking ordinance included: "I did not see the ground sign," "I did not know it was illegal," "It will only be for a couple of minutes," "I don't care," "I don't think anybody uses these parking spaces," and "I couldn't find any other parking space and this one was empty."

It was also concluded that some enforcement of the law was necessary to stop violators from assuming that their violation would not have any negative consequence. A meeting with the local Assistant Chief of Police indicated the department's willingness to increase periodic enforcement in certain areas like supermarkets and shopping malls. According to the police a necessary condition for enforcement was the presence of an upright metal sign.

Based on the data collected through the problem identification phase, participants decided to start a campaign to increase the number of upright metal signs in parking lots. This campaign involved collecting appropriate information to be distributed to business owners and contacting them through letters and personal interviews. The second phase of the intervention process was the negotiation of periodic crackdowns by police officers on selected sites. The consequences of this intervention are described in detail in Suarez de Balcazar, Fawcett, and Balcazar (1988).

Discussion

Problem identification in intervention research involves an interactive process that can lead researchers to generate strategies to address social problems. This process includes gaining entry into a setting, specifying the problem, and analyzing the conditions in which the problem occurs. The emphasis on examining contextual or environmental factors when attempting to define or identify social problems can help researchers avoid the trap of victim blaming. Consumer involvement is also an effective mechanism to protect the integrity of the research process and to increase the likelihood of maintaining the intervention over time.

The case study used to illustrate the process produced some positive results. Participants negotiated the installation of upright metal handicapped-parking signs with several supermarkets and shopping malls. The introduction of upright metal parking signs produced moderate reductions in the percentage of time of illegal use of targeted parking spaces (from an average baseline level of 30% to an average of 24%). Group members negotiated a crackdown with the police department. During the crackdown (over 60 parking tickets were issued in one week), the average of illegal use went down to 13%. A "reduced enforcement" phase was later introduced by the police department (assigning one police car for occasional inspection of supermarkets and shopping malls). During the reduced enforcement phase the average of inappropriate parking went down to 9.5%. It appears that the occasional sighting of a police car issuing tickets in a parking lot had a gradual but significant effect. Follow-up data collected 8 months later indicated that the average percentage of illegal parking was 2% on the targeted sites. Data collected in a control site, selected in a nearby city, suggested that the inappropriate use of handicapped-parking spaces did not vary across experimental conditions (Suarez de Balcazar, Fawcett, & Balcazar, 1988).

In the case study, people with disabilities participated actively in the problem identification, analysis, and intervention phases. The study also yielded important social policy recommendations that were adopted at the local and state levels (Fawcett & Suarez de Balcazar, 1985). The fines for illegal parking in handicapped-parking spaces were eventually increased to $250.

Several potential benefits and limitations of an intervention-research paradigm should be considered. The first consideration is whether participants' involvement in the problem identification and analysis process maximizes the effectiveness of social interventions. This is an empirical question that should be answered based on actual experience with particular populations, problems, and situations. Several studies suggest that active involvement of participants in the problem identification phase and in designing intervention strategies can be beneficial. Such cases include self-management procedures (Baer, 1984) and the quality circles management approach used primarily in the private sector (Peters & Waterman, 1982).

Second, value conflict in the choice of goals (Warwick & Kelman, 1976) may arise. As potential participants and researchers identify and analyze a problem, differences in individuals' perceptions of the problem may persist. Collecting observational data, as was done in the case study (occurrences of illegal parking), assists in an accurate assessment of the problem and helps minimize differences of opinion. In addition, researchers should be sensitive to the needs and values of potential collaborators. For instance, in the case study, people with disabilities provided useful information about the dimensions of the problem (locations of spaces frequently violated, peak hours, etc.). Consumers' participation in the research process allows a more comprehensive and realistic identification and analysis of the problem.

Finally, the degree of experimental control of applied research is limited compared with laboratory or analogue research. However, what is lost in control may be gained in generality, since findings may more closely relate to actual situations. Applied research frequently requires researchers to adopt a more flexible approach to the problem identification phase and to the design of their interventions, since they sometimes have little influence over who receives the intervention or when the intervention takes place (e.g., Balcazar et al., 1990).

Social intervention research is a growing field, and although its goals are ambitious, it has some limitations. One issue is the difficulty in collecting data in natural settings. This process frequently requires strong cooperation from participants who may agree to self-record their own behavior or record relevant community events. It is also important to consider multiple strategies for identifying and analyzing problems such as objective (direct observation) and subjective (surveys, interviews) research techniques.

Skinner (1953) suggested that "the formalized experience of science, added to the practical experience of the individual in a complex set of circumstances, offers the best basis for effective action" (p. 436). This is the framework that characterizes intervention research in community settings. Intervention research is an important strategy to facilitate "empowerment" of community members, as they participate actively in the process of identifying and analyzing problems. The challenge for applied social psychology in the 1990s is to contribute effectively in the development of solutions to relevant social problems.

ACKNOWLEDGMENTS. We specially thank Joe Durlak and Christine Smith for their useful comments and suggestions on earlier versions of this chapter.

References

Agar, M. H. (1980). *The professional stranger: An informal introduction to ethnography.* New York: Academic Press.

Baer, D. M. (1984). Does research on self-control need more self-control? *Analysis and Intervention in Developmental Disabilities, 4,* 211–218.

Baer, D. M., Wolf, M. M., & Risley, T. R. (1968). Some current dimensions of applied behavior analysis. *Journal of Applied Behavior Analysis, 1,* 91–97.

Baer, D. M., Wolf, M. M., & Risley, T. R. (1987). Some still-current dimensions of applied behavior analysis. *Journal of Applied Behavior Analysis, 2,* 313–327.

Bailey, J. S. (1977). *A handbook of research methods in applied behavior analysis* (pp. 1–210).

(Available from the author, Department of Psychology, Florida State University, Tallahassee, FL).

Balcazar, F. E., Seekins T., Fawcett, S. B., & Hopkins, B. L. (1990). Empowering people with physical disabilities through advocacy skills training. *American Journal of Community Psychology, 18,* 281–296.

Balcazar, F. E., Suarez-Balcazar, Y., & Fawcett, S. B. (in press). Intervention research model and the empowerment of black males. In R. Majors and J. U. Gordon (Eds.), *The American black male: His present status and his future.* New York, NY: Nelson Hall.

Briscoe, R. V., Hoffman, D. B., & Bailey, J. S. (1975). Behavioral community psychology: Training a community board to problem solve. *Journal of Applied Behavior Analysis, 8,* 157–168.

Chavis, D. M., Stuckey, P., & Wandersman, A. (1983). Returning basic research to the community: A relationship between scientist and citizen. *American Psychologist, 38,* 424–434.

Crewe, N., & Zola, I. K. (1983). *Independent living for physically disabled people.* San Francisco: Jossey-Bass.

DeJong, G. (1979). Defining and implementing the independent living concept. In N. M. Crew & I. K. Zola (Eds.), *Independent living for physically disabled people* (pp. 4–27). San Francisco: Jossey-Bass.

Department of Housing and Urban Development. (1980). *American National Standards Institute* (Publication No. A117. 1). New York: ANSI.

Deutsch, M., & Hornstein, H. A. (1975). *Applying Social Psychology: Implications for research, practice, and training.* Hillsdale, NJ: Lawrence Erlbaum.

Edwards, J. (1990). Framework for applying social psychology processes to social issues. In J. Edwards, R. S. Tindale, L. Heath, & E. J. Posavac (Eds.), *Social influence processes and prevention* (pp. 1–12). New York: Plenum.

Edwards, J., Tindale, R. S., Heath, L., & Posavac, E. J. (Eds.). (1990). *Social influence processes and prevention.* New York: Plenum.

Fawcett, S. B. (1990). Some emerging standards for community research and action: Aid from a behavioral perspective. In P. Tolan, C. Keys, F. Chertok, & L. Jason (Eds.), *Researching community psychology: Issues of theory and methods* (pp. 64–75). Washington DC: American Psychological Association.

Fawcett, S. B., Mathews, R. M., & Fletcher, R. K. (1980). Some promising dimensions for behavioral community technology. *Journal of Applied Behavior Analysis, 13,* 508–518.

Fawcett, S. B., Seekins, T., Whang, P. L., Muiu, C., & Suarez de Balcazar, Y. (1982). Involving consumers in decision-making. *Social Policy, 13,* 36–41.

Fawcett, S. B., & Suarez de Balcazar, Y. (1985). *Testimony to the special committee on transportation of the Kansas Legislature, Proposal No. 62-Handicapped Parking.* Lawrence: Research and Training Center on Independent Living.

Fawcett, S. B., Suarez-Balcazar, Y., Balcazar, F., White, G., Paine, A., Embree, M. G., & Blanchard, K. A. (in press). Intervention research in communities: Methods and exemplars. In J. Rothman & E. J. Thomas (Eds.), *Intervention research: Creating effective methods for professional practice.* Chicago: University of Chicago Press.

Fawcett, S. B., Suarez de Balcazar, Y., Whang-Ramos, P. L., Seekins, T., Bradford, B., & Mathews, R. M. (1988). The concerns report: Involving consumers in planning for rehabilitation and independent living services. *American Rehabilitation, 14*(13), 17–19.

Geller, R. S., Gruff, C. D., & Nimmer, J. G. (1985). "Flash for life": Community-based prompting for safety belt promotion. *Journal of Applied Behavior Analysis, 18,* 145–159.

Geller, R. S., Winett, R. A., & Everett, P. B. (1982). *Preserving the environment: New strategies for behavior change.* New York: Pergamon Press.

Glenwick, D. S., & Jason, L. A. (Eds.). (1980). *Behavioral community psychology: Progress and prospects.* New York: Praeger.

Goldfried, M. R., & D'Zurilla, T. J. (1969). A behavioral-analytic model for assessing competence. In C. D. Spielberg (Ed.), *Current topics in clinical and community psychology* (Vol. 1, pp. 151–196). New York: Academic Press.

Hornstein, H. A. (1975). Social psychology as social intervention. In M. Deutsch, & H. A. Hornstein (Eds.), *Applying social psychology: Implications for research, practice and training.* Hillsdale, NJ: Lawrence Erlbaum.

Jaccard, J., Turrisi, R., & Wan, C. K. (1990). Implications of behavioral decision theory and social marketing for designing social action programs. In J. Edwards, R. S. Tindale, L. Health, & E. J. Posavac. (Eds.), *Social influence processes and prevention* (Vol. 1, pp. 103–142). New York: Plenum.

Jason, L. A., & Jung, R. (1984). Stimulus control techniques applied to handicapped-designed parking spaces. *Environment and Behavior, 16,* 675–686.

Jason, L. A., & Liotta, R. F. (1982). Reduction of cigarette smoking in a university cafeteria. *Journal of Applied Behavior Analysis, 15,* 573–577.

Kantor, J. R. (1959). *Interbehavioral psychology.* Chicago: Principia Press.

Kelly, J. G. (1986). An ecological paradigm: Defining mental health consultation as a preventative service. In J. G. Kelly & R. E. Hess (Eds.), *The ecology of prevention: Illustrating mental health consultation* (pp. 1–36). New York: Haworth Press.

Kidd, R. F., & Saks, M. J. (1980). *Advances in applied social psychology* (Vol. 1). Hillsdale, NJ: Lawrence Erlbaum.

Lewin, K. (1948). *Resolving social conflicts.* New York: Harper.

Loken, B., Swim, J., & Mittelmark, M. B. (1990). Heart health program: Applying social influence processes in a large-scale community health promotion program. In J. Edwards, R. S. Tindale, L. Heath, & E. J. Posavac (Eds.), *Social Influence Processes and Prevention* (pp. 159–179). New York: Plenum.

Mason, J. E., & Bramble, J. W. (1989). *Understanding and conducting research.* New York: McGraw-Hill.

Miller, G. A. (1969). Psychology as a means of promoting human welfare. *American Psychologists, 24,* 1063–1075.

National Science Foundation (1966). Federal funds for research, development, and other scientific activities. Fiscal year 1967, 1968, 1969. Vol. *15.*

Oskamp, S. (1984). *Applied social psychology.* Englewood Cliffs, NJ: Prentice-Hall.

Peters, T. J., & Waterman, R. H. (1982). *In search of excellence: Lessons from America's best-run companies.* New York: Warner Books.

Rothman, J. (1980). *Social research and development in the human services.* Englewood Cliffs, NJ: Prentice-Hall.

Rothman, J. & Thomas, E. J. (in press). *Intervention research: Creating effective methods for professional practice.* Chicago: University of Chicago Press.

Ryan, W. (1971). *Blaming the victim.* New York: Vintage Books.

Schnelle, J. F., Kirchner, R. E., Jr., Casey, J. D., Uselton, P. H., Jr., & McNees, M. P. (1977). Patrol evaluation research: A multiple-baseline analysis of saturation police patrolling during the day and night hours. *Journal of Applied Behavior Analysis, 10,* 33–40.

Schriner, K. F., & Fawcett, S. B. (1988). Development and validation of a community concerns report method. *Journal of Community Psychology, 16,* 306–316.

Seidman, E., Rappaport, J. (1986). *Redefining social problems.* New York: Plenum.

Seekins, T., Mathews, M. R., & Fawcett, S. B. (1984). Enhancing leadership skills for community self-help organizations through behavioral instructions. *Journal of Community Psychology, 12,* 155–163.

Suarez de Balcazar, Y., Bradford, B., & Fawcett, S. B. (1988). Common concerns of disabled Americans: Issues and options. *Social Policy, 19*(2), 29–35.

Suarez de Balcazar, Y., Fawcett, S. B., & Balcazar, F. E. (1988). Effects of environmental design and police enforcement on violation of a handicapped parking ordinance. *Journal of Applied Behavior Analysis, 21,* 291–298.

Suarez-Balcazar Y., & Fawcett, S. (1990, March). Handicap parking violations: A plan for effective consumer action. *Paraplegia News,* 34–35.

Van Houten, R. (1988). The effects of advance stop lines and sign prompts on pedestrian safety in a crosswalk on a multilane highway. *Journal of Applied Behavior Analysis, 21,* 245–251.

Van Houten, R., & Nau, P. A. (1981). A comparison of the effects of posted feedback and increased police surveillance on highway speeding. *Journal of Applied Behavior Analysis, 14,* 261–271.

Warwick, D. P., & Kelman, H. C. (1976). Ethical issues in social intervention. In W. G. Bennis, H. D. Benne, R. Chin, & K. E. Corey (Eds.), *The planning of change* (3rd ed., pp. 470–496). New York: Holt, Rinehart & Winston.

Weick, K. E. (1984). Small wins: Redefining the scale of social problems. *American Psychologists, 39,* 40–49.

Winett, R. A. (1978). Promoting turning-out lights in unoccupied rooms. *Journal of Environmental Systems, 6,* 237–241.

Wolf, M. M. (1978). Social validity: The case for subjective measurement or how applied behavior analysis is finding its heart. *Journal of Applied Behavior Analysis, 11,* 203–214.

3

Ethical Issues in Community-Based Research and Intervention

Joan E. Sieber and James L. Sorensen

Ethical issues arise at each stage of community-based research and intervention. We divide community-based research and intervention into six stages: (1) selecting the setting in which to address the research problem, (2) designing the research or intervention to fit the setting, (3) recruiting subjects, (4) collecting data, (5) data handling, analysis, storage and ownership, and (6) disseminating findings. In the latter two stages, ethical concerns arise if the data are confidential (see Boruch & Cecil, 1979, for solutions to problems of confidentiality) or if the findings are politically sensitive. However, some of the most complex and poorly understood ethical issues are likely to arise in the first three stages, which are the focus of this chapter.

This chapter provides guidelines for gaining sensitivity to the interests and culture of gatekeepers and subjects[1] in community-based research, and for devel-

---

[1]To some readers the term "subject" may be seen disrespectful. At times the term "respondent" or "participant" is obviously more appropriate. However, for purposes of this chapter, we prefer to use a term that continually reminds the reader that participants in AIDS-related research are far less powerful than the researcher and must be accorded the protection that renders this inequality morally acceptable. While street people and drug addicts do have certain kinds of power in the research process, theirs is the power that comes from being marginal, fearful and streetwise, not the power that comes from privilege and formal education. They did not initiate the idea of doing the research, and they probably will not benefit from it as much as will the investigator.

Joan E. Sieber • Department of Psychology, California State University, Hayward, California 94542.   **James L. Sorensen** • Langley Porter Psychiatric Institute, University of California, San Francisco, California 94110.
Methodological Issues in Applied Psychology, edited by Bryant et al. Plenum Press, New York, 1992.

oping a flexible research plan that is responsive to the exigencies of community-based settings. Throughout this chapter we refer to "gatekeepers." These are the people who let researchers into the community-based setting and help them to establish rapport with the research population—or keep them out. Gatekeepers derive their power from their ability to negotiate conditions that are acceptable to those they serve. They cannot grant favors to a researcher that may cause concern or harm to research participants or to the community. Gatekeepers may occasionally be scientists, such as a researcher who also directs a university-affiliated community clinic. More frequently gatekeepers are nonscientists; they may be so-called street professionals, such as a recovered drug addict or a former prostitute, who now serve as advocate or community outreach person to their own people; they may be ministers of local minority churches, or other kinds of community organizers.

In discussing community-based research, we focus on research on drug abuse and AIDS, distinguishing between street-based and clinic-based projects, which require considerably different skills and methods of gaining access. However, both are settings in which the researcher, in order to enter and obtain valid data, must respect the culture of both the gatekeepers and the subjects. The difficulties of comprehending and responding sensitively to these cultures, and of gaining access and the cooperation of subjects, can be overwhelming, even to the experienced community-based researcher. For the traditional researcher, the task of responding sensitively can amount to having to change some basic beliefs and attitudes about the conduct of social research. In settings where researchers have unilateral power to conduct research, they may be relatively insensitive to their subjects. The "get data" attitude typically conveyed in research training teaches scientists to focus on their predetermined research agenda and to ignore the perceptions and expectations of their subjects. Insensitive researchers become part of the stimulus array to which subjects respond—to the detriment of all concerned. The most polite middle-class subject will gladly deceive an insensitive researcher and certainly a streetwise person will. Ultimately, it is the researcher, not the subject, who is likely to be naive and deceived. Respect and sensitivity to the culture, needs, and interests of subjects, then, are essential on scientific, as well as ethical, grounds. Researchers in all settings do well to resurrect any natural sensitivities to others that they lost in the process of "scientific training," and to further develop those sensitivities according to the cultures they seek to enter.

What Do We Mean by Ethics?

Principles

What do ethics have to do with the culturally sensitive issues just described? Let us first say what we mean by the term "ethics." We take our definition of ethics from the ethical principles and research norms set forth by the National Commission for the Protection of Human Subjects of Biomedical and Behavioral Research (1979).[2]

   A. *Respect for Persons*. This refers to treating individuals as autonomous agents, with courtesy and respect for individuals as persons. People with diminished autonomy, like young children or the mentally ill, are entitled to protection.
   B. *Beneficence*. This principle involves maximizing good outcomes for science, humanity, and the individual research participants, and avoiding or minimizing unnecessary risk, harm, or wrong.
   C. *Justice*. This principle involves the development of fair rules, fair procedures, and fair distribution of costs and benefits. For example, those who bear the risks of research should be those who benefit from it.

Norms of Ethical Research

   These three principles translate into norms of ethical research on humans (the letters after each norm designate the principles on which the norm is based).

   1. Valid research design. The design of ethical research must take into account relevant theory, methods, and prior findings. Invalid research is unethical. (A,B)
   2. Competence of the researcher. The principal investigator needs to be capable of carrying out the procedures and able to assume responsibility for supervising other investigators. (A,B)
   3. Risk–benefit assessment. An assessment of the relative drawbacks and advantages of the study needs to take place from relevant perspectives in addition to that of the researcher. Ethical research will adjust procedures to maximize benefit and minimize risk. (A,B,C)
   4. Selection of subjects. The subjects must be appropriate to the purposes of the study and from the population that is to benefit from the research. Additionally, the researcher should use neither more subjects than necessary nor too few to yield valid inferences about the population. (A,B,C)
   5. Voluntary informed consent. This should be obtained beforehand in the normal conduct of research. *Voluntary* means freely, without threat or undue

[2]Our choice of the NCPHSBBR ethical principles and norms is based on their simplicity, breadth, and generality, which makes it easy to interpret them to reflect the special ethical problems that are likely to arise in AIDS-related research. The researcher may also consult the code of ethics of his or her own professional association.

inducement. *Informed* means that the subject knows what a reasonable person in that situation would want to know before consenting. *Consent* means explicit agreement to participate. Informed consent requires clear, respectful two-way communication that subjects comprehend, not complex technical explanations or legal jargon. (A,B,C)

(A detailed discussion of these principles and research norms and of their application in clinical research appears in Levine, 1986.)

An ethical issue in research, then, is a problem of maximizing the good outcomes for science, subjects, and society, respecting those who participate in the research process, and being fair—not just from the scientist's perspective, but also from the perspective of the culture in which the research is performed—while also meeting the standards of sound scientific practice. Successful translation of the principles and norms for community-based settings hinges on three related ideas that are basic to the rest of this chapter:

1. Ethics and methodology are inextricably related. Unethical methods tend not to yield valid results. This is true in all human research. However, this point is brought home most forcibly in community-based research: entry into the subject population will be blocked by the community if the methods employed are not sensitive to the needs and perspectives of that population.

2. The so-called scientific method by which one conceives of a research problem, designs procedures, and tests hypotheses is merely an iterative subset of the many steps required to carry out community-based research. The researcher enters a community setting with research plans in mind, but these plans must be flexible. Much exploration is required to discover the culture and needs of the subjects in an applied setting before deciding on the exact research methods and procedures. In the process of matching research method with setting, one may have to conceive of many different ways to organize the research before finding a way that satisfies all of the constraints of the community-based setting.

3. Community settings are full of idiosyncrasies and surprises. In each new setting, the discovery of how to gain access and obtain valid, worthwhile data requires the application of patience and cultural sensitivity to both the gatekeepers or professional staff who help provide entry, and to the research population. It is advantageous if the researcher has had prior experience with that population or has been a member of that population; but even prior membership does not mean that the researcher speaks their current language or will be welcomed and trusted.

For the researcher who is accustomed to university-based research, community settings offer unimagined opportunities and unimagined limitations. For example, in San Francisco the city's drug abuse treatment programs collect needle-sharing information from every one of the thousands of admissions each year, and this information is entered into a central computerized data bank. This data bank is a rich archive for research on AIDS prevention, and it has yielded documentation that the reported needle-sharing of patients decreased from 1986 to 1988 (Guydish, Abramowitz, Woods, Black, & Sorensen, 1990). However, the needle-sharing information was gathered by intake workers in treatment programs, and consequently is subject to a number of influences that may have caused patients to underreport their actual needle-sharing behaviors: Patients may have wanted to please the treatment staff or to "look good" in their eyes. Staff may not have asked questions consistently, and unless specifically told to do so, some drug users tend not to count it as sharing if they shared needles only with their spouse or primary sexual partner.

This chapter attempts to provide a perceptual set so that the investigator will more quickly discover such heretofore unimagined aspects of community-based research. But the work of discovery and problem solving remains for each investigator in each new setting. The first step is to find a setting in which the researcher, the gatekeepers, and the subjects may be able to find a way to accommodate one another.

Selecting a Setting for the Research or Intervention

The researcher–intervener no doubt has some goal in mind that suggests possible research sites and populations. For example, one might wish to study the safe-sex knowledge of black teenage crack users or the sex practices of drug-using prostitutes. Perhaps there is an intervention component, such as AIDS education or condom distribution. Even if the researcher does not have an intervention in mind, it might be a requirement of entry that something of value be given to each subject in return for participation, especially if the research is street based.

Community-based research with drug abuse and AIDS usually occurs "on the street" (i.e., in the living situation of the subject) or "in the clinic" (i.e., in drug treatment or in a health care setting). Should the researcher seek a street-based setting or a clinic-based setting? Each setting has relative advantages and disadvantages.

Street-Based Research

The uninitiated researcher might suppose that one can simply "go downtown" and interview street people. Surely such people will welcome the skills and services of a caring professional, and will be delighted to cooperate. This supposition could hardly be less realistic. There are street people who will tell their name and life story, but if the researcher should interview them again a few days later, they will tell a different name and life story. These various personae are ways that many people have of protecting themselves from the law. Their life stories are well rehearsed, and many street people have various "selves" that they will discuss in fascinating detail (Bowser, 1990).

A host of additional problems surround the assumption that one will be perceived as a caring professional and that one's services will be welcomed. Many street people have had their fill of "helping professionals" who have not helped at all; besides, the researcher cannot presume to know what would constitute desired help without seeking the advice of those to be served, and even then persons may not ask for help. One manifestation of the painful past of people living on the street is their belief that it is better to survive on bravado than to trust a stranger. For example, the frightened runaway boy or girl may believe that selling one's body is the best way to get a meal or drugs on a regular basis, despite a distinct probability that he or she will be murdered within a short time.

But perhaps the most serious error of the neophyte community researcher is the assumption that street people are out there alone. Street people live within a culture that has well-defined rules of conduct, communication, and attitudes toward outsiders (Bowser, 1990). Within their community there are close ties and a grapevine that rapidly transmits news about outsiders and about members of the community. Homeless people have friends who look out for one another (Levitas, 1990; Pitt, 1989). The researcher is the outsider and is powerless to achieve valid research or outreach objectives unless the community approves.

How does one become an insider to street culture? It helps to know a gatekeeper. Unless the researcher's activities and objectives are consonant with those of the gatekeeper, no research will occur. Often one needs to put in many hours of social service to that community before discussing the possibility of doing research there. The following example illustrates the objectives of a particular gatekeeper, and the way in which a researcher–intervener established a working relationship with the gatekeeper and the people she served.

The gatekeeper in this instance is the executive director of a prostitute education and advocacy organization. She is an ex-prostitute who has obtained funding for a variety of services to prostitutes, including serving them food and distributing condoms; asking them what she may do to help them; assessing the kinds of education they may need and finding enjoyable ways to provide that education (e.g., quizzes on safe sex, with prizes for those who get all the answers right); responding to problems they may be experiencing (e.g., police confiscating and photocopying their condoms to use as evidence against them, then punching pinholes in the condoms before returning them); solving those problems (e.g., through discussion with the mayor's office and other city agencies); and establishing regular places to meet, serve food, hear concerns, and provide needed resources (Lockett, 1990).

The researcher–intervener is a university-based social scientist who wished to do HIV testing of prostitutes and AIDS education. From her previous work with street drug addicts, she knew that she must learn how to relate to the prostitute population before she could effectively carry out some version of her intended research–intervention. She undertook to assist the gatekeeper so that she could discover how to make her research and intervention plans consonant with the goals and activities of the gatekeeper. Together they developed a plan for AIDS testing and education that was coordinated with and complementary to the gatekeeper's regular activities (Cohen, 1988).

In some cases, gatekeepers are not professionals (street or otherwise) but simply the more capable and influential members of the community. For example, among the homeless, there are some street people who know the ropes well. A researcher who wished to establish a needle exchange program among the homeless conducted conversations with some of these gatekeepers (Case, 1990). She sought information about her potential clientele, their needs and concerns, which of these she could satisfy, and how best to get together with them. After some conversations, she issued a word-of-mouth invitation to a meal at a nearby flophouse. She served hot dogs, sauerkraut, bread, and soda pop in great abundance. This was an opportunity for her to learn about the people who would probably be participating, to learn to recognize faces, to hear people's ideas about how to organize the needle exchange, and to begin to build trust. Subsequent meetings with the gatekeepers enabled her to learn what people thought of the program and how to solve problems that had arisen. Ultimately, the researcher herself became a trusted professional in the community and became a gatekeeper whose requirements other potential researchers and interveners must now satisfy.

Since most gatekeepers are, themselves, interveners—helping professionals, ministers, or street professionals—they may welcome a researcher who will further their cause. A word of caution about causes, however: the researcher may be expected to make the data come out in a way that supports an application for funds, or that otherwise makes the gatekeeper look good. The researcher should expect to bend in various ways to accommodate the needs and interests of the gatekeepers and subjects, but must be wary of the quid pro quo that is immoral or that violates ethical principles of scientific inquiry.

In short, one must devote much effort to cultivating knowledge about one's chosen street setting and to developing a relationship in which research might be permitted. Perhaps by now the reader's fervor to do street-based research has begun to cool and is being replaced by a rising enthusiasm to learn how to conduct research in a clinic.

Clinic-Based Research

Drug treatment and health care programs can be excellent entry points for researchers who want to reach drug abusers. Outpatient drug abusers regularly attend clinics, and residential patients live there. They are accessible because they must comply with clinic rules, and because they develop bonds of trust with the people who treat them. They can also provide access to "street" drug users who are their friends. Thus, such treatment programs can provide an entry point for learning about the problems of AIDS among drug users. A review of 92 HIV seroprevalence studies among drug users indicated that all but 3 were conducted with drug abusers in treatment (Hahn, Oronato, Jones, & Dougherty, 1989). However, there are barriers to clinic-based research as well.

Clinic-based research, like street-based research, is limited by the researcher's ability to accommodate to the requirements of the setting. Depending on the topic of the intended research and the methods the researcher wishes to employ, the clinic gatekeepers decide whether the research can be permitted.

Clinics have interests and vulnerabilities that can make it difficult to conduct research there. Staff are concerned about maintaining confidentiality and controlling the setting. Drug treatment programs need to manage potentially unruly clientele and also need to zealously guard the confidentiality of treatment files. As gatekeepers the program staff keep researchers and drug users from exploiting one another.

The second author of this chapter is Chief of Substance Abuse Services at San Francisco General Hospital (SFGH). To give clear-cut examples of ways that clinic-based research may be arranged, this discussion is based on experience at SFGH. The Substance Abuse Services at SFGH has a methadone maintenance program that treats heroin addicts, half of whom were admitted because of HIV infection. In addition there is an outpatient methadone detoxification clinic that provides 21-day phased withdrawal from heroin, and an outpatient program for people who have problems with cocaine. The program also has a medical clinic for the many patients who have HIV infection. Over the last 10 years, Substance Abuse Services has been the site of research resulting in over 100 publications.

Sometimes a research project simply cannot occur at a program through no fault of the researcher. For example, in Australia innovators reported on the efficacy of integrating a needle exchange with a methadone maintenance program (Wolk, Wodack, Guinan, Macaskill, & Simpson, 1989). Such a project would face considerable barriers in many U.S. programs: current federal policy prohibits using federal resources to evaluate syringe exchanges, many states and municipalities would not allow such an exchange to operate, and treatment program staff might object that the syringe exchange would be inconsistent with the recovery orientation of drug treatment programs.

The attitudes of research staff can also be a barrier to conducting research in a clinic. Researchers can be quite intrusive in a clinic, and they may be ignorant of the standards of care. Researchers at SFGH have attempted to conduct informed consent procedures when patients were in withdrawal or so inebriated that the treatment staff would not even let them in the clinic. In addition, researchers can be quite demanding of staff, putting their research above treatment. Sometimes these conflicts become personnel issues, with line staff resenting the "special" status (or attitudes) of research staff. To conduct research effectively in a clinic, investigators and their staff need to learn the treatment program mores, abide by them, and treat both patients and staff according to the principles of respect, beneficence, and justice that govern research.

Designing Research to Fit the Setting

In community-based research, the selection of hypotheses and methods may be driven by current practice, just as in laboratory-based social psychological research. However, it is typically driven by a different set of current practices— ones grounded in the attempt to solve pressing social problems and grounded in the demands of community-based settings. Bearing in mind that ethical research is beneficent and respectful, one's approaches and goals must be acceptable to the populations studied and to the gatekeepers of the community setting. They must also be conducive to generating useful knowledge.

The vulnerable and powerless populations likely to be studied have been called "fugitive populations" because they fear the establishment and "move on" when they become frightened or distrustful. They will not endure research procedures that fail to benefit them, or that appear to them to pose threats such as disclosure of sensitive information to their neighbors, care providers, or the police. A researcher–intervenor who violates trust not only damages the research, but endangers whatever the street-based or clinic-based gatekeeper is trying to accomplish. For example, in the summer of 1990, a national magazine published a face-front picture of a drug-using prostitute, with her name and the statement that she was infected with HIV but did not tell her customers. The prostitute was subsequently arrested and detained by local police (Lynch, 1990). Gatekeepers cannot permit or condone research that even suggests the possibility that subjects' interests may be compromised.

Many of the theories, research problems and methods discussed in journals that report academically based research are inappropriate to community-based settings. Researchers who seek to explain the behavior of non-middle-class people, but who lack actual knowledge of those populations or of their perspectives, typically misrepresent or blame the victim (Ryan, 1971). Moreover, the testing of some theories would require research procedures that are unacceptably intrusive. Typically inappropriate procedures include the use of deception, studies requiring considerable reading or writing, experimental treatments that make people feel like guinea pigs, research that provides nothing of value to the subjects, and misuse of standard psychological tests (see Huang, Watters, & Case, 1988).

Other research methods—such as long-term follow-up and random assignment—may be difficult but not impossible to apply to these populations. For example, although drug users are extremely difficult to follow in long-term studies, it can be done. Studies at one of the authors' drug treatment programs have typically managed to reach 80% of injection drug users for 12-month follow-ups. This is possible through careful planning. Subjects consent to be in the follow-up at the initial stages of the research and give information that enables them to be followed, for example, how to reach someone who will always know where they are. As the study proceeds, the follow-up information is confirmed and expanded upon. The researchers repeatedly emphasize the project's confidentiality rules, and subjects are compensated more for the longer-term follow-ups. These research procedures, coupled with close relationships with the treatment program allow long-term studies to meet scientifically acceptable standards of attrition.

"Random assignment" and "control groups" in community-based research, or in any field-based social experimentation, mean something quite different from what occurs in most laboratory experiments. Field- or community-based experiments literally tamper with people's lives and must meet a high ethical standard in doing so:

1. All research clients have a right to status quo services and activities. Any social service that currently exists should be available to control group members. No one should be prevented from receiving services; clients in the control group may even be referred to existing services elsewhere.
2. All research clients should be informed about the purposes of the study and about the existence of a control group.
3. Random assignment assures that each participant has an equal chance of being selected to receive what may turn out to be a beneficial or harmful treatment precluding discrimination against any clients. (A detailed discussion of ethics and procedures of random assignment in field experiments appears in Conner, 1982).

One key to ethical random assignment in drug treatment research is to provide two research options that are improvements over the usual treatment. For example, in a study of AIDS prevention methods, patients in a drug treatment program agreed to be randomly assigned to receive a set of informational brochures about AIDS or to receive a 6-hour training program aiming to lower their risk (Sorensen et al., 1989). Subjects in both groups received more AIDS information than they would have if they had not consented to be in the study, and both groups received equal compensation for group attendance and research interviews.

Attempts to use deception can destroy a random assignment study with drug users. In behavioral interventions, noncompliance with random assignment is a key threat to validity, and it is essential for subjects to know the time demands and attendance that the research project requires. If subjects are unaware of assignment options, it may appear to them that the researchers have conducted a secret manipulation, and a streetwise subject population will assume that it was *not* done for their benefit. The up-front notification that there will be randomization makes it likely that those who do not want it will decline to be in the study in the first place, and those who join the study will be more likely to comply with the "luck of the draw" that randomization involves. Traditionally, researchers have assumed that telling subjects too much about possibly unwelcome aspects of participation would bias the sampling. However, experiments in field research on sensitive topics have shown that full informing more than compensates for any initial bias by reducing later attrition and increasing the candor with which subjects respond when they know what to expect (e.g., Singer, 1978).

A Process for Integrating Research into Drug Treatment

We offer these guidelines for researchers who hope to conduct their intervention in a clinic. The steps suggested here will not occur in all programs in the same order, but they seem key to conducting successful clinic-based research with drug abusers. They are based on the system developed at SFGH Substance Abuse Services.

1. Initial Approach

Approach the clinic's research coordinator before the study has been proposed for funding or Institutional Review Board (IRB) approval. In most cases the research coordinator will be the clinic director. Understand that the clinic may be alert for potential conflict between the research and its intervention efforts, and that the research coordinator has responsibility for screening out studies that may be harmful to the patients or the clinic. With that person, review the idea of the research and explain the benefits to the field, to the clinic, and most of all to the clinic's patients. Tell the coordinator what inconveniences there might be to staff or patients, and what ethical concerns may arise. In turn, learn what patient care issues are involved, and the conditions under which the clinic is likely to participate. Presenting to a single coordinator may be less daunting than presenting at a staff meeting, and gives the researcher an opportunity to build an important ally who is on the staff.

2. Contingent Approval

If it appears feasible to do the research at the clinic, it may be appropriate to ask for a letter of support. A letter at this stage might express support for the research and include contingent commitments for participating in the study. For example, the clinic director might say that the research can be done at the clinic if the researcher can get IRB approval; can work out time, space, and access problems with the clinic director; and can obtain research staff so that clinic staff will not be inconvenienced by the research.

3. Management Consent

The researcher should ask about obtaining consent from the managing body of the organization. This may be an administrative group, management team, board of directors, or some other group that conveys clinic approval of research. At this meeting the researcher is likely to be asked about unanticipated aspects of clinic participation. For example, will the researcher need access to clinic charts, need approval of a local research committee, provide acknowledgment to the clinic for its participation in the study, and protect the clinic's identity (in connection with the research results) from inquiring insurance investigators? If negotiations are successful, it is wise to create a letter of cooperation, signed by both the clinic leader and the researcher. The letter can state the intent to cooperate in the study, what each party will give and receive through the study, and any further issues left to be negotiated.

4. Staff Cooperation

Begin meeting with the staff of the treatment program. This is when the researcher and the treatment leaders will resolve such issues as how much time the clinic will allot for each interview, where and when interviews will occur, and exclusionary criteria (e.g., emergency admissions from a hospital's medical wards may be unable to be recruited because of the urgency of their medical problems). This step is vital to the research. If successfully negotiated, the research project can achieve its aims. When poorly conducted, the staff and patients, together, can undermine the study by passive resistance. Consequently, successful researchers attend clinic staff meetings and strive to make their research an ancillary service of the clinic's program, rather than an extra burden for patients and staff.

Designing Street-Based Research

While the street, like the clinic, has its gatekeepers and its own "IRB," its rules and procedures are harder to discover. Earlier, we described how one might gain entry into the community via a gatekeeper. The process of designing the research to fit the setting is a continuation of that process and, in turn, blends into the processes of recruiting research assistants and subjects, and collecting the data. Here, we present a few generalizations about how one might work out the design with the subject population.

Common denominators of successful communication leading to effective research design include meeting with members of the research population on their own turf and engaging in collaborative planning through a series of meetings. At these meetings, the researcher describes the general objectives of the project, seeks advice on how to achieve those objectives, learns about the needs and sensitivities of the research population, and enlists their help with pilot testing and recruitment of subjects. Some more specific strategies are presented below.

Recruiting Subjects

Problems having to do with sampling, recruitment, development of valid instruments and data collection procedures, confidentiality, and community resistance to some aspect of the project are typical in community-based research. The researcher is well advised to keep lines of communication open with gatekeepers, research assistants, and subjects in order to learn of problems as early as possible, and to be flexible about changing the research procedures as required. We hope that the following vignettes, some drawn from street-based research and some from clinic-based research, provide useful insight into what to expect and how to cope.

In recruiting subjects the conscientious social scientist seeks to draw a representative sample, to obtain accurate demographic descriptions of subjects and candid responses to interviews, and to correctly assign subjects to groups. It may prove difficult to accomplish most of these objectives in community-based research.

Sampling

Representative sampling assumes that one has an accurate sample frame—an accurate list of who lives where and the ability to systematically reach a sample of these people. There is no such accurate list of injection drug users. Moreover, addicts tend to move about in cities in search of food, drugs, or other opportunities to satisfy their needs; hence drug users who turn up in one researcher's sample may turn up in another sample taken from the other side of town.

A less systematic but frequently used way to recruit drug users is to advertise in newspapers, on posters, or by word of mouth that persons who meet a given description will be paid to participate in research. Drug users are unlikely to participate without being paid. However, payment creates a new problem: Subjects may lie to get into the study.

Consider the researchers who were interested in interviewing heterosexual injection drug users (P. Case, personal communication, April 19, 1990). They offered to pay $15 for an interview, and found that many gay injection drug users were answering the ad, claiming to be heterosexual. The solution they devised was highly useful and helped the subjects to save face even if they were misrepresenting themselves. The new ad stated that they were looking for both gay and straight male injection drug users. Indeed they were. They had a 10-minute screening interview with all respondents, for which they paid $5. In a face-to-face interview, good rapport can be gained, and sexual orientation can become apparent. This procedure yielded scientifically useful demographic data on both populations. After the screening interview, the straight drug users were invited to participate in a 60-minute interview for $10 more. Everybody got what they wanted. The lesson here is not to exclude people who want to participate and get paid, for they will find ways to muddle your data (Case, 1990).

Focus Groups

Another method of recruitment in community-based research combines recruitment of subjects with development of study design and recruitment of research assistants. Bowser (1990) began the study design and recruitment process for his research on black teenage crack users by inviting prospective subjects to a focus group meeting. He wanted to know their beliefs about crack, where they got it, and how they used it; their knowledge and practice of safe sex; and their sexual behavior in general. He knew that they would welcome attention from him, but was not sure how to organize the interviews and establish rapport. The focus groups met regularly over lunch. Drug abusers often neglect nutrition, but when faced with good food can be ravenously hungry. He learned their concerns about their lives, and communicated ways he would like to help them. He asked their advice on how to organize the interviews and what to ask. He asked what they would like to have in return. He learned what fears subjects had about participating candidly, and discussed ways to demonstrably protect privacy.

Bowser found that many of his focus group participants wanted to learn to be interviewers. Some wanted to get into drug treatment. They worked out the interview protocol, the recruitment strategy, and strategies for providing needed services to participants. Those who became assistants brought the added advantage of access to places, such as crack houses, where the investigator could not go. Moreover, they were known members of the community who could get candid responses to interview questions. These methods resulted in the publication of useful information about the relationship of crack use to high-risk sexual behaviors (Fullilove, Fullilove, Bowser, & Gross, 1990).

Collecting Data

After selecting a setting and negotiating entry, adapting the research project to fit the setting, and arranging an ethical and feasible recruitment process, the next task is collecting data. The data collection process is filled with ethical challenges. Some of the most important of these are protecting confidentiality, coping with the community process, and adapting research measures to obtain valid information.

Confidentiality

The usual problems of confidentiality are dealt with comprehensively elsewhere (e.g., Boruch & Cecil, 1979). The risks and advantages of obtaining certificates of confidentiality to protect data from subpoena are discussed by Melton (1990). In this chapter, we focus only on problems of keeping damaging information from leaking out to other members of the subjects' community.

In community-based research, special problems arise with respect to privacy and confidentiality. The community grapevine is far more active than most professionals imagine, and members of such communities are extremely concerned that they not become the target of that gossip. For example, a VD intervention program could not function openly in the community, as it would stigmatize greatly those who participated. Further, it probably would not work for a researcher to use the typical deceptive tricks such as giving each person who has VD a blue card to bring back to the next session, and each person who doesn't a green card. Before long, everyone in the neighborhood would have figured out what blue cards mean and none of the blue card holders would be back (P. Case, personal communication, April 19, 1990). Routine partner notification could endanger HIV testing and treatment of community members, since word of the program's partner notification policy would spread rapidly, as soon as the first partner was notified.

Drug users themselves may discriminate against those who are infected with HIV. For example, one couple was run out of their hotel with "Go Away AIDS" spray painted on their hotel room door. This was the work of their fellow drug users who believed gossip that one member of the couple had AIDS.

Community research assistants are among those who are interested in gossip. A researcher reports having trained teenage drug users to interview others. They readily learned effective interviewing techniques, and were thrilled to carry a tiny tape recorder in their shirt pocket. Because of their status as interviewers with fancy tape recorders, their cohorts were eager to be interviewed. An interviewer then took the tape recorder home and played juicy parts for others. The juicy parts included interviews with men who named all the women in the neighborhood with whom they (said they had) had sex. The researcher did what damage control he could but realizes that asking the family members of his interviewers not to gossip probably accomplished little.

Community Resistance

Morin (personal communication, March 30, 1990) relates a story of AIDS research that illustrates both how community resistance can ruin the data collection process and how such problems can be overcome. In the mid-1980s, a research project tested AZT, a drug treatment for AIDS, using a double-blind design. The community of HIV-infected people was small and organized. Because they resented the fact that the only way they could get the potentially life-saving drug was if they were randomly assigned to the treatment group in a clinical trial, subjects split and shared their medication, thereby increasing chances that placebo group members would also receive treatment. Later research revealed that the dosage given to the medication group was sufficiently high that a half dose was quite effective. The research, however, was ruined by the sharing of half doses!

When public health planners learned of this community resistance to the research, they changed the procedures. They sponsored meetings between the researchers and community representatives, so that both groups could explain their concerns. Subsequently, the Food and Drug Administration changed its procedures to allow for the compassionate use of such medications, even while clinical trials are still going on. Community forums and meetings between researchers and community representatives became the standard procedure in AIDS research, rather than the exception (see Melton, Levine, Koocher, Rosenthal, & Thompson, 1988, for a detailed discussion of community consultation in socially sensitive research with special reference to clinical trials of treatments for AIDS).

The narrative above illustrates the most effective way to cope with community resistance to research. Through community consultation and collaboration, an investigator can understand the basis of the resistance, acknowledge its validity, and creatively develop ways to accomplish research goals within the norms of the community.

Adapting Research Measures

Sometimes, despite the most careful preparation, the planned research measures are not valid or are not feasible. This frequently occurs in community-based research. When pilot data reveal that the planned measures simply do not work, the researcher learns to step back and consider the options.

For example, the second author is involved in a study of partner notification options for HIV testing in drug programs. What would be the impact if it were required that needle-sharing partners be notified when a drug user is seropositive? An initial interview instrument was developed, pilot tested, and found not to be getting useful data because the subjects could not distinguish between the various testing options. The questionnaire needed to be shortened, clarified, simplified, and retested with a new pilot group. Some of the questions were dropped, and others were made open ended rather than forced-choice response options. Although more difficult to analyze, open-ended questions reflect more accurately the expressed feelings of the research subject. After several iterations the interview format seemed to be working.

The vignette above illustrates some practices that must be followed in any good research, but that are especially crucial in community-based research. The outcome measures must be palatable to the subject population. Subjects will fill out questionnaires, but the data will not be useful unless they understand the questions and can meaningfully respond. The community-based researcher should pilot-test measures and conduct open-ended inquiry, in addition to gathering forced-choice data.

When one's measures and data collection methods yield poor-quality data, other methods need to be considered (e.g., questionnaires, interviews, behavioral observations). In community-based studies it can be more important than in other settings to have multiple methods for gathering information about the same concept. Multitrait–multimethod analysis should be done to determine whether the measures are valid indicators of the characteristics they are intended to measure, or are artifacts of the measurement method (Campbell & Fiske, 1959). When one's measures and methods yield flawed information and all efforts to change them are unsuccessful, one must decide whether to continue with the collection of flawed information or to redesign the study.

Conclusions

The ethics and sensitivity of successful researchers in community settings differ from those of most researchers in other settings, and we suspect that those other researchers might profit from what community-based researchers have learned. Let us first consider how we have interpreted the three principles of ethical research on humans.

Respect. Many scientists assume that a proffered consent form signifies all the respect that is necessary. In community-based research, the researcher must work out research procedures that are respectful of subjects' interests. This is done in collaboration with the gatekeeper and perhaps with representative groups of the subjects.

Beneficence. Most scientists implicitly assume that research produces knowledge and does good for subjects and for society. In community-based research, this cannot be assumed or left to chance. The benefit and lack of risk must reside not just in the eyes of the scientist, but also in those of the gatekeeper and subjects.

Justice. Whom does science benefit; who contributes? In community-based research, gatekeepers and subjects insist that the research benefit the population that participates in the research. More specifically, there should be benefit for each individual who participates.

Second, we interpret the norms of ethical research as they apply to community-based investigation.

Validity. Most researchers assume that subjects are candid, presume to understand the perspective of subjects, and proceed with a design and sampling procedure that takes advantage of all of the techniques of the experimenter's trade. In community-based research, rapport, trust, and understanding of the perspective of the subjects cannot be left to chance. These elements must be carefully established before the research can even begin, and nothing can be done to destroy this basis for candor and cooperation by subjects and gatekeepers. In community-based research, this means that some of the procedures in the experimenter's repertoire (e.g., deception, covert observation, use of invasive questionnaires and tests) are inappropriate, and that much effort to understand the perspective and needs of subjects must precede the final design stage and the conduct of the research.

Competence. The stakes are high in community-based research, not just for contributing meaningfully to science but for shaping the community's image of the scientific enterprise. Because community-based research and intervention is, by nature, in the public eye, it is important that it be carried out by competent scientists. In community-based research, the investigator must have the competence to iteratively redesign the research until it meets the added constraints placed upon it by the community gatekeepers. Scientific competence must be coupled with cultural sensitivity and good communication skills.

Choice of Subjects. All researchers should study the population that is to benefit from the results, but in no other kind of research is this more utterly essential than in community-based research. Moreover, the benefit to the community must be communicated explicitly.

Voluntary Informed Consent. Many researchers have mistaken a consent form for informed consent. Community-based researchers cannot make this mistake. Not only must they engage in clear, respectful, two-way communication, in many cases they must collaboratively design the research with the gatekeepers and perhaps some community members.

Risk–Benefit Assessment. Many researchers mistakenly assume that they can objectively assess the risks and benefits of research. The community-based researcher must recognize that the community's idea of what comprises risk and benefit may differ greatly from that of the investigator. The needs and concerns of the community must be recognized and satisfied.

ACKNOWLEDGMENTS. This work was performed with the support of NSF grant DIR 9012185 and of funds provided by the State of California and allocated on the recommendation of the Universitywide Task Force on AIDS (Grant C89CSH01) to JES, and with the support of the National Institute on Drug Abuse (Grants R18DA06097, R01DA094340) and the National Institutes of Mental Health and Drug Abuse (Grant MH42459) to JLS. The authors appreciate the contribution to this chapter by the staff and patients of Substance Abuse Services, University of California, San Francisco, at San Francisco General Hospital.

References

Boruch, R. F., & Cecil, J. S. (1979). *Assuring the confidentiality of social research data.* Philadelphia: University of Pennsylvania.
Bowser, B. P. (1990). Designing and conducting community-based drug research. In J. E. Sieber, Y. Song-Kim, P. Kelzer, M. Innes, & W. Bergeson (Eds.), *Proceedings of a conference on vulnerable populations and AIDS: Ethical requirements for social and bio-behavioral research and intervention* (pp. 47–54). Hayward, CA. Available from Pioneer Bookstore, California State University Hayward.

Campbell, D. T., & Fiske, D. W. (1959). Convergent and discriminant validation by the multitrait–multimethod matrix. *Psychological Bulletin, 56*, 81–105.

Case, P. (1990). The prevention point needle exchange project. In J. E. Sieber, Y. Song-Kim, P. Kelzer, M. Innes, & W. Bergeson (Eds.), *Proceedings of a conference on vulnerable populations and AIDS: Ethical requirements for social and bio-behavioral research and intervention* (pp. 7–13). Hayward, CA. Available from Pioneer Bookstore, California State University Hayward.

Cohen, J. (1988). Community-based services for women and children at risk for AIDS: Development of resources in San Francisco. In A. Nahmias & F. Schinazi (Eds.), *AIDS in children, adolescents and heterosexual adults: An interdisciplinary perspective* (pp. 86–99). New York: Elsevier.

Conner, R. F. (1982). Random assignment of clients in social experimentation. In J. E. Sieber (Ed.), *The ethics of social research: Surveys and experiments* (pp. 58–77). New York: Springer Verlag.

Fullilove, R. E., Fullilove, M. T., Bowser, B. P., & Gross, S. A. (1990). Risk of sexually transmitted disease among black adolescent crack users in Oakland and San Francisco, Calif. *Journal of the American Medical Association, 263*, 851–855.

Guydish, J. Abramowitz, Z., Woods, W., Black, D. M., & Sorensen, J. (1990). Changes in needle sharing behavior among intravenous drug users: San Francisco, 1986 to 1988. *American Journal of Public Health, 80*, 995–997.

Hahn, R. A., Oronato, I. M., Jones, T. S., & Dougherty, J. (1989). Prevalence of HIV infection among intravenous drug users in the United States. *Journal of the American Medical Association, 261*, 2677–2684.

Huang, K. H. C., Watters, J., & Case, P. (1988). Psychological assessment and AIDS research with intravenous drug users: Challenges in measurement. *Journal of Psychoactive Drugs, 20*, 191–195.

Levine, R. J. (1986). *Ethics and regulation of clinical research*. Baltimore: Urban & Schwarzenberg.

Levitas, M. (1990, June 10). Homeless in America. *New York Times Magazine*, p. 44.

Lockett, G. (1990). Outreach for COYOTE and CAL-PEP. In J. E. Sieber, Y. Song-Kim, P. Kelzer, M. Innes, & W. Bergeson (Eds.), *Proceedings of a conference on vulnerable populations and AIDS: Ethical requirements for social and bio-behavioral research and intervention* (pp. 19–33). Hayward, CA. Available from Pioneer Bookstore, California State University Hayward.

Lynch, A. (1990, July 19). Newsweek paid hooker after photo, interview: Linda Kean's story landed her in jail. *San Francisco Chronicle*, p. A6.

Melton, G. B. (1990). Brief research report: Certificate of confidentiality under the Public Health Service Act: Strong protection but not enough. *Violence and victims, 5*(1), 67–70.

Melton, G. B., Levine, R. J., Koocher, G. P., Rosenthal, R., & Thompson, W. C. (1988). Community consultation in socially sensitive research: Lessons from clinical trials of treatments for AIDS. *American Psychologist, 43*, 573–581.

National Commission for the Protection of Human Subjects of Biomedical and Behavioral Research. (1979, April), *The Belmont Report: Ethical principles and guidelines for the protection of human subjects in research*. Washington, DC: Office for Protection from Research Risks, Department of Health, Education, and Welfare.

Pitt, D. E. (1989, July 23). The social order of the subways' homeless (interview with Marsha A. Martin who researches homeless persons living in New York subways). *New York Times*, pp. E26(N), E26(L).

Ryan, W. (1971). *Blaming the victim*. New York: Pantheon.

Singer, E. (1978). Informed consent: Consequences for response rate and response quality in social surveys. *American Sociological Review, 43*, 144–162.

Sorensen, J. L., Gibson, R. R., Heitzmann, C., Calvillo, A., Dumontet, R., Morales, E., & Acampora, A. (1989). Pilot trial of small group AIDS education with IV drug abusers (abstract). In L. S. Harris (Ed.), *Problems of drug dependence 1988: Proceedings of the Committee on the*

Problems of Drug Dependence (DHHS Publication No. ADM 89-1605). Washington, DC: U.S. Government Printing Office.

Wolk, J., Wodack, A., Guinan, J. J., Macaskill, P., & Simpson, J. M. (1989, June). *The effect of a needle and syringe exchange on a methadone maintenance unit.* Poster presentation at the V International Conference on AIDS, Montreal, Canada.

4

Lessons from the Meta-Analysis of Quasi-Experiments

Paul M. Wortman

Now that we are in the last decade of the century, it is common to ask what one did during the 1980s. To understand my answer to this question, however, it is necessary to make a very brief digression on how I spent the 1970s. Much of the time I was conducting secondary analyses as part of an extended period of postdoctoral work with Donald Campbell and his associates at Northwestern University (Boruch, Wortman, Cordray, and associates, 1981). Toward the end of that decade I and many of my colleagues in applied social psychology and evaluative research were becoming concerned about the utilization of such single, individual studies (Boruch & Wortman, 1979). About that time Gene Glass (1976) published a seminal paper entitled "Primary, Secondary, and Meta-Analysis of Research." It seemed to me that meta-analysis held the promise of greater utilization since it went well beyond the individual research study.

Meta-analysis is a statistical methodology for aggregating the results from many empirical research studies of the same phenomenon (Hedges & Olkin, 1985). It requires the calculation of an average effect size (ES) derived from a set of related dependent measures used in studies testing the same hypothesis. A generic ES in the social sciences is the standard score obtained by subtracting the

A version of this chapter was presented at the American Evaluation Association Annual Meeting in October, 1990. The work on this chapter was supported by Grant Number HS 06264 from the Agency for Health Care Policy and Research.

Paul M. Wortman • Department of Psychology, State University of New York at Stony Brook, Stony Brook, New York 11794.
Methodological Issues in Applied Psychology, edited by Bryant et al. Plenum Press, New York, 1992.

control group mean from the treatment group mean and dividing that difference by the standard deviation of the control group (Glass, McGraw, & Smith, 1981). Multiple ES's can be computed for each relevant outcome measure in a study. In those cases, an average ES should be calculated for the study to preserve independence. Alternatively, separate meta-analyses can be performed for conceptually distinct dependent variables. The ES's are then summed and divided by the total number of studies to obtain an overall average ES. If the results are normally distributed, the percentile rank of the average ES can be obtained from a Z table. A positive ES would usually indicate a beneficial treatment effect, while a negative value would indicate that the treatment was ineffective or even harmful.

So I have spent the past decade investigating the application of research synthesis methods, especially meta-analysis, to the quasi-experimental data often encountered by applied social scientists and evaluation researchers. The focus of this work has been on two important public policy issues in the areas of education and health. The policy issues are the impact of school desegregation on black achievement and the assessment of medical technologies such as coronary artery bypass graft surgery, respectively. This work has resulted in a half-dozen empirical research papers in peer-reviewed journals as well as four chapters in edited volumes. This chapter will summarize the lessons I learned in conducting these meta-analyses.

What are the lessons I and my associates learned? Briefly, they are the following:

- It is possible to meta-analyze quasi-experiments;
- But certain studies should be eliminated if their design is weak.
- Moreover, specific problems or "threats to validity" seem to pervade applied research domains;
- Thus, it is essential that these systematic sources of bias be detected and eliminated.
- Surprisingly even randomized studies may have such systematic flaws.
- And, finally, the replicability of a meta-analysis is lower than one might think—about .70 to .75 based on the agreement among different meta-analysts who used the same data base (Yeaton & Wortman, 1992)—due to the contingent nature of the decisions that are required in extracting and coding information in studies.

The lessons and the various primary sources from which they are drawn are described below. The emphasis is on my experiences in conducting these meta-analyses rather than a detailed recapitulation of the results or extensive discussions and citations of the work of other meta-analytic researchers. While some findings will be presented to illustrate these lessons, those who desire more detailed discussion of the meta-analytic work should consult the original articles.

The Case for Inclusion/Exclusion Criteria

One of the earliest controversies over meta-analysis focused on whether or not one should exclude any studies. Critics such as Mansfield and Busse (1977, p. 3) maintained that the meta-analyst should "eliminate from consideration studies with severe methodological inadequacies." They believed that such "poorly designed" studies were "likely to be more misleading than helpful." Mansfield and Busse recommended that the remaining studies be divided into well-designed and less well designed categories. Separate meta-analyses stratified by design type or quality could then be performed to determine if there is a design effect. If there is, then the results from the well-designed group of studies would be presumed to be more credible.

As a student of Donald Campbell, I naturally felt that the design typology he developed with Julian Stanley in their classic monograph (Campbell & Stanley, 1966) provided a useful framework for testing Mansfield and Busse's assertion. Bill Yeaton and I set out to search for the hypothesized design effect by conducting such a stratified meta-analysis of the medical literature assessing the effectiveness of coronary artery bypass graft surgery (or CABGS). The literature on CABGS proved ideal for this purpose as it is composed of a mix of randomized and quasi-experimental studies, with the latter using the "nonequivalent control group design." Because such a quasi-experimental design includes a control group, an ES can be computed.

The central question concerning a medical technology often is its ability to enhance patient survival. Our meta-analysis of the CABGS literature (Wortman & Yeaton, 1983) found a small mortality benefit of 6.8% for surgery compared to a medical treatment in the randomized trials (see Table 1, line 2). But the effect was a much larger 12.8% in controlled quasi-experimental trials (see Table 1, line 2). Moreover, there was a significant amount of heterogeneity in the quasi-experiments, indicating that some other variable(s), such as type of patient selected in the medical group, may confound or interact with the treatment (see below).

While the survival benefit associated with CABGS has been the major focus in studies of this technology, issues surrounding quality of life have become more prominent in recent assessments of its effectiveness (Fineberg & Hiatt, 1979). In our meta-analysis of outcomes from the CABGS literature, Yeaton and I used the most frequently reported quality-of-life outcome measure—the percentage of patients who were angina free—to estimate this subjective benefit of surgery (Wortman & Yeaton, 1985). The results for both types of studies revealed a statistically significant benefit for surgery, with the quasi-experiments once again producing a larger ES (for anginal relief produced by CABGS) than the randomized studies. We found that those controlled studies not using randomization to assign patients to treatment overestimated quality-of-life benefits by about

Table 1. Mean Percentage Benefits: CABGS and Medical
Control Group by Research Design

Type of benefit	Design	CABGS	Medical	Difference
Mortality	Randomized ($N = 8$)	8.3	15.1	6.8
	Quasi-experiment ($N = 13$)	14.5	27.3	12.8
Quality of life	Randomized ($N = 6$)	42.8	13.0	29.8
	Quasi-experiment ($N = 8$)	57.7	11.5	46.2

Note. All results significant at $p < .05$ using odds ratio (Yusuf et al., 1985).

15% compared to the randomized studies (46.2% vs. 29.8%, respectively), thus replicating the effect of study design found when an objective outcome (i.e., mortality) was synthesized (see Table 1, lines 3 and 4). In this case, the effect is overestimated by slightly more than one-half.

Thus my first lesson from the meta-analysis of quasi-experiments is: *Lesson #1: Studies employing nonrandomized research designs will produce biased ES estimates.*

Validity

My work on CABGS convinced me that the validity framework originally developed by Campbell and Stanley was relevant in determining which studies should be included or excluded in a meta-analysis. The potential application of the most recent validity topology consisting of four categories was described initially as part of a larger review of evaluation research (Wortman, 1983). Fred Bryant and I argued that meta-analysts need to address two sets of decisions, one concerned with "relevance," the other with "acceptability," when evaluating evidence for inclusion in research syntheses (Bryant & Wortman, 1984). Relevance entails the application of criteria derived from the construct and external validity categories; relevant studies are considered suitable for inclusion in the meta-analysis. At that point they must be examined for acceptability by applying criteria from the internal and statistical conclusion validity categories. For each set of decisions, we demonstrated the utility of the validity categories and their associated "threats" for screening the primary studies. We illustrated this approach with examples drawn from a meta-analysis of quasi-experiments on school desegregation and black student achievement (Bryant & Wortman, 1984). The remainder of this section briefly summarizes my extension of the validity framework to meta-analysis (Wortman, 1983).

Construct Validity

The determination of the study's scope is the first task a meta-analyst must address. The result, according to Glass et al. (1981, p. 219), "depends entirely on the exact form of the question being addressed." Once the hypothesis is specified it sets the boundary on what studies should be included in the meta-analysis.

A study is relevant for inclusion in a meta-analysis if it is high in construct validity. Those studies whose independent or dependent variables involve constructs that differ from those specified in the meta-analytic research question should be excluded. Our synthesis of the desegregation literature (Wortman & Bryant, 1985) examined the effects of U.S. public school desegregation on the achievement (i.e., general, reading, or mathematics test scores) of black students bused to previously all-white schools.

Close examination revealed that some studies investigated treatments labeled desegregation or outcomes labeled achievement that were operationalized improperly and were thus irrelevant to the research question. For example, we excluded studies with improper construct validity of treatment (i.e., construct validity of cause) in which interventions did not involve racial desegregation, such as studies of busing per se or studies in which most students in "desegregated" classrooms were actually black. Similarly, we excluded studies in which outcomes were not measured by standardized achievement tests. Thus, studies using IQ scores, grade point averages, dropout rates, and the like were rejected due to improper construct validity of their outcome measures (i.e., construct validity of effect).

Decisions concerning the relevance of a given study's constructs are fundamental in determining whether to include it in a meta-analysis. The restrictiveness in making this decision depends on the specificity of the meta-analytic research question (Wortman, 1983). A highly detailed research question that specifies a precise set of constructs will be fairly restrictive in defining relevant studies. In contrast, a relatively general research question will allow a relatively wide range of constructs and will result in more studies being selected (Cooper, 1982).

External Validity

Meta-analysts must also consider the relevance of a study's settings, populations, and dates of conduct. These "external validity" variables provide exclusion criteria for judgments of relevance similar to those for construct validity. As with construct validity, meta-analysts who formulate highly detailed research questions that specify precise treatment settings, target populations, or time periods will be relatively restrictive in selecting relevant studies. Meta-analysts who formulate relatively general research questions can be more inclusive in selecting relevant evidence. Consequently, investigators with narrower external validity criteria will exclude studies that investigators with broader criteria would include. Such selectivity will obviously limit the generalizability of conclusions drawn from research syntheses (Cooper, 1982).

A given study may be irrelevant on grounds of low external validity if its setting, research population, or historical period differs from those specified in the meta-analytic hypothesis. The specific nature of the research question led Fred Bryant and me to exclude on external validity grounds a number of studies from our meta-analysis of desegregation. For example, we decided to ignore studies that occurred in settings other than U.S. public schools, such as private schools or schools outside the United States. In addition studies were excluded that involved desegregated populations other than blacks or that occurred before the 1954 Supreme Court decision that made desegregation a public policy issue.

Internal Validity

As noted above in the discussion of excluding studies, internal validity considerations figure prominently in the proper conduct of meta-analysis. We rejected relevant desegregation studies that suffered from major threats to their internal validity. For example, we excluded cross-sectional surveys of students because these nonexperimental research designs lacked control groups. Similarly, studies that lacked adequate segregated control groups were excluded. In these cases, comparison groups consisted of district or statewide test norms. Finally, studies were excluded that used different achievement tests for segregated and desegregated students since they suffer from a variety of instrumentation threats, such as differential test reliability that can either produce spurious treatment effects or mask true effects.

Statistical Conclusion Validity

As with judgments about the relevance of a given study's constructs, judgments regarding the acceptability of a given study's statistical comparisons are unavoidable when choosing studies for meta-analysis. Studies will often be excluded from a meta-analysis when they lack the appropriate statistical information to calculate an ES. Even with the clever methods that Glass (1977) and his collaborators (Glass et al., 1981) developed for retrieving this information, it is often impossible to obtain an estimate of the ES. A study may also be unacceptable on grounds of low statistical conclusion validity if the data are improperly analyzed. For example, in our synthesis of desegregation research, Bryant and I excluded summary statements and nonempirical literature reviews that lacked statistical information. Moreover, some of the relevant empirical studies contained insufficient information to derive the means, standard deviations, or sample sizes necessary for calculating an ES, and had to be excluded from our meta-analysis. Although we could have contacted the authors of these studies to request unreported statistics, this strategy goes well beyond the normal role of meta-analysis, and we have not found it to be successful (Bryant & Wortman, 1978; but see Yusuf et al., 1985, p. 559, for an example of a meta-analysis using this approach).

Other relevant studies provided sufficient statistical information, but suffered from threats relating to "violated assumptions of statistical tests" that invalidated their results. These included inadequate sample sizes and inappropriate use of statistical tests. Because inferential statistics are misleading in such cases, we decided to reject these studies. Another similar threat to statistical conclusion validity involved "random heterogeneity in the sample of respondents." For instance, several relevant desegregation studies combined data across different grade levels. Because this approach allows variations in the age of students and the duration of the treatment to influence statistical conclusions, we rejected these studies. A number of related statistical concerns such as testing for homogeneity and adjusting for pretest differences in quasi-experiments will be discussed later.

Another common statistical issue has been the practice of combining multiple results from a single study. Landman and Dawes (1982) noted five different kinds of nonindependence of measures (e.g., multiple measures from the same subject, at multiple points in time, etc.). My approach illustrated above is to stratify or block the meta-analysis into separate strata or variables of interest, such as design methodology (e.g., randomized and quasi-experimental) or type of outcome (e.g., survival and quality of life). Light (1984) maintains that meta-analysis can be more informative than single studies in revealing such interactions.

Using the two validity categories as criteria for assessing the relevance of a study for our meta-analysis resulted in the exclusion of 46 of the 157 studies on desegregation, or 29%. The remaining two validity categories led us (Bryant & Wortman, 1984) to exclude 80 of the remaining 111 studies, or 72%, as unacceptable.

The second lesson I learned in conducting meta-analyses of quasi-experiments is:

Lesson #2: The validity framework provides a useful set of criteria for including or excluding studies.

Estimating Bias

Given the biased estimates found in Lesson #1, one might think I should have abandoned the effort to synthesize quasi-experimental studies. However, one of the earlier lessons I had learned working with Don Campbell on the secondary analysis of quasi-experiments was that it is sometimes possible to adjust for or eliminate the bias in an estimate of treatment effect (cf. Wortman, Reichardt, & St. Pierre, 1978). This required the sources of bias found in individual studies to be consistent across the entire set of studies.

Quasi-Experiments

My work on bypass surgery (see lesson #1 described earlier) demonstrated that study design can affect the results of a meta-analysis. This implied to me that the validity framework might also prove useful in estimating the design effect. For example, the major threat to the internal validity of nonrandomized studies such as the nonequivalent control group commonly found in social science research is differential selection, or "selection-maturation interaction" in the vernacular of Campbell and Stanley (1966). If control and experimental subjects systematically differ on such pretest measures as cognitive ability, then the outcome results using these or related measures will be biased. Since the traditional ES estimate assumes initial group equivalence produced by randomization, some adjustment is needed to remove the selection difference at pretest. Maturation, however, is not a problem here if one accepts the "fan-spread hypothesis" that states a positive correlation between the mean and standard deviation (Wortman & Bryant, 1985, note 2, p. 321).

For such quasi-experimental studies found in applied and evaluative research it is important to remove, or at least adjust for, the pretest differences between the treatment and control groups. It is possible to remove most of the bias due to selection by subtracting the pretest ES for the nonequivalent quasi-experimental control group design. (Other selection interactions with instrumentation or statistical regression to the mean, for example, are also likely and require more complex adjustments; see Wortman et al., 1978, and discussion below.) Such a "pretest-adjusted meta-analysis" was performed for the predominantly quasi-experimental literature dealing with the effects of school desegregation on minority achievement (Wortman & Bryant, 1985). The results are displayed in Table 2 (lines 1 and 2).

Those quasi-experimental studies that did not have an identifiable pretest selection problem (i.e., static group comparison design) had a posttest ES difference of .18, while those judged to have a selection problem had a posttest difference of .55. The overall, average ES was .45 using the Glass method and

Table 2. Pretest-Adjusted Meta-Analysis
of Desegregation Quasi-Experiments

Sample of studies	N of studies	N of cases[a]	ES[b]
All quasi-experiments	31	96	.29[c]
Nonequivalent control group	18	54	.16[d]
NIE core[e]	19	62	.14

[a] Case is distinct grade-level data.
[b] No inferential statistical tests were performed on these results since they were not recommended at that time (see Glass et al., 1981, pp. 197–200) and the methods for doing so had not yet been developed.
[c] Unadjusted effect size (ES) including One Group Pretest–Posttest and Static Group Comparison Designs was .45.
[d] Unadjusted ES was .32.
[e] One study rejected from the sample of Nonequivalent Control Group Designs was included by an expert panel convened by the National Institute of Education to review these results.

.29 when adjusted for pretest differences. For quasi-experiments using the non-equivalent control group design the results were .32 and .16, respectively. Thus, the bias introduced by threats to internal validity can be both substantial and systematic. One cannot assume that these threats will be self-canceling (Staines, 1974). Adjustments to eliminate preexisting group differences should be considered in meta-analyses of quasi-experiments, in particular, if there are insufficient randomized studies.

The relatively small difference between the pretest-adjusted ES and the ES for studies without selection problems in the desegregation meta-analysis may have resulted from differential regression. Given that the students involved in these studies generally score below the mean for their grade, their scores will regress to the higher mean at posttest solely due to measurement error in the tests. Moreover, with an initial difference of .26 standard deviations (i.e., .55 − .29), the control segregated students will regress more. This implies that the pretest correction alone overadjusts slightly. An assumed test reliability of .8 to .9 for these students accounts for the .04 difference in the nonequivalent control studies that used matching on the pretest and those that did not: [(1 − the reliability) × ES difference = (.15) × (.26)]. Thus, the unreliability of the measures should probably be removed before adjusting for a pretest difference.

The pretest adjustment method thus appears to remove the initial differences due to subject nonequivalence. It therefore provides a fairly accurate estimate of the overall actual benefit of desegregation on black achievement. According to Glass et al. (1981, p. 103), each .1 ES may be equal to .1 grade equivalent or 1 month of educational gain. Thus, desegregated students may be gaining about 2 months by attending an integrated environment.

After this initial meta-analysis had been completed, the National Institute of Education (NIE) asked a panel of experts, including the author, to review the results. The NIE panel focused on a subset of the inclusion/exclusion criteria and a subset of the 31 studies used in the original meta-analysis. A similar analysis was performed on the 19 studies selected by the NIE panel of experts (see Table 2, line 3). The pattern of results was quite similar to those presented above for both the original sample and the subset of controlled quasi-experiments. All ES's were positive, indicating a beneficial impact of desegregation on achievement. The ES's are slightly lower, partly due to the inclusion of negative ES's for two studies. The addition of these studies, the elimination of others, and the use of different control groups explains most of the differences among the results of the panelists (Wortman & Bryant, 1985).

The overall mean unadjusted Glass ES was .25. When adjusted for pretest differences, the ES was .14 (see Table 2, line 3). Compared to the original 31 studies, the decrease for the unadjusted Glass ES was .20, but it was only .02 for the pretest-adjusted ES for the controlled studies (see Table 2, lines 2 and 3). It is also worth noting that no inferential statistical tests were performed on these ES's. Such tests were not recommended (Glass et al., 1981, pp. 197–200). Glass et al. (1981, p. 199) maintained that "the typical integrative or meta-analysis seldom meets [the] condition[s] of valid statistical inference." It was not until our meta-analysis was published that the appropriate methods for such tests became available (Hedges & Olkin, 1985). In any case, the important point is that subject nonequivalence is a persistent source of bias in these quasi-experimental studies. For this reason, the pretest adjustment method was employed. This adjusted ES provides a less biased estimate of the overall effectiveness of desegregation.

Thus, my third lesson from the meta-analysis of quasi-experiments is:

Lesson #3: It is possible to adjust for the bias produced by nonrandomized research designs.

Randomized Experiments

Implicit in most of the literature on meta-analysis is the assumption that meta-analysis should be confined to randomized studies. However, randomization does not make a study immune from the problems or threats to validity endemic in quasi-experiments. Among the various ways that randomized designs are compromised, perhaps the most troublesome is the differential attrition of subjects from comparison groups during the actual conduct of an evaluation or experiment. For example, I argued that the process of differential attrition was a plausible explanation of the negative effects found in McCord's (1978) 30-year follow-up of the relationship of counseling to subsequent delinquency in a randomized controlled trial (Wortman, 1978). As a result of this differential attrition process, a well-conceived randomized experimental design may drift toward a quasi-experimental design model with all of its inferential limitations.

This was exactly the situation confronting researchers interested in the evaluation of the potential benefits of coronary artery bypass graft surgery (CABGS) for patients with coronary heart disease (Wortman, 1981). Efforts to compare survival and quality-of-life benefits between patients receiving CABGS and those treated medically in randomized trials were greatly complicated by the substantial percentages of control (i.e., medically treated) patients crossing over to the group receiving surgery.

In our synthesis of the CABGS controlled trials (Wortman & Yeaton, 1983), the average crossover rate from the medical to the surgical group was found to be 21%. This problem was exacerbated by the systematic nature of the attrition, since those medical patients with the worst prognosis typically crossed over (Murphy, Hultgren, Detre, Thomsen, & Takaro, 1977). The net effect of the loss of the most ill patients from the medical group is to raise the survival rate in the medical group, whether crossovers are dropped from the study or included. This would bring the medical group survival rate closer to that for the surgical group, if one assumes that surgery is beneficial, an assumption consistent with the data. Consequently, crossovers will produce an underestimate of any potential benefit due to surgery.

The various factors leading a patient to crossover make it impossible to assess the exact effect of such attrition on survival rate. However, it was possible to estimate the maximum influence that crossovers would have on the mean survival rate of the medical group (Yeaton, Wortman, & Langberg, 1983). We assumed that only those patients in the medical group with the worst prognosis crossed over to receive surgery. Consequently, this assumption implies that the tail of the distribution of survival rates of medical patients is truncated at precisely the point equaling the exact percentage of patients who cross over. Such truncated, standard normal distributions are commonly used to correct statistically for attrition bias in ANOVA and regression models (Hausman & Wise, 1979).

Thus, the crossover rate of 21% (when $p = .21$) found in our synthesis of the results of controlled trials of CABGS (Wortman & Yeaton, 1983) would be associated with a mean shift of .36 (a 36% increase in the standardized mean value), the maximum change attributable solely to crossovers. Using the data reported in Table 1 along with the standard deviation reported by us (Wortman & Yeaton 1983), it is possible to solve the simultaneous equations for the "bias factor" (Ozminkowski, Wortman, & Roloff, 1988) for the CABGS effect size. The computation indicates that the benefit for surgery is underestimated by 1.9%. Thus, the result in Table 1, line 1, for randomized trials should be increased by this amount to yield a mortality benefit of 8.7%.

The lessons I learned from this work are:

Lesson #4: Randomized studies may also produce biased ES estimates; and
Lesson #5: It is also possible to estimate the bias in randomized studies.
Lesson #6: The bias in research designs is systematic.
This last lesson deserves some discussion. The desegregation quasi-experiments generally suffered from selection bias, and that bias systematically overestimated the apparent treatment effect. Similarly, the CABGS randomized trials were systematically biased by a combination of attrition and diffusion that underestimated the effect of the surgery.

Replicability and Coder Reliability

Meta-analysis has been viewed (Glass, 1977) as an objective, scientific method for summarizing the research literature in contrast to the traditional subjective review article. In reviewing the scientific literature on a given topic the researcher is asked to perform an almost impossible cognitive task: combining the results from a large number of studies using different research designs and outcome measures that may vary in both quality and appropriateness. Statistical methods for research synthesis like Glass's meta-analysis appear to eliminate most of the cognitive overload and much of the subjective bias it entails. But the question remains as to how objective are the results from a meta-analysis. One way to approach this issue is to examine the replicability of meta-analyses. There are two factors, in particular, that affect the reproducibility of a meta-analysis—generalizability and reliability. Both of these factors may be viewed as alternative definitions of replicability.

Generalizability

Replication is often considered the ultimate test of the findings in a single study. Implicit in assessing the reproducibility of results is the notion of generalizability or external validity, since the study will, of necessity, be conducted using other subjects (i.e., population) in another location (i.e., setting) at another time. Construct validity may be involved as well, since slightly different treatments or measures may also be used. In this sense, replicability refers to whether meta-analyses of the same literature, but including or excluding different studies, yield the same conclusions (i.e., parallel forms reliability). My work on the CABGS meta-analysis illustrates how external validity issues may affect the replicability of a meta-analysis. This work focused on the patient populations used in the various studies.

Ultimately, decisions concerning external validity rest on the heterogeneity of the results. There are statistical procedures for determining the homogeneity

Table 3. External Validity in Meta-Analysis: CABGS Quasi-Experiments

	Mean % Mortality		
Sample of studies	CABGS	Medical	Difference
All quasi-experiments (N = 13)	14.5	27.3	12.8
Excluding cardiomyopathy (N = 10)	8.8	19.5	10.7
Stable angina (N = 6)	10.3	16.8	6.5
Unstable angina (N = 4)	6.5	23.6	17.1

Note. All results significant at $p < .05$ using odds ratio (Yusuf et al., 1985).

of the results (cf. Hunter et al., 1982). Elashoff (1978) and others (DerSimonian & Laird, 1986) recommend against synthesis when the results are not homogeneous across different patient populations.

Our original analyses reported earlier indicated some statistically significant heterogeneity in the findings for the CABGS quasi-experiments. This indicates that other variables besides surgery may affect the results. In reviewing the studies with the assistance of a medical consultant, Bill Yeaton and I learned that 3 of the 13 quasi-experiments consisted of patients with a severe form of heart disease called cardiomyopathy. We decided to repeat our meta-analysis with these studies removed (see Table 3). The results were nearly identical to our original findings (Table 3, line 2).

Our next step was to stratify the studies according to the most important clinical variable (Chassin et al., 1986)—type of angina (stable or unstable). The results are presented in the bottom two lines of Table 3. There is no significant variability for the studies containing unstable angina patients, while significant variability remains for those with stable angina. Fortunately, the latter results were nearly identical with the randomized studies and only differ slightly (see Table 1, line 1) in magnitude, but not direction. On the other hand, the findings for the patients with unstable angina, although homogeneous, differ from the randomized studies.

There are a couple of lessons to be learned from this experience:
Lesson #7: Replicability can be affected by external validity; but
Lesson #8: Homogeneous findings may still be systematically biased.

Reliability

Another factor that can affect the replicability of meta-analytic findings is the reliability of the data extraction or coding process. In this sense, replicability denotes the degree to which independent meta-analyses of the same set of studies yield the same conclusions (i.e., interrater reliability). Campbell (1975) has noted this problem in "instrumentation" as part of this discussion of "triangulation" or the use of multiple observers. I first encountered the intercoder (or multiple observer) problem in reliability as part of my work on the desegregation meta-analysis (discussed earlier). As noted above, NIE convened an expert panel to review my findings (Wortman & Bryant, 1985). Although they agreed on a subset of the studies I used, they each came up with a different estimate for the effect of desegregation that ranged from .04 to .28. The unreliability among these estimates resulted largely from differences in the choice of control groups and in the choice of dependent measures of achievement.

Bill Yeaton and I decided to examine the coding reliability process more systematically as part of our meta-analyses of occupational stress in health workers (Susanto, Yeaton, & Wortman, 1988). We carefully trained two coders to a high degree of skill (i.e., average agreement or reliability of .90). We were, therefore, quite surprised to observe intercoder reliabilities of .78 for specific measures of stress that would be used in calculating ES estimates. Yeaton and I decided to replicate this procedure on another meta-analysis we were conducting. The results were nearly identical.

We wondered how two different sets of highly reliable coders could end up with such low rates of agreement on variables critical to calculating an ES. When we realized the contingent nature of the decisions made in coding data for meta-analysis, the mystery vanished. The choice of a dependent measure is often dependent on the choice of a control or treatment group. While these dependent decisions are each made at a high level of reliability (say .90), the net effect is a multiplicative one. Thus, if two such contingent decisions are needed, as we think they are, then an initially highly reliable coder will appear unreliable due to the multiplicative effect (i.e., $.90 \times .90 \times .90 = .73$). This model of contingent reliability predicted our results almost exactly.

The lesson I learned should be obvious:

Lesson #9: Meta-analysis requires contingent decisions in coding that will lower the reliability of the process and hence reduce its replicability.

The only way to deal with this problem is either to increase the reliability of the initial level to at least .93 (since $.93 \times .93 \times .93 = .80$—an acceptable level of reliability) or to restrict the number of contingent decisions (for more details, see Yeaton & Wortman, 1992).

Summary

There is no doubt that quantitative methods for synthesizing research results from many studies such as meta-analysis represent a significant innovation. For example, *Psychological Bulletin* has averaged one meta-analysis per issue in recent years. Meta-analysis can eliminate uncertainty surrounding a given study by revealing overall effects from a set of related studies. Alternatively, the allure of such seemingly simple quantitative methods—now available in PC software (Johnson, 1989)—can blind the potential user to the limitations of these methods.

For all its computational simplicity, such methods are usually quite laborious. They require a precise statement of the research question(s) followed by a scouring of the literature for all potential studies. This literature is then subjected to a sequence of judgmental steps that are all open to various threats to validity. These involve the selection of studies addressing the topic or hypothesis and using comparable measures (i.e., construct validity), the use of stratifying or moderating variables (i.e., external validity), the exclusion of studies with weak designs or inappropriate control groups (i.e., internal validity), and the use of an appropriate unit of analysis (i.e., statistical conclusion validity).

The validity concepts developed for assessing the quality of individual studies provide a useful framework for examining these data aggregation approaches. There are, however, other limitations. These involve coding of the studies, the type of inferences that can be made, and problems in adjusting for systematic bias and coder unreliability. It is extremely important that the user of this powerful new technique be aware of these potential problems. The results of meta-analyses are widely published and are assumed by readers to be accurate summaries of the state of science in that area. There is thus an increased responsibility for the meta-analyst to be informed and accurate.

The final lesson I learned from the meta-analysis of quasi-experiments is: *Lesson #10: Meta-analysis is research and, as such, is difficult and time-consuming.*

Table 4. Lessons and Primary Sources from the Meta-Analysis of Quasi-Experiments

Lesson	Source
1. Design effect	Wortman & Yeaton, 1983
2. Validity framework	Wortman, 1983; Bryant & Wortman, 1984
3. Bias adjustment: Quasi-experiments	Wortman & Bryant, 1985
4. Bias in randomized studies	Wortman, 1981
5. Bias adjustment: Randomized studies	Yeaton, Wortman, & Langberg, 1983
6. Bias is systematic	Wortman & Bryant, 1985; Wortman & Yeaton, 1987
7. Generalizability	Wortman & Yeaton 1988
8. Design effect: Homogeneous results	Wortman & Yeaton, 1988
9. Reliability	Yeaton & Wortman, 1990
10. Research process	All of the above

Cooper (1984) has written a monograph describing the similarities between meta-analysis and scientific research. I would go one step further in classifying meta-analysis as a new and important form of research. Like good research, it takes time. I have found that a thorough meta-analysis often takes as long as an original study, about 2 years, to conduct.

In conclusion, while these lessons consist of 10 in number (see Table 4), there is nothing sacred about them. Those of you who have conducted meta-analyses undoubtedly have learned some of these already as well as others not on this list. Those of you about to embark on such a meta-analytic journey will probably find these lessons useful in reaching the promised goal.

References

Boruch, R. F., & Wortman, P. M. (1979). Implications of educational evaluation for evaluation policy. In D. C. Berliner (Ed.), *Review of research in education* (Vol. 7, pp. 309–361).

Boruch, R. F., Wortman, P. M., Cordray, D. S., and associates. (1981). *Reanalyzing program evaluations.* San Francisco: Jossey-Bass.

Bryant F. B., & Wortman, P. M. (1978). Secondary analysis: The case for data archives. *American Psychologist, 33,* 381–387.

Bryant, F. B., & Wortman, P. M. (1984). Methodological issues in the meta-analysis of quasi-experiments. *New Directions for Program Evaluation, 24,* 5–24.

Campbell, D. T. (1975). "Degrees of freedom" and the case study. *Comparative Political Studies, 8,* 178–193.

Campbell, D. T., & Stanley, J. C. (1966). *Experimental and quasi-experimental designs for research.* Chicago: Rand McNally.

Chassin, M. R., park, R. E., Fink, A., Rauchman, S., Keesey, J., & Brook, R. H. (1986). *Indications for selected medical and surgical procedures—A literature review and ratings of appropriateness. Coronary artery bypass graft surgery* (R-3204). Santa Monica, CA: RAND.

Cooper, H. M. (1982). Scientific guidelines for conducting integrative research reviews. *Review of Education Research, 52,* 291–302.

Cooper, H. M. (1984). *The integrative research review: A systematic approach.* Beverly Hills, CA: Sage.

DerSimonian, R., & Laird, N. (1986). Meta-analysis in clinical trials. *Controlled Clinical Trials, 7,* 177–188.

Elashoff, J. D. (1978). Combining results of clinical trials. *Gastroenterology, 75,* 1170–1172.

Fineberg, H. V., & Hiatt, H. H. (1979). Evaluation of medical practices: The case for technology assessment. *New England Journal of Medicine, 301,* 1086–1091.

Glass, G. V. (1976). Primary, secondary, and meta-analysis of research. *Education Research, 5,* 3–8.

Glass, G. V. (1977). Integrating findings: The meta-analysis of research. In L. S. Shulman (Ed.), *Review of research in education* (Vol. 5, pp. 35–79). Itasca, IL: Peacock.

Glass, G. V., McGraw, B., & Smith, M. D. (1981). *Meta-analysis in social research.* Beverly Hills/London: Sage.

Hausman, J. A., & Wise, D. A. (1979). Attrition bias in experimental and panel data: The Gary income maintenance experiment. *Econometrica, 47,* 455–473.

Hedges, L. V., & Olkin, I. (1985). *Statistical methods for meta-analysis.* Orlando, FL: Academic Press.

Hunter, J. E., Schmidt, F. L., & Jackson, G. (1982). *Meta-analysis: Cumulating research findings across studies.* Beverly Hills, CA: Sage.

Johnson, B. T. (1989). DSTAT: Software for the meta-analytic review of research literatures. Hillsdale, NJ: Erlbaum.

Landman, J. T., & Dawes, R. M. (1982). Psychotherapy outcome: Smith and Glass' conclusions stand up under scrutiny. *American Psychologist, 37,* 504–516.

Light, R. J. (1984). Six evaluation issues that synthesis can resolve better than single studies. *New Directions for Program Evaluations, 24,* 57–73.

Mansfield, R. S., & Busse, T. V. (1977). Meta-analysis of research: A rejoinder to Glass. *Education Research, 6,* 3.

McCord, J. (1978). A thirty-year follow-up of treatment effects. *American Psychologist, 33,* 284–289.

Murphy M. I., Hultgren, H. N., Detre, K., Thomsen, J., & Takaro, T. (1977). Special correspondence: A debate on coronary bypass. *New England Journal of Medicine, 297,* 1470.

Ozminkowski, R. J., Wortman, P. M., & Roloff, D. W. (1988). Inborn/outborn status and neonatal survival: A meta-analysis of non-randomized studies. *Statistics in Medicine, 7,* 1207–1221.

Staines, G. L. (1974). The strategic combination argument. In W. Leinfellner and E. Kohler (Eds.), *Developments in the methodology of social science* (pp. 417–430). Dordecht, Holland: Reidel.

Susanto, Y. E., Yeaton, W. H., & Wortman, P. M. (1988). *Multilevel–multifacet meta-analysis: Occupational stress in health care workers.* Unpublished manuscript.

Wortman, P. M. (1978). Differential attrition: Another hazard of follow-up research. *American Psychologist, 33,* 1145–1146.

Wortman, P. M. (1981). Randomized clinical trials. In P. M. Wortman (Ed.), *Methods for evaluating health services* (pp. 41–60). Beverly Hills, CA: Sage.

Wortman, P. M. (1983). Evaluation research: A methodological perspective. *Annual Review of Psychology, 34,* 223–260.

Wortman, P. M., & Bryant, F. B. (1985). School desegregation and black achievement: An integrative review. *Sociological Methods & Research, 13,* 289–324.

Wortman, P. M., Reichardt, C. S., & St. Pierre, R. G. (1978). The first year of the Education Voucher Demonstration: A secondary analysis of student achievement test scores. *Evaluation Quarterly (now Evaluation Review), 2,* 193–214.

Wortman, P. M., & Yeaton, W. H. (1983). Synthesis of results in controlled trials of coronary artery bypass graft surgery. In R. J. Light (Ed.), *Evaluation Studies Review Annual* (Vol. 8, pp. 536–551). Beverly Hills, CA: Sage.

Wortman, P. M., & Yeaton, W. H. (1985). Cumulating quality of life results in controlled trials of coronary artery bypass graft surgery. *Controlled Clinical Trials, 6,* 289–305.

Wortman, P. M., & Yeaton, W. H. (1987). Using research synthesis in medical technology assessment. *International Journal of Technology Assessment in Health Care, 3,* 509–522.

Wortman, P. M., & Yeaton, W. H. (1988). Making meta-analysis useful to physicians: An external validity approach. Unpublished manuscript, University of Michigan, Ann Arbor.

Yeaton, W. H., & Wortman, P. M. (1992). *On the reliability of meta-analytic reviews: The role of intercoder agreement.* Manuscript submitted for review.

Yeaton, W. H., Wortman, P. M., & Langberg, N. (1983). Differential attrition: Estimating the effect of crossovers on the evaluation of a medical technology. *Evaluation Review, 7,* 831–840.

Yusuf, S., Collins, R., Peto, R., Furberg, C., Stampfer, M. J., Goldhaber, S. Z., & Hennekens, C. H. (1985). Intravenous and intracoronary fibrinolytic therapy in acute myocardial infarction: Overview of results on mortality, reinfarction, and side effects from 33 randomized controlled trials. *European Heart Journal, 6,* 556–585.

5

A Structured Diary Methodology for the Study of Daily Events

Anita DeLongis, Kenneth J. Hemphill, and Darrin R. Lehman

In this chapter we consider the use of structured diaries for the study of daily events. Consistent with the book's theme, we draw heavily upon our own experiences in conducting research on daily events using the diary methodology. Particular attention is paid to the utility of the diary approach when the central research question concerns itself with the study of naturally occurring change. It is in cases in which the focus is on examining change, especially across relatively brief periods of time, that the structured diary approach is most useful, and perhaps essential. Without it, we suggest, research findings tend to suffer from serious limitations owing to a lack of ecological validity.

We also address methodological and procedural issues of practical concern in using structured diaries as research instruments. We offer suggestions for improving the quality of data obtained using this methodology, and draw attention to some of the special issues involved in the collection of diary data. First, however, we describe briefly what we mean by a structured diary, and then identify the main areas of research within the social sciences that have used the approach.

The term "structured diary" generally refers to a booklet that contains a series of identical self-report questionnaires, typically at least one for each day of the week. Each questionnaire, or segment of the diary, covers events or experi-

Anita DeLongis, Kenneth J. Hemphill, and Darrin R. Lehman • Department of Psychology, University of British Columbia, Vancouver, British Columbia V6T 1Z4 Canada.
Methodological Issues in Applied Psychology, edited by Bryant et al. Plenum Press, New York, 1992.

ences over some brief time period (e.g., a few hours or a day). Respondents are asked to complete a section of the diary at regular intervals, most often once per day (e.g., DeLongis, Folkman, & Lazarus, 1988). However, some studies have included six or more time-points per day (e.g., Brandstatter, 1983). Although 2 weeks is the typical time frame during which respondents are asked to keep a diary, researchers have asked participants to keep diaries for anywhere from 1 week (e.g., Follick, Ahern, & Laser-Wolston, 1984) to 3 months (e.g., Clark & Watson, 1988; Larsen, 1987). This structured diary methodology will be the focus of this chapter.

A closely related diary methodology is the Experience Sampling Method (ESM; Csikszentmihalyi & Larson, 1987; Csikszentmihalyi, Larson, & Prescott, 1977; Hormuth, 1986; Larson, Zuzanek, & Mannell, 1985; McAdams & Constantian, 1983). ESM involves giving respondents small beepers to carry around with them that signal times when diaries are to be filled out. Respondents are typically asked to record their cognitions, emotions, and behaviors at random times signaled by their beepers. This contrasts with the diary approach described above in that in those studies, respondents are typically asked to make diary entries at predetermined points throughout the day (e.g., meal times), describing their experiences for the entire period between diary entries. Although the initial cost of the beepers is expensive, such a method is ideal for studies in which it is essential to take a snapshot of the person at various random points throughout the day. For a thorough discussion of this method and review of studies using it, see Csikszentmihalyi and Larson (1987).

The use of a diary methodology has been limited largely to a few research domains within the social sciences. Primary among these are the study of mood (and particularly of cyclic changes in mood) (e.g., Campbell, Chew, & Scratchley, 1991; Larson & Kasimatis, 1990), common stressful events (e.g., Bolger, DeLongis, Kessler, & Wethington, 1989), menstrual cycle symptomatology (e.g., McFarlane, Martin, & Williams, 1988), health and illness behavior (e.g., Roghmann & Haggerty, 1972), and personality (Cantor et al., 1991).

Another usage has primarily clinical roots. Many cognitive and behavior therapists ask their patients to keep records, or structured diaries, of their problem behaviors, cognitions, and relevant environmental stimuli. They have done so for a variety of reasons, including to obtain baseline information for assessment purposes. A survey of behavior therapists found that the use of client self-recording (most often via semistructured diaries tailored to the client's specific problem) was second only to clinical interviews in usage as an assessment procedure (Swan & MacDonald, 1978). Not surprisingly, given the strong empirical tradition among cognitive and behavior therapists, this has resulted in a large research literature using the diary approach in therapy outcome studies (e.g., Martin, Nathan, Milech, & van Keppel, 1989), as well as in studies of basic clinical processes (e.g., Johnston, Krech, Tiedemann, & Pelham, 1990).

As with the research domains previously mentioned, a central concern in many of these clinical studies is with examining change.

It is not just cognitive and behavior therapists who have long realized the potential of diaries as clinical tools. Among more psychodynamically oriented clinicians, diaries have been used most frequently as a way of helping patients gain personal insight and express pent-up emotions. The sort of diary used for this purpose differs from that being considered in this chapter in that it is typically unstructured (interestingly, there has recently been a call for just such an open-ended, unstructured diary methodology in stress research (Weber & Laux, 1990]). In fact, its unstructured nature is thought to be one of the reasons for its therapeutic effects. There is increasing evidence that there are beneficial health effects due simply to writing about traumatic experiences (e.g., Pennebaker, 1987, 1989; Pennebaker, Kiecolt-Glaser, & Glaser, 1988). Although studies using the type of structured diary that is the focus of this chapter often have an open-ended question or two, the structured diary has little in common with the sort of diary employed by psychodynamically oriented clinicians, other than that both focus on daily experiences, and in both cases entries are most typically made at least once per day. Therefore, aside from considerations of the potential therapeutic effects of participating in a study that involves frequent recording of one's experiences and behaviors, we limit our present discussion to the use of structured diaries.

It is beyond the scope of this chapter to provide a review of each of these aforementioned literatures. Instead, and in line with the theme of the current volume, we will draw primarily upon examples from our own area of research, the study of everyday stressful experiences. First, we will describe the utility of the diary methodology and then proceed to review the relevant literatures regarding diary construction and research methods.

Why Use a Structured Diary Methodology?

There are five primary reasons for employing a diary methodology in research. First is the need to move outside the confines of the laboratory in order to increase ecological validity. Second, and perhaps equally important, is the need to be able to address questions concerning process and change, and related causal issues. Third, recent findings in the stress field suggest the importance of daily events for health and well-being, and the diary methodology is well suited to their study. Fourth, information gathered across multiple situations, and then aggregated, may provide more reliable and valid indicators of person characteristics than can be obtained from a single assessment. And fifth, in some situations structured diaries can be the method of choice because their use can lead to an increase in the reliability and validity of self-report data. This occurs largely via a reduction in recall error in self-reports of events and experiences. We discuss each of these issues below.

The Confines of the Laboratory

Stress research, for the past several decades, has focused on the impact of stress on health and well-being. A central concern in this literature has been whether our research methods allow us to rule out the possibility that relations found between stress and health outcomes are confounded with preexisting psychological or physical health problems (see, e.g., Dohrenwend, Dohrenwend, Dodson, & Shrout, 1984; Dohrenwend & Shrout, 1985; Lazarus, DeLongis, Folkman, & Gruen, 1985). Are relations found between stress and health merely a reflection of persons who are already distressed or ill having more stress in their lives, possibly because something about their personalities or circumstances or both generates stressful events? Clearly, the ill and psychologically disturbed are more likely, by virtue of these problems, to experience more stress. Various attempts to solve this problem have been made over the past few decades.

One solution to this internal validity problem has been to conduct stress research in the laboratory. Although experimental methodology goes far in solving such problems, the laboratory environment poses a number of constraints for stress researchers. Primary among these are the limitations in the types of stressors to which researchers can ethically expose their subjects (Wortman, Abbey, Holland, Silver, & Janoff-Bulman, 1980) and consequent limitations to ecological validity. The sorts of stressors that can be studied under laboratory conditions are constrained in a number of ways. Because the stressors to which subjects can be ethically exposed must produce relatively minor reactions that will dissipate quickly, many stressors of interest cannot be studied in this setting. Laboratory studies have focused on stressors such as noise (e.g., Glass & Singer, 1972) and emotion-arousing films (e.g., Speisman, Lazarus, Mordkoff, & Davidson, 1964).

Although there are no doubt parallels to these stressors that exist outside of the laboratory, they are of necessity quite different from the types of stressors that have been found in field research both to occur most frequently and to prove most troublesome for respondents. As Wortman et al. (1980, p. 205) pointed out: ". . . researchers struggling with this problem are left with an unappealing choice. If they utilize outcomes that are relatively unimportant, they are likely to produce findings that are ultimately trivial; if they expose subjects to aversive outcomes of real significance, the research may well be unethical."

Field research methods have revealed that chronic stressors (Pearlin, Menaghan, Lieberman, & Mullan, 1981), as well as those that are interpersonal in nature (Bolger, DeLongis, Kessler, & Schilling, 1989), tend to have the strongest impact on health and mood. It is obviously unethical to expose subjects in the lab to a stressor over a length of time even beginning to approach periods typically experienced in life outside the lab, such as in the case of chronic work strain. Similarly, naturally occurring interpersonal stressors typically differ in important ways from those interpersonal stressors that can ethically be created under laboratory conditions. Interpersonal problems, arguments, and tensions developing over long periods of time with no easy solution in sight, and where the potential cost of mishandling the stress is highest, are those most difficult, and perhaps impossible, to study in the lab. Yet, these are the very ones that have serious implications for people's lives, that occur frequently, and that have relevance to current theories of stress and social support (DeLongis & O'Brien, 1990).

Further, as Wortman et al. (1980, p. 204) described, "the unique relationship between the experimenter and the subject, as well as the experimenter's position of authority, may artificially constrain the subject's behavioral responses to any stressors encountered in the laboratory." In sum then, the types of stressors most difficult to study in the lab are the ones that are probably the most important to our research if it is to have relevance to human concerns.

The Study of Process

There are two primary reasons for examining stress in process terms: the need for our findings to have clinical relevance and the need for our methods to reflect current theories of stress, coping, and social support. First, if our findings on the effects of daily events are to have relevance for clinical application, they must address phenomena that are capable of change. That is, if our research focuses only on variables that are stable characteristics of persons and of their environments, our findings are unlikely to have applied value. After all, if factors are stable enough not to require us to examine their fluctuations over time, then individuals are unlikely to be able to modify them.

Certainly, there is a need to study such stable phenomena. For example, factors such as poverty, as difficult as they may be to change, may account for a great deal of the variance in health and well-being. However, the difficulty of conducting research on factors that do shift readily over time should not prevent us from trying to develop methods that allow us to examine these shifts. For example, while personality may be relatively stable across time (e.g., Block, 1971), requiring but a single assessment for adequate measurement, coping tends to vary across situations (e.g., Folkman, Lazarus, Dunkel-Schetter, DeLongis, & Gruen, 1986), requiring multiple assessments across varying stressors for adequate measurement. The treatment implications of findings regarding the efficacy of various modes of coping in particular contexts would likely be clearer than those resulting from knowledge of personality styles, since it is more difficult to change one's personality than to change the way one copes with a particular stressor.

A second reason for studying process concerns current theories on stress, coping, and social support (e.g., Lazarus & Folkman, 1984). These have been largely articulated in process terms. That is, the causes and effects of stress are thought to occur over time, with the immediate effects not necessarily mirroring those occurring weeks, months, or years later. A person may cope in such a way (e.g., with denial) so as not to experience the emotional effects of a stressor initially, but in the weeks or months to come, he or she may be even more vulnerable to distress and the effects of other stressors than the person who engages in immediate emotional expression (e.g., DeLongis, Lehman, Silver, & Wortman, 1992). Given this, if phenomena are studied across one assessment, or even a few, it is possible to miss important aspects of the unfolding of events over time and to draw conclusions that are inaccurate, or at best, incomplete.

The view that cognitions and behaviors are best understood as part of ongoing interactions with the environment, rather than as static events, requires a method in which people are studied over time (see Lazarus, 1990; Lazarus & DeLongis, 1983). By assessing a person repeatedly over time, within-subject analyses become possible that allow questions about process to be more fully addressed. Further, repeated assessments allow comparisons of cognitions and behaviors under different conditions, thus providing some control for the possibility that stable characteristics of a person, or other potential confounds, account for relations among daily events and outcomes (see Dohrenwend & Shrout, 1985; Lazarus et al., 1985).

The Growing Interest in the Effects of Daily Events on Health and Mood

A third reason for the development of the diary methodology is that with attention in the stress and coping field turning toward how stress affects everyday life, a methodology was needed that assessed day-to-day life experiences. One of the primary uses of structured diaries in the past few years has been to study day-to-day stressful events.

In earlier attempts to elucidate the stress–illness relation, researchers embraced a major life events approach (e.g., Holmes & Rahe, 1967). Experiences such as bereavement and job loss were proposed as causal factors in physical illness and psychological symptomatology. Although results were generally consistent with this assertion, the associations typically found in the literature have been weak (Rabkin & Struening, 1976).

One reason for this is that major life events, such as divorce, may have their impact on health and well-being largely via their influence on daily life. The findings of a number of studies (e.g., DeLongis, Coyne, Dakof, Folkman, & Lazarus, 1982; Kanner, Coyne, Schaefer, & Lazarus, 1981; Lehman, 1985; Monroe, 1983) suggest that the relation of major stressful events to illness is accounted for largely by the common, everyday stressful events (or "hassles") that lead up to, or follow from, such major events. These relatively minor events, such as relationship problems or getting stuck in a traffic jam, have been found to have a cumulative and significant influence on psychological and physical well-being (e.g., DeLongis, Folkman, & Lazarus, 1988; Eckenrode, 1984; Stone & Neale, 1984; Zarski, 1984).

Paralleling methodology developed for the study of major life stress, initial work on everyday stress used a methodology that involved widely spaced assessments in which respondents were asked to report their stressful experiences occurring over relatively long periods of time. For example, Pearlin et al. (1981) asked respondents to report on the amount of role strain they had in various life domains at two points in time, 4 years apart. One limitation of such a methodology is its seeming mismatch with current conceptualizations of the stress process. Nonetheless, studies such as these have been quite important in providing strong support for the cumulative impact of chronically occurring common sources of stress, such as chronic marital problems, and have provided the impetus for developing a methodology that was more closely aligned with theory.

But in order to examine the effect of naturally occurring fluctuations in everyday stress on mood and health, a research method is required that allows many closely spaced assessments. House, Strecher, Metzner, and Robbins (1986) have pointed out:

> There are . . . clear limits to what can be learned from such studies . . . when we have access to measures of psychosocial stress at only one point in time and attempt to relate them, cross-sectionally or prospectively, to forms of health behavior, morbidity, and mortality. . . . We must move beyond both cross-sectional and prospective studies that measure stress at only a single point in time toward studies that monitor (stress) at multiple time points. (pp. 72–73)

In studies with few widely spaced assessments, when an effect of everyday events on subsequent illness is found, it is difficult to sort out to what the effect is due. Is it that stable, chronically high levels of negative events produce increased risk, or is it frequent fluctuations in the level of life stress that are most difficult? Surely it is *not* that stress occurring several years prior is producing an increased risk of illness or mood disturbance, particularly when the sort of stress under investigation is relatively minor and common. The effect is no doubt due to what is happening to the person over some period of time, including that between assessments, with the earlier time-point serving as a kind of proxy for events over the intervening period.

A structured diary methodology is uniquely suited to the study of these everyday events, and as interest in these more common events has grown, so have the number of studies that use this methodology.

Increasing Predictive Ability via Aggregation across Time

Even when researchers are not concerned with issues of process and change across time or across different situations, but are rather concerned with relatively stable phenomena, such as personality traits, structured diaries can be the method of choice. By aggregating data obtained across multiple time-points, error or noise in the data can be averaged out. Sampling behavior across time and situations yields greater predictive ability than a one-shot approach can typically provide (Epstein, 1983, 1986).

Recall Error

How accurate are people at reporting their moods, thoughts, and actions retrospectively? To the extent that people are not accurate, research methods that involve frequent self-reports of experiences over relatively short time periods will provide more reliable and valid data than that obtained from a few widely spaced assessments. In general, the literature suggests that people are not particularly adept at recalling events, moods, or cognitions (e.g., Bem & McConnell, 1970; McFarland & Ross, 1985; Wixon & Laird, 1976). Respondents have demonstrated poor recall for experiences as varied as labor pain (Norvell, Gaston-Johansson, & Fridh, 1987), alcohol consumption (Lemmens, Knibbe, & Tan, 1988), menstrual mood changes (McFarlane et al., 1988), and reports of various moods (Hedges, Jandorf, & Stone, 1985; Stone, Hedges, Neale, & Satin, 1985).

Verbrugge (1980a) notes two main types of recall error. The first, memory lapse, occurs when an event is forgotten entirely. The second type of recall error, telescoping, involves remembering the occurrence of the event, but forgetting details such as when it occurred. The use of a diary methodology minimizes both types of recall error, because events and thoughts and feelings about them are reported shortly after their occurrence (McKenzie, 1983; Stanton & Tucci, 1982). We will consider several issues that are related to the accuracy of recall.

First, retrospective contamination has long been recognized as a problem in life events research (Lazarus & DeLongis, 1983). Lehman, Wortman, and Williams (1987) and others (e.g., Taylor, 1983; Thompson & Janigian, 1988) have noted, especially among those who have experienced a major life event, that individuals have a need to search for meaning or understanding in the event. Particularly in situations such as those posed by one's own illness or the illness or death of a loved one, people have a great propensity toward making attributions for the events (Downey, Silver, & Wortman, 1990; Taylor, Lichtman, & Wood, 1984). This process of searching for meaning and making attributions may render people's retrospective reports of their experiences unreliable and invalid. A classic example of this phenomenon can be found in the literature on birth defects. After giving birth to a child with Down's syndrome, it is relatively common for a mother to retrospectively report relatively high levels of stress, or other unrelated problems, during pregnancy (e.g., H. Stone, 1973). Initially, this led researchers to search for the role of stress in the etiology of Down's syndrome.

A second reason for the discrepancy between actual affect, thought, or behavior and retrospective reports of the same is that certain experiences are more salient than others. Thus, low-intensity experiences tend to be less readily attended to, and more easily forgotten, than high-intensity ones. As a result, people's retrospective mood assessments may be more characteristic of peak than of average experiences (Hedges et al., 1985), a point we will return to later in this chapter.

Third, what one remembers during a given mood state is in part determined by what one previously learned or experienced in that state. This phenomenon has been termed *mood, or state-dependent, memory* (see Eich, 1989). If certain types of events have previously co-occurred with particular mood states for a person, memory of those types of events will be more salient for the person when he or she is in that particular mood state and, therefore, will be more likely to be recalled, thus introducing recall bias. The reverse also occurs. That is, the occurrence of events that have been previously associated with a particular mood state will tend to evoke that mood state anew.

A fourth source of recall error is that memory for events and mood may be influenced by stereotypes and cultural beliefs (Wilson, Laser, & Stone, 1982). Thus, women who were asked to report changes in their mood across their menstrual cycle retrospectively indicated that they felt worse in the premenstrual phase than they indicated when they were asked to keep ongoing records of their mood across their cycle (DeLongis, Tal, & Kessler, 1987; McFarlane et al., 1988). Beliefs about hormonal changes presumably influenced respondents to report symptoms consistent with a "premenstrual syndrome." The use of daily diaries is a way to reduce retrospective bias caused by both differential salience and culturally based stereotypes about events.

Fifth, problems of retrospective contamination and systematic error being introduced into the data increase with the length of time over which the respondent is asked to recall past events. For example, something that is initially irritating may be forgotten or positively reframed (Lehman & Hemphill, 1990). Daily diaries, to some extent at least, reduce the amount of retrospective bias because they are typically completed shortly after hassles occur.

A sixth source of recall error stems from what has been termed *mood congruent memory*, in which the affective tone of the material recalled matches the prevalent mood (see Lewis & Williams, 1989). For example, while feeling sad or depressed a person is more likely to recall negative events than when feeling happy (even when more negative events may not have occurred). Although the problems posed for researchers by mood congruent memory cannot be completely eliminated by the use of diaries, their use probably serves to minimize the problem given the relatively short period of recall required.

Finally, as the focus across numerous research domains, particularly with the study of stress, shifts from the study of major life events to more common, everyday events, the issue of recall error is becoming increasingly important. The quotidian nature of these more minor events suggests that such experiences are particularly vulnerable to forgetting and other distortions of memory likely to occur with the passage of time. For example, participants in diary studies report the same rates of chronic health problems as are reported in retrospective interviews, but the incidence of acute conditions, including illnesses that are not disabling and those for which professional health care is not sought, appears lower when derived from retrospective reports of health (Verbrugge, 1980a). Apparently, respondents do not have trouble recalling serious chronic conditions such as arthritis or cancer, but not surprisingly, they have greater difficulty recalling colds, flues, and other commonly occurring, less major health problems. By definition, hassles are the minor irritations and frustrations of daily living, and as such, respondents may find it difficult to remember that something routine was also particularly bothersome (Gavanski & Wells, 1989). Thus, researchers need to take into account the differential salience of various life experiences in designing studies that require respondents to recall past events. To the extent that assessing the quality and quantity of more quotidian experiences is of importance to the investigator, the diary methodology becomes increasingly necessary.

Naturalistic observation may be utilized as an alternative methodology to structured diaries. For example, this method has been employed extensively in the close relationship and marital satisfaction literatures. However, as the phenomena of interest across the field of psychology are increasingly cognitive, and therefore not readily observable, the reliance on observational methods has become somewhat problematic as a stand-alone method, and is increasingly being supplemented by self-reports of cognitive phenomena (e.g., Fincham, Beach, & Baucom, 1987). Further, unless the process of interest unfolds over very brief periods of time, observation is not practical. Even an argument tends to have sequelae that unfold across hours and even days, rather than minutes, which is the time frame within which observational work can typically be conducted. Diary studies enable researchers to investigate exchanges that occur over days, weeks, and even months (DeLongis & Lehman, 1989).

Using the Diary Methodology: Potential Pitfalls and Possible Solutions

Throughout the following section, we draw upon both our own research experiences and those previously reported in the literature by others in discussing what we believe are the most serious issues that arise in using diary methodology. Where possible, we suggest potential solutions to these problems, again based on our own experiences and on the published work of others.

The Effects on Respondents of Participating in a Diary Study

The clinical literature suggests that completing diaries can have therapeutic effects, at least under some conditions. These therapeutic effects are best documented for conditions under which the completer expresses previously undisclosed emotions about traumatic life experiences (e.g., Pennebaker, 1989). However, in most diary studies, participants are asked to describe their reactions to events occurring on that particular day, not to some traumatic event that occurred months or years previously. Therefore, it is unclear to what extent the impressive health gains found in the emotional expression literature can be expected to occur among participants in mood or stress studies using more structured diaries.

Other positive effects of diary keeping have been found in the behavioral self-monitoring literature in which patients, by increasing awareness via record-keeping of their problem behaviors and cognitions, and perhaps of the contingencies that elicit them, are able to create change such that their problematic behaviors and cognitions diminish.

It should also be noted that there are potentially deleterious effects of keeping ongoing records of one's daily events, cognitions, and behaviors. This has been best documented in the pain literature, where an increase in attention to, and awareness of, pain is often associated with an increase in the level of pain experienced (e.g., Kanfer & Goldfoot, 1966). This phenomenon, often referred to as "reactivity" in the clinical literature, is closely related to what diary researchers have termed *sensitization effects*.

Sensitization Effects

Because respondents in diary studies complete questionnaires on a regular basis, it is important to consider sensitization effects. That is, participation in diary studies may result in heightened awareness of the problems, stressful events, or other phenomena being monitored, and may change the very attitudes and behaviors that are being examined (Verbrugge, 1980b). Although research is not entirely consistent (e.g., Lipinski, Black, Nelson, & Ciminero, 1975; Porter, Leviton, Slack, & Graham, 1981), investigators have generally noted increases in symptom reporting across time, often interpreted as resulting from increased awareness and focus on symptoms. In one study, for example, cancer patients who initially completed an inventory about side effects from chemotherapy later rated their nausea from a chemotherapy session as more severe than control subjects who completed a patient convenience report (Gard, Edwards, Harris, & McCormack, 1988). Thus, pretreatment information aimed at increasing sensitization about the chemotherapy experience exacerbated subsequent ratings of side effects. Consistent with this, when respondents are asked about the possibility of sensitization effects, they often report that awareness of symptoms did, in fact, increase during the diary period (Verbrugge, 1980b).

Yet, we have found, using the same measure of physical symptoms as did Verbrugge, that the number of symptoms reported by respondents tended to decline across the study period (DeLongis, 1985). However, our sample was younger and generally healthier than Verbrugge's sample. Whether diary respondents increase, decrease, or show no differences over time in levels of symptom reporting may be affected by the seriousness of the symptoms they experience. That is, when the health problems experienced by respondents are more serious, as in the case of frail, elderly respondents, then attention to one's health may heighten awareness of symptoms that have otherwise been largely ignored. On the other hand, when respondents are basically healthy, and the most serious symptoms experienced tend to be ones associated with tension headaches, respiratory infections, and flues—as in the case of younger participants—then respondents may tend to grow bored with, or tired of, record-keeping, and may tend to report these minor symptoms less often as record-keeping continues over time. Such effects are termed *fatigue effects*, and may offset sensitization effects in these studies, at least within a relatively healthy population.

Studies that involve record-keeping of non-health-related behaviors have found no change over time in the phenomena being recorded. For example, McKenzie (1983) found that participating in diary surveys about telephone usage did not effect telephone call behavior over the period of diary keeping.

What is less clear, however, is whether sensitization effects occur primarily in the early part of the reporting period, or persist throughout the study. If sensitization effects are temporary, or at least remain constant after a certain period of time, researchers could include several sample diaries that are not intended for inclusion in data analysis. Then, after sensitization effects level off, investigators could administer diaries that are to be analyzed. Another possible solution is to include a control group that receives the diary at only the initial and final time points, allowing differences in changes across time between the two groups that might be attributed to the diary procedure to be assessed (e.g., McKenzie, 1983). However, as researchers tend not to report information regarding fatigue and sensitization effects, the data on which such design decisions should be made are lacking.

Cook and Campbell (1979) address a related set of issues under the topic of "testing effects," pointing out the potential problems arising when subjects repeatedly fill out a questionnaire over time, such as the potential for subjects to feel that they must present a consistent picture of themselves over time. We present a number of potential solutions to such problems later in this chapter.

Refusal Rate Problems

Unfortunately, researchers often do not provide information on refusal rates; most simply note the number of people who actually participated in their study. In some instances, it is not even possible to calculate response rates. For example, procedures that are employed in which the potential participant contacts the researchers (e.g., sign-up sheets) make it impossible to determine the total number of people who came into contact with the plea for participation.

Some researchers have reported information about response rates in their diary studies. For example, in a study that required participants to complete six interviews and keep diary records for 20 days (over a period of 6 months), 46% of the couples who were asked to participate actually did so (DeLongis et al., 1988). Eighty-one percent of women in a chosen sorority agreed to participate in a diary study (Cantor et al., 1991). Finally, the compliance rate was 58% among students who were nominated by teachers (Wong & Csikszentmihalyi, 1991).

Some information exists about the types of people who do and do not agree to participate in diary studies. Thus, Csikszentmihalyi and Larson (1987) noted that occupation and gender were important considerations: unskilled blue-collar workers were unlikely to volunteer (12% of target sample). In contrast, 75% of clerical workers and technicians who met eligibility requirements volunteered and completed the study. Among high school students and adults, females were generally more willing to participate than males. With respect to age, Kemsley (1975) reports a response rate of approximately 90% for respondents below the age of 25. This compares to a response rate of 60% for older adults.

Researchers have at least two options in addressing refusal rate problems. First, they can attempt to improve their acceptance rate with a variety of strategies. We have noted in our own work that response rates tend to be higher when an interview immediately precedes the diary completion phase of the study, probably because of rapport built between study participants and the research team during the interview. For example, in a study in which a year had passed since the respondents had been interviewed, little more than a third of the respondents contacted for the diary study agreed to participate (Bolger et al., 1989). On the other hand, Verbrugge (1984) asked respondents to complete diaries during the interview, and had a 91% agreement rate.

Beyond the obvious rapport building that goes on in a good interview, participation in a preinterview may make future participation more likely for another reason as well—one which social psychologists have termed the *foot-in-the-door phenomenon* (Freedman & Fraser, 1966). An affirmative response to a large request will be more likely shortly after one complies with a smaller initial request. Respondents may shift their self-perceptions so that they regard themselves as the sort of person who helps others (Bem, 1972; Snyder & Cunningham, 1975), or may come to view helping situations more positively in general. As well, they may realize that the experience is not as painful and threatening as initially imagined (Rittle, 1981). Whatever the reason for its efficacy, the foot-in-the-door technique seems likely to improve acceptance rates.

A small, but genuine, token of appreciation offered to potential diary completers can also be quite effective in increasing acceptance rates. So, for example, minimal financial remuneration or gifts (such as university pens, key chains, gift certificates, or lottery tickets) can give respondents the sense that their time and help is appreciated. We have received letters and phone calls from respondents thanking us for having sent a pen along with the diary!

Interestingly, social psychological research on the overjustification effect (Deci & Ryan, 1985; Lepper, Greene, & Nisbett, 1973) suggests that researchers should not overemphasize the payment or gift. This body of work makes it clear that external rewards have the potential of reducing intrinsic motivation. These problems can be compounded if respondents view the gifts as an attempt to manipulate their behavior or increase their effort. Interestingly, some respondents, presumably to avoid the discomfort of external justification, actually decline payment.

A second, very different strategy for dealing with refusal rate problems involves acquiring data in order to compare diary participants with those who refuse to participate. In general, it is important to consider whether people who enroll in diary studies are different than those who decline participation or who drop out. By employing the preinterview discussed above, researchers can provide a wealth of information upon which the two groups of people can be compared. In the absence of such a preinterview, refusers can be asked to answer a brief series of questions concerning, for example, their current health status, their education level, and the quality of their marital relationship (see Lehman et al., 1987, for an example of this methodology).

Attrition and Missing Data Problems

Completing one or more questionnaires daily for a period of weeks or longer requires a substantial commitment. Researchers who may otherwise conduct diary studies may be dissuaded from doing so, in part, because of the belief that many respondents will fail to complete the study as requested. Is this belief substantiated; that is, are respondents actually reluctant or unable to report as required? The studies that are available generally do not support such a pessimistic assertion. For instance, Bolger et al. (1989) note that, in a sample of 166 married couples, 74% of those who agreed to complete diaries for a total of 42 days actually did so. Similarly, Clark and Watson (1988) found that all of the 18 Japanese upper-class students who began their 3-month study completed it. In a study of 85 married couples across 6 months (DeLongis et al., 1988), 10 dropped out, yielding an attrition rate of less than 12%. Among another group of Japanese respondents, in which five assessments were taken daily for 2 weeks, 21 of 23 people provided enough data to be analyzed (Hedges et al., 1985). Finally, Verbrugge (1984) notes that, of 589 respondents recruited using a multistage probability sample of metropolitan residents, 492 (or 84%) completed the study. We have noted across a number of studies (e.g., Bishop, 1990; Bolger, De-Longis, Kessler, & Wethington, 1989; DeLongis et al., 1988; Verbrugge, 1985) that most respondents who drop out of diary studies do so in the first week of data collection.

Although these attrition figures paint an optimistic picture, we are not suggesting that it is trivial to retain respondents in long-term diary studies. Some descriptive data are available regarding the types of people who do and do not complete diary studies. Verbrugge (1984) reports that those who complete the study usually have children and are middle-aged. Typically, completers are educated, married, have white-collar jobs, and have good general health status. Dropouts tend to be either under 30 or over 65 years of age, single, dependents or household heads, nonparents, and of low-socioeconomic status. In addition, dropouts report feeling worn out, or have poor health status. For many types of studies, this means that a group that may be of particular interest (e.g., those who are psychologically or physically debilitated during the course of the study) may be unable or unwilling to complete their assigned tasks.

These findings compel us to consider some practical solutions for dealing with problems of attrition. Whenever needed, research staff should be prepared to assist respondents in completing the diary. Such help can take the form of detailed instructions about how to complete the diaries, encouragement in the form of respondent payments, small gifts of appreciation, and thank you phone calls or notes. In some cases frequent reminders in the form of letters and telephone calls, or even daily telephone interviews to replace self-report diaries, are necessary. Finally, it may be useful to emphasize to respondents the importance of the study and their participation in it. At the conclusion of this section, we provide general recommendations especially relevant to populations most likely to drop out of diary studies.

The proportion of missing data obtained in diary studies is as important a design issue as the number of respondents dropping out of the study. Again we note that many researchers do not report such statistics. Of the ones who do, missing data do not appear to be particularly problematic. For example, Hedges et al. (1985) report that, in a sample of 21 participants, the rate of missing data was 14%. Similarly, Eckenrode (1984) found that only 328 out of a possible 2,592 person-days of data (or 13%) were missing.

Verbrugge (1980b) notes that fatigue effects may be a primary reason for missing data in diary studies. She posits that respondents may get tired or bored completing daily reports, and may become less diligent in doing so over time. Fatigue effects might be expected to occur more frequently the longer respondents are required to participate in a study, especially if the daily reports are time-consuming and complex. Verbrugge (1980b) has suggested that "when respondents are monitored and given active encouragement throughout the study period, they produce diaries with few missing and unclear responses" (p. 91).

Even if respondents are not bored or fatigued, missing data can nevertheless arise. For example, sometimes respondents are busy with other things and simply forget to complete the diaries at the prescribed times. The Experience Sampling Method (Csikszentmihalyi & Larson, 1987) described earlier is one way to prevent this problem from occurring via the use of beepers to remind respondents to make diary entries at prescribed times.

Finally, researchers must be aware that if they simply exclude those respondents from their analyses who do not have complete data at all time-points, they risk limiting the external validity of their findings. That is, respondents who conscientiously complete diaries across relatively long periods of time no doubt differ from those whose diaries contain missing data. Comparisons among the two groups on relevant dimensions (e.g., age, sex, health, stress levels) could be made to examine differences between conscientious completers and those respondents with missing data. Generalizability of the findings can then be more accurately determined.

The Spacing and Number of Assessments across Time

Although diary studies can include multiple assessments each day, a more common time frame is once-per-day assessments across a period of several weeks (e.g., Bolger, DeLongis, Kessler, & Wethington, 1990; Eckenrode, 1984; Stone, 1981). Such a design has a number of limitations. Perhaps most pertinent among these is that many of the effects and processes of interest unfold within a day, and research methodology must be sensitive enough to measure these changes or else important information may be lost. Many minor stressful episodes are resolved within a matter of minutes or hours, not days (DeLongis & Lehman, 1989). When the research question of interest involves studying changes over a brief period of time, multiple assessments are necessary each day. For example, a number of studies have found no evidence of a 1-day lagged effect of daily stress, or hassles, on mood (Bolger et al., 1990). With common, everyday stressors, the effects on mood appear to be primarily within days. Thus, if causal issues are to be disentangled in this literature, researchers will need to modify their designs to include more closely spaced assessments.

Because many diary studies require respondents to complete entries at one time-point in the day, usually before going to sleep for the night (e.g., DeLongis et al., 1988), it is important to determine the meaning of once-per-day assessments. For example, when asked to report their mood that day, are respondents able to mentally average across mood fluctuations occurring within the day, or are their reports of "typical" mood systematically biased in some way? To address this question, Hedges et al. (1985) measured momentary mood by getting community residents to complete mood checklists at four time-points throughout the day. Respondents also completed a checklist at the end of the day, in which they were asked to report their typical mood that day. Hedges et al. (1985) considered three possibilities for the meaning of this final report each day. First, the final measure may represent an average of all of the moods reported during the day. Second, it may be indicative of peak periods, that is, the highs and the lows for that given day. Third, a recency effect may occur such that respondents, in completing the final measure, may be biased such that they report moods that were experienced just prior to completion of the final assessment. Hedges et al. (1985) found that peak momentary mood corresponded most closely to absolute final reports within subjects. In contrast, average momentary mood had the highest day-to-day correlation with the final assessment. Hedges et al. interpret these results as supporting the notion that more salient moods are most likely to be remembered, whereas less intense moods are more easily forgotten.

Variations in Mood across the Days of the Week

It has generally been assumed that moods vary across days of the week (Weiss & Brown, 1976; Wilson et al., 1982). In particular, the beginning of the traditional work week is regarded as associated with negative affect. However, few empirical studies have been conducted to determine the accuracy of this so-called blue Monday effect. Such a finding would have relevance to diary studies, given that diaries are typically completed daily for several weeks. Interestingly, available evidence, though scant, suggests that although mood on weekend days is more positive than on other days (Rossi & Rossi, 1977), Mondays are not assessed any differently than other weekdays (Stone et al., 1985). People's beliefs about day-of-the-week effects, however, may lead to exaggerations of retrospectively reported weekend highs and Monday lows, when compared with concurrent reports of mood (McFarlane et al., 1988). In contrast to the findings of these studies, Larsen and Kasimatis (1990) found evidence of a peak in mood around Friday or Saturday, with a trough occurring around Monday or Tuesday. Clearly, a larger empirical base of moods across the days of the week is needed before diary researchers can incorporate day effects into their analyses.

Research Costs

One of the main disadvantages of daily diary studies is that they tend to be expensive. In general, diary studies cost more than single-interview studies (Verbrugge, 1980a). The greater lengths that researchers take to improve research design and facilitate accurate responding (including professional printing, pilot testing, extensive contact with participants, diary pickup by researchers), the more the study will cost. Although researchers may be tempted to deal with the increased cost of diary studies by incorporating a number of major research questions into each diary study, the necessity of minimizing demands upon respondents' time tends to outweigh the potential benefits of such a strategy. Greater demands on respondents' time will almost certainly result in lower participation rates, higher rates of missing data, and higher attrition rates across the study.

Interpersonal Concerns with Diary Completions

An interesting set of problems may arise when married persons (or parents) participate in diary studies. Regardless of whether one or both partners are completing diaries, respondents may be concerned that their spouses (or children) will attempt to read their entries. This will be true especially when sensitive types of behaviors are investigated, such as sexual activity, or when one provides data pertaining to other family members. DeLongis, Bolger, and Kessler (1988) asked husbands and wives to report both their own coping with marital problems and their partners' coping. If, in such studies, participants are not guaranteed that their answers will be confidential, they may be reluctant to mention unfavorable aspects of others' behaviors. One way to increase confidentiality is to give respondents envelopes that are to be sealed subsequent to each form completion. If several days are bound within one booklet, adhesive tabs may be used to seal completed pages (Bolger et al., 1989). A more extreme method for handling this concern is to employ lockboxes. After each entry the respondent places the form into a locked, metal box through a top slot, thus discouraging family members from trying to read the entries. At the end of the study period, the respondent can simply bring in the lockbox, or it can be retrieved by a project staff member. These same methods that can be used to increase respondent confidentiality also serve to inhibit or prevent respondents from examining their own responses at previous time-points. Such examination of prior responses could result in enhanced testing effects (see Cook & Campbell, 1979). If respondents look back over their previous diary entries they may adjust either their prior entries to be more in line with their current views of past events, or they may adjust their current entries in order to present a more consistent picture of themselves.

Accuracy of Diary Entries

Because diary studies involve the investigation of subjective phenomena such as thoughts and feelings, and participants are untrained raters, it is often difficult to determine the validity of responses. One suggestion is that other measurement techniques, such as observational data, peer ratings, and questionnaire ratings may be utilized as checks (Hormuth, 1986). Recent research suggests that, under some conditions, it is possible to improve the accuracy of self-report data if collection of objective measures is also anticipated by the respondents. Thus, Bauman and Dent (1982) found that adolescents who had recently smoked reported a greater amount of smoking if they were informed that carbon monoxide in alveolar air scores would be taken after completing a questionnaire on their smoking behavior.

Referring to the percentage of time that two individuals agree that a particular event has occurred, O'Leary and Wilson (1987) conclude that the reliability of self reports on diary-type measures varies from about 50 to 100%. This great variation in agreement rates appears to be a function of how aware respondents typically are of the type of event under investigation. The more common and automatic the behavior or event is, the lower the agreement rate. For example, the rate of agreement found on face touching was only 52% (Lipinski & Nelson, 1974), while that on pill taking was found to be 98% (Azrin & Powell, 1969). Of course, a common use of diaries is to assess cognitive events, and obtaining observer ratings of internal events is not plausible.

Perhaps respondents will be more likely to report socially undesirable behaviors if they are aware that multiple methods, in addition to their own self-report, will be used to assess the behavior. In any case, a multimethod approach may be preferable to a single-method technique. For example, we have recently collected data in which couples report on each other's coping, and this method seems to hold some promise for improving the interpretability of self-report data obtained in diaries.

General Recommendations

Before a diary study is undertaken, it is advisable to pilot test the methods and procedures on a subsample of respondents. At this stage, researchers are able to query study participants regarding any ambiguities with question wording, sensitivity of the questions, readability of the diary booklet, or perceived relevancy of items. Moreover, pilot testing will enable researchers to determine how long it takes respondents to complete each of the entries. We have done this (DeLongis & O'Brien, 1990) by inviting members of the population of interest to participate in focus groups in which they are asked, in addition to the usual open-ended discussion format (see Morgan, 1988), to complete a copy of the "diary" and to discuss any concerns with us.

After the study has been thoroughly pilot tested, researchers should ensure that participants know what is required of them. When respondents are uncertain as to when booklets are to be completed, or do not understand the amount of time required of them by the study, both dropout rates and rates of missing data are likely to increase. It is helpful to provide respondents with sample diaries. Investigators using Verbrugge's Daily Health Record (DeLongis et al., 1988; Verbrugge, 1985) have mailed to respondents, along with a diary booklet to be completed, a "sample" diary that is already completed in order to provide study participants with an example of the sorts of information being requested of them. In other studies (Bolger et al., 1990), we have mailed a blank "sample" diary to potential respondents to allow them to make an informed decision about whether they would like to participate in the study. Regardless of whether a blank or example diary is provided before the start of data collection, respondents find it helpful to have gone through the diary with an interviewer, ideally face-to-face (e.g., DeLongis, 1988). If face-to-face interviews are not possible, respondents can be mailed a copy of the diary and the interviewer can then discuss it with them over the telephone (e.g., Bolger et al., 1989). In any case, respondents should be given a number to telephone, preferably included on the front of the question booklet, and encouraged to phone the research office if questions arise as they complete the diary.

The diary format may influence compliance. Diaries should be small enough to carry around, especially if multiple completions are required each day. Additionally, instruments should be easy to self-administer, and be short in administration time (Howarth & Schokman-Gates, 1981). On average, forms should take only a couple of minutes to complete, although individual variation among respondents in completion time is to be expected. Moreover, diaries should, if possible, present logically grouped items on the same page (Verbrugge, 1984). Although closed-ended response formats typically make fewer demands on respondents, open-ended items allow for idiosyncrasies particular to the situation (Brandstatter, 1983). Furthermore, respondents seem to like the opportunity, especially if it is left as an option, to describe in an open-ended way any special events or experiences they had during the day. However, given the greater time and mental effort required in responding to open-ended questions, such questions should be kept to a minimum. When they are included, they should be stated in such a way that they very clearly indicate precisely what information is being requested of respondents. The only exception to this general rule is if a final wrap-up question is included in the diary that asks something like "Did anything special happen today that you haven't already told us about? If so, please describe it." Of course, in coding and analyzing data obtained using such a vague question, it must be kept in mind that respondents will vary greatly in how they interpret and respond to the question. One would be hard-pressed, for example, to conclude that nothing "special" ever occurred to a particular respondent if he or she failed to describe any events or experiences in response to such a question. A very busy person, or one who is not particularly comfortable with writing (about themselves or, perhaps, more generally) would be unlikely to say much in response to such a question. We continue to include such questions for a number of reasons, however, including our observation that many respondents seem to find it an important avenue for conveying what they feel is of real importance in their lives.

Response booklets should include roughly 1-week's diaries, with items that are unambiguous. Pre-addressed, stamped envelopes should be provided, and if possible, a pen for diary completion. Researchers will probably find it useful to ask respondents to return completed diary booklets at least once weekly (e.g., Bolger et al., 1989). Some researchers (e.g., Cantor et al., 1991) have even asked respondents to return booklets daily, although this probably works best with student samples and may be more difficult to request of community-residing respondents. Respondents can be encouraged to return their booklets promptly with telephone calls, reminder notes, and once a booklet is returned, a thank you note or small gift to encourage the prompt return of the next week's diary booklet.

An alternative to having respondents mail in completed booklets is to have interviewers pick them up at respondents' homes at regular intervals (e.g., De-Longis et al., 1988). This approach enables interviewers to query respondents about any problems or questions regarding the diary task. Another alternative, one that ensures assessments are completed at the prescribed time, is to call respondents daily and have them complete ratings verbally over the telephone, rather than by written report (e.g., MacDermid, Huston, & McHale, 1990). Such a procedure also minimizes the possibility of missing data. Further, verbal reports reduce the likelihood of contamination from reexamining previous diary entries, because respondents do not have a completed form with which to compare answers (Hedges et al., 1985). In addition, responses provided over the telephone are likely to be less memorable than written ones, and therefore, may produce less reactance in the respondent. Drawbacks of this approach include increased cost in terms of time, effort, and telephone bills. In addition, telephones are not always accessible when ratings are supposed to be made, especially if several assessments per day are required. Finally, it must be recognized that respondents' reports of behaviors, cognitions, emotions, and daily events may all be influenced by the telephone interviewer in ways that are perhaps less likely in a written diary. Particularly in cases where descriptions of intimate experiences and respondents' reactions to them are required, as is often the case in studies of daily events, telephone interviewing will have its limit. Interviewers, thus, must take particular care in such cases not to influence respondents, and researchers must take care to design their studies so that questions are asked in ways that minimize this problem. For example, intimate questions about marital interactions can be introduced with a sentence or two that acknowledges wide individual variation with no one way being better than any other. Perhaps even more important is the need for interviewers to make sure that respondents have privacy before beginning the interview. If a spouse or child is within listening distance to the respondent, respondents will no doubt be constrained from openly and honestly discussing the issues at hand during the interview.

Conclusion

The use of structured diaries for the study of daily events holds many advantages over traditional experimental and survey methodologies. Diary studies are more conducive to the study of naturally occurring change, or process, within hours or days, or even across a few months. In addition, it is less susceptible to a host of recall biases present in research designs that require respondents to remember events and experiences over longer time periods. Although there are costs to employing the diary methodology, which we have reviewed here, the richness of the information gleaned will often outweigh the time, money, and effort required to conduct such research. Diary studies, with their focus on ecologically valid social phenomena, provide an important methodology for basic and applied researchers alike.

ACKNOWLEDGMENTS. Preparation of this chapter was supported by grants from the Social Sciences and Humanities Research Council of Canada to Anita De-

Longis and Darrin R. Lehman. The authors thank Fred B. Bryant and three anonymous reviewers for their insightful comments and suggestions on an earlier draft of this chapter.

References

Azrin, N. H., & Powell, J. (1969). Behavioral engineering: The use of response priming to improve prescribed self-medication. *Journal of Applied Behavior Analysis, 2*, 39–42.

Bauman, K. E., & Dent, C. W. (1982). Influence of an objective measure on self-reports of behavior. *Journal of Applied Psychology, 67*, 623–628.

Bem, D. J. (1972). Self-perception theory. In L. Berkowitz (Ed.), *Advances in experimental social psychology* (Vol. 6, pp. 1–62). New York: Academic Press.

Bem, D. J., & McConnell, H. K. (1970). Testing the self-perception explanation of dissonance phenomena: On the salience of premanipulation attitudes. *Journal of Personality and Social Psychology, 14*, 23–31.

Bishop, C. (1990). *Coping with pain in rheumatoid arthritis.* Unpublished Master's Thesis, University of British Columbia, Vancouver.

Block, J. (1971). *Lives thru time.* Berkeley, CA: Bancroft.

Bolger, N., DeLongis, A., Kessler, R. C., & Schilling, E. A. (1989). Effect of daily stress on negative mood. *Journal of Personality and Social Psychology, 57*, 808–818.

Bolger, N., DeLongis, A., Kessler, R. C., & Wethington, E. (1989). The contagion of stress across multiple roles. *Journal of Marriage and the Family, 51*, 175–183.

Bolger, N., DeLongis, A., Kessler, R. C., & Wethington, E. (1990). The microstructure of daily role-related stress in married couples. In J. Eckenrode & S. Gore (Eds.), *Crossing the boundaries: The transmission of stress between work and family* (pp. 95–116). New York: Plenum.

Brandstatter, H. (1983). Emotional responses to other persons in everyday life situations. *Journal of Personality and Social Psychology, 45*, 871–883.

Campbell, J. D., Chew, B., & Scratchley, L. S. (1991). Cognitive and emotional reactions to daily events: The effects of self-esteem and self-complexity. *Journal of Personality, 59*, 473–505.

Cantor, N., Norem, J., Langston, C., Zirkel, S., Fleeson, W., & Cook-Flannagan, C. (1991). Life tasks and daily life experience. *Journal of Personality, 59*, 425–451.

Clark, L. A., & Watson, D. (1988). Mood and the mundane: Relations between daily life events and self-reported mood. *Journal of Personality and Social Psychology, 54*, 296–308.

Cook, T. D., & Campbell, D. T. (1979). *Quasi-experimentation: Design and analysis issues for field settings.* Boston: Houghton Mifflin.

Csikszentmihalyi, M., & Larson, R. (1987). Validity and reliability of the experience-sampling method. *The Journal of Nervous and Mental Disease, 175*, 526–536.

Csikszentmihalyi, M., Larson, R., & Prescott, S. (1977). The ecology of adolescent activity and experience. *Journal of Youth and Adolescence, 6*, 281–294.

Deci, E. L., & Ryan, R. M. (1985). The general causality orientations scale: Self-determination in personality. *Journal of Research in Personality, 19*, 109–134.

DeLongis, A. (1985). *The relationship of everyday stress to health and well-being: Inter- and intraindividual approaches.* Unpublished doctoral dissertation, University of California, Berkeley.

DeLongis, A., Coyne, J. C., Dakof, G., Folkman, S., & Lazarus, R. S. (1982). Relationship of daily hassles, uplifts, and major life events to health status. *Health Psychology, 1*, 119–136.

DeLongis, A., Folkman, S., & Lazarus, R. S. (1988). The impact of daily stress on health and mood:

Psychological and social resources as mediators. *Journal of Personality and Social Psychology,* *54*, 486–495.

DeLongis, A., & Lehman, D. R. (1989). The usefulness of a structured diary approach in studying marital relationships. *Journal of Family Psychology, 2,* 337–343.

DeLongis, A., Lehman, D. R., Silver, R. C., & Wortman, C. B. (1992). The interpersonal dimensions of coping: The social context of emotional expression following a traumatic event. Manuscript submitted for publication.

DeLongis, A., & O'Brien, T. (1990). An interpersonal framework for stress and coping: An application to the families of Alzheimer's patients. In M. A. P. Stephens, J. H. Crowther, S. E. Hobfoll, & D. L. Tennenbaum (Eds.), *Stress and coping in later life families* (pp. 221–239). Washington, DC: Hemisphere Publishers.

DeLongis, A., Tal, M., & Kessler, R. C. (1987). *Daily coping with marital conflict.* Paper presented at the Annual Convention of the American Psychological Association, New York.

Dohrenwend, B. S., Dohrenwend, B. P., Dodson, M., & Shrout, P. E. (1984). Symptoms, hassles, social supports, and life events: Problem of confounded measures. *Journal of Abnormal Psychology, 93,* 222–230.

Dohrenwend, B. P., & Shrout, P. E. (1985). "Hassles" in the conceptualization and measurement of life stress variables. *American Psychologist, 40,* 780–785.

Downey, G., Silver, R. C., & Wortman, C. B. (1990). Reconsidering the attribution-adjustment relation following a major negative event: Coping with the loss of a child. *Journal of Personality and Social Psychology, 59,* 925–940.

Eckenrode, J. (1984). Impact of chronic and acute stressors on daily reports of mood. *Journal of Personality and Social Psychology, 46,* 907–918.

Eich, E. (1989). Theoretical issues in state dependent memory. In H. L. Roediger III & F. I. M. Craik (Eds.), *Varieties of memory and consciousness: Essays in honor of Endel Tulving* (pp. 331–354). Hillsdale, NJ: Lawrence Erlbaum.

Epstein, S. (1983). Aggregation and beyond: Some basic issues on the prediction of behavior. *Journal of Personality, 51,* 360–392.

Epstein, S. (1986). Does aggregation produce spuriously high estimates of behavior stability? *Journal of Personality and Social Psychology, 50,* 1199–1210.

Fincham, F., Beach, S. R., & Baucom, D. H. (1987). Attribution processes in distressed and nondistressed couples: 4. Self–partner attribution differences. *Journal of Personality and Social Psychology, 52,* 739–748.

Folkman, S., Lazarus, R. S., Dunkel-Schetter, C., DeLongis, A., & Gruen, R. J. (1986). Dynamics of a stressful encounter: Cognitive appraisal, coping, and encounter outcomes. *Journal of Personality and Social Psychology, 50,* 992–1003.

Follick, M. J., Ahern, D. K., & Laser-Wolston, N. (1984). Evaluation of a daily activity diary for chronic pain patients. *Pain, 19,* 373–382.

Freedman, J. L., & Fraser, S. C. (1966). Compliance without pressure: The foot-in-the-door technique. *Journal of Personality and Social Psychology, 4,* 195–202.

Gard, D., Edwards, P. W., Harris, J., & McCormack, G. (1988). Sensitizing effects of pretreatment measures on cancer chemotherapy nausea and vomiting. *Journal of Consulting and Clinical Psychology, 56,* 80–84.

Gavanski, I., & Wells, G. L. (1989). Counterfactual processing of normal and exceptional events. *Journal of Experimental Social Psychology, 25,* 314–325.

Glass, D. C., & Singer, J. E. (1972). *Urban stress.* New York: Academic Press.

Hedges, S. M., Jandorf, L., & Stone, A. A. (1985). Meaning of daily mood assessments. *Journal of Personality and Social Psychology, 48,* 428–434.

Holmes, T. H., & Rahe, R. H. (1967). The social readjustment rating scale. *Journal of Psychosomatic Research, 11,* 213–218.

Hormuth, S. E. (1986). The sampling of experiences in situ. *Journal of Personality*, *54*, 262–293.

House, J. S., Strecher, V., Metzner, H. L., & Robbins, C. A. (1986). Occupational stress and health among men and women in the Tecumseh Community Health Study. *Journal of Health and Social Behavior*, *27*, 62–77.

Howarth, E., & Schokman-Gates, K. (1981). Self-report multiple mood instruments. *British Journal of Psychology*, *72*, 421–441.

Johnston, C., Krech, K., Tiedemann, F., & Pelham, W. E. (1990). Parenting stress: Exploring individual differences. In S. E. Kahn, B. C. Long, & A. DeLongis (Eds.), *Women, stress, and coping: An interdisciplinary research workshop* (pp. 109–117). Vancouver, British Columbia, Canada: AWA.

Kanfer, F. H., & Goldfoot, D. A. (1966). Self control and tolerance of noxious stimulation. *Psychological Reports*, *18*, 79–85.

Kanner, A. D., Coyne, J. C., Schaefer, C., & Lazarus, R. S. (1981). Comparison of two modes of stress measurement: Daily hassles and uplifts versus major life events. *Journal of Behavioral Medicine*, *4*, 1–39.

Kemsley, W. F. F. (1975). Family expenditures survey: A study of differential response based on a comparison of the 1971 sample with the census. *Statistical News*, *31*, 16–21.

Larsen, R. J. (1987). The stability of mood variability: A spectral analytic approach to daily mood assessments. *Journal of Personality and Social Psychology*, *52*, 1195–1204.

Larsen, R. J., & Kasimatis, M. (1990). Individual differences in entrainment of mood to the weekly calendar. *Journal of Personality and Social Psychology*, *58*, 164–171.

Larson, R., Zuzanek, J., & Mannell, R. (1985). Being along versus being with people: Disengagement in the daily experience of older adults. *Journal of Gerontology*, *3*, 375–381.

Lazarus, R. S. (1990). Theory-based stress measurement. *Psychological Inquiry*, *1*, 3–13.

Lazarus, R. S., & DeLongis, A. (1983). Psychological stress and coping in aging. *American Psychologist*, *38*, 245–254.

Lazarus, R. S., DeLongis, A., Folkman, S., & Gruen, R. (1985). Stress and adaptational outcomes: The problem of confounded measures. *American Psychologist*, *40*, 770–779.

Lazarus, R. S., & Folkman, S. (1984). *Stress, appraisal, and coping*. New York: Springer.

Lehman, D. R. (1985). *A comparison of spouse and child loss from motor vehicle crashes*. Unpublished doctoral dissertation, University of Michigan, Ann Arbor.

Lehman, D. R., & Hemphill, K. J. (1990). Recipients' perceptions of support attempts and attributions for support attempts that fail. *Journal of Social and Personal Relationships*, *7*, 563–574.

Lehman, D. R., Wortman, C. B., & Williams, A. F. (1987). Long-term effects of losing a spouse or child in a motor vehicle crash. *Journal of Personality and Social Psychology*, *52*, 218–231.

Lemmens, P., Knibbe, R. A., & Tan, F. (1988). Weekly recall and diary estimates of alcohol consumption in a general population survey. *Journal of Studies on Alcohol*, *49*, 131–135.

Lepper, M. R., Greene, D., & Nisbett, R. E. (1973). Undermining children's intrinsic interest with extrinsic reward: A test of the "overjustification" hypothesis. *Journal of Personality and Social Psychology*, *28*, 129–137.

Lewis, V. E., & Williams, R. N. (1989). Mood-congruent vs. mood-state-dependent learning: Implications for a view of emotion. *Journal of Social Behavior and Personality*, *4*, 157–171.

Lipinski, D. P., Black, J. L., Nelson, R. O., & Ciminero, A. R. (1975). Influence of motivational variables on the reactivity and reliability of self-recording. *Journal of Consulting and Clinical Psychology*, *43*, 637–646.

Lipinski, D., & Nelson, R. (1974). The reactivity and unreliability of self-recording. *Journal of Consulting and Clinical Psychology*, *42*, 110–123.

MacDermid, S. M., Huston, T. L., & McHale, S. M. (1990). Changes in marriage associated with the transition to parenthood: Individual differences as a function of sex-role attitudes and changes in the division of household labor. *Journal of Marriage and the Family*, *52*, 475–486.

Martin, P. R., Nathan, P. R., Milech, D., & van Keppel, M. (1989). Cognitive therapy vs. self-management training in the treatment of chronic headaches. *British Journal of Clinical Psychology, 28,* 347–361.

McAdams, D., & Constantian, C. A. (1983). Intimacy and affiliation motives in daily living: An experience sampling analysis. *Journal of Personality and Social Psychology, 45,* 851–861.

McFarland, C., & Ross, M. (1985). *The relation between current impressions and memories of self and dating partners.* Unpublished manuscript, University of Waterloo, Ontario, Canada.

McFarlane, J., Martin, C. L., & Williams, T. M. (1988). Mood fluctuations: Women versus men and menstrual versus other cycles. *Psychology of Women Quarterly, 12,* 201–223.

McKenzie, J. (1983). The accuracy of telephone call data collected by diary methods. *Journal of Marketing Research, 20,* 417–427.

Monroe, S. M. (1983). Major and minor life events as predictors of psychological distress: Further issues and findings. *Journal of Behavioral Medicine, 6,* 189–205.

Morgan, D. L. (1988). *Focus groups as qualitative research.* Beverly Hills: Sage.

Norvell, K. T., Gaston-Johansson, F., & Fridh, G. (1987). Remembrance of labor pain: How valid are retrospective pain measurements? *Pain, 31,* 77–86.

O'Leary, K. D., & Wilson, G. T. (1987). *Behavior therapy: Application and outcome* (2nd ed.). Englewood Cliffs, NJ: Prentice-Hall.

Pearlin, L. I., Menaghan, E. G., Lieberman, M. A., & Mullan, J. T. (1981). The stress process. *Journal of Health and Social Behavior, 22,* 337–356.

Pennebaker, J. W. (1987). The psychophysiology of confession: Linking inhibitory and psychosomatic processes. *Journal of Personality and Social Psychology, 52,* 781–793.

Pennebaker, J. W. (1989). Confession, inhibition, and disease. In L. Berkowitz (Ed.), *Advances in experimental social psychology* (Vol. 22, pp. 211–244). Orlando, FL: Academic Press.

Pennebaker, J. W., Kiecolt-Glaser, J. K., & Glaser, R. (1988). Disclosure of traumas and immune function: Health implications for psychotherapy. *Journal of Consulting and Clinical Psychology, 56,* 239–245.

Porter, D., Leviton, A., Slack, W. V., & Graham, J. R. (1981). A headache chronicle: The daily recording of headaches and their correlates. *Journal of Chronic Diseases, 34,* 481–486.

Rabkin, J. G., & Struening, E. L. (1976). Life events, stress, and illness. *Science, 194,* 1013–1020.

Rittle, R. H. (1981). Changes in helping behavior: Self versus situational perceptions as mediators of the foot-in-the-door effect. *Personality and Social Psychology Bulletin, 7,* 431–437.

Roghmann, K. J., & Haggerty, R. J. (1972). The diary as a research instrument in the study of health and illness behavior: Experiences with a random sample of young families. *Medical Care, 10,* 143–163.

Rossi, A. S., & Rossi, P. E. (1977). Body time and social time: Mood patterns by menstrual cycle phase and day of the week. *Social Science Research, 6,* 273–308.

Snyder, M., & Cunningham, M. R. (1975). To comply or not to comply: Testing the self-perception of the "foot-in-the-door" phenomenon. *Journal of Personality and Social Psychology, 31,* 64–67.

Speisman, J., Lazarus, R. S., Mordkoff, A., & Davidson, L. (1964). Experimental reduction of stress based on ego defense theory. *Journal of Abnormal and Social Psychology, 68,* 367–380.

Stanton, J. L., & Tucci, L. A. (1982). The measurement of consumption: A comparison of surveys and diaries. *Journal of Marketing Research, 19,* 274–277.

Stone, A. A. (1981). The association between perceptions of daily experiences and self- and spouse-rated mood. *Journal of Research in Personality, 15,* 510–522.

Stone, A. A., Hedges, S. M., Neale, J. M., & Satin, M. S. (1985). Prospective and cross-sectional mood reports offer no evidence of a "blue Monday" phenomenon. *Journal of Personality and Social Psychology, 49,* 129–134.

Stone, A. A., & Neale, J. M. (1984). New measure of daily coping: Development and preliminary results. *Journal of Personality and Social Psychology, 46*, 892–906.

Stone, H. (1973). The birth of a child with Down's Syndrome: A medico-social study of thirty-one children and their families. *Scottish Medical Journal, 18*, 182–187.

Swan, G. E., & MacDonald, M. L. (1978). Behavior therapy in practice: A national survey of behavior therapists. *Behavior Therapy, 9*, 799–807.

Taylor, S. E. (1983). Adjustment to threatening events: A theory of cognitive adaptation. *American Psychologist, 38*, 1161–1173.

Taylor, S. E., Lichtman, R. R., & Wood, J. V. (1984). Attributions, beliefs about control, and adjustment to breast cancer. *Journal of Personality and Social Psychology, 46*, 489–502.

Thompson, S. C., & Janigian, A. S. (1988). Life schemas: A framework for understanding the search for meaning. *Journal of Social and Clinical Psychology, 7*, 260–280.

Verbrugge, L. M. (1980a). Health diaries. *Medical Care, 18*, 73–95.

Verbrugge, L. M. (1980b). Sensitization and fatigue in health diaries. *Proceedings of the American Statistical Association* (Section on Survey Research Methods), 666–671.

Verbrugge, L. M. (1984). Health-diaries—Problems and solutions in study design. In C. F. Cannell & R. M. Groves (Eds.), *Health survey research methods* (pp. 171–192). Rockville, MD: National Center for Health Services Research.

Verbrugge, L. M. (1985). Triggers of symptoms and health care. *Social Science and Medicine, 20*, 855–876.

Weber, H., & Laux, L. (1990). Bringing the person back into stress and coping measurement. *Psychological Inquiry, 1*, 37–40.

Weiss, J., & Brown, P. (1976). Self-insight error in the explanation of mood. Unpublished manuscript, Harvard University, Cambridge, MA.

Wilson, T. D., Laser, P. S., & Stone, J. I. (1982). Judging the predictors of one's mood: Accuracy and the use of shared theories. *Journal of Experimental Social Psychology, 18*, 537–556.

Wixon, D. R., & Laird, J. D. (1976). Awareness and attitude change in the forced-compliance paradigm: The importance of when. *Journal of Personality and Social Psychology, 34*, 376–384.

Wong, M. M., & Csikszentmihalyi, M. (1991). Motivation and academic achievement: The effects of personality traits and the quality of experience. *Journal of Personality, 59*, 539–574.

Wortman, C. B., Abbey, A., Holland, A. E., Silver, R. L., & Janoff-Bulman, R. (1980). Transitions from the laboratory to the field: Problems and progress. In L. Bickman (Ed.), *Applied social psychology annual* (pp. 197–233). Beverly Hills, CA: Sage.

Zarski, J. J. (1984). Hassles and health: A replication. *Health Psychology, 3*, 243–251.

6

Time Series Methods in Applied Social Research

Melvin M. Mark, Lawrence J. Sanna, and R. Lance Shotland

Time series methods represent an important research tool for applied social psychologists. Consider interrupted time series designs, in which one assesses the effect of some intervention on an outcome measured repeatedly over time. Interrupted time series designs have been employed to address such varied questions as: the effect of drunk driving laws (Hilton, 1984; Shore & Maguin, 1988; West, Hepworth, McCall, & Reich, 1989), mandatory seat belt laws (Wagenaar, Maybee, & Sullivan, 1988), and an increase in the legal minimum drinking age (Wagenaar, 1982) on traffic fatalities; the effect of incentive payment (Wagner, Rubin, & Callahan, 1988) and of merit pay (Pearce, Stevenson, & Perry, 1985) on productivity; the effect of publishing offenders' names in a newspaper on the frequency of shoplifting and drunk driving (Ross & White, 1987); the effect of mandatory sentencing on firearms violence (Loftin, Heumann, & McDowall, 1983); the effect of TV public service announcements on inquiries to social service agencies (McAbee & Cafferty, 1982); and even the effect of introducing meditation groups on the crime in an area (Dillbeck et al., 1987). In addition, related time series methods, which focus not on the effects of some abrupt intervention but rather on the covariation between two ongoing time series, have addressed the relationship between such variables as: air pollution and psycho-

Melvin M. Mark, Lawrence J. Sanna, and R. Lance Shotland • Department of Psychology, Pennsylvania State University, University Park, Pennsylvania 16802.

Methodological Issues in Applied Psychology, edited by Bryant et al. Plenum Press, New York, 1992.

logical state (Bullinger, 1989); air pollution, weather, and violent crime (Rotton & Frey, 1985); economic conditions and alcohol-related traffic fatalities (Wagenaar & Streff, 1989); alcohol use and suicide rates (Norstrom, 1988); expenditures on cigarette advertising and cigarette consumption (Chetwynd, Coope, Brodie, & Wells, 1988); and historical economic data and lynchings (Hepworth & West, 1988). As one indication of the potential importance of time series methods, consider that Cook and Campbell (1979) dedicated two chapters of their book on quasi-experimentation to the topic of interrupted time series, and part of another chapter to methods for assessing the relationship between two ongoing time series.

As indicated by our illustrative list of time series studies, time series methods have been used to address a variety of interesting and important questions. We also believe that there exists considerable potential for time series methods in the future, in spite of reductions during the 1980s in governmental funds for the development and maintenance of certain potential data sources. For time series methods to realize their potential in the future, however, may require that we learn the lessons of time series studies of the past. The present chapter offers one attempt to specify some of the lessons of the past, and to point toward better time series studies in the future.

In the present chapter we will not, however, attempt a comprehensive review of problems one may encounter in conducting a time series study. Nor will we present a technical description of time series analyses, which is available elsewhere (e.g., Box & Jenkins, 1976; Cook & Campbell, 1979; McCleary & Hay, 1980). Instead, in the sections that follow, we shall present two case studies and discuss the lessons we have derived from them; we will also briefly report the results of a survey of published time series studies.

Case Study 1: The Impact of a Community Action Group

Several years ago one of the authors (M. Mark), along with Dirk Steiner, conducted a study assessing the effectiveness of a community action group that developed to protest a bank's actions. More generally, we were interested in illustrating interrupted time series methods as a way of studying the effectiveness of community action groups. Although community action groups had generated a fair amount of interest in the scholarly community, little of it addressed the question of the groups' effectiveness (Steiner & Mark, 1985)—a question that should be of great concern to community organizers and activists, as well as to organizational theorists.

The community action group in question arose in a midwestern city of about

10,000 in 1982. It was formed in response to a small local bank's announcement that it intended to raise the mortgage interest rates of a subset of its customers. In particular, the bank notified the 223 mortgage holders whose interest rate had been 11% that their interest rate would increase to 13% in about 4 months.[1] Initially, individual mortgage holders met with bank officials; however, these meetings failed to reach a satisfactory agreement about the mortgage interest rates and a group action followed. There were organized community meetings that received media coverage for several months. The result was a distinct, cohesive community group. Members displayed signs in their yards with the group's name and held numerous public meetings, attended by up to 350 people.

The group organized a "mass withdrawal" against the bank and encouraged community members to discontinue all business with the bank. On the date of the targeted mass withdrawal, group members picketed the bank. Steiner and Mark (1985) examined the extent to which there was an associated decline in the monthly total balance of funds deposited in the bank's passbook savings account as of the last day of the month. We found a statistically significant effect such that the bank's total passbook savings accounts were reduced by $476,840 (relative to an overall mean total savings of $6,053,495). Details of the analysis can be found in Steiner and Mark (1985). In the context of this chapter, the most important question about this study is: What lessons about time series methods does this study illustrate?

Lesson #1: Relevant Record-Changing ≠ Internal Validity Threat of Instrumentation. Most presentations about interrupted time series designs consider changes in record-keeping primarily in the context of the internal validity threat known as instrumentation (e.g., Cook and Campbell, 1979, p. 212). That is, researchers are admonished to assess whether some change in the way the time series variable is recorded coincides with the introduction of the treatment; if so, the record-keeping change (or instrumentation), rather than the treatment, could be responsible for any observed change in the dependent variable.

However, in time series studies, the investigator must be mindful of changes in record-keeping *throughout* the length of the time series, not just those that coincide with the introduction of the treatment. Unknown record-keeping shifts can have several negative consequences, which include inflating error variance and changing the construct represented by the time series.

[1]From the perspective of the bank at least, the mortgage agreements gave the bank legal authority to impose such a change. However, the community action group that developed in response to the bank's move engaged the services of an attorney. The legal suit ultimately resulted in several interest rate options viewed favorably by the group. The Steiner and Mark analysis focused, however, on the group's mass-withdrawal campaign and its effect on bank holding.

Record-keeping shifts influenced the conduct of the Steiner and Mark (1985) study in two ways. First, recall that we analyzed the community action group's effect on passbook savings holdings. We did not employ checking account balances, because of numerous changes in the charges for and regulations about such accounts during the period examined. If only one or two such changes had occurred, it would have been possible to estimate their effects simultaneously with the estimation of the action group's effects (assuming the record-keeping shift and the independent variable of interest are not too highly confounded). That is, we could have estimated the effect on the observed dependent variable both of the action group's efforts and of the record-keeping shift; this would prevent the record-keeping shift from being treated as error that could overwhelm the effect of interest. However, given the frequency of shifts in the checking account data, along with the relatively clean savings account data, we simply elected to ignore the checking account data. (In retrospect, we are not sure we would make the same decision again; instead, we would probably analyze the checking account data in several ways, e.g., ignoring the record-keeping changes in one analysis and in another estimate both treatment effects and effects of record-keeping shifts, and look for congruence across analyses.)

A second way in which record-keeping shifts influenced the Steiner and Mark (1985) study involved the passbook savings data for which analyses were done. Again, however, the problem was not instrumentation, as traditionally defined. That is, the record-keeping shift did not coincide with the group's mass withdrawal. Rather, the change in record-keeping occurred several months *after* the intervention of interest. Specifically, following deregulation of banking, the bank revamped its savings account offerings and undertook an advertising campaign emphasizing the new savings accounts. The savings account data from after this revamping were not directly comparable to those before. Consequently, we had only five usable postintervention observations. As a result, we were unable to apply transfer function models (Box & Tiao, 1975; McCleary & Hay, 1980) that could estimate the temporal pattern of the effect (e.g., such models could test the plausible hypothesis that the action group's efforts had an immediate effect that died out over time). Thus, the occurrence of a record-keeping shift did not threaten the internal validity of the study, but instead limited its external validity in the sense that we were less able to draw confident inferences about the group's effects at later points in time (and, by extension, we learned less about the temporal pattern of community action groups more generally). However, a more serious problem would have arisen if we were not aware of the record-keeping shift that occurred: we would have examined the temporal pattern of the action group's effects, and would have drawn inaccurate inferences, because we would have mistaken the effects of the record-keeping shift for those of the action group.

The point is that time series researchers need to be mindful of record-keeping shifts throughout a time series, that such record-keeping shifts can have serious consequences even if they do not coincide with the introduction of the treatment, and that thoughtful judgment is often required to determine how to deal with the record-keeping shifts that occur.

Lesson #2: Time Series Are Not All Equally Costly, nor Are They Equally Valuable. In the Steiner and Mark (1985) study, we reported the results of a "simple" (Cook & Campbell, 1979, p. 209), or one-group, interrupted time series design. As we noted in the discussion section of that paper, one would often attempt to expand a simple interrupted time series design to include a non-equivalent control group, so as to reduce the plausibility of history as a threat to internal validity (Cook & Campbell, 1979). In the Steiner and Mark (1985) paper, we did not do so, arguing in part that there were no historical events, other than the community group's actions, that could plausibly account for the observed results. We also noted that any comparable control bank could suffer from an unusual form of contamination. That is, the money withdrawn from the targeted bank might be deposited in the control bank (ironically, by choosing a more distant bank that would be less likely to experience this contamination, one would also select a bank that is less likely to serve as a good control for historical forces).

What we did not note in the Steiner and Mark paper is that obtaining data from any control bank would probably have been more "costly" than obtaining data from the bank that was targeted by the community action groups, if indeed obtaining control data was possible at all. Privately held banks are not necessarily ecstatic about collating and disseminating to researchers monthly data on balances held. The data for the bank that was the target of the community group's action was, however, relatively "cheap" for the researchers to obtain. The reason? My coauthor's mother worked at the bank, and her position gave us organizational entree and most likely worked in our favor when the our request for data was considered.

Given (1) the absence of plausible history threats, (2) the likely contamination of possible control banks, and (3) the additional "cost" of control group data, we believe the decision to employ a simple interrupted time series design was reasonable. However, the case illustrates that data from control series or from nonequivalent dependent variables (Cook & Campbell, 1979) may come at a cost, that the cost may be greater than the cost of the primary time series, and that judgments will have to be made about the benefits of obtaining data relative to the costs of acquiring them. Most methodological writings do not address well the issues involved in making such decisions; for an exception, see Cronbach (1982).

Case Study 2: Mass Media Violence and Homicides (or, This Study Makes Me Want to Kill)

Background to the Study

The effects of the mass media on individual behavior, particularly violent behavior, is of great interest to social scientists. A now dated report nevertheless documents this interest, noting that over 2,500 studies have been conducted to investigate whether television violence causes aggression (National Institute of Mental Health, 1982). Not surprisingly, given the volume of the literature on media effects on aggression, this research area includes a multiplicity of research methods. Some reviewers have pointed to this use of multiple methods as a great benefit to the validity of the inferences that can be drawn from this literature. For example, in their review of the effects of television on aggression, Comstock and his colleagues claimed that:

> The great strength of the research on television and aggression is that a full range of possible methods has been employed instead of a single genre and that this variety has yielded interpretable results. . . . The reason this diversity provides strength is that, as we have observed in our analysis, each genre has characteristics that open it to criticism, but which are not the same at all. (Comstock et al., 1978, p. 250)

Reviews such as that of Comstock et al. (1978), which point to the convergence of results across different methods, helped make the idea that mass media violence causes aggression become accepted as true by many social scientists (Freedman, 1984). More recently, however, some reviewers have attacked the earlier reliance on convergence across multiple methods, and have thereby questioned the evidence underlying the conclusion that media violence causes aggression (Cook, 1985; Cook, Kendzierski, & Thomas, 1983; Freedman, 1984). These reviewers have questioned the assumption that (1) if different methods have different shortcomings, then (2) we should place great faith in the findings if results converge across methods. The primary alternative to be considered, of course, is that the different methods used—though they may have unique weaknesses—are each biased in the same direction; that is, each method's problems cause it to give the same, *incorrect* answer.

Consider Cook's (1985; Cook et al., 1983) critical review of research on the relationship between television and aggression. Cook suggests that the two methods widely used to examine this relationship, laboratory experiments and cross-sectional correlational studies, may both be biased in the same direction—that is, toward showing a positive relationship between viewing TV violence and aggression. In the case of laboratory experiments on TV and aggression, researchers typically minimize internal and external inhibition against aggression and amplify the treatment in order to maximize their ability to detect treatment effects. In the case of cross-sectional studies, viewing time is correlated with aggression, and statistical procedures are typically employed in an attempt to "partial out" background differences; as Cook (1985; Cook et al., 1983) notes, such attempts to control statistically for the differences between heavy and light viewers may "underadjust" (Campbell & Boruch, 1975) and, consequently, inflate the observed relationship between television viewing and aggression (see Cook, 1985, and Cook et al., 1983, for more detail, and see Freedman, 1984, for a similar perspective).

In short, the use of multiple methods is not a guarantee of valid conclusions, in the case of mass media violence and aggressive behavior or in any other research area. What is needed is confidence that the different methods employed address the same relationship, but are not biased in the same direction (Cook, 1985; Shotland & Mark, 1987). It is from this perspective that two of the authors (M. Mark and R. Shotland), along with Greg Mumma, several years ago set out to examine time series methods as they had been employed in the literature on mass media violence and aggression (e.g., Phillips, 1983; Phillips & Hensley, 1984).

We had several purposes in doing so. First, we wished to examine time series methods, which have only relatively recently been applied to the media violence and aggression literature, from the same "critical multiplist" perspective as Cook (1985, Cook et al., 1983) employed in examining the other methodologies used in this area. We wanted to examine the question: Is it likely that the time series methods used, which provide results that converge with those of other methods, are also biased toward showing a relationship between media violence and aggression, as Cook has suggested the other methods may be? Second, we wished to apply a multiple-method approach, in this case specifically a multiple-analysis approach, to the time series investigation of media violence effects. In so doing, we wanted to suggest that in a time series analysis such as that conducted by Phillips (1983), in general, no single analysis model can be justified as providing appropriate statistical control; therefore, multiple-analysis models, differing in their assumptions, should be provided.

The Phillips (1983) Study

Using time series regression methods, Phillips (1983) found that during the period 1973–1978, heavyweight championship prizefights were followed 3 days later by a significant increase in the number of homicides. (In a single regression analysis, Phillips estimated the immediate effect of the prizefights, as well as the effect lagged up to 10 days). This effect was found in an analysis that controlled for day-of-week, monthly, yearly, and holiday effects.[2] Our reanalyses of the boxing and homicide data Phillips (1983) examined were in part motivated by skepticism on our part about Phillips's (1983) findings. We were skeptical that heavyweight championship prizefights—many of which were not seen live on network television—would lead to an increase of the violent behaviors involved in homicide. In part, this skepticism arose because of an absence in the voluminous literature on television and aggression of compelling evidence that televised models affect real-life violence (Freedman, 1984). Further, we could not imagine a plausible mechanism that would account for the 3-day lag between the prizefight and the increase in homicide (see Baron & Reiss, 1985b, for a critique of the underdeveloped theoretical mechanisms in aggregate studies of imitative violence). Finally, there appeared to be an inconsistency in Phillips's (1983) results, in that a significant increase was found with a 3-day lag in the overall analyses, while different lags were significant in subgroup analyses. In these subgroup analyses, Phillips (1983) examined separately the effects of fights for which there was a black loser and those for which there was a white loser on the homicides of young black males and young white males. White-loser fights had a significant effect on the homicides of young white males at a 0 and 2-day lag. Black-loser fights had a significant effect on the homicides of young black males at a 4-day and 5-day lag (for the latter, $p < .065$ for a two-tailed test). Nor did the coefficient for the 3-day lag approach significance for either of the subgroup analyses, with $t = 0.20$ and $t = 0.54$ for the white and black victim analyses, respectively. We were puzzled in that the pattern of effects observed in the two subgroup analyses did not seem consistent with the 3-day lag in the overall analysis, which was based on all fights and all homicides.

These considerations led us to reanalyze the data examined by Phillips (1983). We were also motivated by a concern for the application of time series methodology in the study of mass media effects. We shall comment on these concerns as we discuss the results of our analyses.

Method

The dates of championship heavyweight fights were obtained from the *Ring Boxing Encyclopedia and Record Book* (1980). Data for the 2,191 daily counts of

[2]The Phillips (1983) study does not fit the stereotypic image of an interrupted time series design. Typically, such a design involves a single intervention assumed to have an effect of some temporal persistence. In contrast, in Phillips, the intervention consists of a set of events (the heavyweight championship fights, treated in the analysis as a dummy code) assumed to have a transitory rather than a long-term effect. The Phillips analysis is also atypical of the stereotypical interrupted time

U.S. homicides from 1973 to 1978 were generated from the National Center for Health Statistics computerized death certificates, available from the Inter-University Consortium for Political Science Research. The category "Late effect of injury purposefully inflicted by other person" was omitted from the count, given that these deaths are due to violence carried out at an earlier unknown date. These data sources are identical to those used by Phillips (1983) except (1) Phillips used a table from the National Center for Health Statistics (1978; table I-30) for the 1978 data, because the computerized tapes were not available, and (2) it is unclear whether Phillips excluded the "Late effect" category. These data were subjected to a variety of analyses, as we shall now describe.

Analyses and Results

Analysis 1: Direct Replication

We first attempted to perform a direct replication of the analysis reported by Phillips (1983) for all prizefights and homicides combined. A time series regression analysis was used with daily U.S. homicides as the regressors. Predictor variables consisted of a series of dummy variables for day of week, for month, for year, for the public holidays coded by Phillips (New Year's Day, Memorial Day, Independence Day, Labor Day, Thanksgiving, and Christmas Day), and a set of dummy variables to represent the effect of a championship prizefight. The latter was coded to correspond to different lags (i.e., different number of days following the fight); following Phillips, these ranged from -1 to 10.

The results of our reanalysis were generally consistent with those of Phillips. Like Phillips, we found that the coefficient for lag 3 prizefights was significant (for Phillips's analyses, $b = 7.47$, $t = 3.45$, $p < .001$; for ours, $b = 7.41$, $t = 3.53$. $p < .001$), as was the lag 4 coefficient for prizefights ($b = 4.15$, $t = 1.97$, $p < .05$, and $b = 4.35$, $t = 2.07$, $p < .05$, for Phillips's and our analyses, respectively). The other regression coefficients and t values were similar to those found by Phillips, with some difference for the coefficients estimated for year. These differences for the year coefficients may have been due to Phillips's use of interim data for 1978, and did not affect the substantive investigation of the effects of heavyweight championship prizefights on homicides. Instead, what is important is that we replicated Phillips's (1983) basic findings using his analysis model. Thus, we were prepared to attempt replication with alternative statistical analyses.

---

series study, in that Phillips tested for an effect at any lag up to 10 days (see Baron & Reiss, 347, p. 351, for a criticism of Phillips's approach on statistical grounds). Nevertheless, we classify the study as a type of interrupted time series design.

Analysis 2: ARIMA Intervention Analysis

In our second analysis, we employed the ARIMA, or autoregressive integrated moving average, models popularized by Box and Jenkins (1976) and extended by Box and Tiao (1975) to intervention assessment. In this analytic approach, the autocorrelation function (ACF) and partial autocorrelation function (PACF) are examined to estimate the error structure of a time series prior to estimating the effect of an intervention. (For an introduction to this approach, see McCain & McCleary, 1979, and Steiner & Mark, 1985. For more detailed presentations, see McLeary & Hay, 1980; Box & Jenkins, 1976; Box & Tiao, 1975.) If the error structure of a time series contains autocorrelation, bias is introduced such that in the typical case, one overestimates the significance of intervention effects. In a regression analysis such as that of Phillips (1983), one includes control variables (e.g., day-of-the-week dummy codes), and then tests for particular patterns of autocorrelation in the regression residuals (Phillips, 1983, footnote 5, p. 561, reports no evidence of autocorrelation, but see Miller, Heath, Molcan, & Dugoni, 1991). In contrast, in the ARIMA modeling approach, one identifies a model that accounts for autocorrelation, and estimates the intervention parameters in the context of that model.

Following conventional procedures, we estimated an ARIMA model for the daily homicide time series. A separate analysis was then made, using this basic model, for the prizefight variable with 0, 1, 2, 3, and 4 lags (i.e., the 3-day effect was estimated in a separate analysis from the other lagged effects, unlike the Phillips analysis). For the analysis examining the lag 3 prizefight variables, which had been significant in the Phillips analysis, the parameter for the prizefight variable was not significant (while the parameters for the ARIMA model, which controlled for autocorrelation, were). Indeed, while nonsignificant, the sign of the coefficient for the prizefight variable was negative, indicating, if anything, a decrease in homicides following the prizefights. The other analyses for lags 0–4 produced similar results, with nonsignificant, negative coefficients for the prizefight variable.

Thus, the ARIMA analysis resulted in a finding inconsistent with Phillips's conclusion that "heavyweight prize fights provoke a brief, sharp increase in homicides" (Phillips, 1983, p. 567). However, in the absence of some substantive explanation for the inconsistent results, all we could say is that the findings are not robust across analysis methods. While such a conclusion might appropriately lead to greater uncertainty about the relationship between heavyweight championship bouts and homicides, it is not satisfying. Thus we searched for an explanation for the inconsistency across analyses.

Boxing–Homicide: Round 3 . . . The Saga Continues

Subsequent analyses, then, were conducted to probe a possible explanation for the inconsistency between the two preceding analyses. Our first attempt to reconcile the two analyses was based on a comparison of the two methods. We concluded that the ARIMA model approach is better suited to account for cyclical variation than the regression approach (Box & Jenkins, 1975; McLeary & Hay, 1980). This appears especially to be true when one cyclical pattern (e.g., weeks) is not constant in its magnitude, but varies across different phases of another cycle (e.g., month or season). In such a case, the regression approach (in terms of the dummy variables for "day") would underadjust during some parts of the year and overadjust during others, because the same adjustment is made throughout the year.

This belief led us to the first in a series of analyses designed to account for the discrepancy between the results of the regression analysis patterned after Phillips (1983) and the ARIMA analysis. Our basic strategy was to identify a potential artifact, to introduce a "control variable" to account for it in the regression analysis (actually, this usually entailed a set of dummy codes), and to see if inclusion of the control variable removed the significant lagged effect of prizefights on homicides that Phillips found. Following our ideas that the regression model was not well equipped to control for cyclical effects that varied in magnitude as a function of another cycle, we began by expanding the regression model to include a set of variables representing the interaction between day of the week and season. The notion was that, for example, the tendency for there to be more homicides on Saturday than on other days of the week may be greater in summer than in winter. The results of this analysis revealed a pattern that was to become familiar to us. The newly added control variables seemed worthwhile (in that many of the parameters for the relevant dummy codes were significant), the magnitude of the effect for the lagged prizefight variable was reduced, but the prizefight effect remained significant.

Similar results occurred when we added a number of other control variables. We employed variables representing the day-of-week × month-of-year interaction, rather than the day-of-week × season interaction, thinking that season may have been too long a period to capture the phenomenon. Again, many of the day-of-week × month parameters were significant, and the prizefight effect was somewhat reduced in magnitude, but it remained significant.

We were encouraged that there were additional artifacts that needed to be controlled for in the regression analyses, and we were optimistic that we could find the artifact that would remove the prizefight effect. In an attempt to discover the artifact, we looked at the magnitude of the 3-day lagged effect associated with *each* of the prizefights in question, as indexed by how many more homicides were observed than were predicted by Phillips's regression model excluding the prizefight variable (see Phillips, 1983, table 2). We compared this estimate of the "effect" associated with each fight to the time the fight was held.

An apparent pattern emerged. The prizefights with the greatest "effects" (i.e., for which the observed homicides exceeded the predicted by the greatest margin) had taken place primarily on Tuesday and Wednesday nights. Of the six Tuesday or Wednesday fights, five of them were in the top six of the eighteen prizefights in terms of "effect" on homicide. The six Tuesday and Wednesday fights had an average "effect size" (i.e., observed homicides minus predicted) of 15.25, while the average for fights occurring on other days was 2.84.

Now recall that Phillips, and our regression model replication, found the effect of prizefights on homicides to have a 3-day lag. This means that the greater-than-expected number of homicides following the Tuesday and Wednesday fights were taking place on Friday and Saturday, respectively. But what artifact, yet uncontrolled for, could be responsible for the observed prizefight effect? It occurred to us that many homicides are alcohol related; it also occurred to us that some people may consume more alcohol the weekend after they are paid than on other weekends. Working on the assumption that many people are paid monthly, we created a variable representing the first weekend of the month, as well as an interaction term whereby Fridays and Saturdays could have a different effect on the first weekend of the month. The results for this expanded regression model were familiar. The new control variable was significant, and the prizefight effect reduced somewhat in magnitude but remained statistically significant. We repeated the analysis with a new variable representing alternating weekends, on the grounds that many people are paid every 2 weeks. The astute reader will be able to guess the findings: the control variable was significant, but the prizefight effect remained significant.

At about this point in our analyses, we discovered a then-recent article by Baron and Reiss (1985b). Baron and Reiss critiqued and reanalyzed the Phillips (1983) prizefight–homicide study, as well as a study by Bollen and Phillips (1982) that investigated the relationship between publicized stories about suicides and total U.S. suicides. Baron and Reiss showed that the residuals from the Phillips regression model are heteroscedastic, that is, that means and variances are correlated (e.g., Saturday has the highest mean number of homicides of the days of the week, and also has the greatest variance of the days of the week). They suggested that Phillips's model may be inadequate in failing to account for interactions between days of the week and other effects. Consistent with this, they conducted a regression analysis adding the interactions of the prizefight dummy variables and the day of the week. These analyses revealed that the 3-day lag effect occurs only for fights that occurred on Tuesday or Wednesday—a finding consistent with our own suspicions. Moreover, Baron and Reiss conducted a clever analysis designed to demonstrate that the prizefight effect was spurious: they treated each prizefight as though it had occurred one year later than it actually did, except they constrained it so that each prizefight fell on the same day of the week.[3] With this pseudo-prizefight variable, Baron and Reiss (1985b) found a 3-day lag effect that was significant (though reduced in magnitude). They argue that this finding demonstrates the artifactual nature of the Phillips (1983) results.

Given the publication of the Baron and Reiss (1985b) analyses, given our frustration at our inability to identify the artifact that would eliminate the prizefight effect, and given the departure of the colleague most directly involved in the computer analyses of the data set (G. Mumma), this project was then "put on a back burner."[4] From the perspective of the present chapter, the critical question is: What are the lessons for time series studies that can be illustrated with this investigation?

Lesson #1: The Multiplicity of Variables to Control for. Consider the underlying nature of Phillips's (1983) analysis. He had a set of prospective causal events (the heavyweight championship prizefights) that he expected would have an effect on the level of a time series variable (daily homicides). The effect was thought to be temporary; he did not look for a permanent increase in the homicide rate after each fight. However, there was no specific, theory-based prediction about exactly when the effect would occur or for how long; instead, Phillips

---

[3]One fight that occurred on July 1 was instead constrained to fall the same number of days before the holiday.

[4]The relevant issues are far from resolved, however. Phillips and Bollen (1985) responded to the Baron and Reiss (1985b) critique. They pointed out that creating a bogus prizefight variable a year *before* the actual fights does not produce a significant 3-day lag. They also demonstrate that Baron and Reiss's bogus year-after variable does not produce a significant effect when the time series is extended by an additional year. Both of these results diminish the plausibility of the artifact interpretation. Phillips and Bollen (1985) also pointed out that the Baron and Reiss procedure did not account for the results of their subgroup analyses. Phillips and Bollen further demonstrate that the 3-day lag effect holds in an analysis in which heteroscedasticity is removed by applying a square root transform. However, in a reply, Baron and Reiss (1985a) present conceptual arguments against the claims of Phillips and Bollen (1985). Thus, it still seems valuable to have a regression model that would account for the lagged effect of prizefights on homicides. Perhaps this chapter will stimulate the thought needed to identify that model.

Another reanalysis of the Phillips (1983) data, by Miller et al. (1991), came to our attention when revising this chapter. Miller et al. corrected some coding errors made by Phillips and found comparable results in a regression analysis, as they did when they added other control variables (e.g., minor holidays). They also prewhitened the homicide time series by fitting an ARIMA model and removing autocorrelation, and then conducted the regression analysis on the prewhitened series (note that this differs from our ARIMA analyses, in which we estimated each lagged effect of prizefights separately). Miller et al. found the third- and fourth-day prizefights to be nonsignificant in the overall analysis of the prewhitened data, but to be significant for more highly publicized fights. Again, it would be valuable to have a model that would account for the similarities and discrepancies across the various analyses.

tested for effects at up to a lag of 10 days. In addition to being prone to Type I errors (Baron & Reiss, 1985b), this approach suffers from the possibility that: (1) one's regression model does not adequately control for all causes of the dependent variable, (2) the causal event is not randomly distributed (e.g., championship prizefights may tend to be held on certain days of the week or times of the month), and (3) at some lag the causal variable happens to be correlated with underadjustments that occur because the regression model is not correctly specified.

Such problems could be readily overcome if we had a good understanding of the causes of the homicide variable. However, consider the number of control variables that we were able to identify. Beyond those used by Phillips (day of week, month, year, and holidays), we added the interaction of day of week and season, or day of week and month, and, for weekend days, the interaction of day of week and "pay cycle" (i.e., first weekend of the month or every other week). And these control variables were added only by our thinking about possible interaction effects for weekend days, in the context of a short historical period. How many more control variables might one be able to find by focusing on other aspects of the time series (e.g., the possible interaction of day of week or holiday effects with the business cycle)? The point is that, in the absence of a strong theory of the causes of the dependent variable, there are likely to be numerous control variables—and unfortunately, the researcher is likely to be aware of only some of them.

Lesson #2: The Tenuousness of Some Time Series Studies. Because of the preceding problem, we are quite skeptical of a certain type of time series study. In particular, we (see also Baron & Reiss, 1985b; Izenman & Zabell, 1981) question studies that look for a temporary effect of a causal variable that is not randomly distributed. Especially where there is no a priori specification of the lag between the treatment and the effect (Baron & Reiss, 1985b), such studies run the risk of a confound of the "independent" variable and causal factors that are not controlled for.

Lesson #3: The Desirability of "Dry-Run" Pseudo-Variables. To address the possibility of validity threats such as selection-maturation in nonequivalent control groups designs, Bob Boruch and others (e.g., Boruch & Rindskopf, 1984) have advocated the use of "dry-run experiments" when possible. In a dry-run experiment, one uses multiple pretest observations, but treats them *as though* one were the posttest (i.e., data are analyzed as though the treatment had occurred, even though it had not yet occurred at the time of the second measurement). If the results suggest a treatment effect, a threat such as selection-maturation is implied, because there should obviously be no treatment effect before the treatment occurs.

Baron and Reiss (1985b) apparently independently developed the analogous strategy for time series, in their creation of a pseudo-prizefight variable, in which the fights were treated as though they occurred a year later than they did (also see Phillips & Bollens's, 1985, extension). While this approach has its limits (Baron & Reiss, 1985a), it is a useful heuristic for judging the plausibility of the alternative interpretation that one's results are artifactually due to a confound with uncontrolled cyclical variation. Thus, we advocate the more widespread adoption of this approach.

Lesson #4: Congruence–Incongruence of Results across Analyses. In our reanalysis of the Phillips (1983) study, we found a considerable inconsistency between the results of the original regression model, which found a significant increase in homicides at a 3-day lag, and the ARIMA model analysis, which found a nonsignificant increase. We are unaware of any simulations or analytic work comparing the results of these two approaches under various conditions. Any such work would likely conclude that the degree of congruence between the two depends at least in part on the extent to which the regression model provides a good model of the causal influences that operate on the time series variable.

At present, we advocate that, if the time series analyst believes a reasonable regression model can be employed (and this implies that the regression model adequately accounts for autocorrelation), then the ARIMA modeling approach should also be undertaken. If the two analytic approaches converge on the same answer, at least one has more confidence that the results do not depend on the specifics of the analysis employed. If the results are not consistent, one can attempt to argue for the superiority of one analysis over another. And at least one will not be misled by having only the results of one analysis.

Unlike the incongruence observed across the regression model and ARIMA analyses, our experience with ARIMA analyses has been that one finds quite similar results for alternative ARIMA models. For instance, in the Steiner and Mark (1985) study, we reported similar estimates of the treatment effect across three different ARIMA analyses. Similar results have been reported for simulated time series by Harrop and Velicer (1985), suggesting that minor misspecification of an ARIMA model is not likely to have major consequences for hypothesis testing.

Lesson #5: Let the Timid Beware. Although we do not have systematic empirical evidence, our strong impression is that time series studies are more likely to be reanalyzed than are most other kinds of social science research. We have already mentioned our own attempts to reanalyze Phillips (1983), as well as Miller et al's. (1991) reanalysis of Phillips (1983) and Baron and Reiss's (1985b) reanalysis of Phillips (1983) and Bollen and Phillips (1982). Other examples of reanalyses of time series studies include Kessler and Stipp's (1984) reanalysis of Phillips (1982), McCleary and Musheno's (1980) reanalysis of Aaronson, Dienes, and Musheno (1978), Hay and McCleary's (1979) reanalysis of Deutsch and Alt (1977), O'Grady's (1988) reanalysis of Polyson, Peterson, and Marshall (1986), and Hepworth and West's (1988) reanalysis of Hovland and Sears (1940). We suspect that part of the explanation of the reanalyses of time series studies is the public availability of the archival data used in many studies. In addition, published studies often rely on a single analysis, leaving the possibility of criticism from other scholars who would specify a different model. Of course, such critical reanalyses can be applauded from the perspective of the sociology of science (e.g., Cook, 1985).

Beyond Case Studies: A Cursory Review of Time Series Studies in Psychology

When we began work on this chapter, as quantitative researchers we had some reservations about the case study approach to be undertaken. Perhaps as a compensatory mechanism, we felt it would be desirable to review more systematically the time series literature (we should note that since then we have become persuaded of the advantages of the case study approach as used in this volume). As part of our review of the literature, we conducted a computer-based search of *PsycLIT*, the computerized version of *Psych Abstracts*, and coded the abstracts in terms of a number of variables. The results of that exercise reveal some interesting things about the time series literature in psychology. We must admit, however, that the results should be interpreted with some caution: only articles abstracted in *PsycLIT* were considered; our operational definition of a time series article was generous, as described below; and we reviewed only the *PsycLIT* abstracts, not the entire articles, so doubtlessly some errors were made because some abstracts excluded information. Despite these caveats, we believe the results of our coding reveal some interesting characteristics of the time series literature in psychology.

We conducted our computer-based search of *PsycLIT* using the key word "time series." The search yielded 328 abstracts from articles abstracted between January, 1983, and March, 1990. Of the 328 abstracts, 26 were dropped from consideration either because the topic of time series was mentioned tangentially (e.g., as a suggested avenue for future research in a substantive review article) or because the study was clearly not a time series study (e.g., it included only two observations). Thus the final data set included 302 abstracts.

Abstracts were coded in terms of research area (e.g., criminal justice, public health) and data source (archival data, investigator-collected data, secondary analysis of another investigator's data, source unclear, and no data [as in some methodological articles]). The coding of primary interest concerned the nature of the article's research question or focus. We employed the following classification of the articles' primary focus:

1. Methodology, including articles about the analysis of time series studies, and articles overviewing time series methods and advocating their use in a particular research area.
2. Outcome studies, that is, those studies that focused on the effect of some intervention on a dependent variable in time series form (these studies are characterized by interrupted time series designs).
3. Outcome and moderation studies, that is, those that examined whether an intervention interacted with another variable or, in other words, if the effect of the intervention was moderated by a third variable (e.g., is the effect of the intervention greater for males than females?).
4. Outcome and mediation studies, that is, those that assessed the effect of an intervention on an outcome and investigated some intervening process thought to mediate the treatment–outcome relationship (see, e.g., Baron & Kenny, 1986, on the distinction between moderation and mediation).
5. Correlational studies, that is, those that investigated the relationship between two ongoing time series (e.g., air pollution and crime; note that we coded such studies as correlational even if the investigator described the relationship in causal terms).
6. Descriptive studies, that is, studies that simply reported the pattern of a variable across time (e.g., are SAT scores declining?).

In addition, we used the same classification scheme to code an article's secondary focus, if there was one.

What did our coding tell us? First, somewhat like the weather, time series seems to be a topic that people talk about more than they do anything about. The most frequent primary focus,[5] by far, was methodological (with 41% of the 302 abstracts). These articles included fairly general discussions of time series methods, technical work on issues in time series analysis, and debates on the need for and type of statistical analysis of time series data in the applied behavior analysis literature.

The second most frequent category of time series study in our abstracts was correlational (28%). Correlational studies were particularly common in the areas of suicide–homicide research (i.e., 73% of the 15 studies in this area) and social–personality psychology (i.e., 54% of the 28 studies in this area). Illustrative topics for the two research areas, respectively, include the relationship

[5]Of the 302 abstracts, 50 were coded as having a secondary focus. Most commonly, if a study had a secondary focus, that focus was correlational (for 40% of the abstracts that had a secondary focus, the focus was correlational). Most such articles had a primary focus on methodology or on outcome.

between economic conditions and suicide, and the relationship between major life events, stressors, and daily reports of mood.

Although each of the three categories involving outcome studies (outcome, outcome and moderation, outcome and mediation) occurred less frequently than did the category of correlational studies, if we combine these three there are nearly as many outcome studies as correlational, with 26% of the 302 abstracts falling in one of the outcome categories. Most of these studies were outcome studies only, with no focus on moderation or mediation (67% of the combined outcome studies, or 18% of the total sample, focused on outcome alone). Such outcome studies were particularly common in criminal justice (53% of the 17 criminal justice articles) and industrial–organizational psychology/occupational safety (44% of the 9 articles), and were also relatively frequent in educational psychology (35% of 17 articles) and clinical–counseling psychology (32% of 57 articles).

Relative to the studies focusing on outcome only, fewer than half as many studies focused on outcome and moderation (32% of the combined outcome studies, or 8% of all articles). Although this was not the most common focus of any research area, outcome and moderation studies were relatively more frequent in the areas of public health, educational psychology, and experimental psychology (constituting from 13 to 19% of the articles in these areas). A closer examination revealed that for the outcome and moderation studies, common moderator variables examined included sex and age of subjects, region, and miscellaneous individual difference variables (e.g., locus of control).

Only one study out of the 302 articles examined outcome and mediation. In that study (Zettle & Hayes, 1987), three components of cognitive therapy were presented to depressed subjects in various sequential combinations, and measures of presumed mediating variables were taken repeatedly. That is, the study assessed the mechanisms through which the components of cognitive therapy initiated therapeutic change.[6]

Few of the articles were primarily descriptive studies (4% of the 302). These studies examined the changes in a variable over time, such as the frequency of references to the MMPI or the Rorschach in *Psych Abstracts*.

Of the 75 studies using archival data, 57% were correlational, 20% outcome, and 16% outcome and moderation. Of the 125 studies using investigator–collected data, 31% were correlational, 30% outcome, and 10% outcome and moderation. For articles in the areas of suicide–homicide and criminal justice, over 80% employed archival data. In contrast, over 55% of the articles in

---

[6]Four additional abstracts included explicit tests of mediation, but in the context of a correlational rather than an outcome study. That is, these four assessed presumed mechanisms that mediated the relationship between two ongoing time series variables, typically employing some form of causal modeling.

clinical–counseling psychology, over 70% of the articles in experimental psychology, and over 80% of the articles in educational psychology employed investigator-collected data.

Now, what lessons are there in this cursory review of time series abstracts?

Lesson #1: Mediation Is Rarely Assessed in Time Series Studies. Cook and Campbell (1979, p. 230) noted that archival data "have an 'outcome' rather than a 'process' flavor. . . . Consequently, current archives may not be useful to those who favor testing causal explanations involving psychological constructs." The paucity of outcome and mediation studies is testimony to the accuracy of this statement. However, given the number of studies employing investigator-collected data, and given the emphasis on process in contemporary psychological research both theoretical and applied, one might have expected to find more emphasis on mediation among researchers collecting their own data.

Perhaps the results show the need for the further development and dissemination of methods to assess mediation in the context of interrupted time series studies. Emphasis might also be given to multiple-method investigations, with time series methods assessing a causal relationship, and more microlevel, perhaps even qualitative methods focusing on mediating processes. Such multiple-method investigations may be particularly important to supplement time series studies in which aggregate data are used to draw inferences about individual-level phenomena (Barton & Reiss, 1985b).

Lesson #2: The Potential Role of Moderation in Theory-Testing. We were frankly surprised that the percentage of outcome studies that had a focus on moderation was as high as it was. However, a closer look at the moderator variables employed dampens optimism about the amount of illumination to result. Common moderator variables were sex, age, and geographic region. Most of these seem to have been employed because the data were archived by such subgroups (e.g., male and females), or because it was an obvious way of classifying one's subjects.

Assessing moderation can be a highly useful way of testing theory or of achieving construct validity (Cook & Campbell, 1979, pp. 68–70; Mark, 1990; Mark, Hofmann, & Reichardt, 1992). However, to do so well requires: (1) explicating plausible process theories, (2) establishing the theories' implications for moderation (e.g., a theory might specify that a persuasive intervention would work better for those high in need for cognition; Cacioppo & Petty, 1982), (3) obtaining the relevant data (e.g., time series evidence of effectiveness for those low and for those high in need for cognition), and (4) comparing the observed results with the predicted pattern (Mark, 1990; Mark et al., 1992). We have not carefully examined all the articles to see how well this is done; however, our impression is that the assessment of moderation was often motivated by convenience at least as much as by thoughtful efforts to probe explanatory mechanisms. In any event, we feel that particularly for outcome studies using investigator-collected data, more theoretically directed attention could be given to moderation.

Lesson #3: Local Research Traditions May Imply Local Lessons. Different research areas were characterized by different types of studies. For instance, the typical empirical time series study in clinical–counseling psychology was an outcome study using investigator–collected data. In contrast, the typical suicide–homicide study employed archival data to assess the correlation between two time series.

Just as different areas or research traditions have different modal study types, so too may the conduct of time series studies have somewhat different lessons in different traditions. We invite the reader to consider critically the extent to which the lessons we have discussed apply to his or her area of research. We also invite the reader to undertake now, and in the future, the rewarding task of reviewing the methodological lessons of his or her own time series investigations.

ACKNOWLEDGMENTS. We thank Dirk Steiner and Greg Mumma for their contribution to research described in this chapter, and Linda Heath and two anonymous reviewers for their helpful comments on a previous draft.

References

Aaronson, D., Dienes, C. T., & Musheno, M. C. (1978). Changing the public drunkenness laws: The impact of decriminalization. *Law and Society Review*, *12*, 405–436.

Baron, J. N., & Reiss, P. C. (1985a). Reply to Phillips and Bollen. *American Sociological Review*, *50*, 372–376.

Baron, J. N., & Reiss, P. C. (1985b). Same time, next year: Aggregate analyses of the mass media and violent behavior. *American Sociological Review*, *50*, 347–363.

Baron, R. M., & Kenny, D. A. (1986). The moderator–mediator variable distinction in social psychological research: Conceptual, strategic, and statistical considerations. *Journal of Personality and Social Psychology*, *51*, 1173–1182.

Bollen, K. A., & Phillips, D. P. (1982). Imitative suicides: A national study of the effects of television news stories. *American Sociological Review*, *47*, 802–809.

Boruch, R. F., & Rindskopf, D. (1984). Data analysis. In L. Rutman (Ed.), *Evaluation research methods* (2nd ed., pp. 121–157). Newbury Park, CA: Sage.

Box, G. E. P., & Jenkins, G. M. (1976). *Time-series analysis: Forecasting and control.* San Francisco: Holden-Day.

Box, G. E. P., & Tiao, G. C. (1975). Intervention analysis with applications to economic and environmental problems. *Journal of the American Statistical Association*, *70*, 70–92.

Bullinger, M. (1989). Psychological effects of air pollution on healthy residents: A time-series approach. *Journal of Environmental Psychology*, *9*, 103–118.

Campbell, D. T., & Boruch, R. F. (1975). Making the case of randomized assignment to treatments by considering the alternatives: Six ways in which quasi-experimental evaluations tend to underestimate effects. In C. A. Bennett & A. A. Lumsdaine (Eds.), *Evaluation and experience: Some critical issues in assessing social programs* (pp. 195–296). New York: Academic Press.

Cacioppo, J. T., & Petty, R. E. (1982). The need for cognition. *Journal of Personality and Social Psychology*, *42*, 116–131.

Chetwynd, J., Coope, P., Brodie, R. J., & Wells, E. (1988). Impact of cigarette advertising on aggregate demand for cigarettes in New Zealand. *British Journal of Addiction*, *83*, 409–414.

Comstock, G. A., Chaffee, S. H., Katzman, N. I., McCombs, M. E., & Roberts, D. F. (1978). *Television and human behavior*. New York: Columbia University Press.

Cook, T. D. (1985). Post positivist critical multiplism. In R. L. Shotland & M. M. Mark (Eds.), *Social science and social policy* (pp. 21–62). Newbury Park, CA: Sage.

Cook, T. D., & Campbell, D. T. (1979). *Quasi-experimentation: Design & analysis issues for field settings*. Boston: Houghton Mifflin.

Cook, T. D., Kendzierski, D. A., & Thomas, S. V. (1983). The implicit assumptions of television research: An analysis of the 1982 NIMH report on "television and behavior." *Public Opinion Quarterly*, *47*, 161–201.

Cronbach, L. J. (1982). *Designing evaluations of educational and social programs*. San Francisco, CA: Jossey-Bass.

Deutsch, S. J., & Alt, F. B. (1977). The effect of Massachusetts' gun control law on gun-related crimes in the city of Boston. *Evaluation Quarterly*, *3*, 315–328.

Dillbeck, M. C., Cavanaugh, K. L., Glenn, T., Orme, T., David, M., & Mittefehldt, V. (1987). Consciousness as a field: The Transcendental Meditation and TM-Sidhi program and changes in social indicators. *Journal of Mind and Behavior*, *8*, 67–103.

Freedman, J. L. (1984). Effect of television violence on aggressiveness. *Psychological Bulletin*, *96*, 227–246.

Harrop, J. W., & Velicer, W. F. (1985). A comparison of alternative approaches to the analysis of interrupted time-series. *Multivariate Behavioral Research*, *20*, 27–44.

Hay, R. A., & McCleary, R. (1979). Box–Tiao time series models for impact assessment: A comment on the recent work of Deutsch and Alt. *Evaluation Quarterly*, *3*, 277–314.

Hepworth, J. T., & West, S. G. (1988). Lynchings and the economy: A time-series reanalysis of Hovland and Sears (1940). *Journal of Personality and Social Psychology*, *55*, 239–247.

Hilton, M. E. (1984). The impact of recent changes in California drinking–driving laws on fatal accident levels during the first postintervention year: An interrupted time series analysis. *Law and Society Review*, *18*, 605–627.

Hovland, C. J., & Sears, R. R. (1940). Minor studies in aggression: VI. Correlation of lynchings with economic indices. *Journal of Psychology*, *9*, 301–310.

Izenman, A. J., & Zabell, S. L. (1981). Babies in a blackout: The genesis of a misconception. *Social Science Research*, *10*, 282–299.

Kessler, R. C., & Stipp, H. (1984). The impact of fictional television suicide stories on U.S. fatalities: A replication. *American Journal of Sociology*, *90*, 151–167.

Loftin, C., Heumann, M., & McDowall, D. (1983). Mandatory sentencing and firearms violence: Evaluation an alternative to gun control. *Law and Society Review*, *17*, 287–318.

Mark, M. M. (1990). From program theory to *tests* of program theory. In L. Bickman (Ed.), *Program theory* (pp. 37–51). San Francisco: Jossey-Bass.

Mark, M. M., Hofmann, D. A., & Reichardt, C. S. (1992). Testing theories in theory-driven evaluations: (Tests of) moderation in all things. In H. T. Chen & P. H. Rossi (Eds.). *Using theory to improve program and policy evaluations* (pp. 71–84). New York: Greenwood Press.

McAbee, T. A., & Cafferty, T. P. (1982). Television public service announcements as outreach for potential clients. *American Journal of Community Psychology*, *10*, 723–738.

McCain, L. J., & McCleary, R. (1979). The statistical analysis of the simple interrupted time series experiment. In T. D. Cook & D. T. Campbell (Eds.), *Quasi-experimentation: Design & analysis issues for field settings* (pp. 233–293). Boston: Houghton Mifflin.

McCleary, R., & Hay, R. A. (1980). *Applied time series analysis for the social sciences.* Beverly Hills, CA: Sage.

McCleary, R., & Musheno, M. C. (1980). Floor effects in the time series quasi-experiment. *Political Methodology, 7,* 351–362.

Miller, T. Q., Heath, L., Molcan, T. R., & Dugoni, B. L. (1991). Imitative violence in the real world: A reanalysis of homicide rates following championship prize fights. *Aggressive Behavior, 17,* 121–134.

National Center for Health Statistics (1978). *Vital statistics of the United States.* Washington, DC: U.S. Government Printing Office.

National Institute of Mental Health (1982). *Television and behavior: Ten years of scientific progress and implications for the eighties (Vol. 1). Summary Report.* Washington, DC: U.S. Government Printing Office.

Norstrom, T. (1988). Alcohol and suicide in Scandinavia. *British Journal of Addiction, 83,* 553–559.

O'Grady, K. E. (1988). "MMPI and Rorschach: Three decades of research": A time series reanalysis. *Professional Psychology Research and Practice, 19,* 132–133.

Pearce, J. L., Stevenson, W. B., & Perry, J. L. (1985). Managerial compensation based on organizational performance: A time series analysis of the effects of merit pay. *Academy of Management Journal, 28,* 261–278.

Phillips, D. P. (1982). The impact of fictional television stories on U.S. adult fatalities: New evidence on the effect of the mass media on violence. *American Journal of Sociology, 87,* 1340–1359.

Phillips, D. P. (1983). The impact of mass media violence on U.S. homicides. *American Sociological Review, 48,* 560–568.

Phillips, D. P., & Bollen, K. A. (1985). Same time, last year: Selective data dredging for negative findings. *American Sociological Review, 50,* 364–371.

Phillips, D. P., & Hensley, J. E. (1984). When violence is rewarded or punished: The impact of mass media stories on homicide. *Journal of Communication, 34,* 101–116.

Polyson, J., Peterson, R., & Marshall, C. (1986). MMPI and Rorschach: Three decades of research. *Professional Psychology Research and Practice, 17,* 476–478.

Ross, A. S., & White, S. (1987). Shoplifting, impaired driving, and refusing the breathalyzer: On seeing one's name in a public place. *Evaluation Review, 11,* 254–260.

Rotton, J., & Frey, J. (1985). Air pollution, weather, and violent crimes: Concomitant time-series analysis of archival data. *Journal of Personality and Society Psychology, 49,* 1207–1220.

Shore, E. R., & Maguin, E. (1988). Deterrence of drinking–driving: The effect of changes in the Kansas driving under the influence law. *Evaluation and Program Planning, 11,* 245–254.

Shotland, R. L., & Mark, M. M. (1987). Improving inferences from multiple methods. In M. M. Mark & R. L. Shotland (Eds.), *Multiple methods in program evaluation* (pp. 77–94). San Francisco: Jossey-Bass.

Steiner, D. D., & Mark, M. M. (1985). The impact of a community action group: An illustration of the potential of time series analysis for the study of community groups. *American Journal of Community Psychology, 13,* 13–30.

The ringing boxing encyclopedia and record book (1980). New York: Atheneum.

Wagner, J. A., Rubin, P. A., & Callahan, T. J. (1988). Incentive payment and nonmanagerial productivity: An interrupted time series analysis of magnitude and trend. *Organizational Behavior and Human Decision Processes, 42,* 47–74.

Wasserman, I. M. (1984). Imitation and suicide: A reexamination of the Werther effect. *American Sociological Review, 49,* 427–436.

Wegenaar, A. C. (1982). Preventing highway crashes by raising the legal minimum age for drinking: An empirical confirmation. *Journal of Safety Research, 13*, 57–71.

Wegenaar, A. C., Maybee, R. G., & Sullivan, K. P. (1988). Mandatory seat belt laws in eight states: A time series evaluation. *Journal of Safety Research, 19*, 51–70.

Wegenaar, A. C., & Streff, F. M. (1989). Macroeconomic conditions and alcohol-impaired driving. *Journal of Studies on Alcohol, 50*, 217–225.

West, S. G., Hepworth, J. T., McCall, M. A., & Reich, J. W. (1989). An evaluation of Arizona's July 1982 drunk driving law: Effects on the city of Phoenix. *Journal of Applied Social Psychology, 19*, 1212–1237.

Zettle, R. D., & Hayes, S. C. (1987). Component and process analysis of cognitive therapy. *Psychological Reports, 61*, 939–953.

7

Structural Equations Modeling
A New Friend?

Richard E. Olmstead and Peter M. Bentler

In the spring of 1990, the Hubble Space Telescope was put into orbit, the culmination of work by a multitude of astronomers, engineers, technicians, and researchers over a period of many years. Its proponents hail it as a key tool to understanding the universe, while its critics write it off as a monumental waste of resources that will never fulfill the expectations of those who designed it. Almost immediately after it went on-line, concern arose about the robustness of its inner workings, yet the demand for access to this device is immense.

As a tool, structural equations modeling (SEM) has a fair amount in common with the Space Telescope.[1] Although the theoretical foundations for this method predate the manned spaced program (see Bentler, 1986), it has only been in the last 10 years that the majority of social science researchers have become aware of the existence of SEM. Those who have been introduced to it are often fascinated by the possible uses of the method for their particular research interests. On the other hand, many are baffled by the mechanics and theory of the

[1]The initial draft of this manuscript was written soon after the launch of the Hubble Space Telescope. Though many months have passed, the analogy of SEM to the HST remains appropriate. Both continue to be criticized for being flawed and/or limited in various ways, yet the use of both continues to grow and successful applications of each are demonstrated regularly. It appears that any device that provides scientists a novel perspective will almost certainly be utilized even in the face of the device's imperfections.

Richard E. Olmstead and Peter M. Bentler • Department of Psychology, University of California, Los Angeles, California 90024

Methodological Issues in Applied Psychology, edited by Bryant et al. Plenum Press, New York, 1992.

method, an arcane world of matrices, beta weights, and factor loadings where obtaining significance can be a hindrance and not a goal. Although there are critics of both the theory (Freedman, 1987) and the practice (Cliff, 1983) of SEM, the most common hesitation to use the method may be due to lack of experience.

This chapter provides a basic introduction to SEM using a concrete research example, namely, a study of friendship development. It will not include a detailed exposition of the mechanics or theory of the method. Readers are encouraged to seek out this information (e.g., Anderson & Gerbing, 1988; Bentler & Chou, 1987; Loehlin, 1987) if they intend to utilize SEM in the future; it is also recommended that they increase their familiarity with the associated techniques of factor analysis and multiple regression. Two major computer programs are available for doing SEM—EQS (Bentler, 1989) and LISREL (Joreskog & Sorbom, 1988)—and the guides that accompany these products are very good sources of information. The EQS manual is recommended for those who have limited experience with matrix algebra.

SEM: An Overview

Linear structural equations models (SEM) are often called "causal models" because the models are intended to represent the causal structure underlying some interesting set of data. Causality is actually relevant only in that the model itself is created according to causal hypotheses. Then, data are used to evaluate the model against reality. If the data are consistent with the model, one's causal hypotheses remain plausible, that is, the causal structure cannot be rejected. If the data are inconsistent with the model, the causal hypotheses cannot all be true simultaneously. As a whole, they must be rejected. Some insight as to how this is accomplished can be seen when one considers causal hypotheses and their representation in path diagrams, equations and their generation of model-implied correlations, and the estimation and testing of models.

Causal Hypotheses and Path Diagrams

The basic elements of an SEM are variables, factors, and possible specifications of interrelations among these. A *variable* is, as usual, a measurement of some observed phenomenon on a number of subjects. Thus height, IQ, GPA, rating of presidential leadership, judgments of physical beauty, interpersonal skills, and level of anger could all be variables in a social psychological structural model since different subjects would have different scores on these variables. *Factors,* sometimes called latent variables, are unmeasured but hypothesized underlying constructs that one might have measured directly but that one can observe only indirectly. Thus, intelligence is more typically a factor, a hypothesized differential ability that people manifest to a greater or lesser extent on various IQ tests, such as the Stanford–Binet or Wechsler scales of intelligence. The IQ tests are just observed variables that we may use to infer intelligence.

It will be apparent that if one measures, say, 10 variables in a sample of 100 subjects, one has a 100 by 10 data matrix of measures. These measures could be the object of study in an SEM, providing one has clear hypotheses about how these variables are interrelated. In practice the 100 by 10 data matrix would be reduced to a 10 by 10 symmetric matrix whose entries are the variances and covariances (a *covariance* is a correlation times the standard deviations of the two variables) of the 10 variables. Thus, in the data the variables are simply correlated, but the task of a model is to explain or account for those same correlations.

In order to develop an explanatory model, one must begin by formulating an explicit theoretical framework for the topic being studied, based on past research, relevant theories, personal hunches, and so forth. This framework, initially phrased in verbal form, identifies factors pertinent to the topic and indicates how they might be related to one another. These verbal statements constitute the causal hypotheses of a model. These can then be specified by a path diagram such as that in Figure 1. Influences in such a diagram are either unidirectional or bidirectional, as shown by the relevant type of arrow. A unidirectional arrow from one variable to another is a statement that one variable is hypothesized to influence the other. Thus, the path $X \rightarrow Y$ says that X is hypothesized to influence Y. On the other hand, directionality of causation is not specified for the relationship between X and $W: X \leftrightarrow W$. In either case the actual magnitude of the influence, and its sign, may or may not be specified.

The assumptions of causality that determine the path diagram can be a priori based on educated theory or logical constraints. For example, if A = Upper-Body Strength and B = Push-Up Performance, a diagram could indicate that $A \rightarrow B$. One does not need a fancy "causal" theory to realize that the reverse path would make no sense in this situation since it is hard to imagine how one's performance on a push-up task could lead to one's upper-body strength. In other instances, one may infer causality from the design of the study. For example, if some variables are measured at time 1, but others are measured at time 2 (say, a month later), it is easy to hypothesize that the effects flow from time 1 to time 2, but almost impossible to imagine that the effects could flow backward in time. It also should be noted that the actual location of the variables and paths on a page is completely arbitrary, and is essentially an exercise in graphical beauty. It is the connections that matter.

As noted above, some constructs cannot be measured precisely by a given measure. In the previous example, how could one know a student's "upper-body strength"? All one would ever have is some type of performance indicators such

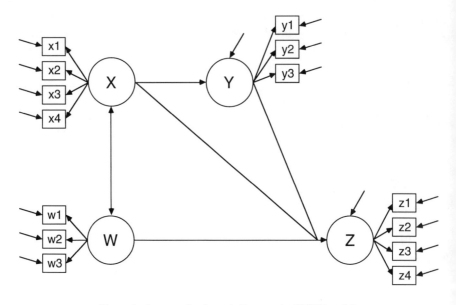

Figure 1. An example of a path diagram: the WXYZ model.

as bench press, chin-up, or curl results, that is, indicators of the true strength. In this case we might consider Upper-Body Strength as a latent factor, designated as UBS. And we might say that $ubs1 \leftarrow UBS \rightarrow ubs2$, where $ubs1$ is a bench-press score and $ubs2$ is a curl score obtained one afternoon in a gym. Every physical education student would recognize that neither $ubs1$ nor $ubs2$ would be exact indicators of their upper-body strength, since they may have been sick at the time of testing, had a poor grip on the hardware, and so on. In social psychology and in much of social science, there is a recognition that many variables are inevitably measured with error, and that the measure is not to be confused with the latent construct that one is truly after. Intelligence is not the IQ test; one track meet cannot establish one's running competence; inflation is not identical to the increase in the cost of cars, though that might be one indicator of it.

Path diagrams typically show latent variables, or factors, in circles or ovals, while measured variables appear in squares or rectangles. In Figure 1, there are four factors (W, X, Y, and Z). In each case it will be noted that there are arrows going from the factor to several indicators (measured variables, in rectangles). Thus we see that four variables, $x1$ through $x4$, are intended to be indicators of the latent factor X, and that three variables, $y1$ through $y3$, indicate latent factor Y, and so on.

Factors and measured variables may impact each other in a number of ways constrained only by the theoretical beliefs of the investigator. In Figure 1, factor to factor and factor to measured variable paths are specified, but other relationships might be imagined. For example, a specific indicator of Y might have a unique and direct influence on an indicator of Z. Thus the path $y2 \rightarrow z4$ could be added. Additionally, measured variables can impact factors: perhaps $w1 \rightarrow$ Y.

An important feature of SEM and hence path diagrams is that they allow variables to influence each other indirectly. For example, with $X \rightarrow Z$ and $X \rightarrow Y$ $\rightarrow Z$, the influence of X on Z is both direct and indirect (mediated by Y). The sum of all the indirect effects, plus the direct effect, is called the total effect of one variable on another.

Some influences among variables are, further, outside the scope of one's theory, and one may be hesitant to specify causal influences among the variables. Nonetheless, the variables may be related or correlated. For example, height and weight might be correlated (tall people tend to be heavier), but one might hesitate to say that height $\rightarrow$ weight in a sample of adults. In that case, one would simply draw height $\leftrightarrow$ weight, connected by a two-way arrow, indicating an association that is not interpreted causally. In Figure 1, X and W are simply correlated, but all other paths are hypothesized to be causal or directional.

A figure can also show an arrow emanating from nowhere aiming at a variable. In Figure 1, the arrow in the upper left corner aiming at $x1$ is one such arrow. This is a so-called residual variable. It indicates that while one has hypothesized a number of influences on a given variable, there may be still other influences that one has not measured in the model, as well as random noise. These are captured in the arrow from a residual variable.

A complete diagram such as Figure 1 is called a path diagram, and it represents all the hypothesized interrelations among variables in a domain that one wants to study. If the theory that leads to Figure 1 is uninteresting or inadequate, there is not much point to actually testing it against data. But hopefully, the theory is well justified, and data will inform about the theory as well as the modeling process.

Equations and Model-Implied Correlations

A path diagram is completely synonymous with a set of equations. That is, if $X \rightarrow Z$, we can write $Z = bX$, where b is a coefficient representing the strength of the effect of X on Z. If W and X affect Z, that is, $X \rightarrow Z \leftarrow W$, we could write $Z = bX + aW$, where now a is a coefficient representing the effect of W on Z. To be complete one should also add a residual, say e, indicating that one's prediction is not perfect. That is, $Z = bX + aW + e$. In looking at a path diagram, we could search out each dependent variable that has an arrow aiming at it, and write its corresponding equation. The set of such equations, along with the variances and covariances (correlations) of the independent variables, represents the complete model.

If one knew everything about the model, one would have actual numbers in place of the arrows, that is, values for the coefficients, variances, and covariances. For example, $a = .5$ and $b = -.3$ might be the values in the previous example. Such values allow one to generate predictions as to how all of the variables in the model are correlated, and what their variances are. Suppose in Figure 1 that $x1 = a*X$ and $x2 = b*X$, where $a = .6$ and $b = .9$. This says, first, that $x2$ is a better indicator of X than is $x1$ (just as a midterm might be a better indicator of knowledge than a final, perhaps because the final was conducted under very bad testing conditions). Second, it says that, under the model, $x1$ and $x2$ are expected to correlate $.6 \times .9 = .54$. There exist path-tracing rules emanating from the work of Sewell Wright, who invented path analysis as the method for doing these calculations graphically (here, go back from $x1$ to X, and then go forward to $x2$, and multiply the product of the path values) that permit making a prediction of every possible association among variables in the diagram. Alternatively, there are algebraic ways of doing the same thing. These methods are beyond the scope of the current chapter.

Estimation and Testing

We do not know the numbers associated with a path diagram. That's where the data come in, and where some of the space-science magic of SEM appears. The unknown parameters of the model (the coefficients, variances, covariances) are estimated so that the data are reproduced as closely as possible. This is done with some standard statistical method such as the method of least squares, or the method of "maximum-likelihood." In practice, the data that are being evaluated are not the raw scores of persons for the variables, but rather the variances and covariances (correlations) among these variables in the sample. This is why SEM is sometimes called "covariance structure" modeling. Now suppose the estimated model is very close to the data (sample variances and covariances). Then the model must be quite good. If we can accept the model, its parameters can be interpreted, for example, as to whether a particular variable has a strong effect on another or only a minimal effect. On the other hand, suppose that the estimated model is very far away from the data. Then the model is not a very good representation of the data, and we can reject the model. In addition, there is not much point to interpreting the size of the coefficients in a model that does not describe the data accurately.

SEM in Practice

Given a domain of interest, how does a researcher proceed to utilize SEM? The process is quite straightforward actually. Suppose one were interested in the relationships between W, X, Y, and Z. Specifying the causal patterns presents no problem given the vast amount of uncontradictory research on W, X, Y, and Z that has preceded our efforts. Our choice of measures for the latent constructs is simple, as they need only be normally distributed and good representations (both mathematically and conceptually) of their respective factors. Of the many choices for good indicators that are available, a minimum of three per factor will be chosen.

After independently sampling 500 to 1,000 cases (SEM works best with large samples) we are ready to begin the analysis. An important requirement of the model is that it is "identified" so that the parameter estimates are assured to be unique. When latent factors are included in a model it is important to fix either the estimate of the factor variance or one of the factor loadings. It is also a general requirements that each factor have more than two indicators, although paths to other factors and variables can serve this purpose. The data and the model are submitted to a program like LISREL or EQS, where convergence of the algorithm is achieved with a minimum of computing time even when starting with estimates far different from the final values. While the possibility existed that the WXYZ model would not fit well, it does fit well by the main criterion: a standard statistic usually used to evaluate the degree of closeness of data to an estimated model, namely, the chi-square statistic.

When fit is not achieved, misspecifications exist in the model. For example, one may have omitted a crucial causal path. The model may have to be modified to yield a new path diagram that is reestimated and again evaluated. The WXYZ model might have required one or two of these cycles before good fit was achieved. In this process, one might make undue use of chance features of the data and this is, of course, to be avoided. Fortunately, both EQS and LISREL will usually recommend only logical changes to models like that of the WXYZ phenomenon.

One should now cross-validate the model results in another sample, so another 500 to 1,000 independent cases are collected and the model is retested. In the end one has a model that is both theoretically cogent, and empirically validated, an amazing breakthrough in our knowledge about WXYZ. This straightforward process will now be illustrated with a "real-world" study of friendship development.

A Brief Review of the Theoretical Basis of the Friendship Model

For the most part, researchers in interpersonal attraction have confined themselves to the study of acquaintanceships. Huston (1974) noted that the vast majority of findings about attraction involved strangers whose interaction was limited to the typically short duration of the study. In many cases, the subjects related their attraction for a stranger whom they hadn't met and who, in fact, existed only on paper (e.g., Byrne, 1971). The generalizability of these "paper stranger" experiments to the phenomenon of initial attraction outside the laboratory is largely unknown and may be limited (Levinger, 1972).

Same-sex friendship has received some attention though most of the data has been provided by young adults. Theories about the onset of friendship are usually inferred from acquaintanceship-type studies. Another area of concern is the factors that maintain or attenuate levels of attraction through the course of an ongoing relationship. Unfortunately, as Berscheid (1985) states, "longitudinal studies of attraction are notable in their rarity."

Causes and Correlates of Attraction and Friendship

A large number of variables have been hypothesized to affect both initial attraction and its ongoing maintenance. Five of those most commonly studied are summarized below.

Similarity

Arguably, the most commonly studied factor in relation to attraction is similarity. Of all measures of similarity, attitudinal similarity has received the most extensive study. It is typically measured by the degree of agreement of a number of items that assess various attitudes on a number of topics (e.g., politics, religion). Many experiments have manipulated similarity as an independent variable by using a paper stranger whose attitudes can be more or less like those of a subject who subsequently is induced to indicate his or her attraction for this imaginary person. In general, these experiments indicate that increased similarity leads to increased liking (Byrne, 1971). Attitudinal similarity has been shown to be positively correlated with attraction outside the laboratory as well (Newcomb, 1961). Attitudinal similarity, however, may not be an important determinant of the success of ongoing relationships (Hill, Rubin, & Peplau, 1976).

Other types of similarity have been investigated. Similarity in personality traits has been demonstrated as being positively associated with friendship (Duck & Craig, 1978; Reader & English, 1947); however, there is evidence that personality similarity between friends is more imagined than real (Miller, Campbell, Twedt, O'Connell, 1966). Warner and Parmelee (1979) found that similarity of activity preferences was more common among friends than similarity of attitudes. There is evidence that friends have similar social skills (Henderson & Furnham, 1982). The theories that have been put forth to explain the similarity–attraction relationship have been many (e.g., Aronson & Worchel, 1966; Byrne & Clore, 1970), but none can completely explain the diverse collection of results that have been obtained.

Physical Attractiveness

The potency of physical attractiveness for producing attraction is considerable and is not limited to sexual attraction. People assume those who are physically attractive have a host of other positive characteristics (Dion, Berscheid, & Walster, 1972). In fact, the advantages of being physically attractive extend to a variety of situations and apparently throughout life (Hatfield & Sprecher, 1986).

An underlying assumption that exists in most of the literature is that physical attractiveness is unidimensional. Ashmore and Del Boca (1987) suggest that this is not the case. They hypothesize that there are a number of dimensions on which a person can be more or less physically attractive, for example, cuteness and sexiness. Although the data collected in support of these ideas are meager at this point, conceptualizing physical attractiveness in this multidimensional way may prove fruitful.

Proximity

A third variable that apparently affects levels of attraction two people have for each other is proximity. Proximity is defined as the physical distance between the "home bases" of two people (e.g., apartments in a complex or desks in an office). The distinction is made between functional or travel distance versus absolute or point-to-point distance. Increased proximity has been shown to relate to increased attraction in studies that have looked at functional distance (Festinger, Schachter, & Back, 1950; Nahemow & Lawton, 1975) and alphabetical seating arrangements (Segal, 1974).

Of the reasons suggested to explain why proximity should lead to attraction, two are, perhaps, the most obvious: accessibility and familiarity. With regard to accessibility, a person who is given the choice of visiting two people will make the trip that requires less effort, all other factors being equal. On the other hand, there is evidence indicating a person will like an object (or person) more with increased exposure to that object (Saegert, Swap, & Zajonc, 1968). Thus, proximity will increase attraction through familiarity.

Communication

A good friend is often described as "someone I can talk to," indicating a strong relationship between communication and friendship. That friendship should lead to communication is accepted as given; it would be an unusual situation indeed if a person was attracted to another and yet had no desire to communicate with him or her. The reverse relation, that communication should lead to attraction, is not as incontrovertible but is nonetheless sensible.

Most of the research in support of this supposition involves self-disclosures. The findings have indicated that "appropriate" self-disclosures will lead to increased liking, although what will be considered "appropriate" will depend on the context and the perceiver (Jones & Archer, 1976; Taylor, Gould, & Brounstein, 1981). Self-disclosure rates may be related to the physical attractiveness of the listener (Brundage, Derlega, & Cash, 1977). Another way communication may lead to attraction is by way of familiarity. Zajonc's (1968) mere exposure hypothesis would predict that any conversation, even about the most mundane topics, may lead to increased attraction at least during the early stages of a relationship.

The fact that communication will normally occur between two people in the initial stages of a relationship points to one of the major ways the "paper stranger" experiments lack realism. Sunnafrank (1984) has investigated the effects of attitudinal similarity and communication on attraction. His findings indicate that communication tends to substantially decrease the difference in liking for (attitudinally) similar and dissimilar others to nonsignificant levels. These findings contradict those of earlier studies (e.g., Newcomb, 1961), but even if attitudinal similarity is important for attraction, communication is a likely avenue by which people become aware of such similarity.

Common Fate

Commonality of circumstances and its effect on attraction has not received much exposure in the attraction literature. Common fate is, perhaps, best thought of as the amount of time two (or more) people spend together in the same environment. Thus, it is inevitably correlated with proximity. One might expect similarity and attraction to increase the amount of common fate between two people, as well as the converse—that common fate would result in increases in attraction and similarity (at least attitudinal similarity). Common fate should increase familiarity, with consequent effects on attraction. In addition, if the common fate condition is a product of some imposed grouping, past studies have shown that, in general, there is increased liking among members of the group (Tajfel, 1982). Such in-group–out-group effects may affect the amount of perceived similarity and, hence, attraction (Hensley & Duval, 1976). Finally, common fate provides increased opportunities for communication.

Creating a Model

Although there are other variables that have been hypothesized to facilitate or hamper attraction (see Berscheid & Walster, 1978, for a review), the five described above are perhaps the most theoretically supported and empirically consistent. Unfortunately, the contribution of each when the levels of the others are free to vary (as would be the case in a real-life situation) is not well documented. To date, it is rare for studies of attraction and friendship to examine the effects of more than two of these variables at a time.

Devising a model that relates attraction to all five of the variables discussed is not as simple as creating the WXYZ model. In this case many of the pairwise

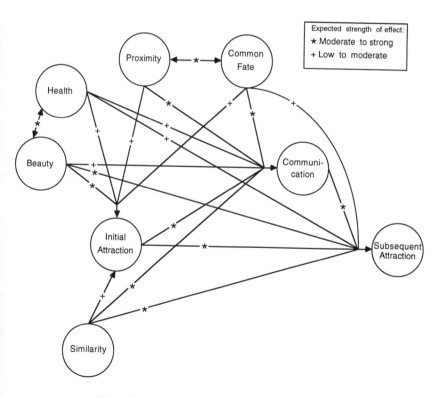

Figure 2. Hypothesized model of friendship development.

associations between the factors have yet to be examined empirically, so any model that is devised will be very tentative in nature. Figure 2 represents a possible model for early and subsequent attraction between friends with the expected strengths of the relationships between factors (all relationships are predicted to be positive). This is based on one part popular theory, one part personal theory, and one part guessing. Physical Attractiveness is represented by two separate factors, Health and Beauty. The most notable feature of the model is that it specifies many indirect effects via Communication.

Data Collection: Friendship at Camp

Data Source

Data were collected from 333 females attending one of four sessions of a girls-only summer camp on an island off the coast of southern California. The average age of the subjects was 12.8 years, and the sample was predominantly white and from middle-class backgrounds.

The campers were presented with a questionnaire within a few hours of their arrival. Later this same day each subject was photographed. The day before the campers were to leave they filled out a second questionnaire and were thanked for their participation. The camp sessions lasted either 10 or 11 days.

Measures

The initial questionnaire included a section where each subject was asked to answer questions about five other people at the camp. The five names were chosen at random from all those who attended that particular camp session. In addition, each subject was allowed to list the names of up to five other people they had met for the first time who were at the camp and similarly answer questions about them. The second questionnaire included questions about all of the people they provided information about initially (a minimum of the five randomly chosen campers and any others chosen on the first questionnaire).

Four hundred thirty-four dyads were formed subject to informational availability, that is, both the rater and the person rated (target) must have participated in the study. Each subject could appear in more than one dyad as either a rater or a target. This method assumes that a subject's ratings of one person is independent of their ratings for another person. If this belief is untenable, an assumption of SEM is violated. On the other hand, if dyads are randomly selected from the total set such that no person appears more than once as a rater or a target, the sample size is reduced to under 300, which is somewhat small for SEM. Faced with this trade-off, the assumption of independence will be made.[2]

Although data were collected with regard to all the factors in the model in Figure 2, it was not possible to create three or more good indicators for each factor. Similarity, Proximity and Common Fate each have only one indicator available; thus, they must be represented as measured variables and not latent constructs. Communication has merely two indicators, but the path from Communication to Subsequent Attraction will work as an indicator for the purpose of "identifying" the structural model. Enough indicators are available for Health, Beauty, Initial Attraction and Subsequent Attraction. The actual measures that are available to test the model appear below:

- Initial Attraction: The rater responded to five 9-point scales for each target (I think ____ is a great person; I trust ____ 's judgment; I think most people would like ____ ; I would prefer to work with ____ on a job; If I were going to do something fun, I would want ____ there). The indicators of this factor are the scores from these single items abbreviated great1, judge1, like1, work1, and fun1.

- Subsequent Attraction: The second questionnaire included a repeat of the attraction questions above. The indicators are great2, judge2, like2, work2, and fun2.

- Health–Beauty: The photographs that were taken were rated by UCLA undergraduates[3] using six scales (physically attractive, cute, beautiful, healthy, in shape physically, and mature). Each photograph was rated by a minimum of 12 people (maximum 16), and these ratings were averaged over the number of judges to obtain six averaged scale scores. Three are the indicators of Beauty (physatt, cute, beauty) and three are indicators of Health (health, shape, mature).

- Communication: The second questionnaire asked the raters two questions about their communication with each target during the camp session. One question inquired about the amount of conversation (amount), and the other involved the depth of self-disclosure that took place (depth).

- Similarity: The first questionnaire included 162 items relating to activities preferences, attitudes, and beliefs. The difference between the rater and target's response to each item was squared. These values were summed and the square root of this number was subtracted from the maximum score possible (i.e., if all the responses were maximally different).

- Proximity: The physical distance in feet between the rater's tent and the target's tent was measured. Proximity $= 10 - \log$ (distance in feet $+ 1$).

---

[2]An analysis using the smaller sample yielded equivalent results.
[3]Admittedly, using judges with ages more similar to the subjects might have led to different ratings, but, as often happens in research, one must make do with those who are easily available.

- Common Fate: This is a measure of the time the rater and target spent in mutual activities between the administration of the two questionnaires.

For a more complete description of the design, measures, and methods of this study, see Olmstead and Collins (1992).

It is often recommended that the factor structure of indicators of latent constructs be confirmed prior to SEM. In doing this for the friendship model it was discovered that postulating two separate physical attractiveness factors may not be valid, at least for these data. Exploratory factor analyses indicated that there was a slight indication of two factors (with physatt, cute, and beauty loading on one and health, shape, and mature on the other). But this evidence was not strong enough to warrant the inclusion of two factors of physical attractiveness in the model. The model to be tested, therefore, will have one factor of Physical Attractiveness with six indicators.

At this point, the measured variables need to be checked for normality. Although there was some skew to the indicators of Subsequent Attraction and kurtosis to amount and depth of Communication and Proximity, there were no obvious indications of nonnormality. Although SEM methods exist that do not require an assumption about the distribution of the variables (Bentler, 1983; Browne, 1984), most do. The method of estimation chosen to analyze the friendship data, maximum likelihood, assumes normality, but has been shown to provide acceptable estimates even with nonnormal data (Huba & Harlow, 1987). Serious violations to normality, however, may cause problems and, given that many measures in social science research probably fail to possess interval-scale qualities, this is always a concern.

The Modeling Process

Testing the Initial Model

Figure 3 is the model of friendship development that will be tested. In comparison with Figure 2, this model captures much of the intentions of the initial model, though there are a few substantial differences. Some hypotheses are made given the specific sample and not the overall theory of friendship development. For example, Proximity can impact Initial Attraction because the campers were already assigned a tent before the first questionnaire was given. However, the measure of Common Fate involves events afterward, so no path to Initial Attraction is specified. The parameters specified in this model are free to be estimated, while those not appearing in the diagram are fixed at zero. One factor loading for each factor was fixed for identification purposes (namely, physatt, great1, great2, and amount). In addition, error terms are included for

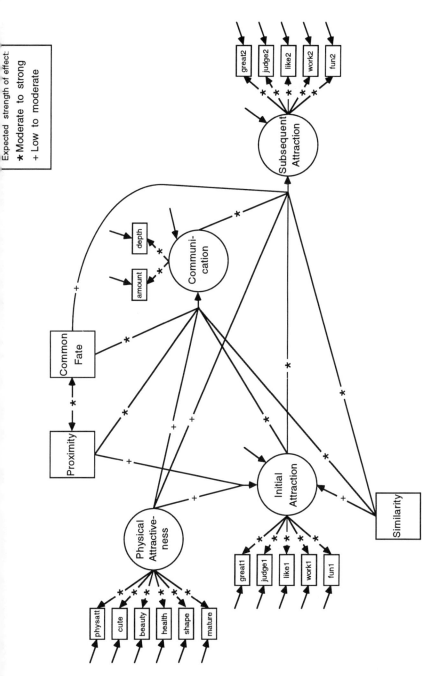

Figure 3. Revised model of friendship to be tested.

each dependent variable and factor. In the case of the same measures across time (e.g., great1 and great2), these error terms are allowed to correlate. The fact that the original theoretical model could not be tested with the data at hand is somewhat disappointing but not unusual. It is frequently easier to create models than it is to collect appropriate data.

The program EQS (Bentler, 1989) was used to test the model as specified above. The program had no problems in solving the structural equations necessary to reach a converged solution. If problems had been experienced, the model might have required modifications for identification purposes, or initial values of the free parameters other than those supplied by the program would have to be tried. This is not too uncommon, especially for larger models (i.e., more factors and measured variables). The chi-square of the initial model was 1,173, based on 172 degrees of freedom. This is very significant, indicating poor fit.

Lack of fit of the initial model is, unfortunately, an all-too-common experience in modeling efforts. A potential problem with the chi-square test is that it is a direct function of sample size. With a very large sample, even trivial model misspecifications will lead to large chi-squares, compared to degrees of freedom, and almost any model will have to be rejected because of the high power of the tests. Yet, for all practical purposes, the model may describe most key features of the data. Fortunately, alternatives to chi-square statistics have been developed. In addition to being less dependent on sample size, a more assumption-free measure of model adequacy is given by so-called fit indices, which are normed to lie in the range from 0–1, with 1 indicating a perfect fit and 0 indicating a terrible fit. Fits above .9 are typically considered to be quite good (Bentler, 1990). Alternative measures of fit are available with EQS, including the Bentler–Bonett Normed Fit Index (NFI) and Comparative Fit Index (CFI), which for the model were .89 and .90, respectively (see Bentler, 1990, for more information about these and other fit indices). These values indicate reasonable fit and suggest that good fit is possible with some modifications to the original model.

The Final Model

Improvements to the model involve one of two actions. One is the addition of more constraints, that is, fixing paths or correlations that were formerly free to vary but appear to be negligible in magnitude. This will increase the degrees of freedom in the model, while possibly decreasing the fit only minimumly. The converse action is the addition of more paths or correlations, generally those that were fixed to zero originally. This will increase the fit of the model but sometimes not enough to make the loss in degrees of freedom worthwhile. In practice, these procedures are implemented through statistical methods known as the Wald (W) and Lagrange Multiplier (LM) tests (Chou & Bentler, 1990).

The initial model of friendship was improved through a series of alternative applications of the LM and W tests. Although the program may indicate many possible changes, it is important to consider the theoretical basis of each parameter before it is released or dropped. For example, the LM test indicated that a path from Similarity to the indicator Health would be an improvement, yet there appears to be no mechanism through which such an effect could exist. Obviously, the fewer ad hoc parameters that are added before satisfactory fit is reached, the better from a theoretical standpoint.

Table 1 describes the changes made to the original model.[4] Of the parameters dropped, two are of importance. First, the hypothesis of strong effect of Common Fate on Communication was not borne out. Second, even though there was a significant effect of Proximity on Subsequent Attraction it was in the opposite direction as expected. In examining the correlations between Proximity and the indicators of Subsequent Attraction and models with and without this path, it was determined that this was probably a case of "classical suppression" (see Cohen & Cohen, 1975). Most of the parameters added were correlations between errors and are generally very interpretable. The fit to this final model is good ($\chi^2 = 192.4$, $df = 160$, $p = .041$, NFI $= .98$, CFI $= 1.00$). The final model is shown in Figure 4.

Many parameters were added to the original model to obtain a good fit. This is a difficult trade-off. On one hand, fit by the chi-square criterion is the generally accepted yardstick. On the other hand, one does not want to engage in too much post hoc fitting. In fact, efforts to increase fit for the friendship model stopped short of the $p > .05$ level because the remaining paths suggested for inclusion could not be readily rationalized.

One way to justify the inclusion of post hoc paths is to assess whether these modifications lead to serious changes in the basic structure of the initial model. In this case, when the estimates of parameters common to both models are correlated there is a very high degree of agreement ($r = .99$). This indicates that the adjustments to the model do not lead to a distortion of those relationships that are of primary interest. Even so, after-the-fact model modifications can and should be questioned.

A major advantage of SEM, as discussed previously, is the possibility of examining indirect effects. Table 2 lists the important direct and indirect effects on the two factors representing Communication and Subsequent Attraction. For

---

[4]Those parameters listed in Table 1 are not illustrated in Figure 4 (with the exception of the correlation between Physical Attractiveness and Proximity), nor are the three correlations between errors specified in the original model. The parameter estimates for these correlations in the final model were .135, .115, and .118 for judge1–judge2, like1–like2, and work1–work2, respectively. The significance level for these estimates is $p < .05$ for the first and third and $p < .05$, one-tailed, for the second.

Table 1. Differences between Initial and Final Models

Differences	Parameter estimate[a]
Initial parameters dropped:	
Paths:	
Similarity to Initial Attraction	.051
Common Fate to Communication	.012
Physical Attractiveness to Communication	.026
Common Fate to Subsequent Attraction	.006
Proximity to Subsequent Attraction	−.165*
Physical Attractiveness to Subsequent Attraction	.027
Correlated errors:	
great1–great2	.073
fun1–fun2	.036
Parameters added:	
Paths:	
Proximity to great1	.076**
Proximity to great2	.040*
Physical Attractiveness to judge1	−.057**
Correlations:	
Physical Attractiveness-Proximity	−.077*
Correlated errors:	
judge1–work1	.235**
work1–fun1	.411**
judge1–work2	.157**
fun1–beauty	.111**
fun1–shape	.056*
mature–physatt	−.689**
beau–cute	.424**
health–cute	.104**
mature–cute	−.774**
mature–beauty	−.395**
shape–health	.835**
mature–amount	.181*
beauty–depth	−.102*
great2–work2	−.261**
great2–fun2	−.736**
judge2–fun2	−.628**

[a] For those parameters listed as fixed at zero, this is the estimate in the initial model.
*$p < .05$. **$p < .01$.

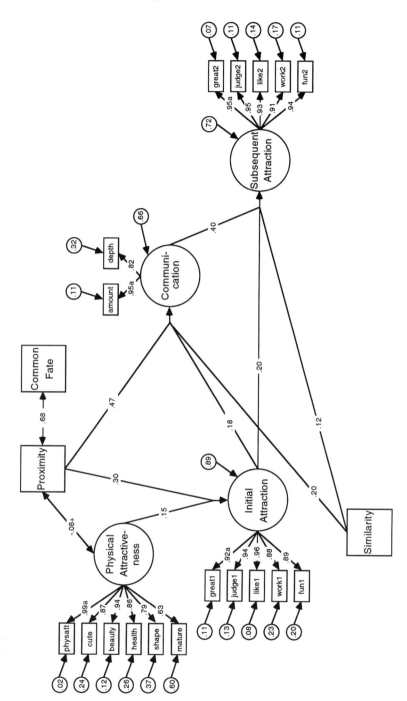

Figure 4. Standardized final model. (a, fixed for identification purposes. All parameters are significant at $p < .01$ except $+ : p < .05$. Residual variances are in small circles.)

Table 2. Effect Decomposition for the Final Model

Dependent factor	Source of influence	Type of effect		
		Direct	Indirect[a]	Total
Comm	Similarity	.203**		.203
	Proximity	.470**	.054*	.524
	Ini Att	.179**		.179
	Phys Att		.026*	.026
Sub Att	Similarity	.122**	.080**	.202
	Proximity		.266**	.266
	Ini Att	.196**	.071**	.267
	Phys Att		.039**	.039
	Comm	.395**		.395

Note. Comm = Communication; Ini Att = Initial Attraction; Phys Att = Physical Attractiveness; Sub Att = Subsequent Attraction.
[a] Total of all indirect effects.
*$p < .05$. **$p < .01$.

some variables, the indirect effects provide substantial contributions to the total effect.

Discussion

Interpreting the Friendship Model

The results of the modeling effort indicate many intriguing relationships among the variables that directly relate to past studies and theories of attraction and friendship. The hypothesized model was mostly confirmed. The structural paths were not particularly strong though the relative magnitudes were as expected, for the most part.

The importance of communication as a mediator of attraction was confirmed. Proximity affected subsequent attraction largely by way of communication and, although similarity and initial attraction primarily impacted subsequent attraction directly, they had substantial indirect effects through this route as well.

The findings with regard to initial attraction are quite interesting as well. The fact that similarity had no effect on initial attraction is not surprising given there was little possibility that the rater could be aware of her similarity to the target. On the other hand, the information that was available immediately was utilized, namely, proximity and physical attractiveness. The "paper stranger" studies fail to take this into account, and this is evidence of their lack of generalizability to naturalistic settings.

A stronger effect of initial attraction upon subsequent attraction was expected, but the current results may be explainable by the context of the study. The time period between the first and second measures of attraction was limited to eight or nine days. It is unlikely that friendship choice would be stable in such a short period. In addition, although the mean attraction ratings did increase from the initial meeting to the end of the session, so did the variance of the scores. The raters may have become more selective in whom they liked a great deal.

Physical attractiveness had a lone effect on initial attraction (save small indirect effects), which contradicts past findings where physical attractiveness is shown to be quite powerful. Again, many of these studies did not involve actual interaction, merely the presentation of photographs. It appears that physical attractiveness loses its importance as other information about the person becomes available, at least for same-sex friendships. One caveat to these findings, though, is the fact that the ratings of physical attractiveness were done by judges not of the same age group as the subjects.

Common fate did not evidence a great deal of association to the other variables and factors with the exception of proximity. Common fate's lack of influence on communication may be due to the type of activities that were engaged in at the camp. These were primarily activities where communication is not likely, for example, skin diving. Even so, familiarity should have been increased, which in theory, increases attraction. This model indicates that convenience may be more important than familiarity.

These results are, of course, from a specific sample in a specific context. Cross-validation would be a wonderful idea, especially in the face of the number of post hoc paths; however, there are no data remaining to do so (and at this point no resources available to collect more). The generalizability of this model is not known, although one might expect that its key features, such as the important link of communication, may apply to other populations and situations. A review of those parameters that were added to the original model is an important step that has been omitted here.

The Use of SEM

In creating the friendship model and by using SEM to test it, it was possible to analyze a number of hypotheses about the relationship between a larger set of the major variables associated with attraction phenomenon than has been examined previously. Even if the current model for friendship development turns out to be incomplete or incorrect in major ways, the utility of SEM as a procedure for specifying and evaluating social psychological theories should now be clear.

Additionally, it should be clear that implementing SEM is much easier for a fantasy WXYZ model under ideal circumstances than for most models devised by real researchers and tested with data provided by real subjects. Models are often inadequate due to incompleteness of theoretical specification or inappropriateness of statistical assumptions. Specifying directions of influences among applied social psychological variables is often quite difficult. Not only are social psychological theories frequently insufficient to the task of specifying simultaneous relationships among a set of variables, the applied researcher may be able to rationalize just about any direction of influence. In such cases, SEM is not a suitable methodology.

The process of SEM is not guaranteed to be free from problems even if a theoretical model is readily devised. Initially, identification problems may plague the modeling attempts, especially if the model is large or the researcher is new to the method. Of course, the test of the model is limited by the measures and data available. Additionally, when a model fits marginally there is no standard of how to proceed. First of all, fit indices vary in their appropriateness under different conditions and thus the "distance" one is away from acceptable fit may not be obvious. Some model modification is often necessary, but any paths added post hoc will need to be defended.

As an approach, SEM is still an emerging idea. Debate concerning the theory and the practice of modeling techniques will, no doubt, continue for some time. The empirical evidence indicates that the method is quite viable and will probably come to be commonly accepted as an important component of research strategy. In fact, to borrow a phrase that is more likely to appear in a physical sciences research proposal, SEM may be a key tool in increasing our understanding of the universe . . . at least that part of interest to social scientists.

References

Anderson, J. C., & Gerbing, D. W. (1988). Structural equation modeling in practice: A review and recommended two-step approach. *Psychological Bulletin, 103,* 411–423.

Aronson, E., & Worchel, P. (1966). Similarity vs. liking as determinants of interpersonal attractiveness. *Psychonomic Science, 5,* 157–158.

Ashmore, R. D., & Del Boca, F. K. (1987). *Thinking about physical attractiveness: Superficial? perhaps; simple? not at all.* Paper presented at American Psychological Association Convention, New York.

Bentler, P. M. (1983). Some contributions to efficient statistics for structural models: Specification and estimation of moment structures. *Psychometrika, 48,* 493–517.

Bentler, P. M. (1986). Structural modeling and Psychometrika: An historical perspective on growth and achievements. *Psychometrika, 51,* 35–51.

Bentler, P. M. (1989). *EQS, Structural equations program manual.* Los Angeles, CA: BMDP Statistical Software.

Bentler, P. M. (1990). Comparative fit indexes in structural models. *Psychological Bulletin, 107,* 238–246.

Bentler, P. M., & Chou, C.-P. (1987). Practical issues in structural modeling. *Sociological Methods and Research, 16,* 78–117.

Berscheid, E. (1985). Interpersonal attraction. In G. Lindzay & E. Aronson (Eds.), *Handbook of social psychology* (Vol. 2, 3rd ed., pp. 413–484). New York: Random House.

Berscheid, E., & Walster, E. (1978). *Interpersonal attraction* (2nd ed.). Reading, MA: Addison-Wesley.

Browne, M. W. (1984). Asymptotically distribution-free methods for the analysis of covariance structures. *British Journal of Mathematical and Statistical Psychology, 37*, 62–83.

Brundage, L. E., Derlega, V. J., & Cash, T. F. (1977). The effects of physical attractiveness and need for approval on self-disclosure. *Personality and Social Psychology Bulletin, 3*, 63–66.

Byrne, D. (1971). *The attraction paradigm.* New York: Academic Press.

Byrne, D., & Clore, G. L. (1970). A reinforcement model of evaluative responses. *Personality: An International Journal, 1*, 103–128.

Chou, C-P., & Bentler, P. M. (1990). Model modification in covariance structure modeling: A comparison among likelihood ratio, Lagrange Multiplier, and Wald tests. *Multivariate Behavioral Research, 25*, 115–136.

Cliff, N. (1983). Come cautions concerning the application of causal modeling methods. *Multivariate Behavioral Research, 18*, 115–126.

Cohen, J., & Cohen, P. (1975). *Applied multiple regression/correlation analysis for the behavioral sciences.* Hillsdale, NJ: Erlbaum.

Dion, K., Berscheid, E., & Walster, E. (1972). What is beautiful is good. *Journal of Personality and Social Psychology, 24*(3), 285–290.

Duck, S. W., & Craig, G. (1978). Personality similarity and the development of friendship: A longitudinal study. *British Journal of Social and Clinical Psychology, 17*, 237–242.

Festinger, L., Schachter, S., & Back, K. (1950). *Social pressures in informal groups: A study of human factors in housing.* Stanford, CA: Stanford University Press.

Freedman, D. A. (1987). As others see us: A case in path analysis. *Journal of Educational Statistics, 12*, 101–128.

Hatfield, E., & Sprecher, S. (1986). *Mirror, mirror: The importance of looks in everyday life.* Albany: State University of New York Press.

Henderson, M., & Furnham, A. (1982). Similarity and attraction: The relationship between personality, beliefs, skills, needs and friendship choice. *Journal of Adolescence, 5*, 111–123.

Hensley, V., & Duval, S. (1976). Some perceptual determinants of perceived similarity, liking, and correctness. *Journal of Personality and Social Psychology, 34*(2), 159–168.

Hill, C. T., Rubin, Z., & Peplau, L. A. (1976). Breakups before marriage: The end of 103 affairs. *Journal of Social Issues, 32*(1), 147–168.

Huba, G. J., & Harlow, L. L. (1987). Robust structural equation models: Implications for developmental psychology. *Child Development, 58*, 147–166.

Huston, T. L. (1974). A perspective on interpersonal attraction. In T. L. Huston (Ed.), *Foundations of interpersonal attraction* (pp. 3–28). New York: Academic Press.

Jones, E. E., & Archer, R. L. (1976). Are there special effects of personalistic self-disclosure? *Journal of Experimental Social Psychology, 12*, 180–193.

Joreskog, K. G., & Sorbom, D. (1988). *LISREL 7, A guide to the program and applications.* Chicago: SPSS.

Levinger, G. (1972). Little sand box and big quarry: Comment on Byrne's paradigmatic spade for research on interpersonal attraction. *Representative Research in Social Psychology, 3*, 3–19.

Loehlin, J. C. (1987). *Latent variable models: An introduction to factor, path, and structural analysis.* Hillsdale, NJ: Erlbaum.

Miller, N., Campbell, D. T., Twedt, H., & O'Connell, E. J., (1966). Similarity, contrast, and complementarity in friendship choice. *Journal of Personality and Social Psychology, 3*(1), 3–12.

Nahemow, L., & Lawton, M. P. (1975). Similarity and propinquity in friendship formation. *Journal of Personality and Social Psychology, 32*(2), 205–213.

Newcomb, T. M. (1961). *The acquaintance process.* New York: Holt, Rinehart & Winston.

Olmstead, R. E., & Collins, B. E. (1992). *Modeling interpersonal attraction: A field study.* Unpublished manuscript.

Reader, N., & English, H. B. (1947). Personality factors in adolescent female friendships. *Journal of Consulting Psychology, 11,* 212–220.

Saegert, S., Swap, W., & Zajonc, R. B. (1973). Exposure, context, and interpersonal attraction. *Journal of Personality and Social Psychology, 25*(2), 234–242.

Segal, M. W. (1974). Alphabet and attraction: An unobtrusive measure of the effect of propinquity in a field setting. *Journal of Personality and Social Psychology, 30*(5), 654–657.

Sunnafrank, M. (1984). A communication-based perspective on attitude similarity and interpersonal attraction in early acquaintance. *Communication Monographs, 51,* 372–380.

Tajfel, H. (Ed.). (1982). *Social identity and intergroup relations.* Cambridge, MA: Cambridge University Press.

Taylor, D. A., Gould, R. J., & Brounstein, P. J. (1981). Effects of personalistic self-disclosure. *Personality and Social Psychology Bulletin, 7,* 487–492.

Warner, C., & Parmelee, P. (1979). Similarity of activity preferences among friends: Those who play together stay together. *Social Psychology Quarterly, 42*(1), 62–66.

Zajonc, R. B. (1968). Attitudinal effects of mere exposure. *Journal of Personality and Social Psychology 9*(2) (Monograph Supplement 2), 1–27.

8

Research without Control Groups
A Control Construct Design

Jack McKillip

The benefits and costs of control groups shift as research is moved from laboratory to field settings. In field research, experimental and control groups are more likely to differ systematically on important dimensions other than independent variables. Comparisons between groups may not yield the unbiased estimates of impact that accompany controlled laboratory research. At the same time, logistic considerations affect the cost of each observation more dramatically in field settings than in a laboratory. If gathering control group information requires additional data collection sites, costs of individual control observations may be significantly higher than costs of additional experimental group observations. Possibilities of nonequivalence and of increased costs suggest a need for unbiased research designs that do not require control groups. This chapter (1) briefly reviews problems using control groups in field research, (2) describes a research design that has the potential for providing unbiased estimates of impact without use of a control group, and (3) illustrates the use of the design with a study of a responsible alcohol-use media campaign.

Jack McKillip • Department of Psychology, Southern Illinois University at Carbondale, Carbondale, Illinois 62901
Methodological Issues in Applied Psychology, edited by Bryant et al. Plenum Press, New York, 1992.

Problems with Control Groups

Nonequivalence of control and experimental groups can occur because individuals have greater freedom to agree to and to drop out of field than laboratory research. Even if random assignment is accomplished, differential attrition can cause experimental versus control group comparisons to be biased. The classic New Jersey Negative Income Tax Study found attrition varied from 8% in the "best" experimental group to 25% in the control group.

Nonequivalence in field settings also occurs because of a shift from the individual to larger units of intervention. Experimental programming is targeted broadly at communities, housing units, or market segments. In such cases, random assignment is rarely attempted. There are only a few "units" available and these are often separated by distance, language, or other barriers.

The Stanford Three Communities Project (Farquhar et al., 1977) provides a good example of difficulties related to comparisons between experimental and control groups in the field. In this case intervention was at the level of a town; two experimental towns and one control town were selected for study. Extensive media programming about cardiovascular disease risk factors was provided in the experimental towns over a 2-year period. The control town, which was separated from the two experimental towns by geographical barriers and served by different media outlets, received no project-based media programming. Analyses revealed effects attributed to the media intervention on measures of knowledge and self-reported change in diet.

By comparing groups from different geographical areas, interpretation of the results of the Stanford Three Communities Project was obscured for at least three reasons:

1. Historical events localized in a single town might have influenced the dependent measures. Such effects might be particularly likely in the less closely monitored control town.
2. Because there were only three towns in the study, observations were analyzed at the level of the individual. Since residents of a single town share sources of variance in addition to the "independent variable" (Leventhal, Safr, Cleary, & Gutmann, 1980), analyses may have violated statistical assumptions about independence of observations. Ignoring group effects in statistical analyses can result in inappropriately small error terms and increased likelihood of attributing unreliable effects to experimental interventions (Judd & Kenny, 1981).
3. On the other hand, lack of attention to the experimental intervention by residents of the experimental towns or unanticipated health education activities of residents of the control town may have led to underestimates

of the effects of the media intervention. Nonattending residents of experimental towns and self-educating residents of the control town lessen between-town differences and inflate error terms. Both effects make it less likely that experimental impacts would be identified.

Along with potential experimental versus control group comparison biases, the Stanford Three Communities Project demonstrates another drawback of use of control groups in field studies. Control groups can significantly increase logistic and financial costs of study. Program staff must travel to control units to identify and observe subjects who are not the focus of the intervention. Such costs often keep applied researchers from collecting control group information (e.g., Bertrand, Stover, & Porter, 1989). If the Stanford Three Communities Project were to avoid statistical analysis problems, for example by increasing units to five experimental and five control towns, the cost of the multimillion-dollar intervention would have more than tripled.

Control Construct Design

Because of inference and logistic problems that between-group designs often cause in the field, I have recently proposed use of a control construct design (McKillip, 1989; McKillip & Baldwin, 1990). The design combines characteristics of what Cook and Campbell (1979) label a "nonequivalent dependent variable design" with those of a single-subjects designs (Barlow & Herson, 1984). Rather than estimating no-treatment baselines from groups not exposed to an intervention, the design uses measures of the experimental subjects, themselves, that are not the focus of the intervention. The design uses control constructs rather than control groups to estimate impact. As I have used the control construct design:

1. Multiple constructs are observed during the entire length of a study, including those related to the experimental programming (experimental construct) and constructs that could, but will not, be the focus of an intervention (control constructs).
2. Observations are made at multiple intervals before and after the intervention. At each interval, a different sample of the study population is observed.
3. The intervention is introduced abruptly.
4. The impact of programming is tested for by a specific form of the Construct × Time of Observation interaction in an ANOVA statistical analysis format.

Control Constructs

In the control construct design, measures of control constructs serve the same function as control groups in traditional between-group designs. Change in levels of the control constructs estimate the change that would have occurred in the experimental construct without an intervention. The important consideration when choosing control constructs is to select issues that could change as a result of an intervention similar to that under investigation, but not as a result of the experimental programming. An experimental effect is indicated if the level of the experimental construct increases with the experimental programming but the levels of the control constructs remain stable.

A good control construct is similar to the experimental construct in terms of historical interest, social desirability, and measurement reliability, but measures a different "true score." Error components that systematically bias experimental and control group comparisons, such as history, maturation, or testing, are controlled to the extent that they affect both experimental and control constructs equally. Error components that inflate error terms are controlled by the within-subjects factor of the control construct design. To the extent that experimental and control constructs are correlated at the level of the individual, the design has increased power from its ability to control for subject heterogeneity (Lipsey, 1990, McKillip & Baldwin, 1990). Because of the desire to choose constructs that share error but not true score variation with the experimental construct, at least two control constructs should be used.

For example, an evaluation of a women's safety-education intervention might choose women's job advancement and self-examination for breast cancer as control constructs to compare to the experimental construct of violence against women. During the time of the experimental intervention an unrelated event may make "women's issue" more salient, affecting experimental and control constructs. Such an irrelevant historical event could bias comparison between an experimental group that experiences both the intervention and the confounding event, and a control group that experiences neither. However, if both control and experimental constructs are affected by a confounding event, comparisons between the constructs would not be biased.

Multiple Observations

The control construct design makes observations at multiple intervals during the pre- and the postintervention time periods. Multiple observations allow for greater confidence in estimates of the level of dependent variables before and after an intervention than a design that includes only one pre- and one postobservation. In this latter case, pre–post comparisons confound the effect of an intervention with incidental, between-observation changes. Such changes may be trivial in a research laboratory but can be substantial in a field setting. Making multiple observations within pre- and postintervention time periods allows the field researcher to separate experimental effects from normal interval-to-interval variation. Multiple observation intervals increase the reliability and power of the control construct design to estimate experimental impacts.

A drawback of making multiple observations in field research is the reactivity of the measurement process. Repeated self-report on attitudes or behaviors may produce changes by itself or in interaction with an intervention. Anticipating that the unit of intervention will include many individuals (e.g., a town), the control construct design observes different samples of respondents at each measurement interval. Using a single measurement on each respondent minimizes the importance of testing and other threats that complicate strict within-group designs.

The control construct design has some of the strengths of time series designs and avoids some of its complications. Multiple observation helps isolate time-correlated trends from experimental impact, such as maturation. Use of a different sample of respondents at each interval limits the serial dependency of adjacent observations that complicates interrupted time series analysis (McCleary & Hay, 1980). However, the validity of comparisons among samples from the same population depends on the comparability of each sample. Random sampling at each time period is important. The control construct design requires comparison of samples on attrition and on important demographic characteristics to test the appropriateness of the comparability assumption (Jurs & Glass, 1971; St. Pierre & Proper, 1978).

Abrupt Intervention

An abrupt, rather than gradual, introduction of experimental programming greatly clarifies inferences of impact on time-related measurements. The combination of multiple observations and abrupt intervention allows the control construct design to take advantage of similarities with time series analyses noted above. Abrupt impacts produce changes in the level of time series that distinguish experimental effects from a wide range of gradual and cyclical factors. An abrupt intervention should produce a change from the pre- to postintervention mean for the experimental construct time series without producing similar changes in the control construct time series.

In addition to a distinction between abrupt and gradual experimental impacts, time series analyses often distinguish between temporary and permanent changes. Temporary changes fade as the time series returns to its preintervention level. Permanent changes are easier to detect because there is a long-term change in the level of the time series. Whether an impact is expected to be permanent or temporary results from theoretical understanding of and experience with an intervention.

Contrast Weighting

The use of an abrupt onset with multiple observations during the pre- and postintervention periods permits use of an array of statistical analysis strategies. Among them are (1) contrast weighting in ANOVA, described here (Winer, 1971, pp. 170–185); (2) ANCOVA, with the control constructs as covariates; and (3) stepdown analysis (Stevens, 1986, chap. 10).

In a control construct design, ANOVA includes one between-group factor (Time of Observation), and one within-group factor (Constructs). Time of Observation has $k - 1$ degrees of freedom, where k is the number of both pre- and postintervention observations. Constructs have $j - 1$ degrees of freedom, where j is the number of both experimental and control constructs used.

ANOVA effects that have more than 1 degree of freedom have lower power (Lipsey, 1990) and can be difficult to interpret without further analysis. The use of contrast weights avoids both of these problems. Contrasts with 1 degree of freedom are constructed for both main effects and their interaction by weighting cell values to reflect the specific comparisons built into the control construct design. For the Constructs factor, the experimental construct measure is contrasted with the control construct measures. Where there is one experimental construct and two control constructs, the former receives a weight of 2 and the latter each a weight of -1. The use of contrast weights collapses the three construct time series into a single series that reflects standing on the experimental construct relative to the control constructs. Weights of 3, -1, -1, and -1 would be used with one experimental construct and three control constructs. The absolute size of the weights is not important. It is important that the sum of the weights for any effect be zero.

The specific form of an experimental impact is modeled by weights assigned to values of the Time of Observation factor. For example, an abrupt, permanent impact can be modeled by assigning weights of -1, -1, and -1 to preintervention observations and weights of $+1$, $+1$, and $+1$ to postintervention observations. Weights should sum to zero. Alternately, an abrupt but temporary impact could be modeled by assigning weights of -3, -3, and -3 to preintervention observations and weights of $+5$, $+3$, and $+1$ to postintervention observations (McKillip & Baldwin, 1990). In either case, variation due to Time of Observation is collapsed into a single, powerful pre-versus postintervention contrast (Lipsey, 1990).

In the control contrast design the hypothesized effect of an intervention is

**Table 1. Example of ANOVA Interaction Contrast
Weights for an Abrupt, Temporary Impact in
a Control Contrast Design**

Construct (weight)	Time of Observation (weight)					
	1 (−3)	2 (−3)	3 (−3)	4[a] (5)	5 (3)	6 (1)
Experimental (2)	−6	−6	−6	10	6	2
Control (−1)	3	3	3	−5	−3	−1
Control (−1)	3	3	3	−5	−3	−1

[a] Intervention begins.

revealed as part of an interaction between Time of Observation and Constructs. Graphically, this effect is revealed by an increase in the experimental construct time series at the start of the intervention with no change in the control construct measure time series. Whether the intervention effect is maintained or lessened depends on the type of intervention and the length of the time series. In an ANOVA, the overall interaction has $(k - 1) \times (j - 1)$ degrees of freedom and usually does not provide a sensitive test of impact.

A specific test of an experimental impact is provided by weighting the Constructs × Time of Observation interaction cell values by both main-effects weights. The weight for each individual cell is determined by the product of the marginal cell weights. Table 1 presents an example of contrast weights for a control construct design with one experimental and two control constructs, three pre- and three postintervention observations, and the hypothesis of an abrupt, temporary experimental impact. In the example, the weight for the experimental construct at the fourth observation is 2×5, or 10. The weight for each of the control construct measures is -1×5, or -5. The resulting interaction contrast is tested against the normal interaction error term. The contrast weighting in ANOVA is available as an option in most statistical analysis packages.

Illustrating the Control Construct Design:
A Health Media Campaign

Health promotion campaigns have become increasingly popular on college campuses, although without a substantial body of research that supports their efficacy (Braverman & Campbell, 1989; McGuire, 1986). Typically, campaigns seek to educate students about a health topic and to persuade them to adopt related attitudes and behaviors. Campaigns use media such as radio, newspapers, posters, and promotional activities such as information booths, sponsored work-shops, and formal presentations to get their message across (e.g., McKillip, Lockhart, Eckert, & Phillips, 1985).

The use of a control construct design in media research is illustrated by this example of a campaign to support responsible alcohol-use attitudes and behaviors during a student festival at Southern Illinois University at Carbondale (SIUC) during spring 1989 (McKillip et al., 1990). The target population for the campaign was the university's entire student body, and the intervention used media available to all students. A design requiring a nontreated comparison group would have required observations of students from another university, obtainable only at considerable expense and logistic difficulty. In addition, such a design has the inference problems discussed for the Stanford Three Community Project. Rather than use a nonequivalent control group design, the study used a control construct design.

Research Methodology

Control Constructs

Three health constructs were measured: responsible alcohol use, good nutrition, and stress reduction. Responsible alcohol use was the experimental construct; good nutrition and stress reduction the control constructs. Responsible alcohol-use measures asked about: "not getting drunk when drinking." Nutrition measures asked about: "eating the right foods." Stress reduction measures asked about: "managing the stress of college."

Three dependent variables were collected for each construct: (1) content of media health messages actually available to students, (2) students' awareness of health messages, and (3) the importance students attach to the health construct. Roberts and Maccoby (1985) indicate that changes on all three of these variables are needed for a causal inference of intervention impact. A researcher must show (1) that the intervention produced a change in the overall content of the media available to the target population, (2) that the audience attended to the changed media, and (3) that the audience changed on a dimension related to the content of the media. This last aspect was measured by the perceived importance of the health topic to the respondent (McCombs, 1981).

Health Message Content. The university's student newspaper, which is published every weekday during the academic year, was monitored during the five study weeks as the measure of health message promotion. The number of square inches was measured for articles and advertisements related to the health constructs of alcohol use, nutrition, and stress.

Awareness of Health Messages. Respondents to a telephone survey were asked (1) if they had seen an article or advertisement related to each of the health topics, and (2) if they had seen posters on campus related to each of the topics. Responses were made on a scale from (4) "definitely yes" to (1) "definitely no." Answers were combined for an index of message awareness.

Importance of Health Topics. As a measure of campaign impact, telephone survey respondents were asked how important each of the three health constructs were on a 5-point scale from (5) "extremely important" to (1) "not at all important."

Multiple Observations

Comparable Samples. Respondents were selected from the spring 1989 on-campus enrollment of Southern Illinois University at Carbondale. Separate random samples of 190 student phone numbers within the calling area of the university were drawn for each of 10 calling dates, indicating comparability of samples. Each sample had equal numbers of men and women and equal numbers of freshmen, sophomores, juniors, seniors, and graduate students. From the original sample of 1,900, interviews were completed with 698 (40%). The completion rate was lowered because each sample of students was phoned on only one evening. Because of the cultural context of the health promotion campaign, 89 international students were dropped from the study, leaving a final sample of 609.

Analyses revealed that gender, race, academic class of respondents, and refusals did not differ over the 10 calling dates. Of the final sample, 88% were white and 12% were minority group members. In total, 297 men (49%) and 312 women (51%) were interviewed.

Date of Observation. Interviewers telephoned a different random sample of students on each of the 10 Tuesday and Thursday evenings from March 28 to April 27, 1989. Tuesday interviews concerned health messages since the previous Friday. Thursday interviews concerned messages since the previous Tuesday. All calls to a particular random sample were made during a single evening. Interviewers had completed nine hours of prestudy training based on Guenzel, Berckmans, and Cannell's (1983) manual.

Abrupt Intervention

April 22 was Springfest on the SIUC campus, an annual university-sponsored student celebration that included entertainment, carnival rides, and thousands of non-SIUC student visitors. The Wellness Center (Cohen, 1980) sponsored a six-day responsible alcohol-use multimedia campaign with the theme: "Some people enjoy a drink, nobody enjoys a drunk." The campaign used newspaper advertising, posters, and cafeteria table tents. Advertising and promotional activity ran from April 14 through April 21, covering the April 18 and April 20 interview calling dates.

Contrast Weighting

Statistical analyses were accomplished by means of contrast weighting in an ANOVA (Winer, 1971). Three levels of the within-subject Health Construct factor were coded: (1) responsible alcohol use, $+2$; (2) good nutrition, -1; and (3) stress management, -1. These weights produce a main-effect contrast for each respondent comparing scores on responsible alcohol-use measures with a combination of those of good nutrition and stress management.

The six precampaign levels of the between-subjects Date of Observation factor were weighted -2, and the four postcampaign levels were weighted 3. These weights model a hypothesized abrupt, permanent intervention impact.

The overall Health Construct $\times$ Date of Observation interaction in an ANOVA, with 27 degrees of freedom, does not provide a sensitive test of the specific interaction effect hypothesized: an increase in the responsible alcohol-use trend line on April 18, and no change in the two control construct trend lines. A sensitive test is provided by using main-effect contrast weights to produce an interaction effect with 1 degree of freedom. Contrast coding was accomplished using the SPSS MANOVA procedure. An example of appropriate SPSS control language is given in Table 2.

In addition to the Health Construct and the Date of Observation factors, analyses were conducted including respondent Gender as a between-subjects variable. While Gender main effects were observed, there were no interactions between Gender and other study variables.

Research Findings

Health Media Content

In order to test whether campaign activities increased exposure to the target health construct, the SIUC student paper was monitored daily throughout the study period. Articles and advertisements were identified for the three health constructs of alcohol use, nutrition, and stress. Table 3 presents the mean area covered by newspaper articles and advertisements during the study for each health topic. Analysis revealed a significant difference between newspaper

Table 2. Example of SPSS Control Language for ANOVA with Contrast Weighting for a Construct X Date of Observation Interaction

```
MANOVA   EXPCON, CONTROL1, CONTROL 2 BY DATE(1, 10)/           [1]
         TRANSFORM (EXPCON, CONTROL1, CONTROL2)                [2]
           = SPECIAL(1   1   1
                     2 -1 -1
                     0   1 -1)
         PRINT=TRANSFORM                                       [3]
         SIGNIF(SINGLEDF)
         CELLINFO(MEANS)/
         CONTRASTS (DATE)= SPECIAL(1 1 1 1 1 1 1 1 1 1
           -2 -2 -2 -2 -2 -2  3  3  3  3                       [4]
            2 -2  0  0  0  0  0  0  0  0                        [5]
            0  0  2 -2  0  0  0  0  0  0
            0  0  0  0  2 -2  0  0  0  0
            0  0  0  0  0  0  2 -2  0  0
            0  0  0  0  0  0  0  0  2 -2
            0  0  0  0  0  0  2  2 -2 -2
            2  2 -2 -2  0  0  0  0  0  0
            0  0  2  2 -2 -2  0  0  0  0)/
         DESIGN=DATE/                                          [6]
```

Note. Brackets, [ ], indicate notes for this table only. They are not part of the SPSS language. The example anticipates two control constructs and 10 observation dates with intervention after the sixth date.
[1] Uses SPSS MANOVA procedure. EXPCON is name of the experimental construct; CONTROL1 and CONTROL2 are names of control constructs.
[2] Creates Constructs contrast. The first row of contrasts (1 1 1) are mandatory; the second row gives the contrast weights; the third row is mandatory but can take any values not fully colinear with the second row.
[3] Prints the tranformation in [2] and the interaction cell means. SPSS names the contrasts in [2] as T1, T2, and T3, respectively.
[4] Similar to [2], but creates the Date of Observation contrast weights.
[5] Eight additional, and arbitrary, contrasts must be listed. Take care that all are independent of [4]. SPSSX will report effects for each of these contrasts. They may be meaningless.
[6] The critical test of the interaction hypothesis is refered to as the T2 univariate effect of the first parameter of the Date effect in the SPSS print out.

coverage during the campaign and the noncampaign weeks only for responsible alcohol use.

Awareness of Health Messages

Using contrast weights, analyses of the index of message awareness for health topics over the 10 calling dates revealed a significant abrupt, permanent impact for responsible alcohol use as compared to the control health constructs ($F(1,531) = 89.6$, $p < .001$, $r = .38$). Using Cohen's (1988) criteria, the

**Table 3. Mean Daily Square inches of Newspaper Coverage
for Health Constructs by Study Period**

Study period	Responsible alcohol use	Good nutrition	Stress reduction
Precampaign	21.6	15.9	3.7
Campaign	330.4	2.7	6.4
Postcampaign	35.7	16.0	3.0

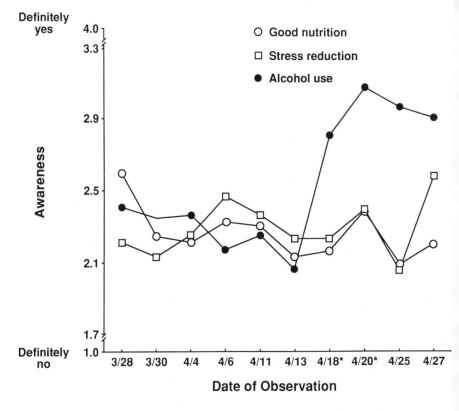

Figure 1. Mean awareness score as a function of Health Construct and Date of Observation. The responsible alcohol-use campaign period covered the 4/18 and 4/20 dates.

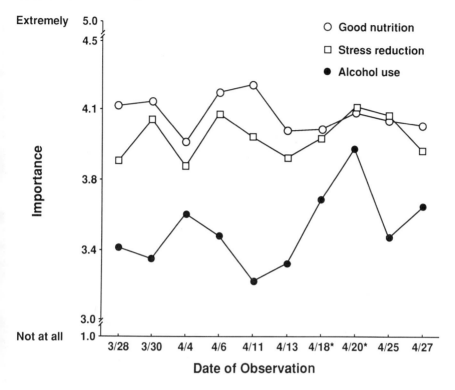

Figure 2. Mean importance rating as a function of Health Construct and Date of Observation. The responsible alcohol-use campaign period covered the 4/18 and 4/20 dates.

responsible alcohol-use awareness effect is large. Message awareness scores are shown in Figure 1. While awareness scores for good nutrition and stress management are relatively stable, scores for responsible alcohol use show an abrupt rise during the campaign period and then a gradual decay.

Importance of Health Constructs

As the measure of the impact of the health promotion campaigns, telephone respondents were asked to rate the importance of each of the three health constructs. Contrast-weighted analyses of importance ratings for the health topics over the 10 calling dates revealed a significant increase for responsible alcohol use to the control health constructs ($F(1,582) = 5.90, p < .02, r = .10$). Using Cohen's (1988) criteria, the importance impact of the responsible alcohol-use campaign was small. Health construct importance scores are shown in Figure 2.

While the visual and statistical impression is not as strong as for the message awareness index, a reliable increase in the importance of the topic to respondents is indicated only for the alcohol construct during the campaign period. This effect dissipated quickly.

Discussion

Use of the control construct design to evaluate this responsible alcohol-use campaign yielded fairly clear evidence of impact. First, the campaign significantly increased media related to responsible alcohol use. Second, students were aware of the change in message promotion. Third, students changed on the attitudinal indicator of the importance of responsible alcohol use.

A number of studies in this rural but comprehensive university setting have shown that multimedia health promotion campaigns can increase audience exposure to and awareness of health messages (McKillip & Baldwin, 1990; McKillip, Landis, & Phillips, 1984; McKillip et al., 1985). Such exposure effects are clear and large.

The question remains as to the impact of health promotion campaigns beyond audience awareness. The current study found a reliable but modest increase in the importance of responsible alcohol use to college students due to a promotional campaign. McKillip and Baldwin (1990) found modest increases in the frequency of discussion of use of condoms to prevent sexually transmitted disease infection and changes in supportive beliefs as a result of a similar promotional campaign. Both studies used control construct designs and both studies found modest indications of impact.

Whether these effect sizes are impressive depends on what alternative interventions are available. Most health promotion efforts yield modest effects, if any. As Lipsey (1990) has pointed out, effect sizes are as much a function of background noise as they are of intervention impact. Certainly, health promotion messages compete in an arena that is both crowded and contradictory. On the positive side, Kaplan and Abramson (1989) have demonstrated that small but continuing educational impacts can be expected to have large, long-term effects.

Limitations and Extensions of the Control Construct Design

The purpose of this chapter is to introduce a design for use when nonequivalent control groups are either inappropriate or too expensive. Assuming that it is easier and less expensive to add dependent measures than to replicate an entire observation procedure with an additional group of people, the control construct design presents an alternative based on the traditional scientific logic of comparative observation. The design maintains the quasi-experimental ability to rule out a number of threats to causal inference while demanding that only a single population be observed.

The justification for additional dependent measures in the control construct design is somewhat different from more typical interest in triangulation or multiplism (Cook, 1984). In the traditional approach, multiple measures are included because of overlapping true score and different error components. In the control construct design, multiple measures are added because of overlapping error components and different true scores. This difference is similar to that between convergent and discriminant validity in a multitrait–multimethod matrix (Campbell & Fiske, 1959). The tradition method can be said to look for high monotrait–heteromethod correlations, and the control construct design looks for high heterotrait–monomethod correlations.

Just as comparisons between experimental and nonequivalent control groups depend for credibility on the similarity of the subjects in each group, the credibility of comparisons between experimental and control constructs depends on similarity. Appropriate control construct measures should be as sensitive to social desirability, target population interests, and a host of "methodological artifacts" as experimental construct measures. If control constructs are less sensitive to these factors than the treated construct, comparisons may overestimate treatment effects. If control constructs are more sensitive, treatment effects may be underestimated. As illustrated in the present chapter, control and experimental construct measures have been simple, one- or two-item indices, with only theoretical validity. McKillip and Baldwin (1989) found effects with multi-item measures of belief, but not attitude or behavioral intention. The utility of the design with psychometrically sophisticated measures needs to be investigated.

An empirical test of the assumption of similarity between control and experimental constructs is to mount additional interventions aimed at each of the control constructs. In this case the previous experimental construct serves as a control construct. McKillip (1989) describes a design that uses a sequence of interventions aimed at multiple constructs as a multiple-baseline design across behaviors. McKillip et al. (1985) provide an example of this design.

The control construct design is not an alternative to random assignment, nor is it a substitute for nonequivalent control groups in many situations. Any field research study, where random assignment is possible or where nonequivalent control groups are feasible and appropriate, will be strengthened by the inclusion of control constructs as part of the design and the statistical analyses. Field research will be improved if, in addition to measuring targeted constructs, researchers include measures that share similar error components but different true scores.

References

Barlow, D. H., & Hersen, M. (1984). *Single case experimental designs (2nd ed.)*. New York: Pergamon Press.

Bertrand, J. T., Stover, J., & Porter, R. (1989). Methodologies for evaluating the impact of contraceptive social marketing programs. *Evaluation Review, 13,* 323–354.

Braverman, M. T., & Campbell, D. T. (1989). Facilitating the development of health promotion programs: Recommendations for researchers and funders. In M. T. Braverman (Ed.), *Evaluating health promotion programs* (pp. 5–18). New Directions for Program Evaluation, no. 43. San Francisco: Jossey-Bass.

Campbell, D. T., & Fiske, D. W. (1959). Convergent and discriminant validation by the multitrait–multimethod matrix. *Psychological Bulletin, 56,* 81–105.

Cohen, J. (1988). *Statistical power analysis for the behavioral sciences* (2nd ed.) Hillsdale, NJ: Lawrence Erlbaum.

Cohen, M. S. (1980). The student wellness resource center: A holistic approach to wellness. *Health Values, 4,* 209–212.

Cook, T. D. (1984). Post-positivist critical multiplism. In L. Shotland & M. M. Mark (Eds.), *Social science and social policy* (pp. 21–62). Newbury Park, CA: Sage.

Cook, T. D., & Campbell, D. T. (1979). *Quasiexperimentation: Design and analysis issues for field settings*. Chicago: Rand McNally.

Farquhar, J. W., Maccoby, N., Wood, P. D., Alexander, J. K., Breitrose, H., Brown, B. W., Haskell, W. L., McAlister, A. L., Meyer, A. J., Nash, J. D., & Stern, M. P. (1977). Community education for cardiovascular health. *Lancet, 1,* 1192–1195.

Guenzel, P. J., Berckmans, T. R., & Cannell, C. F. (1983). *General interviewing techniques*. Ann Arbor, MI: Institute for Social Research.

Judd, C. M., & Kenny, D. A. (1981). *Estimating the effects of social interventions*. Cambridge: Cambridge University Press.

Jurs, S. G., & Glass, G. V. (1971). The effect of experimental mortality on the internal and external validity of the randomized comparative experiment. *Journal of Experimental Education, 40,* 62–66.

Kaplan, E. H., & Abramson, P. R. (1989). So what if the program ain't perfect? A mathematical model of AIDS education. *Evaluation Review, 13,* 107–122.

Leventhal, H., Safr, M. A., Cleary, P. D., & Gutmann, M. (1980). Cardiovascular risk modification by community-based programs for life style change. Comments on the Stanford study. *Journal of Consulting and Clinical Psychology, 48,* 150–158.

Lipsey, M. W. (1990). *Design sensitivity*. Newbury Park, CA: Sage.

McCleary, R., & Hay, R. A. (1980). *Applied time series analysis for the social Sciences*. Newbury Park, CA: Sage.

McCombs, M. E. (1981). The agenda setting approach. In D. D. Nimmo & K. R. Sanders (Eds.), *Handbook of political communication* (pp. 121–140). Newbury Park, CA: Sage.

McGuire, W. J. (1986). The myth of massive media impact: Savagings and salvagings. In G. Comstock (Ed.), *Public communication behavior* (pp. 172–257). Orlando, FL: Academic Press.

McKillip, J. (1989). Evaluation of health promotion media campaigns. In M. Braverman (Ed.), *Evaluating health promotion programs* (pp. 89–100). New Directions for Program Evaluation, no. 43. San Francisco: Jossey-Bass.

McKillip, J., & Baldwin, K. (1990). Evaluation of an STD education media campaign: A control construct design. *Evaluation Review, 14,* 331–346.

McKillip, J., Devera, K., Presley, C., Rester, B., Watkins, J., & Klosterman, B. (1990). *Evaluation of AIDS education and of moderate drinking health promotion campaigns on a college campus.* Read at the meeting of the Midwestern Psychological Association, Chicago.

McKillip, J., Landis, S. M., & Phillips, J. (1984). The role of advertising in birth control use and sexual decision making. *Journal of Sex Education and Therapy, 10,* 44–48.

McKillip, J., Lockhart, D. C., Eckert, P. S., & Phillips, J. (1985). Evaluation of a responsible alcohol use media campaign on a college campus. *Journal of Alcohol and Drug Education, 30,* 88–97.

Roberts, D. F., & Maccoby, N. (1985). Effects of mass communication. In G. Lindzey & E. Aronson (Eds.), *Handbook of Social Psychology (Vol. 11,* pp. 539–598). New York: Random House.

St. Pierre, R. G., & Proper, E. C. (1978). Attrition: Identification and exploration in the national Follow Through evaluation. *Evaluation Quarterly, 2,* 153–166.

Stevens, J. (1986). Applied multivariate statistics for the social sciences. Hillsdale NJ: Lawrence Erlbaum.

Winer, B. J. (1971). *Statistical principles in experimental design.* New York: McGraw Hill.

9

Statistical Analysis for Single-Case Designs

Paul R. Yarnold

As a graduate student majoring in academic social psychology I was exposed to a wondrous assemblage of theories that seemed to offer practically limitless resources with which to help solve important, large-scale, real-world problems. Initially I found it mildly disturbing that many of these theories were validated using primarily experimental methodologies involving samples (sometimes very large samples) that usually consisted of college undergraduates. Indeed, I felt that the most appropriate context in which to validate these theories was the applied setting—where the important, large-scale, real-world problems actually occurred. The ready availability of large random samples of college undergraduates in close proximity to social psychology laboratories, however, constituted an irresistible opportunity to initiate laboratory-based research programs of my own, that actively continue today. I benefit from this approach, of course, vis-à-vis numerous substantive and methodological insights that ultimately improve my ability to do science.

After graduating and accepting a position as an applied social psychologist in the Division of General Internal Medicine, it quickly became obvious that the focus of the real world is often on single individuals, in contrast to the sample-based focus of many laboratories. For example, clinical psychologists, medical specialists such as internists, psychiatrists, or cardiologists, ergonomics engineers, sports psychologists, and vocational and educational counselors all repre-

Paul R. Yarnold • Division of General Internal Medicine, Northwestern University Medical School, Chicago, Illinois 60611

Methodological Issues in Applied Psychology, edited by Bryant et al. Plenum Press, New York, 1992.

sent professionals in applied disciplines that generally receive individual cases for assessment. For every individual case a profile of measures is often obtained and evaluated in order to gain insight regarding each case's uniqueness. I have come to realize that the N-of-1 focus of applied social science is also reflected in many other areas of applied science: geologists aspire to predict the behavior of an individual volcano; meteorologists aspire to predict the behavior of an individual storm; archaeologists seek to classify an individual skeleton; rocket scientists strive to fix an individual space shuttle.

The Need for Statistical Analysis in N-of-1 Research

There are many instances of N-of-1 phenomena for which no statistical analysis is required in order to determine whether a specific criterion has been achieved. For example, when a rocket's nozzle is correctly designed, the rocket does not explode. When a fractured tibia is correctly set, the patient recovers and walks. When a cross between a peach and a plum is successful, the result is a nectarine. When one is pregnant, one is pregnant. Such phenomena share the characteristic that the difference between the criterion (e.g., being pregnant) and its alternative (e.g., not being pregnant) is so large that a discontinuity clearly exists between them.[1]

There are, however, an even greater number of phenomena for which the difference between the criterion and its alternative is less clear. For example, by how many points must a slumping baseball player's batting average improve before a batting coach can conclude that an intervention has been successful? By how many points must a student's reading achievement score increase before an educator can conclude that an intervention has been effective? By how many points must a diabetic's fasting blood sugar score increase before an internist can conclude that an intervention has been beneficial? It is to these "gray" questions that the present chapter speaks.

Invariably, research involving N-of-1 designs of this latter type is a double-edged sword. On the one hand, many practitioners argue that the bottom-line applied question is not whether an observed change in a score is statistically significant, but rather whether the change in that score is great enough to satisfy the patient, business, court, or whomever is concerned (Michael, 1974). In contrast, others argue that visual inspection can be unreliable between and within observers, and may be insensitive to small yet statistically significant changes that are theoretically important in evaluating intervention effectiveness (Baer, 1977; Cook & Campbell, 1978; DeProspero & Cohen, 1979). These views

---

[1]It is possible that such phenomena might be fruitfully modeled using catastrophe theory (Saunders, 1980). The application of catastrophe theory to single-subject designs represents an intriguing idea that, while falling outside of the domain of this manuscript, appears worthy of future consideration.

reflect the fundamental difference between *statistical* and *practical* significance: whereas the primary concern in applied *practice* is practical significance, the primary concern in applied *research* is statistical significance.

As is often the case, the most adaptive position probably lies somewhere between these extremes. It might be difficult, for example, to justify continuing an intervention that, although resulting in statistically significant increases in observed scores, requires (via extrapolation) an unreasonably enormous number of additional trials to reach the clinically desired level of change. Similarly, it might be difficult to justify expressing strong faith in a subjective judgment for which statistical findings were equivocal—or even contradictory. Some phenomena, such as might occur in medical matters, where incorrect decisions may lead to death, are so salient that all judgments (subjective or objective) are considered. Other phenomena, such as might occur in the context of manufacturing quality assurance, may naturally reflect an economic "cost–benefit ratio" problem for which statistical criteria are most appropriate. Still other phenomena, such as might occur in the context of religious or aesthetic issues, may naturally be subjective and nonquantitative.

In general, however, the historical tendency of modern humankind has been toward ever-increasing quantification. This tendency is most pronounced in the physical sciences but is prevalent to the extent that it is difficult to think of any aspect of life (human or nonhuman) that has evaded quantification. Recent American history suggests an increasing societal interest in quantification, and of particular relevance is the rapidly accelerating use of quantitative information in litigation involving claims of, for example, malpractice and discrimination. Thus, it appears inevitable that quantitative N-of-1 techniques will eventually find increased application in ever-broadening domains of life.

Corroborating circumstantial evidence in this regard is the recent proliferation of statistical procedures that have been developed for single-subject research (Barlow & Hersen, 1984; Davidson & Costello, 1969; Kazdin, 1982). Unfortunately, these techniques are typically based upon analysis of variance or time series methodologies, which require relatively large numbers of data points. It was this shortcoming, in fact, that motivated the development of the classical test theory methodology reviewed in this chapter. Before discussing the classical test method, however, it is important to review the nature of the hypotheses that may be addressed using this technique.

Hypotheses in N-of-1 Research

Regardless of the particular area of application, there are basically three different types of hypotheses that can be considered in N-of-1 research: (1) K *hypotheses,* which entail a single case measured on multiple dependent variables at one point in time; (2) T *hypotheses,* which entail a single case measured on one dependent variable across multiple time points; and (3) *KT hypotheses,* which entail a single case measured on multiple dependent variables across multiple time points.

K Hypotheses

The simplest case of a *K* hypothesis involves a single individual tested once on two variables; the alternative hypothesis is that the individual scored at significantly different levels on the two variables (*K* denotes the number of variables). The following two examples illustrate possible single-subject research problems involving *K* hypotheses.

A sports psychologist is called on to cure a big-league pitcher who is in a slump. As a first step, the psychologist administers a questionnaire designed to assess the pitcher's level of confidence across five important domains: pitch selection, pitch accuracy, pitch speed, getting the big out, and holding a lead. The psychologist can then compare the pitcher's responses across these five questionnaire items (*K* hypotheses) to look for areas in which the pitcher has or does not have a relative confidence problem.

A criminal justice researcher examines an individual judge's past sentencing record across 24 defendants all convicted of the same crime. The question of interest is whether one or more of the defendants received significantly heavier or lighter sentences than one or more of the other defendants (here the 24 defendants are the *K* measures).

T Hypotheses

The simplest case of a *T* hypothesis involves a single individual tested twice on one variable; the alternative hypothesis is that the individual scored at significantly different levels on the variable at the two testings (*T* denotes the number of testings). The following two examples illustrate possible single-subject research problems involving *T* hypotheses.

A psychotherapist wishes to gain a child's confidence before embarking on an intensive course of psychotherapy. So, the therapist decides to devote as many initial sessions as it takes until the child feels significantly more comfortable. The therapist and the child spend each of these initial sessions sitting together on the floor talking. As a measure of the child's level of comfort, at the end of each session the therapist keeps track of where the child was sitting and then later measures the distance between them: sitting distance at the first meeting constitutes a baseline measure. The problem is determining when the child has significantly decreased the sitting distance from the therapist relative to this baseline. Once the child is sitting significantly closer to the therapist, then the therapist will begin psychotherapy.

An exercise physiologist wants to improve the cardiovascular fitness of a client. An aerobic exercise program is designed for the client, who is instructed to return once a month for 3 months to be tested for cardiovascular fitness (assessed as the maximum heart rate achieved on a treadmill). To evaluate the success of the exercise program, the physiologist could compare the client's maximum heart rate between the three monthly measurements (T hypotheses) in search of a significant increase.

KT Hypotheses

The simplest case of a KT hypothesis involves a single individual tested twice on two variables; the alternative hypothesis is that the individual scored at significantly different levels on the two variables at the two testings. The following two examples illustrate possible single-subject research problems involving KT hypotheses.

A counseling psychologist is given the task of training an individual factory worker to handle more effectively the stress of tight production schedules, without reducing the worker's high level of productivity. Before intervening, the psychologist assesses both the worker's coping skills as well as the worker's productivity level. The psychologist then initiates a formal intervention aimed at improving the worker's coping skills. After this intervention, the psychologist again measures the worker's coping skills and productivity level. The key statistical issues concern whether coping skills increase over time, and whether productivity declines over time.

A school psychologist wishes to evaluate the effect of eliminating bilingual education upon a Hispanic child's relative English and Spanish language skills. The child is given an age-normed standardized English and Spanish language achievement test when bilingual education is first terminated, and again 1 year later. The question is whether the child's age-adjusted skills in English improve over time, and whether the child's age-adjusted skills in Spanish decline over time.

N-of-1 designs may involve any number of variables and testing periods, and in applied settings are often quite complex. My experience applying social psychology to real-world problems has led to K, T, and KT hypotheses that could not be addressed using conventional statistical procedures. Necessity being the mother of invention, new statistical procedures thus needed to be developed. After describing these new procedures for statistical analysis of K, T, and KT hypotheses in the context of applied social psychological research, I discuss directions for future research concerning these procedures that were made apparent by their use with applied data.

Statistical Analysis for *K* Hypotheses

Consider, for example, the hypothetical situation of a personnel director for an oil firm attempting to fill a vacant position as a full-time field technician whose job would involve independent mapping of a remote wilderness area in Alaska. This position requires technical expertise in areas such as mapping, orienteering, camping, first aid, and survival, which a large pool of applicants possess. As an adjunct in the hiring decision, each applicant completed a pre-employment survey called the Successful Applicant Map (SAM), which provides standardized (z) scores on $K = 4$ subscales: hard-working (HW), team-work (TW), leadership (L), and adjustment to stress (ATS) (Yarnold, Bryant, & Lyons, 1988). Experience suggests that individuals with equivalent positive scores on HW and ATS and equivalent negative scores on TW and L, are best suited for this line of work. Thus, the personnel director wishes to reduce the pool of possible employees to applicants for whom HW and ATS are positive, TW and L are negative, and for whom (HW = ATS) > (TW = L).

In this example, applicants for whom HW or ATS are negative, or for whom TW or L are positive, are automatically eliminated. Similarly, applicants for whom HW ≤ TW, HW ≤ L, ATS ≤ TW, or ATS ≤ L are automatically eliminated (note that none of these evaluations require statistical analysis, since these decisions are based on absolute criteria). What is left is a subset of applicants for each of whom it is necessary to statistically compare HW, ATS, TW, and L scores. Individuals for whom HW and ATS are statistically comparable ($p > .05$), TW and L are statistically comparable ($p > .05$), and HW and ATS are both significantly greater than TW and L (p's $< .05$) will constitute the final subset of applicants who meet the SAM criteria.

The only statistical analysis of which I am aware that enables statistical evaluation of the difference between two scores for a single individual is based upon *classical test theory* (Magnusson, 1967, pp. 90–93). In a nutshell, classical test theory holds that an observed score for an individual on a measure of a particular construct is constituted by (1) the true value of the underlying construct in the individual (i.e., true score) and (2) unmeasured sources of variability (i.e., error score); that is, observed score = true score + error score. The null hypothesis evaluated by classical test theory is that the two scores are from parallel tests, which are theoretically equivalent with respect to content and style of items, have equivalent means and variances (for samples), and measure the same true score (true, observed, and error scores are assumed to be continuous). Any nonzero differences between the two scores are assumed to occur as a result of the unreliability of the tests, that is, as a function of their sensitivity to extraneous factors.

Under these assumptions, the estimated standard deviation of the distribution of difference scores resulting from the comparison of two parallel z scores is calculated using

$$s_e = [2(1 - r_{tt})]^{-2}, \tag{1}$$

where s_e is the standard deviation of the distribution of difference scores, and r_{tt} is the mean reliability of the two scores (see Magnusson, 1967). In order to obtain the critical difference score ($p < .05$) to compare two z scores, s_e is multiplied by 1.64 for a one-tailed (a priori) confirmatory hypothesis, or by 1.96 for a two tailed (post hoc) exploratory hypothesis. If the absolute value of the observed difference between an individual's two scores exceeds the critical difference score, then those two scores are significantly different ($p < .05$).

In the present example it is necessary to compare two scores a total of six times (HW versus ATS, TW, & L; ATS versus TW & L; TW versus L), such that the Type I error rate for the complete analysis of an individual's SAM profile would be $p < 6(.05)$, or $p < .30$. To guard against such alpha inflation associated with multiple tests of statistical hypotheses, Yarnold (1982) extended this classical test theory procedure to cases involving $K > 1$. For a set of K variables, there are a total of $K(K-1)/2$ unique, nontrivial difference scores between variables (i.e., excluding redundant difference scores and excluding difference scores that represent a particular variable minus itself). The standard deviation of this set of unique, nontrivial difference scores for a profile of K measures is calculated using

$$s_e(K) = [K(1 - r_{tt})]^{-2}, \tag{2}$$

where r_{tt} is the mean reliability of all K scales. Assuming that in the present example the mean internal consistency reliability of the four SAM subscales was $r_{tt} = 0.80$, $s_e(K) = 0.894$. For any single individual, any $|HW - TW|$, $|HW - L|$, $|ATS - TW|$, or $|ATS - L|$ that exceeds $1.64s_e(K)$ (here, 1.467) is statistically significant at an overall $p < .05$ (one-tailed hypotheses); and any $|HW - ATS|$ or $|TW - L|$ that exceeds $1.96s_e(K)$ (here, 1.753) is statistically significant at an overall $p < .05$ (two-tailed hypotheses).

Other writers have considered the problem of testing differences between variables within single cases. For example, Barlow and Hersen 1984), Kazdin (1982), and Payne and Jones (1957) discuss nonparametric procedures, t test, and regression in the context of statistically evaluating the comparability of two sets of K variables, where $K \gg 1$ (the symbol "$\gg$" means "much greater than"; see Strahan, 1975, for an excellent example of t test in this context). None of these procedures, however, allow a comparison of two scores, or of all possible pairs of scores, as is possible using classical test theory procedures for N-of-1 designs.

Statistical Analysis for T Hypotheses

While K hypotheses involve multiple measures for a single case at one point in time, T hypotheses involve one measure for a single case across multiple time points. Consider, for example, the hypothetical situation of a clinical outpatient (client) undertaking therapy designed to reduce interpersonal hostility. Immediately preceding therapy the client was administered the Structured Interview (a standardized clinical interview designed to elicit aggressive, time-urgent, hostile behavior) and assigned a hostility score (Blumenthal, O'Toole, & Haney, 1984). The client then underwent 10 consecutive weekly 1-hour sessions designed to improve the ability to recognize the types of social interactions that elicit hostility and to improve the ability to cope with such interactions when they are unavoidable. One week following the end of therapy, the client was readministered the Structured Interview and assigned a second hostility score. In this example the clinician wishes to determine whether therapy resulted in a statistically significant decrease in the client's posttherapy hostility score relative to the pretherapy hostility score.

As was true for statistical analysis of K hypotheses, the only statistical analysis of which I am aware that enables evaluation of the difference between one score at two testings for a single individual is based upon classical test theory (Yarnold, 1988). As was true in the analysis of K hypotheses, the null hypothesis evaluated by this classical test theory procedure for T hypotheses is that the two scores are from parallel tests, and that no developmental changes in the individual that are predictive of scores have occurred in the time between testings. Under these assumptions the estimated standard deviation of the distribution of difference scores arising from the comparison of one z score from two testings is calculated using equation (1), and the standard deviation of the distribution of all $T(T-1)/2$ unique, nontrivial difference scores occurring for a profile of $T > 2$ testings is calculated using equation (2) with T substituted for K. In the present example, if the 2-week test–retest reliability of the measure was $r_{tt} = 0.90$, the client's standardized hostility score would need to decline by $1.64(0.447) = 0.73$ z units to be statistically significant at $p < .05$.

Other writers have considered the problem of assessing differences between testings for single cases. For example, Barlow and Hersen (1984) and Kazdin (1982) discuss alternative within-subjects statistical procedures, such as t test and time series, that may be used in statistical evaluation of designs involving $T \gg 1$. As was true for analysis of K hypotheses, however, these alternative procedures do not allow a comparison of single scores at two testings, or of scores at all possible pairs of testings, as is possible using classical test theory procedures.

Statistical Analysis for *KT* Hypotheses

While *K* hypotheses concern differences across multiple measures at one time point, and *T* hypotheses concern differences in one measure across multiple time points, *KT* hypotheses concern the interaction between these two, namely, differences across multiple variables and across multiple time points, for a single case. Consider, for example, the hypothetical situation of a medical resident undergoing formal training designed to enhance interpersonal communication skills. At the beginning of a 1-month rotation, the resident unknowingly interacted with a confederate who played the role of a standardized patient. Behavioral observation by two experimentally blind independent raters was employed to rate the resident on medical thoroughness (MT) and on interpersonal communication (IC). Following the 1-month training rotation, the resident again unknowingly interacted with another confederate standardized patient, and was re-rated on MT and IC. In this example, the educator wishes to determine (a) if the resident scored higher on MT than on IC before the rotation (i.e., if the resident showed a relative deficit in IC relative to MT, or vice versa, before the rotation); (2) if the resident received a higher IC rating after the rotation than before the rotation (i.e., if the rotation had the intended affect of increasing IC skills); (3) if the resident received a lower MT rating after the rotation than before the rotation (i.e., if the increased emphasis on IC skills had the unintended effect of reducing MT performance); and (4) whether the resident scored higher on MT than on IC after the rotation (i.e., if the resident showed a relative deficit in IC relative to MT, or vice versa, after the rotation).

Classical test theory (Yarnold, 1988) provides a procedure for testing all $KT(KT-1)/2$ unique, nontrivial difference scores that arise in a design involving $K \geq 1$ variables at $T > 1$ testings. Specifically, the standard deviation of the distribution of difference scores arising in such designs is calculated using

$$s_e(KT) = [KT(1 - r_{tt})]^{-2}. \tag{3}$$

In the present example, if the mean interrater reliability for MT and IC at the two testings was $r_{tt} = 0.68$, any pair of the resident's scores would need to differ by $1.64(1.131) = 1.86$ absolute *z* units to be statistically significant ($p < .05$) for a one-tailed test, and any pair of scores would need to differ by $1.96(1.131) = 2.22$ absolute *z* units to be statistically significant ($p < .05$) for a two-tailed test.

I know of no alternative N-of-1 statistical procedure that allows for statistical evaluation of any pair, or of all possible pairs, of K scores at T time periods, as is possible using classical test theory methods.

Considerations for Future Research

Use of these methodologies with actual applied data suggests several guidelines to follow when testing K, T, and KT hypotheses. These concrete applications have also highlighted several previously unresolved issues that reflect interesting directions for future research concerning classical test theory procedures for statistical analysis of N-of-1 designs. Issues warranting attention and additional research, discussed respectively below, include (1) minimizing the magnitude of the critical difference score, (2) standardizing data, (3) selecting the reliability index, and (4) N-of-1 analysis as a data-screening tool.

Minimizing the Magnitude of the Critical Difference Score

Just as is true in $N > 1$ research, a fundamental problem facing researchers conducting single-subject research involves minimization of error variance. Reducing sources of error makes the observed score more accurately reflect the true score for an individual, and reduces the magnitude of the critical difference score that must be achieved to establish statistical significance. The most obvious recourse to restrict the magnitude of the critical difference score involves the use of parsimonious confirmatory (one-tailed) hypotheses. Below I discuss several issues relevant to minimizing the magnitude of the critical difference score, beginning with the comparative influence of parsimony (i.e., magnitude of K and T) versus precision (i.e., the reliability of the measures). Next, I discuss the importance of a priori design in establishing statistical significance criteria. Finally, a procedure for dealing with alpha inflation associated with multiple tests of hypotheses is discussed.

The Role of K, T, and r_{tt}

Real-world applications often reflect complex KT designs, for which the magnitude of the critical difference score increases as a *synergistic* function of the number of variables (K) and the testing periods (T) constituting the design, and decreases as a *linear* function of the mean reliability of the variables (r_{tt}). In practice, due to various cost constraints, there is often an inverse relationship between (1) K and T and (2) r_{tt}. For example, in situations where subjects will provide a fixed amount of time for researchers to collect data, one may either (1)

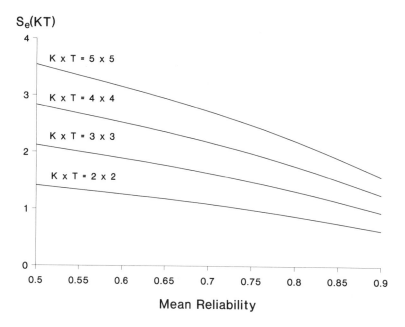

Figure 1. Nomograph giving the standard deviation of the distribution of difference scores (ordinate) as a function of parsimony (i.e., the number of levels of K and of T)—indicated by the curves—and as a function of the mean reliability of the measures (abscissa).

ensure that the variables are reliable (e.g., by assessing each dimension using a large number of items) or (2) assess a larger number of less reliable variables. In practice it is often true that reducing the number of variables and testing periods will have greater effect than increasing the mean reliability in decreasing the magnitude of the critical difference score necessary to achieve statistical significance in a given design. Figure 1, for example, illustrates the simultaneous effect of decreasing K and T (from 5 × 5, to 4 × 4, 3 × 3, and finally 2 × 2) and increasing r_{tt} (from 0.50, to 0.60, 0.70, 0.80, and finally 0.90) on $s_e(KT)$, the standard deviation of the distribution of difference scores.

As seen in Figure 1, decreasing K and T each by one has the same effect on $s_e(KT)$ as an increase by 0.18 in r_{tt}; decreasing K and T each by two has the same effect on $s_e(KT)$ as an increase by 0.32 in r_{tt}; and decreasing K and T each by three has the same effect on $s_e(KT)$ as an increase by 0.42 in r_{tt}. Using the Spearman–Brown prophesy formula,[2] it is estimated that it would be necessary

---

[2]The Spearman–Brown prophecy formula allows one to estimate the magnitude of the increase in the reliability of a measure that would theoretically be achieved by increasing the number of items constituting that measure by a specified amount (for a discussion, see Magnusson, 1967, p. 74).

to increase the number of items used to assess each K by 2.1 times in order to increase r_{tt} by 0.18; by 4.6 times to increase r_{tt} by 0.32; and by 11.5 times to increase r_{tt} by 0.42. Thus, the power of this classical test theory methodology decreases dramatically for studies involving many unreliable variables and many testing periods, and is maximized in studies involving only a few highly reliable variables and a small number of testing sessions.

The Importance of an Exhaustive A Priori Design

By the nature of real-world applications, it is not always possible for the statistician to influence the design of an N-of-1 study [see Barlow & Hersen (1984), Davidson & Costello (1969), and Kazdin (1982) for discussion of how to construct N-of-1 designs]. It is not unusual, for example, for statisticians to be called in as consultants on projects for which data have already been collected. In clinical or business applications, it is not uncommon for the original design to be completely abandoned in favor of a newly discovered or conceived design. Nevertheless, when the opportunity to assist in the design of an N-of-1 study arises, the importance of an exhaustive a priori design should be stressed.

If it is possible, for example, for the number of testing sessions initially planned for a study to be increased depending upon the outcome of the initial testing sessions (e.g., clinical trials), the critical difference score should be computed based on the projected total number of testing sessions (i.e., including the additional testing sessions), rather than upon the number of initial testing sessions. By using the projected total number of testing sessions the critical difference score will be appropriate in the event that the additional testing sessions are conducted. If, instead, the critical difference score was based on the number of initial testing sessions, and it was later determined that additional testing sessions were appropriate, then the larger T at the conclusion of the study might make earlier initial findings—based upon a smaller T—invalid (i.e., effects that were statistically significant using the smaller critical difference score for the initial testings might be statistically insignificant using the larger critical difference score for the actual total number of testings).

Representing the extreme case of a sequential N-of-1 design, clinicians, educators, and researchers occasionally continue an intervention until the subject achieves some criterion: for example, instruction in interpersonal communication skills for a medical resident might continue until the resident demonstrates a statistically significant ($p < .05$) improvement in interpersonal communication proficiency relative to baseline. With each additional application of the intervention (unit of education and subsequent testing session), T increases, and thus so increases the magnitude of the critical difference score necessary to reach the criterion. Before conducting this sequential procedure the critical difference score should be computed for every level of T: $T = 2, 3, \ldots, X$, where X

represents a level of T specified a priori as being so high as to consider the intervention a failure and to halt the study.

Multiple Hypotheses and Subjects

The classical test theory procedures ensure that $p < .05$ (or whatever Type I error rate is desired) when a single hypothesis is evaluated for a single subject (even though, for example, a design involving $K = 2$ and $T = 4$ has 28 unique nontrivial difference scores, this KT design constitutes a single hypothesis). N-of-1 studies that involve (1) more than one hypothesis per subject (e.g., a K hypothesis and a KT hypothesis), or (2) more than one subject, have actual overall Type I error rates that are greater than desired as a consequence of the evaluation of multiple tests of statistical hypotheses. Thus, in order to maintain an overall $p < .05$ for studies involving multiple tests of statistical hypotheses it is necessary to adjust the criterion for achieving statistical significance.

An obvious method for ensuring an overall desired Type I error rate, that should be investigated in future research, is an adaptation of the Bonferroni procedure (e.g., Holland & Copenhaver, 1987). In this procedure the desired alpha for the entire study (e.g., $p < .05$) is divided by the total number of tests of statistical hypotheses conducted; the resultant is referred to as the Bonferroni-adjusted alpha criterion. Individual statistical tests with associated generalized Type I error rates that are less than or equal to the Bonferroni-adjusted alpha criterion are considered statistically significant at an overall $p < .05$.

Imagine, for example, a study involving N-of-1 analysis of a K hypothesis for each of five cases [note that (1) these could also be T hypotheses, KT hypotheses, or a combination of all three types of hypotheses, so long as there was only one hypothesis per subject, and (2) the following is also appropriate for a study involving a single subject and five hypotheses]. In order to ensure the desired overall Type I error rate of $p < .05$ in this example, the Bonferroni-adjusted alpha criterion would be $p < (.05/5)$, or $p < .01$. Thus, when computing the critical difference score for each of the five cases (or hypotheses), the standard deviation of the distribution of difference scores—$s_e(K)$—would be multiplied by 2.58 for a two-tailed hypothesis and by 2.33 for a one-tailed hypothesis (these are the values of z corresponding to $p < .01$). Had each subject been evaluated with respect to a K, a T, and a KT hypothesis (i.e., three statistical tests per subject), the Bonferroni-adjusted alpha criterion would be $p < .0033$, and the standard deviation of the distribution of difference scores (for each hypothesis) would be multiplied by 2.93 for a two-tailed test and by 2.71 for a one-tailed test.

Whereas the Bonferroni procedure guarantees a known overall Type I error rate, this procedure may be unnecessarily conservative. Thus, future research should pursue the development of a sequentially rejective Bonferroni-type procedure, which would ensure the desired overall Type I error rate, yet afford increased power (e.g., Holland & Copenhaver, 1987).

Standardizing Data

In prior discussions of N-of-1 methodology the issue of how to standardize data has never been formally addressed. There are several methodologies for deriving standardized data, each with different theoretical perspectives on what the data represent. As might be expected, consideration of the context underlying K, T, and KT hypotheses suggests that different standardizations are appropriate for different types of hypotheses. Accordingly, below I discuss the most appropriate standardization methodology separately by type of hypothesis.

K Hypotheses

In the simplest case of a K hypothesis, a single individual has been measured on two different variables (K_1 and K_2), which may reflect responses to single items, or may reflect composites of responses to many items with or without differential item weighting. A common reference system is necessary to compare the individual's scores on K_1 versus K_2, and for K hypotheses the normative perspective is most intuitive (Cattell, 1952). Under normative standardization, raw scores on K_1 and K_2 are transformed into corresponding standardized scores that reflect their magnitude relative to the population of scores— provided by a population of individuals—for K_1 and K_2. Thus, the individual is perceived as having scored at one percentile level relative to the population on K_1, and as having scored at another percentile level relative to the population on K_2; statistical analysis is employed to ascertain whether or not these percentile levels are significantly different.

To normatively standardize an individual's scores it is most desirable to use normatively appropriate population parameters (*mu* and *sigma*). In applied research involving normal individuals and widely used tests (e.g., MMPI, WISC, or Strong–Campbell), normative parameters are often easily obtained. For more specialized tests, and for special subgroups of the population, normative parameters may be unavailable. If a random sample of individuals representing the special subgroup of the population has received scores on K_1 and K_2, the population parameters may be estimated. If prior published research has assessed K_1 and K_2 for the special subgroup of the population, it may be possible to use meta-analytic procedures to estimate the population parameters (Hedges & Olkin, 1985; Hunter, Schmidt, & Jackson, 1982).

Sometimes, however, it may be impossible to obtain estimates of normative parameters. For example, the N-of-1 study may represent the first use of either K_1 or K_2. In such cases the only recourse is to adopt an ipsative reference system with which to compare K_1 and K_2 (Cattell, 1952). Under ipsative standardization, raw scores on K_1 and K_2 are transformed into corresponding standard scores that reflect their magnitude relative to the population of scores—provided by the individual—on a population of variables. Thus, the individual is perceived as having scored at one percentile level on K_1 relative to his or her scores on all variables, and as having scored at another percentile level on K_2 relative to his or her scores on all variables; statistical analysis is employed to determine whether or not these percentile levels are significantly different.

To ipsatively standardize an individual's scores it is necessary that the scores are measured in a comparable context. That is, before ipsative standardization occurs, K_1 and K_2 should be separately transformed into corresponding equivalents on an absolute scale where zero represents the theoretical minimum score (MIN) that can be attained, and 1 represents the theoretical maximum score (MAX) that can be attained. For any original (or "raw") score—denoted as "X"—this transformation is accomplished using the following expression:

$$X_{ABS} = 1 - (MAX - X)/(MAX - MIN), \qquad (4)$$

where X_{ABS} is the value of X on the absolute scale (scores on this absolute scale are referred to as idiothetic; Lamiell, 1981; Rogers & Widiger, 1989). For example, a raw score of 5 on a scale with $MAX = 20$ and $MIN = 1$ would be $1 - (15/19) = 0.21$ on the absolute scale.

Once K_1 and K_2 have been placed on a common scale, the mechanics underlying their conversion into ipsative standard scores parallel mechanics underlying normative standardization, except that the mean and standard deviation are computed based on the individual's K_1 and K_2 scores, rather than on scores from a sample of individuals. This procedure has not yet been attempted with actual data, and constitutes an interesting direction for future research.

T Hypotheses

In the simplest case of a T hypothesis, a single individual has been measured on one (single- or multi-item) variable at two testing periods (T_1 and T_2). A common reference system is necessary to compare the individual's score at T_1 versus T_2, and for T hypotheses the ipsative perspective is most intuitive (Cattell, 1952). Under ipsative standardization, raw scores on the variable at T_1 and T_2 are transformed into corresponding standard scores that reflect their magnitude relative to the population of scores on the variable for the individual. Thus, the individual is perceived as having scored at one percentile level on the variable at

T_1 relative to the population of his or her scores on this variable across all time points, and as having scored at another percentile level on the variable at T_2 relative to his or her scores on this variable across all time points; statistical analysis is employed to evaluate whether or not these percentile levels are significantly different (see Mueser, Yarnold, & Foy, 1991, for an example of this analysis).

Normative standardization, while less intuitive, may also be employed in designs involving T hypotheses. In this case, the individual's scores on the variable would be standardized using normative or sample statistics as for designs involving K hypotheses. The same normative parameters would be used to standardize the individual's scores at T_1 and at T_2. The resulting standard scores reflect the magnitude of the individual's scores at T_1 and at T_2 relative to the population of scores—provided by a population of individuals—on this variable at a single point in time. Thus, the individual is perceived as having scored at one percentile level relative to the population on the variable at T_1, and as having scored at another percentile level relative to the population on the variable at T_2; statistical analysis is employed to discover whether or not these percentile levels are significantly different.

For some measures, normative statistics are available for individuals at different developmental levels and/or chronological ages. If the T hypothesis involves assessing an individual's score at the different stages for which normative statistics are available, then normative standardization seems more intuitively appealing. Rather than standardize the individual's score at T_1 and at T_2 using normative parameters from a single point in time, T_1 would be standardized using normative parameters appropriate for T_1, and the same would be true for T_2. This approach has not yet been attempted, and represents an interesting direction for future research.

KT Hypotheses

In the simplest case of a KT hypothesis, a single individual has been measured on two (single- or multi-item) variables at two testings: K_1T_1 (K_1 at T_1), K_1T_2 (K_1 at T_2), K_2T_1 (K_2 at T_1), and K_2T_2 (K_2 at T_2). The most desirable basis for standardization in such designs involves normative parameters for each K at every specific T; that is, normatively standardize K_1 and K_2 at T_1, and normatively standardize K_1 and K_2 at T_2. If normative parameters are not available for each K at every T, ipsative standardization over T—separately for each K—represents the best alternative. An interesting, as of yet untested method of standardization in KT problems involving the first use of at least one K involves (1) ipsative standardization of K_1 and K_2 at T_1 and ipsative standardization of K_1 and K_2 at T_2; and (2) ipsative standardization of the variables created in (1) over T (this methodology is referred to as double-centered; Harris, 1953).

Selecting the Reliability Index

As was true for choice of standardization, prior discussions of N-of-1 methodologies have not addressed the issue of the most appropriate r_{tt} estimate to employ for a specific type of hypothesis. In the broadest sense, all reliability estimates address the precision of measurement achieved by a variable, and are thus consistent with the theory underlying classical test theory methodology. Nevertheless, different r_{tt} estimates are more or less intuitively appropriate for different N-of-1 hypotheses.

Numerous techniques for estimating r_{tt} of a (typically multi-item) variable are available that assess its internal consistency, precision, or stability (Allen & Yen, 1979; Cronbach, Rajaratnam, & Gleser, 1963; Magnusson, 1967). *Cronbach's alpha* is the best known measure of internal consistency, and estimates the relationship between random parallel tests. *Parallel forms* (considered the best) and *split-half* methodologies are more often employed to obtain precision estimates. The Kuder–Richardson "Formula 20" (KR_{20}) provides the mean of the distribution of coefficients that would be obtained if one were to compute every possible split-half coefficient for the variable, and on this basis is preferred over precision estimates based on random or hand-selected split-halfs which may reflect bias or otherwise be nonrepresentative. Finally, *test–retest* methodology is conventionally employed to estimate the stability of a variable across multiple testings.

In applied research, it is not often the case that one has a selection of r_{tt} estimates from which to choose: indeed, no prior estimate of r_{tt} based on a representative sample is typically available. As in the case of estimating parameters for standardization, if a representative sample is available, then numerous r_{tt} estimates can be obtained; if a representative sample is not available, it may be possible to use meta-analytic procedures to estimate one or more types of r_{tt} (see T hypotheses, below, for discussion concerning one possible recourse if none of these conditions are true). If, however, several r_{tt} estimates are available, the N-of-1 analyses should be conducted separately using each available estimate, and any inconsistencies between analyses considered in the context of the hypotheses. Despite the pragmatic constraints typical of applied research, it remains important to consider the most appropriate reliability index for each type of N-of-1 hypothesis.

K Hypotheses. Because K hypotheses involve comparisons between variables assessed at a single point in time, test–retest r_{tt} probably reflects the least appropriate estimate. If the items constituting the variables are homogeneous (i.e., measure the same underlying construct), then Cronbach's alpha appears to be the most appropriate r_{tt} estimate. If the items constituting the variables are not homogeneous, parallel forms or KR_{20} methodologies appear to be most appropriate.

T Hypotheses. Test–retest methodology is the most obvious selection of r_{tt} estimate for problems involving T hypotheses. A problem exists if the test–retest interval in the N-of-1 study is different than the test–retest interval upon which r_{tt} is based. In such cases, and in cases where no other estimate of r_{tt} is available (e.g., as in the first use of a variable), Mueser et al. (1991) recommend use of the *lag-1 autocorrelation function*—the correlation between the individual's jth and $(j+1)$th scores for all sequential pairs of $(j, j+1)$ scores (McDowall, McCleary, Meidinger, & Hay, 1980)—as an estimate of test–retest r_{tt}.

KT Hypotheses. Least obvious is the most appropriate selection of r_{tt} for designs involving KT hypotheses. Consistent with the discussion concerning standardization in these designs, precision coefficients (parallel forms or KR_{20}) are probably most appropriate if they are available for developmental classes that mirror those reflected in the N-of-1 study; test–retest coefficients are the next best alternative.

Multivariate Reliability. For problems involving $K > 1$, Yarnold (1984) has derived the *profile reliability coefficient*, $r_{tt}(K)$, that estimates the split-half r_{tt} of the profile of K variables (this may be thought of as an estimate of multivariate reliability, and may also be used with parallel forms or test–retest data). Interesting directions for future research include (1) development of a KR_{20} analogue to $r_{tt}(K)$ (e.g., KR_{20K}) and (2) formal justification for and evaluation of substitution of KR_{20K} for r_{tt} in N-of-1 formulae. Since the reliability of a profile of variables is greater than the mean reliability of the individual variables constituting the profile, the critical difference score will be lowest when the profile reliability coefficient is employed.

N-of-1 Analysis as a Screening Tool

Finally, it is important to note that N-of-1 procedures may be useful—in the sense of a "preprocessor"—in preliminary analysis stages of research involving multiple subjects. Discussed below, N-of-1 methods can be employed to individually assign subjects into groups (e.g., subjects who responded significantly to the intervention versus subjects that did not respond). This may dramatically increase the reliability of group classification and therefore increase the power of multisubject statistical procedures. Also discussed below, in $N > 1$ research it is sometimes the case that there are substantially more variables than subjects. In such cases, N-of-1 methods may be used as a screen for variables, helping identify a subset of variables that are especially sensitive to each subject's condition (e.g., on which the subject scores as an outlier or experiences significant change).

Screening for Subjects

Imagine that an investigator is planning a multisubject study in which subjects will be classified into groups on the basis of whether they scored higher (group 1) or lower (group 2) on K_1 than on K_2. In the area of sex roles, for example, subjects are classified as instrumentally typed when they score higher on a measure of instrumentality (I) than on a measure of expressiveness (E), and are classified as expressively typed when scoring higher on E than on I (Cook, 1985). This absolute definition of these sex-role constructs results in unreliable classification of individuals whose I and E scores are nearly identical, and these subjects are thus excluded from study (e.g., Yarnold, Nightingale, Curry, & Martin, 1990). Different researchers use different criteria for exclusion, making direct comparisons across studies more difficult than if a uniform exclusion criterion had been adopted. In situations such as these, N-of-1 procedures may instead be used to exclude all individuals whose K_1 (I) and K_2 (E) scores are not significantly different. Used in this way, N-of-1 procedures can increase the reliability of group classification for multisubject studies. This methodology has not yet been empirically evaluated, and reflects an interesting focus for future research.

Screening for Variables

In situations where few subjects are available (e.g., due to rarity or cost), investigators often adopt the case study approach and assess each subject using a large number of variables—many if not all of which are exploratory—in the hopes of obtaining a clearer understanding of the nature of the topic under investigation and a better understanding of what the particular subject is like (e.g., early research concerning AIDS). The present N-of-1 methodologies may be used to objectively identify variables that may be of importance in this regard, in at least two possible ways. First, the ipsative methodology described for K hypotheses may be used to identify variables on which the subject scores significantly high or low, in an absolute sense, relative to other variables; the pattern of results from this analysis would then be examined in an attempt to identify an underlying theme(s) that could explain such a pattern. Second, in clinical trials the T and KT hypothesis-testing approaches may be used to identify variables that are influenced by the intervention(s), and thus provide indirect information concerning the nature of the subject's condition. These methodologies have not yet been empirically evaluated, and represent interesting avenues for future research.

Summary

Consistent with the theme of this volume, the application of social psychology/personality to real-world problems led to the development of new procedures for statistical analysis of N-of-1 designs, and creation of these procedures has uncovered numerous methodological issues that are in need of further research. Ultimately, further research concerning N-of-1 methodologies must occur, since the bottom line for applied scientists involves treatment of individual problems. Indeed, as stated by Yarnold (1988, p. 919): "As the ability of the sciences to measure and manipulate increases, so will the need for more advanced N-of-1 measurement methodologies. Thus, these and related methodologies will be receiving more attention as the sciences advance."

ACKNOWLEDGMENTS. This work was supported in part by grants from the Merck Company Foundation to the National Fund for Medical Education (30188A), and from the National Science Foundation (SES-8822337). Appreciation is extended to Fred Bryant and the anonymous reviewers, whose enthusiastic and insightful comments greatly improved an earlier draft of this chapter.

References

Allen, M. J., & Yen, W. M. (1979). *Introduction to measurement theory*. Monterey, CA: Books/Cole.

Baer, D. M. (1977). Perhaps it would be better not to know everything. *Journal of Applied Behavior Analysis, 10*, 167–172.

Barlow, D. H., & Hersen, M. (1984). *Single case experimental designs: Strategies for studying behavior change* (2nd Ed.). New York: Pergamon Press.

Blumenthal, J. A., O'Toole, L. C., & Haney, T. (1984). Behavioral assessment of the Type A behavior pattern. *Psychosomatic Medicine, 46*, 415–423.

Cattell, R. B. (1952). Psychological measurement: Normative, ipsative, interactive. *Psychological Review, 51*, 292–303.

Cook, E. P. (1985). *Psychological androgyny*. New York: Pergamon Press.

Cook, T. D., & Campbell, D. T. (1978). *Quasi-experimentation: Design and analysis issues for field settings*. Chicago: Rand McNally.

Cronbach, L. J., Rajaratnam, N., & Gleser, G. C. (1963). Theory of generalizability: A liberalization of reliability theory. *British Journal of Statistical Psychology, 15*, 137–163.

Davidson, P. O., & Costello, C. G. (Eds.). (1969). *N=1: Experimental studies of single cases*. New York: Van Nostrand.

DeProspero, A., & Cohen, S. (1979). Inconsistent visual analysis of intrasubject data. *Journal of Applied Behavior Analysis, 12*, 573–579.

Harris, C. W. (1953). Relations among factors of raw, deviation, and double-centered score matrices. *Journal of Experimental Education, 22*, 53–58.

Hedges, L. V., & Olkin, I. (1985). *Statistical methods for meta-analysis*. Orlando, FL: Academic Press.

Holland, B. S., & Copenhaver, M. D. (1987). An improved sequentially rejective Bonferroni test procedure. *Biometrics, 43*, 417–423.

Hunter, J. E., Schmidt, F. L., & Jackson, G. B. (1982). *Meta-analysis: Cumulating research findings across studies*. Beverly Hills, CA: Sage.

Kazdin, A. E. (1982). *Single-case research designs: Methods for clinical and applied settings*. Oxford: Oxford University Press.

Lamiell, J. T. (1981). Toward an idiothetic psychology of personality. *American Psychologist, 36,* 276–289.

Magnusson, D. (1967). *Test theory*. Reading, MA: Addison-Wesley.

McDowall, D., McCleary, R., Meidinger, E. E., & May, R. A. (1980). *Interrupted time series analysis*. Beverly Hills, CA: Sage.

Michael, J. (1974). Statistical inference for individual organism research: Mixed blessing or curse? *Journal of Applied Behavior Analysis, 7,* 647–653.

Mueser, K. T., Yarnold, P. R., & Foy, D. W. (1991). Statistical analysis for single-case designs: Evaluating outcome of imaginal exposure treatment of chronic PTSD. *Behavior Modification, 15,* 134–155.

Payne, R. W., & Jones, H. G. (1957). Statistics for the investigation of individual cases. *Journal of Clinical Psychology, 13,* 115–121.

Rogers, J. H., & Widiger, T. A. (1989). Comparing idiothetic, ipsative, and normative indices of consistency. *Journal of Personality, 57,* 847–869.

Saunders, P. T. (1980). *An introduction to catastrophie theory*. Cambridge: Cambridge University Press.

Strahan, R. F. (1975). Remarks on Bem's measurement of psychological androgyny: Alternative methods and a supplementary analysis. *Journal of Clinical and Consulting Psychology, 43,* 568–571.

Yarnold, P. R. (1982). On testing inter-scale difference scores within a profile. *Educational and Psychological Measurement, 42,* 1037–1044.

Yarnold, P. R. (1984). The reliability of a profile. *Educational and Psychological Measurement, 44,* 49–59.

Yarnold, P. R. (1988). Classical test theory methods for repeated-measures N=1 research designs. *Educational and Psychological Measurement, 48,* 913–919.

Yarnold, P. R., Bryant, F. B., & Lyons, J. S. (1988). *SAM: The Successful Applicant Map*. Chicago: TGP.

Yarnold, P. R., Nightingale, S. N., Curry, R. H., & Martin, G. J. (1990). Psychological androgyny and preference for intubation in a hypothetical case of end-stage lung disease. *Medical Decision Making, 10,* 215–222.

10

Qualitative Activist Research
Reflections on Methods and Politics

Michelle Fine and Virginia Vanderslice

This chapter presents an analysis in which we presume that applied social psychological research is designed not only to explain, but also to provoke social change. Drawing on the early writings of Kurt Lewin (1948), and later from Carolyn Payton (1984), we view the tasks of such researchers to be the facilitation and documentation of structural and social change processes. In this chapter, we review our methodology, *qualitative activist research,* through a single-case study of our work with a public urban school district in the midst of restructuring its high schools. This chapter attempts to portray critically the themes, tensions, and productive possibilities that emerge once an activist research stance is assumed.

Qualitative Activist Research

In his early writings, Kurt Lewin (1948) reflected radically on the purposes of social research. He insisted that such work focus on the transformation of inequitable social arrangements:

> This and similar experiences have convinced me that we should consider action, research and training as a triangle . . . (p. 211)

Michelle Fine • CUNY Graduate School and University Center, New York, New York 10036   **Virginia Vanderslice** • Praxis Associates, Philadelphia, Pennsylvania 19119
Methodological Issues in Applied Psychology, edited by Bryant et al. Plenum Press, New York, 1992.

It is . . . clear that [a large-scale effort of social research on intergroup relations] demands from the social scientists an utmost amount of courage. It needs courage as Plato defines it: "Wisdom concerning dangers." It needs the best of what the best among us can give, and the help of everybody. (p. 216)

Since that time Lewin's politics and passions have, for the most part, been tamed, contained, and domesticated within the notion of action research in which it is assumed that social research is best situated within a change process.

More recently the passions and politics of Lewin's early writings have been resurrected within Afro-American scholarship, feminist theory, and from critical theorists within the field of education, where scholars have been advocating research as praxis. Consider Patti Lather's (1986) argument:

I base my argument for a research approach openly committed to a more just social order on two assumptions. First, we are in a post-positivist period in the human sciences, a period marked by such methodological and epistemological ferment. There has been, however, little exploration of the methodological implications of the search for an emancipatory social science. Such a social science would allow us not only to understand the maldistribution of power and resources underlying our society but also to change that maldistribution to help create a more equal world. Second, research that is explicitly committed to critiquing the status quo and building a more just society—that is, research as praxis—adds an important voice to that ferment. (p. 258)

Lather argues not only for research *on* change, but for research *as* change. Explicit in such a position is a commitment by researchers to disrupt and transform existing social arrangements, and to design research to understand how such change occurs. Here, all researchers, not just activists, are viewed as persons who explicitly carry passions, politics, and, as we have learned to call them, "biases." We infuse these beliefs into the questions we ask (and those we don't), the methods we deploy (and those we reject), the interpretations we advance (and those we never imagine), and the writings we produce (and those we bury in our desk drawers).

Some of the most compelling thinking on the complicated role of researchers *in* our texts comes from Donna Haraway (1988), biologist and epistemologist, who caricatures those researchers who write as if they carry no authorial perspective, as if they were simply vessels for transmitting "the facts." Haraway describes this narrative stance as the God trick, "that mode of seeing that pretends to offer a vision that is from everywhere and nowhere, equally and fully" (p. 584). By refusing to acknowledge their own stances, such researchers reproduce and conceal privileged biases, reifying a pernicious distinction between "biased" and "objective" research.

We are, like Haraway, quite serious about social research designed to facilitate and document social–organizational change. And yet we have both been thoroughly socialized as traditional social psychologists; that is, we learned that we were not supposed to allow our biases—much less our passions and involvements—to influence our scholarship. Anthropologists (Clifford, 990; Geertz, 1973; Mascia-Lees, Sharpe, & Cohen, 1989), sociologists (Becker, 1986; Reinharz, 1988; Stacey, 1988), and some psychologists (Mishler, 1979; Morawski, 1990; Semin & Gergen, 1990; Wexler, 1981) are now deeply embedded in critical conversations about the ways in which researchers are implicated in constructing the narratives that we produce as social science "truths." In this chapter, we intend to enter that conversation as social psychologists, and press a bit further, asking about how activist researchers can construct the very scenes which we study, and the very narratives we publish (see Newberg, 1991).

The Assumptions of Qualitative Activist Research

In many respects, the work we are calling qualitative activist research draws upon a rich—if marginal—heritage within social psychology (see Clark & Clark, 1947; Deutsch, 1976; Lewin, 1948; Lykes, 1986; Mishler, 1979; Morawski, 1990; Stewart & Healy, 1989). At the same time, we consider this work to challenge fundamentally many of the basic driving tenets of social psychology. As a preface to our assumptions, it seems important to reiterate that the goal of qualitative activist research is fundamentally at odds with that of traditional social psychology. Traditional social psychology, even in its most action research mode, has sought only to document change. In contrast, being explicit about the desire to both facilitate and document social change processes systematically transforms how we as social psychologists do our work, particularly because the process of change is seen as unending, ongoing, continually self-reflective, and always transforming. In an effort to unpack the challenge of activist research, we elaborate below its assumptions through three broad categories: the transforming role of researchers, the reconceptualizing of data collection, and the grounding of theories of social change.

The Transforming Role of Researchers

Within activist research, the role of researcher changes dramatically. First, activist researchers self-consciously import a set of biases that drive, but do not limit, their research. Further, such researchers actively participate in the change efforts they study, in ways that inform but do not narrow their understanding.

On Bias

It is typically understood, within the social sciences, that for objectivity to be achieved, researchers can hold no biases on the topic under study; that is researchers need to be "naive," which is assumed a precursor to "being open."

As a corollary, it is presumed that biased research is distinguishable from objective research. The former is tainted because the researcher, a priori, held a position on the issue under study, and then allowed that position to infiltrate her work (Rosaldo, 1989). Objective research, in contrast, is considered methodologically and analytically pure, uncontaminated and uninfluenced by any position ever held by the researcher.

In a space between these two polar positions, Abbey Stewart and Joseph Healy, Jr., write:

> Over the past few intensely self-critical and self-reflective decades, psychologists have understood more and more that our own historical situation influences our work. . . . We have learned to accept that this influence is present both in terms of the questions we are able to think to ask, or the theoretical frameworks we adopt and in the kinds of topics our values and experiences lead us to consider worthy of study. (Stewart & Healy, 1989, p. 30)

Qualitative activist research begins with the assumption that all social research is drenched in biases, and that these biases seep into our work whether out of knowledge or ignorance, insidership or outsidership, centrality or marginality, passion or disregard. We assert further that such biases do shape the questions we ask, the methodologies we deploy, and the interpretations we generate.

Given our press to understand biases—rather than deny or confess them—we believe that it is our responsibility as researchers to be clear not only about our original perspectives on the topic under study, but also about the areas in which we seek and find intellectual surprises through our research.

On Participation

This second feature of activist research pulls yet another sacred cord of traditional psychology; that is, we think it imperative for activist researchers to be engaged in, if somewhat detachable from, the change effort. Like Lewin, we believe that this calls forth, from researchers, a fair amount of "courage." While clearly there are dangers in deep participation in the projects we study, there are equally compelling dangers in being sheltered from participation.

Psychology has, for so long, so deeply isolated itself from social movements that our work suffers from the bias of ignorance and privilege, instead of the bias of engagement and risk. Psychologists have been shielded from the extraordinary benefits of knowledge, access, tensions, and, ultimately, we would assert, morality that come with researchers' engagement in social change projects. The role we play within these projects is, of course, fragile, bordered, and constantly being negotiated. And yet we nevertheless believe that to participate is to understand more deeply (if every partially) the processes of change. Part of our research process, therefore, involves ongoing conversations with informants, in which we all air, challenge, and rethink our original and rotated assumptions.

Reconceptualizing the Collection of Data

A second feature of activist research is that data collection is positioned as a strategy for change. That is, within the framework of activist research, data collection becomes an intervention which intentionally interrupts the belief in "one voice"—organizational unity—or in "two voices"—right versus wrong perspectives. By pulling for multiple perspectives embedded in qualitative data, activist researchers try to understand how diverse constituencies "make sense" of their organization, and of possibilities for change.

On Data Collection as an Intervention

In our work we use varied strategies of data collection—distribution of surveys, archival analyses, individual and group interviews, observations, and qualitative feedback sessions—as pivotal to the change efforts. Within activist research, the very processes of change involve the gathering and legitimating of multiple perspectives, collected both by us, as researchers, and by the many informants within our research–change projects.

By engaging all stakeholders in the research process a number of things can happen. These stakeholders come to recognize that their belief in a single, coherent institutional voice is actually a piece of ideology rather than a "real" reflection of institutional coherence. Further, they can interrupt the dichotomy of Right versus Wrong positions as they become aware of, and even invested in, understanding the kaleidoscopic voices within the institution. Drawing from poststructural theory, we take as given, then, that no one organization (nor person) can be assumed unitary. That is, multiple consciousness flows through all organizations (and individuals).

As theorist Linda Brodkey (1987) writes: "Knowledge of multiple subject positions makes possible both the practical and the theoretical critiques that interrupt the assumption of unchanging, irreversible, and asymmetrical social and political relations between the privileged and unprivileged subjects" (p. 127). Activist research becomes the strategy to unearth these multiple perspectives and grant them the legitimacy that dominant perspectives typically hold alone and unchallenged. This search for multiplicity runs in direct contrast to psychology's typical search for single and parsimonious stories of truth.

On Qualitative Data

Elliot Mischler has argued that if the task of social scientists is to understand human action and experience, then such understandings must be sought in local contexts, discourses, patterns of knowledge, and strategies for "meaning making", not imposed through a set of predetermined categories generated via abstractions of remote scholars. Mischler (1979) writes:

> This ordinary and common sense understanding of meaning as context-dependent has been excluded from the main tradition of theory and research in the social and psychological sciences and in the application of this tradition to educational research. As theorists and researchers, we tend to behave as if context were the enemy of understanding rather than the resource of understanding which is in our every day lives. (p. 2)

Implicit in the tasks of activist researchers, to facilitate and document the processes of social change, lies the search for contextually generated, qualitative categories of knowledge.

To understand the revealing, and radical, value of qualitative data, we draw from the work of social psychologists Susan Condor and Celia Kitzinger, both of whom are interested in understanding "ways of making meaning" from groups situated outside the social science mainstream. Condor (1986) has studied how New Right women make sense of the politics of gender. She argues that to assume these women to be the inverse of feminists, in their meaning-making strategies, is simply wrongheaded. Her research suggests, instead, that the very dimensions of meaning making by New Right women are so at variance from those of feminists, and even of more mainstream women, that handing these women an Attitudes Toward Women scale, which drives them immediately to the "nonfeminist" end of the continuum, without first understanding the contours of their local meanings, is a serious epistemological error.

Celia Kitzinger (1987), like Condor, is most interested in local meaning making, particularly in how lesbian women construct personal and political identities. She advocates Q-sort methodology because it is sufficiently open-ended to yield from informants those dimensions of social experience that *they* consider most self-defining. Strongly committed to "bottom up" generation of categories, Kitzinger (1987) writes:

> [S]ocial scientific accounts of lesbianism serve two major functions: the clarification of science as the only legitimate form of knowledge, and the depoliticization of potential social disruption through its relocation in a private and personal domain. The scientific reports cited to illustrate this thesis depend for their data, however, on accounts provided by lesbians, responding to the scientists' requests to describe themselves, their biographies, their sexual experience, their beliefs, hopes, fears and ambitions. (p. 66)
>
> Interviews with lesbians can, then, within the theoretical framework of this study, be carried out without checks for reliability or validity as these are usually understood, because the aim is not to obtain "the truth" about lesbianism but to collect and explore the variety of accounts people construct about lesbianism. (p. 71)

Like Mishler, Condor, and Kitzinger, in our own work with public schools, it has become clear that in order to unearth the multiple perspectives which linger within any one institution, we have had to utilize both observational and interview skills to extract qualitatively the local definitions of problems, local images of solutions, and local dimensions of what is meaningful.

We did, initially, administer standardized surveys about job satisfaction and dissatisfaction, morale, and organizational development across 22 schools. And from these, we learned quite a bit about the schools, gathering standard information that proved to be quite useful comparatively. But when we wanted to understand a single school enough to engage with its educators in a process of fundamental restructuring of curriculum, instruction, assessment, and governance, not only did we need to know how this school compared with the other 21 schools, but more fundamentally we needed to gather qualitatively an archive of its local messages, meanings, visions, moments of despair, political mine fields, and collective satisfactions.

Generating Grounded Theory at Multiple Levels of Power and Practice

Central to the work of activist research lies a commitment to grounded theory (Glaser & Strauss, 1967) in which theory is constructed, at once, at the level of *practice* (in this case, at the school level), and of *power* (in this case, at the district, union, and state levels). That is, as we help schools study and approach "what could be," we collectively document those district, union, and state policies that get in the way of change, and those that facilitate it. Activist research involves the dialectical gathering and sharing of information across sites of power and practice, so that no one side of the institution is ever engaged in an image of possibility without the rest of the system at least on deck to listen, and be a part of the transformative process. To initiate activist research at the school-level alone could be irresponsible, in so far as we could easily "take" the schools toward images of possibility that the district, union, or state would never tolerate. Similarly, to initiate activist research at the district (state/union) level alone could yield unduly narrow images. Districts, as the seat of policy setting, monitoring and power, do not know, intimately, where they need to change, give up monitoring, and share power until they hear from schools—the site of practice.

On Conversations

Finally, activist research is orchestrated around all constituencies being engaged in ongoing, critical, and collective "power-sensitive conversations"

about the organization as it is, as it could be, and as it needs to be. Drawing again
from Donna Haraway (1988):

> Above all, rational knowledge does not pretend to disengagement: to be
> from everywhere and so nowhere, to be free from interpretation, from being
> represented, to be fully self-contained or fully formalizable. Rational knowl-
> edge is a process of ongoing critical interpretation among "fields" of interpreters
> and decoders. Rational knowledge is power-sensitive conversation. Decoding
> and transcoding; translation and criticism; all are necessary. So science becomes
> the paradigmatic model, not of closure, but of that which is contestable and
> contested. (p. 590)

When we organize our work through such conversations, critical reflections
across multiple perspectives become commonplace, and they nurture organizational health.

Assumptions in Summary

In sum, by positioning data generation and data collection as change strategies, activist researchers explicitly challenge a number of traditional epistemological assumptions of psychology. First, explicit about and interested in bias, we
reject the search for "truth." Second, committed to critical participation of researchers in the change process, we challenge the assumption that involvement
disqualifies researchers. Third, by pressing for ongoing data collection as intervention, which changes intentionally that which we study, we abandon the desire
to capture, freeze, and write up a social situation. Fourth, eager to involve all
stakeholders as researchers, we confront critically the claim that researchers as
outsiders essentially know better and more than informants. And fifth, interested
in engaging critical, ongoing, power-sensitive conversations throughout the
project, we abandon the illusion that a single piece of research is ever complete
or final, or that formative feedback is contaminating.

Our desire, simply, is to facilitate, through qualitative activist research, a set
of institutional processes that will generate contexts for change, document processes of change, and create the conditions for participants to engage in ongoing
reflection on changes. Echoing Carolyn Payton (1984), who pleaded with psychologists almost 10 years ago, we see activist research as a professional responsibility:

> Please keep in mind that almost two decades ago the APA grappled with
> the question of the propriety of psychologists as a group advocating social
> change or taking part in political advocacy, and a process for dealing with such
> matters was suggested. Yet, here we are in 1983 still denying that we have any
> responsibility for or obligation to the society in which we live. We behave as if,
> along with study in this discipline, we inherit a dispensation from considering

all matters concerning social consciousness barring those related to guild issues. (Payton, 1984, p. 394)

The Philadelphia Schools Collaborative

In the late 1980s, the School District of Philadelphia responded both to national attention to high school dropouts, truancy, and absenteeism, and to a concern that the city's 22 neighborhood high schools were in serious need of rethinking and revising. Funded by a 3-year, $8.3 million grant from the Pew Charitable Trust, the district initiated a restructuring project administered by the Philadelphia Schools Collaborative (PSC), a 501 (c) (3) responsible to the funders and the school district. The goal of the collaborative was no less than the full restructuring of all 22 schools.

Operationally, the primary strategic objectives of restructuring included: (1) teacher-driven *structural change* of the existing schools with existing faculties and students from large anonymous institutions into smaller, semiautonomous "intellectual communities" for teachers and students; (2) transformed *governance structures,* from traditional hierarchies to shared decision-making democracies involving teachers, parents, and community members; (3) reinvigorated *instructional renewal* aimed at creating classroom practices that are active, cooperative, and nontracked; (4) *strengthened collaborative relationships* between schools and their local communities; and, (5) the *braiding of standardized and performance-based assessments* in classrooms and schools with more systematic use of interactive evaluations, group exhibitions, individual portfolios, and the like.

The first year of the project demanded that we (the PSC) pursue simultaneously two primary change strategies. One was directed at teacher-driven, school-based change and the other at system change within the district. At the school level each of the 22 high schools assembled a renewal team comprising 10 people (the principal, a vice principal, two department heads, a representative from the building committee, and five teachers) charged with directing the renewal effort in their respective schools. Because ninth grade was identified as *the critical year* in which many students fail and/or drop out, each team was invited to develop a plan for radically transforming their ninth grades for the following year. Through school-based, teacher-driven renewal plans, each school had the opportunity to move at its chosen pace toward locally generated, contextually rich "models," with technical and consultative assistance from the collaborative.

In concert with deep school-based change, the PSC focused attention on creating a top level joint committee of district and union administrators that could legitimate and facilitate change and remove bureaucratic obstacles to restructuring efforts across these 22 schools. It was essential for the top school district administrators and the union leadership to be the key members of this committee, since restructuring wouldn't work without labor–management cooperation.

Activist Research

As activist researchers we were intensely involved in facilitating the change process, rather than being passive observers and recorders. Michelle's work focused on the district and union leadership, working with them toward creating contexts *for* initiating and sustaining change; engaging them in discussions and decisions about how to move the restructuring agenda; and, exposing teachers across schools throughout the district to examples of the "best of practice" around the country, as a way of encouraging them to imagine and create alternatives to urban educational failure.

Ginny's involvement was at the school level: supporting energized faculty; unfreezing teachers who had little faith that anything could change (many of them were content, if not happy, with things the way they were because they had adapted to it over the years); helping teachers and administrators imagine how the school could be; and, then, planning and implementing a process for creating the school they designed.

Through our active and collaborative participation we modeled behaviors that reflected the principles to which we were committed. In our different but complementary capacities as participants in the change process, we asked questions rather than freezing on answers; we offered reflective definitions of "success" as evolving rather than moving from one predetermined step to another; we stood dually, and together, for an investment in change happening at the same time as we committed to an openness in *how* it happened (as long as the process was empowering rather than disempowering for teachers).

We now turn to our work with an individual school to illustrate the organizational change processes and what we mean by *qualitative activist research.*

Phoenix High: Rising from the Ashes

Phoenix High School serves nearly 1,000 students in an urban community that was once entirely white working class, and is now 41% Hispanic, 15% black, and 7% Asian. Phoenix High suffered from a burnt out faculty, extremely low student attendance rates (average daily attendance for the previous year was just over 60%), and extremely high dropout rates (out of 380 entering ninth graders, 73 graduated in 1990).

Phoenix was targeted as a school in which broad and deep restructuring was needed. Having been unsuccessful in stemming the mounting tide of student failure, at the same time, Phoenix had a number of ingredients that seemed promising in terms of facilitating radical change. Specifically, Phoenix had a new and energetic principal who was deeply committed to providing students with a successful educational experience and enjoyed a strong core of teachers poised to provide restructuring leadership within the school.

In November 1989, Ginny became the activist researcher at the individual school level, when assigned to Phoenix as an organizational change consultant. At the same time, Michelle was working at the PSC on district- and union-level strategies to help create and sustain a district-level climate compatible with and supportive of restructuring.

Teachers as Researchers

The Phoenix High restructuring process engaged 35 faculty (out of 54), and a few staff, parents, and community members in an intensive experience of planned change over the summer and across the school year. A key feature of this planning model involved transforming participants into researchers. We did this in three ways. First, we provided them with mountains of quantitative data about student performance, so that *as researchers* they could develop their own interpretations and conclusions. Quantitative archival data provided by the district at the request of the Phoenix staff confirmed their sense that Phoenix was a "dumping-ground" school. They learned, for instance, that over 40% of entering ninth graders were over 15 and a half years old; that 75% of entering ninth graders had missed an average of one day of school a week the previous year; and, that about 75% of students coming from their "feeder" middle schools fell in the bottom two-thirds of their class, many having failed at least once already. For the first time teachers were asked to use these data in the role of *planners* of a more effective high school. This use of data differed significantly from their previous encounters with district-generated data in which educators had been presented with predetermined statistics and interpretations that they experienced as a way of pointing blame at them for the data. They had never been asked what data they would like, were never asked to engage in interpretation, and had never used data for planning their own institutional images.

Next, these educators, parents, and community members became data-collecting researchers. Our initial plan had been to train a small group of three to four teachers as interviewers and to send them out to collect data from parents and community members prior to the retreat. Teachers on the planning team, however, insisted that turning all participants into researchers would be a much more powerful strategy for getting staff to understand the community in which their students lived. According to the plan the team worked out, all participants were assigned to three- to four-person teams that were to complete two tasks.

They were to contact and interview by phone, or in person, as many students and parents as they could from a list of current and incoming ninth graders, coded for regular versus irregular attendance and dropouts. Invited to add, subtract, or change questions on the interview format, staff were given pointers about interviewing do's and don't's, such as finding some common ground with informants before moving onto the questions, and being aware of cultural differences in Hispanic and Asian homes. Community members and parents told them what to expect and how to best present themselves if they visited people in their homes. One community worker told the teachers, "If you go into a Hispanic home and both the mother and father are present, direct your questions to the father out of respect for his position in the family or he will be insulted."

For most of the staff, this information was enlightening. Only two staff members were Hispanic, whereas many of the people they would be calling and/or visiting were Hispanic. If they interviewed exclusively by phone, they also were required to spend at least one hour in the community, observing community life.

This dimension of our work created the major turning point for the staff. By becoming researchers they changed their thinking about students, the community, and one another. Staff who had initially feared, and therefore resisted, going into the community were convinced by conversations with parents and community members that it was safe to make home and community visits. They came back with both wonderful and depressing stories about their experiences and the data they collected. And they came back anxious to share and compare.

One group was unable to locate any of the people on their list, and ended up in a community center. They were not only well received, but people made it clear to them how impressed they were that teachers took the time to come into the community. Another group described finding a student of one of the teachers on a local street corner, and the teacher and student sat on a doorstep on the street and talked about the school.

The process of doing these interviews allowed educators who had worked together for an average of 15 years to construct a unified, yet complex picture of the many dimensions of the school's community and students' lives. They developed a new sense of their collective potential for connecting school and community. As researchers, staff began to believe not only that the school could be different, but also that they weren't alone in their desire to make it so. Where they had previously presumed they were working against the community, and that parents didn't care, they now found interested community members who were anxious to be of assistance, and parents who were willing to be involved if only someone would tell them how. The interviewing experience forced them to confront individually the narrowness of their own attitudes and beliefs about students, their families, and the community and to concretize, collectively, the concerns and needs their school would have to address with community resources. As a direct result of this interviewing experience, many of the participants voiced the strong opinion that all teachers should be required to do interviews in the community at least once a year. As one announced, "this experience has changed my entire outlook on teaching at this school." We believe it is safe to suggest that few, if any, of these teacher–researcher transformations would have occurred if the data from the community had been collected by others and presented to the teachers.

The process of doing these interviews in teams and entering the community together also seemed to provoke a change in the relationships among the staff participating in the retreat. Following this experience, the tone of the group changed. Staff members who had previously kept an uneasy distance from one another began joking with each other. One staff member, who was generally viewed as antagonistic in his relationship with the renewal leadership group, publicly announced appreciation for another member's leadership role in the group. Staff who had expressed negative attitudes about the school began to find constructive channels for their energy. A teacher who had started the retreat with a strongly negative comment became one of the leaders in suggesting deep, creative, positive changes.

The third strategy for engaging teachers as researchers involved their reading about alternative educational images and talking with teachers and administrators who had already developed and worked within schools that were structured and governed dramatically differently from Phoenix. The idea for developing a "reader" on current educational change strategies came from teachers on the planning committee who wanted to use the reading process to "inspire participants and give them a common language for talking about change." They believed that the readings would also challenge teachers' beliefs in the inevitability of a "48-minute class," seven- or eight-period days, teaching only one subject at a time, grading by standardized tests only, and so forth. They were right. Learning about and examining a variety of images allowed Phoenix teachers to cull elements that they believed could be used to better respond to their students' needs. It also gave them evidence for replacing some of their assumptions about how schools *had* to be structured; it freed and inspired them to imagine a radically different school. For example, Mark Weiss, the principal from Bronx Regional High School, talked with them in detail about the "family groups" that made up the core of his school's organizational structure. At Bronx Regional all adults (custodians, aides, secretaries, counselors, and administrators) at the school are responsible for a "family" of 15 students. Principal Nancy Mohr and a teacher from University Heights High School talked about their version of family groups consisting of about 18 students and a teacher who meet every day, offering students one credit per year. In some schools family groups carry a curriculum and attached credits. In others they proceed according to the students' agendas. In all cases, family groups are used as a means of creating strong connections and relationships between students and adults.

As a result of this input, Phoenix teachers decided, after much discussion and within clearly defined constraints, to adopt the family group as a keystone of their new school. Family groups would involve *all* teachers, administrators, counselors, and aides with a group of about 10 students for 4 years. They viewed this as a way to create a sense of community for students within the school and for teachers to connect more fully with students' personal lives within and outside of school. Some adult would know each student's situation, would miss them when they didn't show up, and would be able to talk with them about their problems and celebrate their successes.

Research to Legitimate Multiple Perspectives: At the School and at the District

One of the major goals and outcomes of the Phoenix planning process was that through research multiple perspectives were aired and given legitimacy. The group of 40 then struggled to invent a common vision that incorporated those diverse perspectives. Differences were construed not as roadblocks or battle grounds, but as the basis for creative ideas.

To illustrate: the group decided to break the school into four houses, each of which would be built around a different career-related theme. One teacher suggested forming an "academic" house for students who were college bound. "This is essential if Phoenix High is ever going to attract some students who are higher achievers. Currently such students choose to attend other high schools." A sizable group of teachers felt that there weren't enough students enrolled to warrant such a deeply tracked, "creaming" program and that it was much more important to figure out how to respond better to the students that currently attended Phoenix. "We need to concentrate on the students who are here, not the students we *wish* we had." And the principal held a very strong position that establishing such a house would re-create tracking and drain the best students away from the other houses. A lengthy discussion ensued, in which all viewpoints were considered. The group settled on an explicit "requirement" for *each* house to include in its design a programmatic response for students interested in going to college.

Phoenix, like each school with which we worked, affected and was affected by the District. Our research questions, therefore, traveled dialectically from district level to school and back again. With each iteration of a question, multiple perspectives could be solicited at the school and district levels. So, for instance, Phoenix High wanted to understand the patterns of what they knew to be an extremely transient and, therefore, mobile population. They requested that the district provide archival statistical runs of Phoenix ninth graders by race or ethnicity in terms of percentage of enrollees who started in September and were still on the books in May.

Just asking this question, even prior to getting the data, provoked a diverse set of responses. A colleague from the N.Y.C. Board of Education warned that "if you do that analysis by race or ethnicity, you're opening yourself up to a lawsuit." Some felt the question to be inherently racist, while others considered it quite culturally sensitive.

As requested, the "data junkies" from the district produced reports which suggested that, in fact, 80% of September enrollees were still on roll in May. A 20% mobility rate did not seem high relative to the district range.

Educators from Phoenix were astonished by this report. They examined the same data only to find that:

• The mobile 20% were in and out an average of three times per year, causing enormous disruption.
• being "on the roll" in May meant attending school, on average, 3 days per week.
• Some September through May enrollees were migrant farming for all of January and February.

Supported by those data, Phoenix staff came back to the collaborative with a set of possible interventions, and more research questions. "Can we offer short, intensive courses for students who will not be in school from January through March, and can we evaluate those courses ourselves?" "Can we create and evaluate 'special transition' classes for the mobile 20%?" "Can we conduct research with these students, parents, and Latino policymakers on this topic?"

As a result, the district is conducting statistical analyses of Latino mobility and financial analyses of what it would cost to create *continuity of education* (when parents move so often), and qualitative interviews with students, drop-outs, and graduates are underway. The research questions floated across lines of policy, power, and practice from school to district. New layers of questions continue to surface about literacy, bilingual programs, the need for social service infusion within the schools, and the like, and we continue to legitimate multiple perspectives.

The Dialectic of Theory and Practice in Activist Research: On Surprises

Because of our bias toward participatory democracy and teacher empower-ment, we began with a clear interest in a bottom-up change strategy, initiated through school-based, teacher-driven, renewal teams. Throughout our work, however, we met a series of intellectual surprises that interrupted and transformed our initial biases.

Our first "surprise" occurred when Ginny entered Phoenix as a consultant. After only a few meetings with the renewal team, it was clear that, despite their commitment to restructuring, the team had neither the group nor the organizational change skills to effectively involve the full staff in envisioning and creating a radically different educational environment. They were faced with inventing changes for a staff who voiced only limited visions of "what could be," who seemed to be extraordinarily complacent, and who said they wanted someone else to tell them what to do. And then they resisted the plans the team suggested. While the team was "spinning its wheels," the principal, pressed by the seriousness of Phoenix's situation, had worked around them to develop the only significant programmatic changes that were underway in the school.

So, in the face of our notion that the change process should be teacher driven, we discovered that this conceptualization of the change process was severely limited by teachers' history and adaptation within a system that had rarely solicited their input. As consultants, we found, reluctantly, that we needed to take much more active leadership roles, working closely with staff, in order to crack through the sense of disillusionment and despair that had encrusted the school over the past 20 years. We had learned that to fully restructure a school, one needs to radically interrupt the culture—which was much more ingrained than we had anticipated—as well as create new governance structures and educational practices. At Phoenix we realized that if this was going to happen, a large portion of the staff would have to work together intensively to study and transform their historic and current structures, to rethink their practices, and to develop and sustain a new culture. So bottom-up change became the occasion for deep and intensive, change-oriented, but guided, work.

Indeed, the intensive staff planning project at Phoenix was initiated by the consultants. Once the principal and renewal team agreed to it, the process was designed through the organizational change knowledge of the consultant, with teachers' knowledge of themselves and their colleagues, as well as their personal analyses of factors that had made them willing to believe things could change. The planning team discussed, disagreed, argued, and provided mutual support for each other until we arrived at a design that we all believed would work. The design process became a microcosm of the process of legitimizing multiple perspectives with insiders and outsiders and creating a unified picture in which those perspectives could coexist.

Another "surprise" modified our practice. Our commitment to empowerment focused our attention initially on the site of practice—teachers in individual schools. By so doing, we miscalculated how much work needed to be done at the district level. A bottom-up strategy alone could potentially block, or at least sidetrack, the change process if people at the top who controlled the educational system were not ready to support change. It was one thing for teachers to press for change as part of a legitimized change process. It is quite another for them to have to "demand" change when they are potentially vulnerable. Instead of working together to create a more equitable system that would work better for everyone, a bottom-up strategy alone could have created an aggressive stance on the part of teachers and a defensive stance on the part of administrators, distracting both groups from the real work of creating collaborative, constructive change. This is why so much of our work was directed at multiple levels.

We worked with groups of teachers and administrators, within and across individual schools, to facilitate their ability to imagine and to create "new" schools. This included team building, data gathering, model development, small- and large-group process work, and consultation with individual schools. At the same time, we worked with district officials and the teachers' union leaders toward a public commitment to a highly decentralized and teacher-driven model of school management. We worked toward redeploying resources, working out joint agreements about the district and union roles in restructuring, and making necessary changes at the top level of both organizations to enable teachers and administrators to fully rethink teaching and learning processes and environments.

Our final surprise comes from the success of our work. Since Phoenix, we have tried to distill the elements of the planing design that were critical to our work there. However, to the extent that we can identify such factors, we create a tension in our own and in teachers' involvement in activist research. That is, can we define ahead of time the elements necessary to stimulate deep school change and still provoke sufficient self-reflection and a sense of ownership that came with "discovering" the process at Phoenix? The point here is that activist researchers, in formulating grounded theories, must never assume the theory of change is complete, but rather always evolving. And that "discovery" and "ownership" are as important as the products produced.

From our experience, then, we found that awareness of our initial biases provided us with a strong foundation for organizational change. These biases represented starting points which did not (from what we can tell) dramatically limit our perspective because we were, collectively and often, self-reflective and critical. As activist researchers, our commitment to rethinking continually what we saw meant that we attended to the many "surprises" that confronted us, by participating in conversations with educators, policymakers, and organizational consultants. Those very surprises became the bases for ever revising our collaborative emergent theory of restructuring.

Reflections on Activist Research

In this chapter we have summarized how we envision, and how we work, within this frame of activist research. It may be helpful, in conclusion, to distinguish activist work from more standard forms of applied social research. Allow us to use an example:

We recently attended a meeting of researchers and community organizers interested in understanding how the redistribution and infusion of state monies into low-income districts would affect student outcomes. These were the individuals who had been deeply involved in getting "equitable formula" legislation passed, and in understanding the impact of "more money" on student outcomes.

The conversation spiraled around how to assess the infusion of monies as it affects student outcomes. Boxes were drawn on the board with Money as the independent variable, Educational Administration/Curriculum/Practices as the mediating variables, and Student Outcomes (test scores, promotion, graduation, dropout, attendance) as the outcome variables.

Those of us who worked in and around school districts worried, knowing that while more money is absolutely essential to the transformation of districts and schools, most districts would not automatically transform how they do business just because more money arrived; that "new money" would be poured into "old categories" and we might not see much change. We voiced this worry, perhaps overstated, when we expressed: "If we merely 'measure' the impact of money on student outcomes we will probably see little change. In five years, we will bemoan how we used to be liberals who thought more money was the answer, but now we are wiser conservatives, who know that money doesn't matter." Not just critical, we suggested that we, as a group, should try to get a small grant to work with a select sample of districts on rethinking how, why, and for what monies are spent. By transforming educators into researchers of their own districts and schools, we could help them think through the process of restructuring districts and schools, and then assess how increased budgets could enhance (or not) student outcomes.

Clearly we had transgressed, stepped over the border between researchers and agents of change. The agenda was applied research—the study of a "real phenomenon" in the field. And yet, it was clear to us that unless activist research, collaboratively undertaken with a set of districts, was pursued, the likely outcome in five years would suggest erroneously that "more money" was *not* the answer to educational improvement.

That meeting was just another example of how the noninvolvement of researchers can, and often does, inadvertently breed conservative research. It is incumbent upon us, as social psychologists, not simply to study and report change as we find it, but rather to use our knowledge and experience collaboratively with those in the field to create effective change strategies, to reflect critically on those strategies, and to further refine our understanding of change to inform our next attempts to create positive social change. Psychology has suffered long from the bias of noninvolvement. We invite you, with this essay, to imagine delighting in the passions, pleasures, pains, and possibilities of activist research.

References

Becker, H. (1986). *Writing for social scientists: How to start and finish your thesis, book or article.* Chicago: University of Chicago Press.

Brodkey, L. (1987). Writing critical ethnographic narratives. *Anthropology and Education Quarterly, 18*(2), 67–76.

Clark, K., & Clark, M. (1947). "Racial identification and preference in negro children." In T. Newcomb & E. L. Hatley (Eds.), *Readings in Social Psychology* (pp. 169–178). New York: Holt.

Clifford, J. (1990). *Formal semantics and pragmatics for natural language and querying.* Cambridge: Cambridge University Press.

Condor, S. (1986). Sex roles belief and "traditional" women: Feminist and intergroup perspectives. In S. Wilkinson (Ed.), *Feminist social psychology: Developing theory and practice* (pp. 97–118). Philadelphia: Open University Press.

Deutsch, M. (1976). Equity, equality, and need: What determines which value will be used as the basis of distributive justice? *Journal of Social Issues, 31*(3), 137–149.

Geertz, C. (1973). *Interpretation of culture.* New York: Basic.

Glaser, B., & Strauss, A. (1967). *Discovery of grounded theory: Strategies for qualitative research.* Chicago: Aldine de Gruyter.

Haraway, D. (1988). Situated knowledges: The science question in feminism and the privilege of partial perspective. *Feminist Studies, 14,* 575–597.

Kitzinger, C. (1987). *The social construction of lesbianism.* Newbury Park, CA: Sage.

Lather, P. (1986). Research as praxis. *Harvard Educational Review, 56,* 257–277.

Lewin, K. (1948). *Resolving social conflicts, Selected papers on group dynamics.* New York: Harper.

Lykes, M. B. (1986, October). *The will to resist: Preservation of self and culture in Guatemala.* Paper presented at Latin American Studies Association Meeting, Boston.

Lykes, M. B. (1989). Dialogue with Guatemalan indian women: Critical perspectives on constructing collaborative research. In R. Unger (Ed.), *Representations: Social constructions of gender* (pp. 167–184). Farmingdale: Baywood Press.

Mascia-Lees, F., Sharpe, P., & Cohen C. (1989). The post-modernist turn in anthropology: Cautions from a feminist perspective. *Signs: Journal of Women in Culture and Society, 15*(1), 7–32.

Mischler, E. (1979). Meaning in context: Is there any other kind? *Harvard Educational Review, 49*(1), 1–19.

Morawski, J. (1990). Toward the unimagined: Feminism and epistemology in psychology. In R. Hare-Mustin & J. Marecek (Eds.), *Making a difference: Psychology and the construction of gender* (pp. 159–183). New Haven, CT: Yale University Press.

Newberg, N. (1991). Bridging the gap. An organizational inquiry into an urban school system. In S. Schon (Ed.), *Reflective turn: Case studies of reflection in and on practice* (pp. 65–83). New York: Teachers College Press.

Payton, C. (1984). Who must do the hard things? *American Psychologist 39*(4), 391–397.

Reinharz, S. (1988, October 22–24). *The concept of voice.* Paper presented at Human Diversity: Perspectives on People in Context, University of Maryland, College Park.

Rosaldo, R. (1989). *Culture and truth: The remaking of social analysis.* Boston: Beacon Press.

Semin, G., & Gergen, K. (1990). *Everyday understanding: Social and scientific implications.* London: Sage Publications.

Stacey J. (1988). Can there be a feminist ethnography? *Women's Studies International Forum, 11*(1), 21–27.

Stewart, A., & Healy, J. (1989). Linking individual development with social changes. *American Psychologist, 44*(1), 30–42.

Wexler, P. (1981). Toward a critical social psychology. *Psychology and Social Theory,* Spring-Summer *1,* 52–68.

11

"Thought Experiments" and Applied Social Psychology

R. Scott Tindale and David A. Vollrath

One of the key functions of applied social psychological research is to provide policymakers with information relevant to potential outcomes associated with new or changing policies. Unfortunately, most policy decisions are made in a limited time frame, which rarely allows for appropriate studies to be conducted. Thus, if research results are used at all in policy decisions, they are usually based on extrapolations from previous research. However, the circumstances surrounding previous research endeavors rarely provide a close match to the current situation. This has led some to doubt the efficacy of social psychological research for informing social policy (e.g., Gergen, 1973; Hendrick, 1976). For example, the U.S. Supreme Court recently made a ruling on the use of "death-qualified" juries that conflicted with the majority of psychological research findings (Bersoff, 1987). The lack of research *directly* addressing the question involved in that specific case (whether the presence of jurors opposed to the death penalty would have influenced the final jury verdict) was cited as one reason for ignoring the previous findings.

In addition, many applied social research questions pose numerous problems for direct empirical investigation. Both practical and ethical constraints make empirical (especially experimental) investigations of many natural settings difficult, if not impossible. For example, manipulating aspects of a real jury trial

R. Scott Tindale • Department of Psychology, Loyola University of Chicago, Chicago, Illinois 60626.   **David A. Vollrath** • Division of Business and Economics, Indiana University at South Bend, South Bend, Indiana 46634.
Methodological Issues in Applied Psychology, edited by Bryant et al. Plenum Press, New York, 1992.

or directly observing meetings of the National Security Council are not ethically feasible. Furthermore, one trial or meeting would not provide the generality necessary for providing valid and reliable information to policymakers. Thus, a priori, clear-cut, empirical evidence addressing a particular policy has been, and will continue to be, a rare phenomenon.

One potential solution to this recurring problem involves the use of "thought experiments" (Davis, 1980; Davis & Kerr, 1986). Thought experiments (in the present context, computer simulations) refer to the use of formal theory (or theories) and previous empirical research to generate plausible "conceptual" answers to as yet (empirically) unresearched questions (Davis, 1980). The use of such techniques is not new to social psychology, or to psychology in general (see, e.g., Abelson, 1968; Anderson & Bower, 1973; Stasser, 1988). However, most simulation work in psychology has involved theory generation or testing (e.g., Hastie, 1988; Stasser & Davis, 1981). The use of thought experiments to directly address applied social psychological questions has been rare, which is surprising given the frequent use of simulations in other applied fields (e.g., economics, meteorology, engineering). With the current ease of access to personal computers, the time seems right for applied social psychologists to begin taking advantage of simulation methodologies.

In order to demonstrate the usefulness of the thought experiment approach, the current chapter describes two applied issues, both concerning the criminal justice system, where thought experiments were performed in attempts to provide policy-relevant information. The first example (Vollrath & Davis, 1979) dealt with the potential implications of proposed changes to the grand jury system. The second example (Tindale & Nagao, 1986) focused on the potential efficacy of "scientific jury selection"—the use of social science technologies to aid in selecting juries. We begin with a brief discussion of the theory of group performance on which both studies were based.

Social Decision Scheme Theory

In essence, social decision scheme theory (Davis, 1973) provides for models, or social decision schemes, which map members' preferences into group responses. In the general case, imagine that an individual decision maker must select one of n mutually exclusive and exhaustive response alternatives, A_j, $j = 1, 2, 3, \ldots, n$. We assume that the individual decisions are characterized by a discrete probability distribution, $p = (p_1, p_2, \ldots p_n)$ over the A_j alternatives. Similarly, we assume a discrete probability distribution for group decisions, $P = (P_1, P_2, \ldots, P_n)$. In some cases, such as a trial jury, the number of response alternatives available for groups (guilty, not guilty, or hung) may be different from the number defined for individuals (guilty or not guilty).

Prior to discussion, the r group members may array themselves over the n response alternatives in

$$M = \binom{n + r - 1}{r} \tag{1}$$

different ways. For example, at the outset, guilt preferences in a 12-person jury may be distributed over the two possible alternatives (guilty, not guilty) in 13 different ways, that is, (12,0), (11,1), (10,2), (9,3), (8,4), . . . , (1,11), (0,12). Such an array will be referred to as a distinguishable distribution, where response alternatives, but not individual people, are distinguishable. The probability, π_i, of the ith distribution, $i = 1, 2, \ldots, m$, of member preferences occurring may sometimes be estimated directly by counting the relative frequency $\hat{\pi}_i$, with which the ith array occurs. However, in other instances, π_i, must be estimated indirectly using the multinomial distribution

$$\pi_i = \binom{r}{r_1\, r_2\, \ldots\, r_n} p_1^{r_1}\, p_2^{r_2}\, \cdots\, p_n^{r_n}, \tag{2}$$

and substituting appropriately the observed relative rfrequencies $(p_1, p_2, \ldots, p_n)$ from an independent sample of individual decisions. Given a particular distribution of opinions in a group, the relevant problem is to ascertain the probability that the group will choose a given alternative. This process is obviously a function of the social interaction as well as various prescribed rules or laws governing the particular group. Although the process is probably rather complex, it can be given an explicit summary form by defining the conditional probability, d_{ij}, of the group choosing the jth response alternative given the ith distinguishable distribution. The general statement of the theoretical relation between the initial individual preference distribution and the final group outcome may be cast as an $m \times n$ stochastic matrix, D, called a social decision scheme matrix. Two examples of social decision scheme matrices for 12-person juries are presented in Table 1.

The first decision scheme, D_1, represents the formalization of the familiar "majority-wins" decision rule. As can be seen from Table 1, when a simple majority in favor of guilty (or not guilty) exists, juries are assumed to choose that alternative with probability near 1.0. However, when groups are evenly split (i.e., (6,6)), no simple majority exists and a subscheme is necessary. In D_1, the subscheme we have illustrated is "otherwise hung." Thus, juries with even splits are assumed to hang with a probability near 1.0. Decision scheme D_2 represents the formalization of a "two-thirds majority, otherwise defendant protection" rule. Under this decision rule, juries are assumed to choose a verdict with probability near 1.0 if a two-thirds majority or greater favors that alternative. The defendant

Table 1. Sample Social Decision Schemes
for 12-Person Juries

Initial verdict distribution (G. NG)	D_1			D_2		
	G	NG	H	G	NG	H
(12, 0)	1.00	.00	.00	1.00	.00	.00
(11, 1)	1.00	.00	.00	1.00	.00	.00
(10, 2)	1.00	.00	.00	1.00	.00	.00
(9, 3)	1.00	.00	.00	1.00	.00	.00
(8, 4)	1.00	.00	.00	1.00	.00	.00
(7, 5)	1.00	.00	.00	.00	.75	.25
(6, 6)	.00	.00	1.00	.00	.75	.25
(5, 7)	.00	1.00	.00	.00	.75	.25
(4, 8)	.00	1.00	.00	.00	1.00	.00
(3, 9)	.00	1.00	.00	.00	1.00	.00
(2, 10)	.00	1.00	.00	.00	1.00	.00
(1, 11)	.00	1.00	.00	.00	1.00	.00
(0, 12)	.00	1.00	.00	.00	1.00	.00

Note. D_1 = Simple Majority Wins—Otherwise Hung; D_2 = Two-Thirds Majority Wins—Otherwise Defendant Protection; G = Guilty, NG = Not Guilty, H = Hung.

protection subscheme specifies that if a two-thirds majority does not exist, juries will either choose not guilty (probability = .75) or hang (probability = .25). Note that unlike decision scheme D_1, D_2 is asymmetrical in that it favors the defendant.

The predicted distribution of group decisions, P_G, given a particular social decision scheme, is given by

$$P_G = \pi \cdot D. \tag{3}$$

Comparisons with an observed distribution of group decisions on the same task can then be used to assess the adequacy of the social combination rules embodied in each of the a priori social decision schemes tested. This type of social decision scheme analysis is known as model testing (Kerr, Stasser, & Davis, 1979).

However, the social decision scheme approach can also be used to simulate the effects of a number of different variables (group size, assigned decision rule, sampling members from different populations) on the predicted distribution of group decisions. In addition, the effects of such variables can be assessed for different social interaction processes, as defined by different social decision schemes. The thought experiments discussed here used social decision scheme theory in these ways.

Thought Experiments

Grand Jury Size and Decision Rule

Background Information and Issues

Within our criminal justice system, grand juries decide whether to return indictments against a person who has been arrested for (or is suspected of) a particular crime. If indicted, the defendant is then tried before a petit jury to assess his or her guilt or innocence. States differ in terms of the specific features of grand juries, with some requiring no grand juries at all. Federal grand juries consist of 16 to 23 citizens, who serve for 18 months. Although grand juries sometimes operate autonomously, a prosecutor directs the proceedings of most cases. Witnesses and records can be subpoenaed to appear before grand juries, which hear evidence in secret with relatively few rules to govern procedure and testimony. Witnesses are not accompanied by legal counsel, although they may consult periodically outside the hearings. At the close of hearings, the grand jurors retire to decide whether an indictment should be returned.

Throughout their history, grand juries have been criticized on a number of dimensions, including being a "rubber stamp" for prosecutors and instigating pointless and potentially damaging "fishing expeditions" for evidence. Various reforms have been proposed to alleviate some of these problems, such as providing counsel for witnesses and standardizing investigation procedures. One such proposal, H.R. 94 (1977), which was introduced in the 95th Congress, included changes in the *size and decision rule* requirements for federal grand juries.[1] These proposed changes were the focus of the thought experiments described below.

Size and decision rule have been shown capable of affecting verdicts of petit juries, in both empirical investigations and previous thought experiments (Vollrath & Davis, 1980). In common with petit juries, grand jury size and decision rule can be modeled within social decision scheme theory. However, a number of important differences exist between petit and grand juries. First, grand juries cannot hang: either a true bill (indictment) or no true bill is returned. Second, petit juries are typically a constant size, while grand juries may range between 16 and 23 members. Finally, petit juries have a fixed decision rule (typically unanimity, but occasionally two-thirds or five-sixths majorities are used), while grand juries simply need 12 of those members present to agree that a true bill should be returned. Given that grand juries can differ in size, the decision rule "slides" from a three-fourths majority (12/16) to a simple majority (12/23) rule.

Among other changes, H.R. 94 proposed that the grand jury size range be

---

[1]This bill was eventually not passed by the House of Representatives.

changed to a minimum of 9 and a maximum of 15 members. In addition, rather than the sliding decision rule currently used, the bill proposed that two-thirds of those present must vote for indictment before a true bill would be returned. Thus, the proposal would have fixed the *relative frequency* of jurors concurring, whereas the present system fixes the *absolute frequency* of jurors favoring indictment. In addition, the new bill proposed a maximum grand jury size that is smaller than the minimum size currently used. Besides evaluating the current and proposed systems, Vollrath and Davis (1979) also assessed a composite system which combined the current size range (16–25) with a fixed two-thirds majority decision rule.

Simulation Results and Implications

Several simulations examined the probability of grand jury indictment as a function of the probability that a randomly selected grand juror would vote for

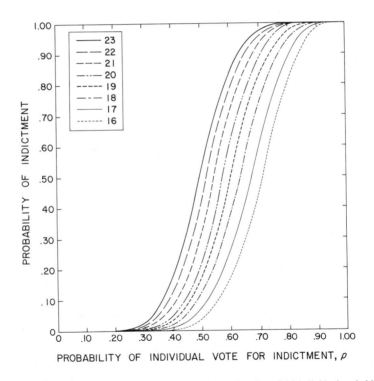

Figure 1. The probability of indictment by a grand jury as a function of the individual probability of indictment under the current system. (From Vollrath & Davis, 1979. Copyright Plenum Press. Reprinted with permission.)

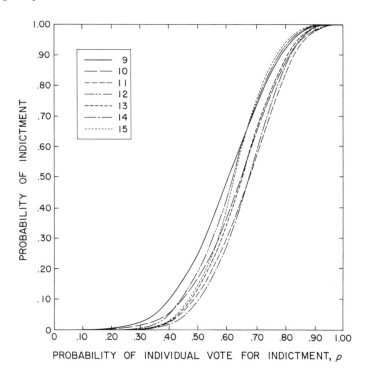

PROBABILITY OF INDIVIDUAL VOTE FOR INDICTMENT, p

Figure 2. The probability of indictment by a grand jury as a function of the individual probability of indictment under the system proposed in H.R. 94. (From Vollrath & Davis, 1979. Copyright Plenum Press. Reprinted with permission.)

indictment within each of the systems described above. Figure 1 represents the current system, Figure 2 represents the system proposed in H.R. 94, and Figure 3 represents the composite system. For the current system, Figure 1 shows that the probability of indictment by a grand jury increases as jury size increases. Thus, larger grand juries are more likely than smaller juries to indict in the current system. However, a more complex pattern is observed for both the system proposed in H.R. 94 and the composite system (see Figures 2 and 3, respectively). For both of these systems, if the probability of an individual juror voting for indictment is low (below .60), increases in jury size tend to decrease the probability of an indictment by the grand jury as a whole. However, when individual jurors are likely to vote for indictment (above .70), larger grand juries are more likely than smaller juries to indict. Thus, the shifting decision rule in the current system produced consistent changes in indictment probabilities across group sizes, while the fixed decision rule in the other systems produced variable changes across group size as a function of individual indictment probabilities.

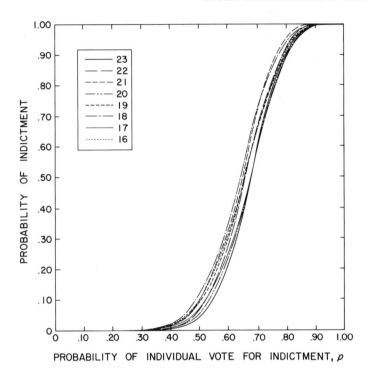

Figure 3. The probability of indictment by a grand jury as a function of the individual probability of indictment under the composite system. (From Vollrath & Davis, 1979. Copyright Plenum Press. Reprinted with permission.)

The separate curves for each group size make it difficult to compare the three different systems directly. Although one could collapse across size to make such comparisons, it is highly unlikely that each group size would be equally likely. However, through the use of archival records, Vollrath and Davis (1979) obtained an estimate of the average federal grand jury size for a given year. Assuming that excuses from service on the grand jury are independent events, a binomial probability distribution was used to generate the probabilities associated with the occurrence of each group size, using the average size as the expected value. Thus, a single curve representing the probabilities of the grand jury returning a true bill across individual member indictment probabilities was generated for each system. These curves are presented in Figure 4.

As Figure 4 indicates, the current system consistently leads to higher indictment probabilities than the other two systems. Comparing the system proposed in H.R. 94 and the composite system, the H.R. 94 system produced higher indict-

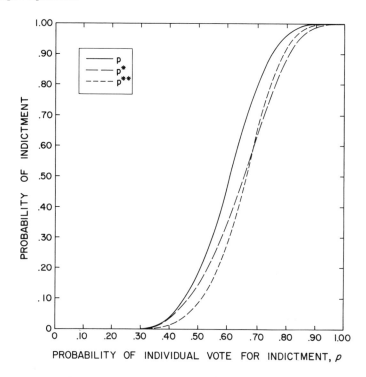

Figure 4. The probability of indictment by a grand jury as a function of the individual probability of indictment under each system collapsed across group sizes weighted by estimated probabilities of occurrence. The current system is represented by p, the system proposed under H.R. 94 by p^*, and the composite system by p^{**}. (From Vollrath & Davis, 1979. Copyright Plenum Press. Reprinted with permission.)

ment probabilities when individual member indictment probabilities were low, with the reverse being true when individual indictment probabilities were high.

These simulations imply that the present system leads to a greater number of indictments than would either of the other two systems. This seems to be a function of the current system's absolute decision rule (only 12 members need vote for indictment regardless of group's size) as compared to the relative (two-thirds of present members) rule used in the other systems. The larger jury sizes used in the composite system, as compared to those used in the H.R. 94 system, lead to greater indictment probabilities when individual indictment probabilities are high. They also lead to lower jury indictment probabilities when individual indictment probabilities are lower. Assuming that individual juror indictment probabilities represent the strength of the evidence, the larger group sizes in the composite system, relative to those proposed in H.R. 94, increase the probability of indictment for strong cases and decrease it for weak cases. Similar effects of group size have been demonstrated for petit juries as well (Vollrath & Davis, 1980). Thus, these different indictment rates for alternative systems of grand jury size and assigned decision rule should be considered in the process of legislative reform.

Scientific Jury Selection

Background Information and Relevant Issues

Scientific jury selection (SJS) (Schulman, Shaver, Colman, Emrick, & Christie, 1973) involves the use of social science and statistical techniques to aid lawyers during the jury selection process. Since it was first used in the early 1970s, it has generated a fair amount of controversy in both the legal and psychological literature (Etzioni, 1974; Moskitis, 1976; Saks, 1976; Saks & Hastie, 1978). The legal concerns have been mainly ethical in nature, while psychologists have generally questioned the validity and usefulness of the method. The thought experiments discussed here were directed toward the latter. SJS has been used in three areas of the jury selection process. (See Kairys, Schulman, & Harris, 1975, or McConahay, Mullen, & Frederick, 1977, for a more thorough discussion of SJS and how it has been used.) First, SJS has been used to question the representativeness of the jury panel (the list of people who could potentially be called for jury duty). This is typically done by comparing the composition of the community (by sex, age, race, etc.) with that of the panel. If it can be demonstrated that a particular subgroup in the community is "substantially" underrepresented in the panel, then the composition of the panel can be challenged, leading to the drawing of a new panel if the motion is accepted. The second aspect of jury selection for which SJS has been used is to support motions for change of venue (i.e., moving the trial to a new location). Using survey sampling, attitude assessment, and statistical inference, researchers have, at times, shown evidence of pretrial publicity bias, or general prejudice that has been used to support such motions (see McConahay et al., 1977, for an example).

Although proponents of the SJS method have argued that these first two uses are probably the most important (McConahay et al., 1977), most of the controversy surrounding SJS has focused on its use in the actual selection of the jury (or voir dire). The major contribution SJS makes to this phase of the selection procedure is a sample survey of the community, consisting of a variety of demographic and trial-relevant attitude questions. The results are then used as a data base from which profiles of good and bad jurors (for one side or the other) can be developed. Typically, multiple regression or profile analysis techniques are used to identify a particular set of demographic variables that are presumed to predict trial-relevant attitudes. The latter results not only assist attorneys in their choice of questions to ask during the voir dire, but also aid their later selection of jurors to be seated (see Kairys et al, 1975, for additional techniques used in this phase of the selection process).

Users of the SJS method have argued, often with cautious reservation, for the utility of the method by pointing to the verdicts that have been obtained— usually acquittals or hung juries—in the various cases in which it has been used (e.g., Christie, 1976; Schulman et al., 1973; McConahay et al., 1977). This supposed success has led some critics to argue for laws against its use for ethical reasons (i.e., it creates biased juries; Etzioni, 1974). However, Saks (1976) and others have argued that there is little scientific evidence to support claims of the utility of SJS. Saks has argued that the cases in which SJS has supposedly been successful were weak to begin with, and involved political or racial issues where certain attitudes may play a meager role. He has also shown that, when compared to trial evidence, demographics and attitudes account for only a small percentage of the variance in individual mock juror verdicts. Thus, Saks suggests that, with few exceptions, lawyers would be better off spending their time and effort on obtaining and presenting evidence than on using SJS to select favorable jurors.

A variety of problems exist in attempting to empirically assess the effectiveness of any multifaceted procedure. Although Saks (1976) points out that the case study approach cannot be used to scientifically assess the effectiveness of SJS, the survey and laboratory studies to date are also lacking in regard to assessing the complete SJS method (Horowitz, 1980; Saks, 1976). Not only are they limited to a single aspect of the SJS method (i.e., the predictability of verdicts from demographic and attitude information), but they also only focus on the individual unit of analysis. Since group decisions have frequently been shown to differ from those made by individuals (Tindale, 1989; Tindale & Davis, 1985), a true assessment of SJS would need to focus on *jury* rather than *juror* verdicts.

Unfortunately, the odds of obtaining an empirical data base assessing the effects of the complete SJS method on jury verdicts (or even mock jury verdicts) in the near future are rather low. First, experimentally assessing such effects in natural courtroom settings poses both economic and ethical problems (imagine being the defendant in a case where the prosecution is randomly assigned the SJS method and the defense is not). Unfortunately, the prospects for studying SJS in the laboratory do not seem much better. Group studies are hard to coordinate and are costly in terms of space and subjects. In addition, accurate simulations of courtroom settings often require the assistance of attorneys, judges, and the like, which increases both cost and coordination problems. Although it is clear that such empirical studies can be done and are needed (see Hastie, Penrod, & Pennington, 1983, for an excellent example), the inherent difficulties suggest that a coherent body of such empirical literature will be slow to develop, especially because multiple studies would be necessary to gain some degree of generality across different types of cases.

However, policy decisions (such as whether to outlaw or restrict certain jury selection practices) must be made regardless of the information base available. Therefore, Tindale and Nagao (1986) attempted to provide information relevant to questions concerning the potential utility of SJS using the thought experiment approach. Using social decision scheme theory and a related computer program (SCHEME; Nagao & Hinsz, 1980), the simulations attempted to address the potential effects on jury verdicts of (1) changes of venue (or a redrawing of the jury panel), (2) the use of SJS to select jurors, and (3) a combination of both of the preceding. We should note that our primary focus was not on the particular techniques involved in bringing about a change in venue or selecting the "right" jurors, but rather on the potential consequences of such procedures when they are *successful* to some degree. As we will show, even the modest success of SJS can have rather dramatic effects on jury verdicts under some circumstances.

Simulation Results and Implications

The following simulations (or thought experiments) were based on a number of assumptions. First, a two-thirds majority—otherwise defendant protection decision scheme (scheme D_2 in Table 1) was used for all of the simulations, due to its previous empirical success at accurately describing mock jury verdict distributions (e.g., Davis, Kerr, Stasser, Meek, & Holt, 1977). Second, since SJS has typically been employed by the defense, all simulations assumed that only the defense used SJS. Similar results (although not identical due to the asymmetrical nature of the D_2 decision scheme) would have been produced by attributing the use of SJS to only the prosecution. Third, all of the simulations assumed that the SJS techniques "worked" in so far as they allowed the identification of favorable jurors, although the degree to which SJS worked is specified in each simulation. Fourth, except where noted, the effects of trial evidence were controlled by assuming that the prosecution and defense cases for a given trial were equally strong (i.e., the probability of an individual guilty vote in an unbiased population would be .50). Fifth, all juries were assumed to contain 12 members unless otherwise indicated. Finally, potential jurors are assumed to be randomly selected from the relevant jury panel.

The first simulation focused on the potential effects on jury verdicts of using SJS to obtain a change of venue or a redrawing of the jury panel. A successful use of SJS in this regard would lead to a jury panel with less initial bias than the original panel. Three different jury panel distributions (potentially representing different populations of potential jurors located in different areas) were used. The first can be conceived of as representing opinions in a locale where the crime may have been committed and/or where prejudicial pretrial publicity has effectively resulted in a guilt-biased population. In this instance, 80% of the potential jurors would favor a guilty verdict prior to jury deliberations. The second panel, where 60% of the potential jurors favor guilty, can be conceived of as representing a nearby locale where some guilt bias exists, but not as strongly as in the original trial locale. Finally, the third panel represents an unbiased population where the distribution of potential juror verdict preferences reflects the actual strength of the evidence (assumed to be equivalent and resulting in a 50% preference for guilt).

The probabilities of a guilty, not-guilty, or no-decision (hung) jury verdict for each of the three populations are displayed in Figure 5. It is clear that the jury verdict distributions vary as a function of the population from which jurors are selected. It is interesting to note that with no change of venue, or redrawing of the jury panel, the bias evidenced at the *juror* level (80% guilt rate) is actually exacerbated for juries (93% guilt rate). However, simply finding or producing a less biased panel increased the probability of a not-guilty verdict by almost 39%. Moreover, with an unbiased jury panel, the probability of a not-guilty verdict became considerably higher than a guilty verdict. In addition, the likelihood of a jury hanging (an outcome generally considered as favorable to the defendant) also increased as the panels became less biased. Thus, theoretically, the successful use of SJS for obtaining a change of venue or redrawing of the jury panel could have rather dramatic effects on trial outcomes.

The second simulation focused on the more controversial aspect of SJS— that is, helping to select the specific jurors to be impaneled. One way of conceptualizing how SJS aids in the jury selection processes is to assume that it allows the defense to place a greater number of "favorable" jurors on the jury (see Tindale & Nagao, 1986, and the third simulation below for other ways of simulating this aspect of SJS). Proponents of SJS (Christie, 1976) have reported relatively good matches between predicted juror positions and jurors' initial verdict preferences (e.g., 8 out of 12 in the Gainsville Eight trial; Christie, 1976, p. 274). This seems to imply that SJS would allow for placing *multiple* jurors favoring a particular side onto the jury. Although such predictions may not be that accurate in all cases, a very modest assumption would be that using SJS instead of random selection would lead to *one more* juror favoring the defense being placed onto the jury.

Figure 6 shows the jury verdict consequences of using SJS to replace one guilty-voting juror with one not-guilty-voting juror for both 12-person (top panel) and 6-person (bottom panel) juries, across all values of the probability of an individual guilty vote (reflecting the strength of evidence against a defendant). We included the six-person jury simulations since some states do allow for juries

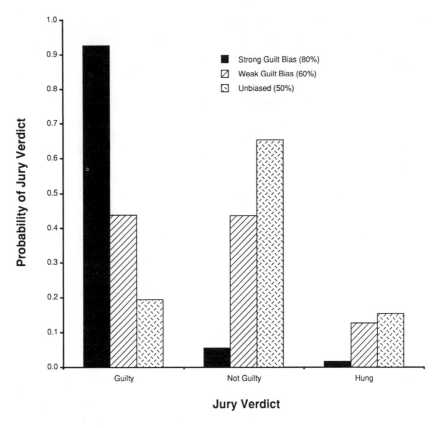

Figure 5. Predicted jury verdict consequences as a results of a change in venue. (From Tindale & Nagao, 1986. Copyright Academic Press. Reprinted with permission.)

as small as (but no smaller than) six members. As indicated in the figure, for very weak or very strong cases, the addition of one not-guilty juror had very little effect. However, the effect on jury verdicts was quite substantial (especially for six-person juries) in the middle ranges of the probability-of-guilt continuum. The largest difference in conviction rates was approximately 19% for 12-person juries and 30% for 6-person juries when the probability of a guilty vote was .65. This is particularly interesting because the majority of cases actually going to trial (i.e., not being dismissed or plea bargained to a lesser charge) would probably fall in that range (moderately strong case against the defendant) where the greatest differences occurred. Thus, these results indicate that even relatively weak assumptions concerning the potency of SJS in placing defense-favorable jurors on

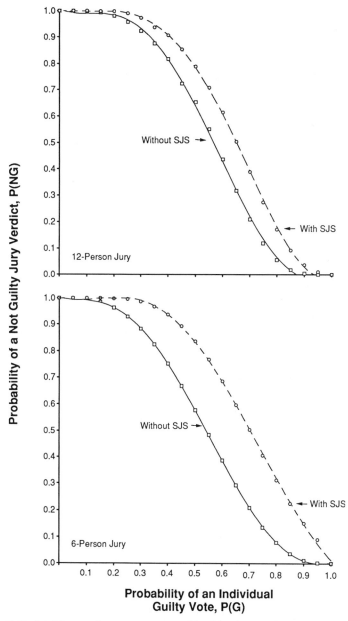

Figure 6. Predicted jury verdict consequences resulting from the use of SJS to replace one guilty-voting juror with one not-guilty-voting juror. (From Tindale & Nagao, 1986. Copyright Academic Press. Reprinted with permission.)

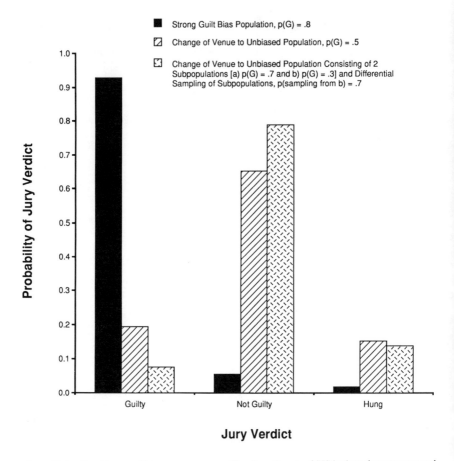

Figure 7. Predicted jury verdict consequences resulting from the use of SJS both to change venue and differentially sample jurors. (From Tindale & Nagao, 1986. Copyright Academic Press. Reprinted with permission.)

the jury can produce dramatic changes at the jury level, especially when jury size is decreased.[2]

The final set of SJS simulations focused on the verdict consequences of using SJS both to obtain a change of venue and to select individual jurors. The results of these simulations are reported in Figure 7. The solid black bars repre-

---

[2]It should be noted that adding one more not-guilty juror to a 6-person jury would probably be more difficult than adding such a juror to a 12-person jury. Thus, the 6-person jury simulation theoretically assumes a somewhat more effective use of SJS.

sent the original population, which is strongly biased against the defendant (80% initially favoring guilt). The hatched bars show the jury verdict probabilities associated with obtaining a change of venue to an unbiased population (50% initially favoring guilt). For the juror selection portion of the simulation, we assumed that the unbiased population could be divided into two subpopulations; one with 70% of the individuals favoring guilty and one with 30% favoring guilty. In addition, we assumed that SJS would allow the defense to sample more heavily (70%) from the less guilt-prone subpopulation. The cross-hatched bars represent the additional effects on jury verdicts associated with using SJS to select jurors, as described above.

While Figure 7 demonstrates the relatively large effects of removing bias from the jury panel by means of a change of venue, it also shows that using SJS for subsequent juror selection can still be effective. The additional increment in the probability of a not-guilty jury verdict (hatched vs. cross-hatched bars) resulting from the use of SJS for selection purposes after a change of venue was approximately 12%. Although considerably smaller than the change-of-venue effect, the additional effect of using SJS to select jurors was still substantial.

Overall, these simulations point out some interesting aspects of the potential efficacy of using SJS. First, consistent with the claims of many SJS proponents (e.g., Schulman et al., 1973; McConahay et al., 1977), the effects of achieving a less biased jury panel are considerably stronger than those effects attributable to using SJS to select jurors, a point often ignored in the controversy surrounding SJS. However, substantial effects were also found for using SJS to select the actual jurors, especially for juries of size six. It should also be noted that these effects were found using rather conservative assumptions about the effectiveness of the SJS method. Thus, it would seem that the conclusions by Saks (1976) and others concerning the futility of using SJS are, at least, premature, if not generally inaccurate.

Summary and Conclusions

The two sets of simulations described here demonstrate the utility of the "thought experiment" approach for addressing applied social psychological issues. Grand jury reform and scientific jury selection represent applied issues that would be difficult to investigate empirically in a timely and precise manner. However, key aspects of both issues were easily and economically addressed via computer simulations. In addition, the grand jury simulation shows how thought experiments can potentially evaluate social policies *before* they are implemented. Such evaluation techniques seem particularly useful for policies involving high implementation costs—economic as well as social.

The thought experiments described here deal with legal issues. However, simulation technologies are domain independent. All that is needed for their implementation is a well-defined theory or model relevant to a particular issue. As Davis and Kerr (1986, p. 344) suggest, thought experiments could revolutionize evaluation research, much as new statistical and qualitative methods have. The range of uses for thought experiments is broad, including, but not limited to, applied issues in business, government, neighborhoods, and families. Social psychological domains such as decision making, person perception, category accessibility, attitude change, conflict resolution, and the like have all been addressed with enough theoretical rigor to allow for application-oriented simulations (see Hastie, 1988, and Smith, 1988 for examples of basic research simulations in some of these areas).

However, there are a number of limitations and necessary prerequisites which constrain the types of questions to which this methodology can be applied. First, a formal theory or model relevant to the particular issue must be available. The model does not need to be mathematical (as was the case in our two examples), but it does need to be defined well enough to provide clear, logical deductions. Second, most formal models or theories require estimates of parameters or a priori conditions. Thus, empirical or archival data for such estimates are necessary to use the method effectively. Finally, researchers must know applied domains well enough to include the practically important aspects of systems in their simulations.

Thus, the thought experiment approach is not currently useful in all domains, and may often only address a limited range of questions. Nonetheless, thought experiments can be quite valuable in identifying areas where more work is needed. Applying formal models or theories to applied issues can highlight vague or inconsistent areas for reconceptualization. Furthermore, parameters that cannot be estimated from current data illuminate needs for further empirical research. Consequently, thought experiments, together with other methods, can advance social psychological theory and research as well as enhance our capabilities to apply social science knowledge to real-world problems.

References

Abelson, R. P. (1968). Simulation of social behavior. In G. Lindsey and E. Aronson (Eds.), *Handbook of social psychology* (Vol. 2, pp. 274–356). Reading, MA: Addison-Wesley.

Anderson, J. R., & Bower, G. H. (1973). *Human associative memory.* Hillsdale, NJ: Lawrence Erlbaum.

Bersoff, D. N. (1987). Social science data and the Supreme Court: *Lockhart* as a case in point. *American Psychologist, 42,* 52–58.

Christie, R. (1976). Probability vs. precedence: The social psychology of jury selection. In G. Bermant, C. Nemeth, & N. Vidmar (Eds.), *Psychology and the law* (pp. 245–281). Lexington, MA: Lexington Books.

Davis, J. H. (1973). Group decision and social interaction: A theory of social decision schemes. *Psychological Review, 80,* 97–125.

Davis, J. H. (1980). Group decision and procedural justice. In M. Fishbein (Ed.), *Progress in social psychology* (Vol. 1, pp. 157–229). Hillsdale, NJ: Erlbaum.

Davis, J. H., & Kerr, N. L. (1986). Thought experiments and the problem of sparse data in small group performance research. In P. S. Goodman (Ed.), *Designing effective work groups* (pp. 305–349). San Francisco: Jossey-Bass.

Davis, J. H., Kerr, N. L., Stasser, G., Meek, D., & Holt, R. (1977). Victim consequences, sentence severity, and decision processes in mock juries. *Organizational Behavior and Human Performance, 18,* 346–365.

Etzioni, A. (1974). Creating an imbalance. *Trial, 10,* 28–30.

Gergen, K. J. (1973). Social psychology as history. *Journal of Personality and Social Psychology, 26,* 309–320.

Hastie, R. (1988). A computer simulation model of person memory. *Journal of Experimental Social Psychology, 24,* 423–447.

Hastie, R., Penrod, S., & Pennington, N. (1983). *Inside the jury.* Cambridge, MA: Harvard University Press.

Hendrick, C. (1976). Social psychology as history and as traditional science: An appraisal. *Personality and Social Psychology Bulletin, 2,* 392–403.

Horowitz, I. A. (1980). Juror selection: A comparison of two methods in several criminal cases. *Journal of Applied Social Psychology, 10,* 86–99.

Kairys, D., Schulman, J., & Harring, S. (Eds.). (1975). *The jury system: New methods for reducing prejudice.* Philadelphia: Philadelphia Resistance Print Shop.

Kerr, N. L., Stasser, G., & Davis, J. H. (1979). Model testing, model fitting, and social decision schemes. *Organizational Behavior and Human Performance, 23,* 399–410.

McConahay, J., Mullin, C., & Frederick, J. (1977). The uses of social science in trials with political and racial overtones: The trial of Joan Little. *Law and Contemporary Problems, 41,* 205–229.

Moskitis, R. L. (1976). The constitutional need for discovery of pre-voir dire juror studies. *Southern California Law Review, 49,* 597–633.

Nagao, D. H., & Hinsz, V. B. (1980). SCHEME: An interactive FORTRAN program to analyze and simulate group decision data. *Behavior Research Methods and Instrumentation, 12,* 484–486.

Saks, M. (1976). The limits of scientific jury selection: Ethical and empirical. *Jurimetrics Journal, 17,* 3–22.

Saks, M., & Hastie, R. (1978). *Social psychology in court.* Princeton, NJ: Van Nostrand-Reinhold.

Schulman, J., Shaver, P., Colman, R., Emrick, B., & Christie, R. (1973, May). Recipe for a jury. *Psychology Today,* pp. 34–44, 77, 79–84.

Smith, E. R. (1988). Category accessibility effects in a simulated exemplar-based memory. *Journal of Experimental Social Psychology, 24,* 448–463.

Stasser, G. (1988). Computer simulation as a research tool: The DISCUSS model of group decision making. *Journal of Experimental Social Psychology, 24,* 393–422.

Stasser, G., & Davis, J. H. (1981). Group decision making and social influence: A social interaction sequence model. *Psychological Review, 88,* 523–551.

Tindale, R. S. (1989). Group vs. individual information processing: The effects of outcome feedback on decision making. *Organizational Behavior and Human Decision Processes, 44,* 454–473.

Tindale, R. S., & Davis, J. H. (1985). Individual and group reward allocation decisions in two situational contexts: The effects of relative need and performance. *Journal of Personality and Social Psychology, 48,* 1148–1161.

Tindale, R. S., & Nagao, D. H. (1986). An assessment of the potential utility of "Scientific Jury Selection": A "Thought Experiment" approach. *Organizational Behavior and Human Decision Processes, 37,* 409–425.

U.S. Congress. House. (1977). H.R. 94. 95th Congress, 1st session.
Vollrath, D. A., & Davis, J. H. (1979). Evaluating proposals for social change with minimal data: An example from grand jury reform proposals. *Law and Human Behavior, 3,* 121–134.
Vollrath, D. A., & Davis, J. H. (1980). Jury size and decision rule. In R. R. Simon (Ed.), *The jury: Its role in American society* (pp. 73–106). Lexington, MA: Lexington Books.

12

Computer Networks in Field Research

Sara Kiesler, John Walsh, and Lee Sproull

In applied social research, the questions we can ask and the data we can collect depend on our tools. Computers have made possible many new tools—for instrument design, sampling, scheduling research, coding and editing, data entry, data cleaning, scale and index construction, data base organization and retrieval, statistical analysis, documentation, and report writing (Karweit & Meyers, 1983, pp. 379–414). In the past two decades, these tools have led to efficiencies and a scale of research heretofore impossible, but the data collection process remains much as it was. Today, most field researchers rely on paper questionnaires, personal observations, and interviews carried out face-to-face or by telephone. For example, of the 90 articles published in the *Journal of Applied Social Psychology* in 1989, 46 report data from a paper-and-pencil survey or face-to-face interview; in another 22, investigators used a personality inventory or similar paper-and-pencil instrument as part of experimental research. In this chapter we consider new tools for data collection based on networking and computers.[1] These tools can increase the efficiency and scale of research. More interesting, they make possible new ways of collecting data and give access to data that in the past were virtually unobtainable.

[1]The first half of this chapter is based on Kiesler and Sproull (1986) and Turner, Dubnoff, and Kiesler (1987). More detailed discussion of the data and issues raised in the second half of the chapter is contained in Sproull and Kiesler (1991).

Sara Kiesler • Department of Social and Decision Sciences, Carnegie Mellon University, Pittsburgh, Pennsylvania 15213.   **John Walsh** • Department of Sociology, University of Illinois at Chicago, Chicago, Illinois 60680.   **Lee Sproull** • School of Management, Boston University, Boston, Massachusetts 02215.
Methodological Issues in Applied Psychology, edited by Bryant et al. Plenum Press, New York, 1992.

Development of Networks

In 1889, Herman Hollerith patented a punch-card data tabulating system that increased the speed of data enumeration and expanded the scope of data analysis over previous hand-tabulation systems. Its use in the 1890 U.S.census reduced analysis time by a third from the previous census and allayed fears that the 1890 analysis would not be finished before the 1900 census (Beniger, 1986). The 1890 census case prefigured how later computing technology would improve the scope and efficiency of social research data processing and analysis (it also prefigured some later surprises, when technology, introduced to reduce costs, ended up increasing them instead). By the 1970s most social researchers used descendants of Hollerith's machine for data processing. As the cost of computing declined, universities and private research organizations bought more computers and processed more information with them. Personal computing proliferated in the 1980s. Today most applied social researchers have access to at least one personal computer.

Computer scientists developed another technology in the 1960s and early 1970s that changed their behavior at least as much as personal computing did: computer networking. With the invention of networking, it became possible to exchange data and messages with remote computers. Computer networks made computer resources accessible independent of geography. Thus today, small university libraries can access up-to-date lists of publications on their computer system. Individual researchers can link into their university's network with a portable computer and a telephone call. The first extensive computer network, the ARPANET, begun in 1969, was intended to let researchers log on to remote computers and share scarce resources such as large programs, data bases, or special hardware. Although this kind of linking and sharing did come to pass on the ARPANET, to everyone's surprise the most popular and extensively used feature of the network was computer mail (Licklider & Vezza, 1978). Soon the designation "computer network" came to have both technical and social meanings. Technically, a computer network is a package of "computing machinery" that connects computers to one another through a transport medium carrying packets of information through nodes and pathways. Socially, a network is an artifact connecting people to one another in diverse forums to exchange benefit. A network community is a social group consisting of people who use computer-based communication regularly. Such a community has norms and social structure. Its membership may or may not have a nonnetworked counterpart (even so, a network community often has many more members than its nonnetworked counterpart). Technical components of a network provide the necessary infrastructure to connect people but by themselves do not create a network community.

Network computer mail made it possible for a computer scientist at one location to send a free-text message on any topic over the network to a computer scientist at a different location. It also made it possible, by using distribution lists stored in computer memory, to send the same message to many people just as easily as to one person. Once computer mail was available on the ARPANET, large numbers of computer scientists around the country could exchange ideas spontaneously and rapidly on topics ranging from system design to programming bugs to movie reviews. Graduate students "visited" different laboratories by computer. Scientists could choose their colleagues based on shared interest rather than proximity (Lederberg, 1978). A large network community formed, filled with friends who didn't know each other and collaborators who had never met in person. We are now beginning to see similar network communities developing in groups and organizations that make extensive use of computer mail (Finholt & Sproull, 1990).

Three key technical changes in computer technology made possible network communities, as well as the new tools for research we will be discussing. One was networking; the second was improvements in computer power, including memory and processing capability; the third was communication software such as computer mail. Before these innovations, a computer "understood" and did computations on standardized, fixed-format information. A researcher can interact with such a computer to find out, for example, how many subjects failed to complete a long questionnaire (the computer counts and reports how many answers are incomplete). Networking, computer power, and computer mail programs made possible a marriage of computer and communication technologies.

Now, a computer is not limited to prespecified formats; it does not have to make computations, and it does not have to understand the information on which it acts. Like other communication technologies, it can accept and move information *in vivo*, leaving people to make sense of it. Yet networks differ from other communication technologies. Unlike telephones, facsimile machines, and so forth, they are designed to use computer processing power and programs for storing and manipulating information about the information exchanged among people: for doing such things as storing messages and interaction records in computer files; imbedding documents in messages; listing files by date, subject, or person; searching for people using the network; creating distribution lists; and editing communications and data. Processing power and programs minimize the effort of search and distribution, expand access to information and ideas, and increase flexibility in using communications.

It is not necessary to have a network to do computer-based field research. Researchers already use stand-alone computers as data collection devices. For instance, they may have respondents sit down at a personal computer and type in answers to a questionnaire (for a review see Synodinos & Brennan, 1988). Networked computers offer advantages beyond stand-alone machines. They make it possible to administer questionnaires as easily to many people as to a few, nearby or remotely. Researchers can conduct interviews remotely, or run panels, focus groups, or long-distance experiments. To aid data collection, programs within networks can help locate respondents manually or automatically, deliver survey instruments to unknown locations, and control their timing or trigger delivery of an instrument to certain behaviors or events. Repeat mailings can be generated automatically if responses have not been received by a certain time. Meanwhile, respondents can respond at once or at their own convenience. Once the responses are collected either on site or remotely, they can be forwarded automatically to computer files for statistical analysis, to other sites or researchers, or to a data base that can be shared by many researchers. Programs can make remote, unobtrusive observations possible too: they can "watch" people interacting on-line or collect public conversation records, and they can manipulate these data statistically to insure confidentiality.

Of course, the sampling frame for studies using such tools is restricted to members of networked groups, organizations, or communities. Until such time as network communication is as easy and ubiquitous as the telephone, computer-based research will be infeasible for general purposes such as citywide citizen surveys. More limited applications, however, are increasingly appropriate. Below we consider the characteristics, advantages, and disadvantages of network-based field research. We emphasize especially the remote computer-based survey because it is the tool with which social researchers have had the most experience. We do not discuss how to design and construct computer-based surveys or tests, a topic too broad for the space limitations of this chapter (see Kiesler & Sproull, 1986; Sproull, 1986; Synodinos & Brennan, 1990; Waller & Reise, 1989; Walsh, Kiesler, Sproull, & Hesse, in press).

Data Collection on Networks

The full application of computers to research has been limited by the fact that raw data are collected off-line. But with a computer, a respondent can self-administer a questionnaire on-line. Add network technology, and the computer survey can reduce barriers of distance, time, and sample size more easily and more quickly than other ways of delivering surveys. As an example, in one organization whose CEO wanted to survey his employees directly, the CEO sent a questionnaire using the firm's network to the 9,000 employees of the firm, reaching them all over the world in minutes.

The technology most like a network-based computer survey is computer-assisted telephone interviewing (CATI; e.g., Groves & Mathiowetz, 1984). In CATI, the interviewer telephones respondents and types their oral responses directly into a computer. However, in CATI a person (the interviewer) stands between the respondent and the data to be analyzed. In a computer survey, respondents enter their own data directly into the computer. When people are linked by a computer network, the computer survey can be administered to any person having access to the network.

Advantages of Network Data Collection

Reduced Research Costs

If only because it can reduce research costs, network data collection someday may become widespread. Once respondents have access to a networked computer, relatively lower marginal costs of collecting and transmitting data digitally can be substituted for the substantial costs of interviewing people in person, telephoning them, observing them by following them around physically, or sending questionnaires through the mail or distributing them in person. In addition, it has been estimated that 20–40% of the total computing costs of conducting a survey may derive from transforming data collected off-line into a form that can be processed by the computer (Ferrara & Nolan, 1974, p. 27). A network survey eliminates data entry costs and can substantially reduce coding and cleaning costs as well. Some open-ended material will still need to be hand coded, but even this task can be aided by computerized text-processing and analysis programs (Carley, 1988).

From the respondents' perspective, if computing and using computer mail are part of their ordinary work or home activities, then the effort required to respond to a network survey can be low (the opposite is true if people have to learn special procedures or take special steps to receive and complete a network survey). A major advantage for respondents of network surveys may be in reducing the effort of answering questions. Because questionnaires can be customized, the respondent need not work through a long and imposing booklet and items constructed for many kinds of people. The computer can screen responses as they occur to determine whether or not a longer series of items is needed; then it transparently skips unnecessary items. Thus, a researcher's questionnaire can be long and complex while still being brief and simple for most respondents.

Improved Data Quality

Because of its flexibility, a network survey can be adapted not just to questionnaire formats suitable for polling, personality inventories, and the like but also to interview formats. Interviews typically are more interactive than questionnaires: items "branch" and "skip" in different directions depending on the respondent's responses. Also, interviewers can explain items that are not clear, and they can ask ("probe") respondents to say more about their answers.

Rhoda, did your parents talk to you about sex when you were
growing up?

no

    Children often consciously or unconsciously interpret
their parents' silence concerning sex as an indication that
sex is bad or at the least is something not to be talked
about. Obviously, parents who are uncomfortable talking
about sex or who are themselves misinformed may also transmit
negative messages. One way or the other, it isn't very
useful to blame them for this. I suspect they tried their
best and were probably only acting like their own parents.
Now it is up to you to improve on it for yourself.

    Did you learn about sex from other sources such as
books, friends, siblings, school, etc?

yes

    Do you feel the information you got was accurate?

yes

    I'm really pleased to hear that. Most of my clients do
not feel that way. Although accurate information about sex
is highly desirable and often helps sexual performance, it is
sometimes not sufficient to insure a pleasurable sex life.

    Have you experienced any sex related events such as rape
or incest that were traumatic for you?

1 You have   2 You have not   3 You don't want to talk
about it

1   [Here the client's answer triggers a "sexual trauma dialogue plan". . .]

    Ron, are you aware of what happened?

no

    I'm not sure why you haven't discussed this, however
there are often valid reasons to avoid such a discussion.
The most immediate reason may be that discussing or even
thinking about what happened can bring back many of the
emotions and fears related to it. I'm a little concerned
that I've raised an issue that you might not be ready to deal
with. If one or both of you feel this way, it may be better
to further delay discussion. It may also be highly advisable
to seek human help concerning this.

    Rhoda, do you want to continue talking about this now?

no

    Fine, let me just say that even if we were to discuss
the details of what happened, it would be very difficult for
me to know how your sex life would have developed had this
trauma not occurred. I hope that it is reassuring for you to
know that there are many women who experienced a sexual
trauma but were able to develop their orgasmic capacity.

[At this point the therapy pertaining to orgasmic concerns resumes.]

Figure 1. Excerpt from a computer-administered sex counseling interview. Responses of the couple
to the computer are given in italics. From Servan-Schreiber & Binik, 1989, pp. 254–255.

An assumption in the statistical analysis of interview data is that all respondents are responding to the same stimulus. A significant disadvantage of face-to-face interviews is that interviewers' behaviors differ both randomly and systematically. These differences contribute a nontrivial interview variance component to the obtained data (e.g., Bailey, Moore, & Bailar, 1978, Groves & Kahn, 1979; Turner & Martin, 1984, pp. 109–111, 136–138; U.S. Bureau of the Census, 1968, 1979). But computer interviews are like self-administered paper questionnaires in that they can deliver a completely standardized stimulus; that is, each respondent sees questions presented in precisely the same manner. At the same time, with some programming, computer interviews can incorporate branches, skips, optional explanatory material, probes, and on-line help. To a surprising degree, a computer interview can simulate an interested and sympathetic interviewer.

Figure 1 shows an excerpt from a computer interview with a married couple in the highly sensitive domain of sex counseling. An experimental study of this program showed significant changes in participants' attitudes after trying it. Whereas before using the program the subjects thought a computer counselor would be little better than reading a book on sex, afterwards they thought it much better though not quite as good as having a marriage counselor (Binik, Westbury, & Servan-Schreiber, 1989).

Improved Assessment of Measurement Error

Among the factors that affect survey and interview responses are question wording and order (e.g., Rugg, 1941; Schuman & Presser, 1981). In studies designed to investigate these issues, two or more randomly assigned groups of respondents can be given questionnaires with different wordings or different orderings of the survey questions. A panel of the National Academy of Sciences has recommended that such experimentation should become a routine part of all survey data collection in order to provide a reasonable accounting for the measurement errors that affect survey estimates (Turner & Martin, 1984, pp. 316–318). Although it is possible to conduct these experiments using personal interviews, telephone interviews, or self-administered paper questionnaires, the mechanics of juggling multiple survey forms make such efforts costly and difficult to execute. As a result, despite their theoretical advantage, these experiments are done infrequently. In contrast, the computer survey makes the use of alternative question wordings, orderings, and skip patterns inexpensive to both researcher and respondents.

More Feasible Measurement of Ongoing and Daily Events

Surveys of experience taken while events are happening are superior to retrospective surveys (see Dawes, 1988, pp. 106–120). They help to reduce underreporting and inaccuracies because of memory lapses, telescoping of time in memory, or current mood. Health diary surveys produce greater reporting of minor health problems, diffuse symptoms, and time lost from acute conditions than do retrospective surveys. In surveys of mental health, the diary method has been used successfully to map the relations between "daily hassles," mood, and health. Unfortunately, it is extremely expensive and difficult to arrange and supervise ongoing or frequently repeated surveys or interviews, or daily diaries, even when they are partially automated, for example, with beepers to remind respondents to complete items (e.g., Hannaway, 1989). And when paper-based, they suffer from the same defects as other self-administered questionnaires— skips and branches are difficult to administer, incomplete and inconsistent responses are common, and response rates are relatively low.

If frequent administration of items were more practical, we could do more research on ongoing and daily events and we could better address questions about how the frequency, magnitude, or severity of daily events and ongoing changes in peoples' environments affect them. Network data collection tools can make this approach much more feasible. For example, in a network survey we conducted, each questionnaire was triggered by a particular event in an employee's workday—a request for technical information or help. We were able to collect data on the triggering event as well as on consequent events at a cost that was not much greater than a single interview done in person. The more than 200 employees we surveyed in this manner were located in 60 different cities and countries. Observing events for these employees, let alone surveying them about the events, would have been impossible without this technology.

Better Measurement of Sensitive Data

Because computer-mediated communications hide much social information— situational definitions, audience reminders, social status attributes, and so forth—respondents may experience less evaluation anxiety and less self-consciousness than when they respond through other forms of survey administration (Erdman, Klein, & Greist, 1985; Plutchik & Karasu, 1991; Sproull & Kiesler, 1986; Walsh et al., in press). Respondents seem to feel they are safe and that the information they are giving is private. Research consistently shows that computer surveys and interviews not only elicit good response rates, but also that answers are more detailed, more disclosing, more extreme, and less socially desirable than comparable paper questionnaires or face-to-face interviews (see Table 1) (Kiesler & Sproull, 1986; Martin & Nagao, 1989; Sproull, 1986; Waterton & Duffy, 1984). In the Waterton and Duffy study, for example, men from Edinburgh reported more alcohol use when interviewed with a computer than by a person, and the reports on the computer better approximated alcohol sales in the city (see Table 2). In a study we conducted for our university, staff and

**Table 1. Percentages Who Responded "True" to Questions
about Good Behavior**

	Paper survey	Computer survey
I am always careful about my dress.	50	20
I always try to practice what I preach.	79	72
I would never think of letting someone else be punished for my wrongdoings.	87	57
I never resent being asked to return a favor.	74	59

Note. From Kiesler & Sproull, 1986.

students reported more illicit drug use when surveyed through the network than through a mailed paper-and-pencil questionnaire, even though the paper survey was self-administered, anonymous, and untraceable.

One way to think about sensitivity in measurement is in terms of response effects, which are entailed in every survey administration (Bradburn, 1983, p. 289; Kiesler & Sproull, 1986). Thus self-administered paper questionnaires, which are impersonal but also relatively private, are not very motivating to respondents. Compared with other methods, paper questionnaires elicit fewer responses and less accuracy overall, but better responses to sensitive questions. Face-to-face interviews are more motivating but also increase anxiety. They tend to elicit more total responses and more accurate reports of unthreatening information but less disclosure of sensitive information. In comparison, computer surveys and interviews can be highly motivating while minimizing anxiety. They therefore elicit a high number of responses, good accuracy, and much disclosure.

**Table 2. Weekly Consumption of Alcohol
Reported by a Sample of Men in Scotland**

	Personal interview	Computer interview
Glasses of beer	15.0	19.0
Glasses of wine	1.2	1.7
Shots of whiskey	3.4	5.4

Note. Half the men were given the questions on a computer, and half were given the questions in person. From Waterton & Duffy, 1984.

Disadvantages of Network Data Collection

Limited Populations

A major shortcoming of doing network-based field research is that potential populations are limited to people who are actively connected to a computer network and routinely use network communications. Access and routine communication are important since nominal membership in a network is insufficient for contacting respondents, enabling them to respond, and motivating them to do so (having the computer mail address of someone who never reads computer mail is much like having the telephone number of someone who is never home). Although there are some interesting studies that can be done using "reading the questionnaire" as a variable (see Salancik, 1983, for more on this research strategy), generally we are interested in the substance of the questionnaire.

Currently, scientists and members of large corporations, government organizations, and universities seem to be the primary users of computer mail (we know of no general survey of computer mail use that would allow us to specify the base rates). We therefore suspect that networks are a poor medium for doing election polls or general market surveys, for example. However, the telephone once was seen as a business tool and for a long time was considered an invalid medium for surveys because of income bias. Computer mail may never become as ubiquitous as the telephone, but increased diffusion will increase the potential populations for study.

There is a kind of backhanded advantage to the current state, in that researchers will be tempted to confine their network-based research to groups and organizations in which people use computer mail and other computer communication programs frequently. In these kinds of settings, a critical mass of network communications is more likely to exist as are genuine network communities (e.g., project groups or scientists interested in a particular specialty). Studies of active social groups are likely to yield much higher response rates than studies of people who just happen to subscribe to the same computer mail service. Previous research has shown that surveys administered to respondents who feel an attachment or commitment to an organization in which a survey is done, or to the subject matter of the survey, give higher response rates (Goyder, 1987; Larson & Catton, 1959). Previous findings of high response rates in network surveys (Kiesler & Sproull, 1986; Sproull, 1986; Walsh et al., in press) may be the result of studying populations that are somewhat community minded. When researchers begin to study nominal groups and unrelated collections of people who happen to have accounts on a network, they are likely to see the same decline in response rates that has been observed in surveys employing similar nominal populations (Goyder, 1987; Steeh, 1981; Thomsen & Siring, 1980).

A major constraint to the use of any computer-based technology for doing research is that it generally requires the respondent to read questions from a computer screen, and usually, to type responses into the computer. Currently available technology will not work with blind people or with anyone who is illiterate. The technology, however, does not require English to be the language of the survey. In fact, computer surveys may be more flexible in this regard than previous methods. With appropriate branching, respondents can choose their language and we need not send multiple copies of the instrument to each respondent or have multilingual interviewers.

The loss of the blind in network surveys is similar to the loss of the hearing impaired in telephone and face-to-face surveys. Either loss can be minimized with special (probably costly) equipment. Literacy is a bigger relative disadvantage in that it is not required in telephone or face-to-face surveys but is required for network surveys. National statistics on literacy collected by the U.S. Census Bureau indicate that less than 1% of the American adult population is unable to read and write (U.S. Bureau of the Census, 1971). Because the definition of literacy in this statistic is not very stringent, this doubtless is a lower-bound estimate of the fraction of the population that would be inaccessible to a computer survey. Nonetheless, it does provide crude guidelines as to the subpopulation that would be most difficult to survey using this technology. For example, illiteracy is higher among older people and among immigrants.

Threats to Privacy

In network-based field research, it is very difficult to guarantee complete anonymity. If a questionnaire is sent to individual computer mailboxes and respondents mail back their replies over the network, no respondent can be truly anonymous. Techniques can be used to increase the protection of privacy. For instance, we have asked respondents to send their completed questionnaires to a special computer mailbox, where a program automatically strips off all identifying information. But questionnaires can be intercepted and techniques can be circumvented. We might send potential respondents computer mail asking them to log on to a public account and complete and mail back their survey questionnaire from that account. Yet still it is possible to learn who was logged on to the public account at what time. While the actual incidence of violating anonymity probably will be rare, its potential may discourage respondents. So far, just the opposite seems true: in our studies, respondents act less afraid of privacy violations when they type responses into a computer than when they give them on paper or to a person.

A potentially serious disadvantage to network-based field research is that guidelines, laws, and procedures protecting confidentiality and informed consent may be inadequately suited to the new technology. Networks give people access, in principle, to ever-increasing information about others. The potential for access can be abused by researchers and others who snoop in people's mail files or access data bases containing personal information without permission from the persons whose information these data bases contain. Network technology can be used to collect data automatically and unobtrusively to provide statistical reports on how employees spend their time in and away from the office, when and where they travel, whom they talk to, what they read, how they spend their money, and how healthy they are. Laws, regulations, and procedures, although improved in recent years, still do not cover all the possibilities for abuse. Lawmakers must continually try to catch up to advances in computer and communication capabilities. Most applied social researchers have little knowledge and experience of potential privacy issues in domains of new technology; they will not even find an adequate discussion in the research literature of how new privacy laws and actual behavior by government officials and others may affect their network research. (A good introduction to this topic is Katz, 1988. Also, potential problems and actual cases involving privacy are discussed on the Internet bulletin board, "Risks.")

A related issue is that of acceptable levels of informed consent for respondents. Today, researchers obtain consent from each respondent to a survey; we say it is informed because the respondent understands what will be done with responses. Usually they will be used for a specific research project. Data-collecting organizations, including universities, protect the confidentiality of the information obtained from respondents, but guarantee only that information about specific individuals or corporations will not be released in such a way that they can be identified. The extent to which informed consent can be given to unknown future uses of survey data, in particular to their use by other investigators or merger with other data sources, is of great concern to survey researchers. Controlling the eventual uses of merged, widely distributed data sets will be difficult. One natural response is to say, "Well, we'll just keep our data at home." But there are strong pressures in the opposite direction. The National Science Foundation now requires that data collected with the support of the economics program be archived in machine-readable form, and that any professional article citing program support be accompanied by a fully documented disk describing the underlying data. In the social sciences, a 1985 report of the National Research Council's Committee on National Statistics recommended that "sharing data should be a regular practice" and that a "comprehensive reference service for computer-readable social science data should be developed" (Fienberg, Martin, & Straf, 1985; for more discussion of data base-related policy issues see National Research Council, 1989).

New Data and Different Questions

Research efficiency and technical advantages probably will be the primary factors that move social researchers toward or away from computer-based data collection tools. Yet the way such tools allow researchers to collect new kinds of data and ask questions that have been difficult to ask in the past also may prove important. In our own research program, we did find efficiency changes in data collection, but these were not the most interesting changes. Below we draw on our studies of network communication to illustrate both quantitative changes in our ability to study remote or rare phenomena and qualitative changes in our ability to study social phenomena. In some cases we have gained a new perspective on complex phenomena such as organizational participation and commitment; social scientists have long had an interest in these topics but they have proved difficult to study in the field.

Reaching Remote People through Surveys

To conduct a network survey of oceanographers we sent a computer questionnaire to a stratified random sample of 338 scientists and technicians who used SCIENCEnet (Hesse, Sproull, Kiesler, & Walsh, in press). These scientists were working in many regions of the world including New Zealand and the Arctic, and some were on ships, yet our response rate was good—76%. Respondents could complete and return the survey by computer or, if they wished, they could print a hard copy of the survey and return it using postal mail. Our response rates (and early returns) were highly correlated with respondents' routine use of computer mail and with their responding by computer, but not with their geographical distance. Thus, the computer medium seems to have made possible and even encouraged high levels of survey participation among respondents who would have been more difficult to include using traditional methods. Unexpectedly, an additional 104 persons who were not in our sample requested a copy of the survey, filled it out, and returned it on their own initiative. We realized then that because the survey was sent on a network and was announced on a computer bulletin board read by many scientists, members of the network who were not selected into the sample could also participate in the study. This phenomenon of voluntary participation in a survey meant to be a random sample survey is one we have never before observed and seems to have been a direct consequence of using a computer forum. Almost all (96%) of the self-selected respondents replied by computer rather than on paper. By comparison, 58% of the random sample respondents replied by computer and 42% replied on paper.

Surveys using self-selected groups, such as questionnaire polls of magazine readers, broadcast polls of radio listeners, and newsletter surveys by members of Congress to their constituents, frequently are used to give people a voice. Although such surveys are not properly scientific, they are nonetheless used to gather information on people considered likely to vote, buy consumer goods, and so forth. Like these other forums, networks can be a medium for giving people a voice at little cost, especially among populations similar to the scientist group we studied—people who are very literate, and comfortable with a survey format and expressing themselves in text (Tallent & Reiss, 1959). The sciences also support norms of communication (Hagstrom, 1965; Hargens, 1975). We would expect to see similar behavior in other professional settings where computer mail has been institutionalized; it is an open question whether spontaneous survey participation would occur in more reserved cultures or in autocratic, hierarchical organizations.

To investigate their motivations for participating, we compared the spontaneous, self-selected respondents in our study of oceanographers with the random sample respondents (Walsh et al., in press). In many respects the two groups were similar, but the self-selected group were especially active in the oceanographic community and seemed to be motivated to make their opinions known on the topics covered by the survey. For example, they left fewer items blank and wrote longer open-ended answers. Of course, this comparison has many limitations, mostly connected to the fact that we did not plan it before collecting our data. But our experience suggests some future possibilities for research involving self-selected samples. Survey researchers view self-selected samples as "really terrible" (Bradburn & Sudman, 1988), but when random samples are not available (as is the case now with samples of people at risk for AIDS) they may be all we have. The situation would be somewhat improved if we could estimate the bias in these samples. This is usually impossible, but using a network we can conduct planned comparisons of self-selected and random sample respondents.

Event-Driven Computer Surveys

Event-driven surveys are usually conducted in face-to-face settings where the event of interest can be observed (e.g., exit polling on election day or market basket surveys in grocery stores). With network-based communication, it is possible to observe behaviors on the network and then send questionnaires triggered by these events. This is how we and David Constant are studying discretionary information sharing at a Fortune 500 high-technology firm. First, during a specified period (several months), we monitored all the messages sent to public distribution lists. Whenever an employee sent a message requesting help in answering a question or finding information (a message sent to all members of the organization), we sent a network survey questionnaire to the person who had asked the question. We also asked the employee to save any answers that the query generated. Next, we sent a (slightly different) survey to every person who replied to the request for help. After a week, we sent a second survey to the question asker to get his or her reaction to the replies.

Using this method, we were able to survey people while their behavior (asking or replying to a question) was still fresh in their minds. Also, because we have an exact record of the behavior—the text of the question and the text of replies—as well as self-reports from the surveys, we were able to study how variance in the nature of the behavior affected survey responses. This made possible such questions as: Are longer answers, or answers from more people, considered more valuable? Does the form of the answer make a difference to the question asker? We were also able to evaluate the contribution of asker attributes and replier attributes to perceptions of questions and answers.

We are using this study to evaluate contrary predictions made by theories of economic exchange and theories of altruism (both of which were generated from observations in noncomputer interactions), as well as to examine hypotheses about the quantity and quality of discretionary information sharing in organizations.

Ethnographic Studies of On-Line Behavior

Because social interaction on a network can be stored in computer memory, network-based field research can be used to "capture" interactions, even those that occur rarely and are too costly to measure using traditional methods. If the researchers' interests are in private conversations and exchanges, they can ask people to forward or save their computer mail messages (e.g., Sproull & Kiesler, 1986). Messages can be moved automatically to computer files, where identifying information is stripped and data prepared for statistical and content analysis.

Researchers in anthropology (Collier, 1967) and qualitative sociology (Whyte, 1984) have used photographs of the social situation being studied to elicit additional information from respondents. We used a similar technique with computer mail messages (Sproull, 1986; Sproull & Kiesler, 1986). We asked respondents to save a week's computer mail, and then used these messages as a focal point for interview questions. Like photographs, computer mail captures a snapshot of social interaction. We can examine the interaction indirectly by asking the respondent why the message was sent, what the respondent's relationship with the sender (or receiver) is, how typical the message is, and so forth.

Researchers have direct access to social interaction and groups through private and public computer bulletin boards ("bboards"), conferences, and distribution lists in network communities (our university subscribes to more than

---
Message offers item for sale:

Date: 31 Oct 90 17:47:30 EST

To: BBoard-Market

From: William.Walker@A.GZ.CX.CMU.EDU

Subject: Body Armor

MIL-B-44053 spec vest, life-saving multiple layers of Kevlar aramid ballistic cloth. Protects against typical missile fragmentation from mines, grenades, mortar shells and artillery fire. It may decrease the severity of wounds from rifles and machine guns and can stop small arms fire from an angle or if the projectile has low velocity. Outer shell features nylon webbing grenade hangers above each pocket. Size L(41-45). Never used. $550

One of 8 messages advising against purchase :

Date: Fri, 2 Nov 1990 14:51-EST

From: Clayton.Bridges@GZ1.SP.CS.CMU.EDU

    Caveat Emptor on Mr. Walker's offer.

The August 90 Consumer Report has a penetrating article on the MIL-B-44053 spec vest which reveals serious design flaws. The article is a synopsis of a US Army study which discovered that flawed construction techniques "seriously endangered the lives of Army personnel dependent on the vest for protection." Even the present mail-order prices for these vests is too high now. Soldier of Fortune predicts that the MIL-B-44053 vests will eventually be dumped for as little as $80 for the minimal protection they offer.

    The interested consumer should look instead to the MIL-B-44068/A spec vest, which the study showed to be correctly designed, and can be had for as little as $350 (last time I checked).

    If Walker knew about this study, he is a rip-off artist of the worst kind. Enough said.

Angry message from seller (excerpt)

Message Date: 2 Nov 90 15:37:09 EST

From: William.Walker@A.GP.CS.CMU.EDU

So, who appointed you "Miss Body Armor Consumer Advocate Know-It-All, USA"? Anybody who would order from a police-supply catalog -- sheesh. The vests you typically see in these publications are NIJ-0042 spec or of that ilk. That's fine for stopping the a random shotgun blast or two, and maybe deflecting a .38 slug if the angle's wide (you'll still eat big on the backface deformation), but its just not the kind of thing I'd want when some 'SLiberty bag-lady starts hosing down the 71-A with one of those ghetto .802 knockoffs the kids are making these days instead of bolo ties and potholders. . ..The price on the vest stands at $550, firm. Serious inquiries only, I'm not here to entertain a bunch of milk-babies with M1 tank jokes. --will

---

Peer pressure, 2 of several such messages:

Date: Fri, 2 Nov 90 16:54:19 -0500 (EST)
From: Barbara Clarkson <bc1w+@andrew.cmu.edu>
re: welsh's scathing reply

I think I need body armor to READ that! Milk-baby? Uh ...
yeah. Just don't call me a panty-waist (or is it waste??)
or I'll tell my mommy on you.
--Barb--
PS What are you people DOING out there, anyway?

Date: Sat, 3 Nov 90 19:24:18 -0500 (EST)
From: Brian Michael Keesey <bk1a+@andrew.cmu.edu>

excuse me. . . is this really important????????
---brian

Seller tries to end messages:

Date: 3 Nov 90 21:34:20 EST
From: William.Walker@A.GZ.CS.CMU.EDU

We have a happy new owner. No further discussion will be
required.

"Discussion" continues:

Date: Sun, 4 Nov 90 19:44:59 EST
From: Christopher.Medea@A.GZ.CS.CMU.EDU

I disagree. I think discussion of these consumer related
topics is entirely appropriate to cmu.market. I think this
discussion prevented me from making the mistake of my life.
    By the way, now that SCS has instituted austerity
measures in the supply closet, where can you get teflon-
coated bullets. There is a thesis-defense coming up soon...

Date: Mon, 5 Nov 90 00:09:51 -0500 (EST)
From: Michael Jacks <mj5z+@ANDREW.CMU.EDU>

    If I recall Mr. Walker's original post he claimed that
it would stop shards from quite an array of common war
materials. Against bullets he claimed effectiveness ranging
from almost worthwhile to fatal. Just where are all of these
vests going? I guess I missed all the inner-city mortar
bombardments in the headlines. This stuff is a bit bulky to
wear to the laundromat just in case someone opens up on a
dryer. Or have the neighbors been laying mines again?
Just curious,
Mike Jacks

Figure 2. Excerpts from a board discussion of an unusual item offered for sale on the computer network "classifieds" at Carnegie Mellon. In addition to the messages shown, there were 10 from other people.

2,000 bboards). The fact that all these interactions are stored and can be read on-line makes it possible for researchers to unobtrusively study the emergence and dynamics of such interactions and groups and to study their various "cultures." Within so-called electronic groups, one can examine many kinds of behavior, including decision making, problem solving, bargaining, selling, scapegoating, and certain behaviors that would be difficult to observe in any other circumstance.

In Figure 2, we show a discussion that took place over a few days on the "market" bboard, which faculty, staff, and students use to advertise items for sale. This discussion has some unusual attributes: the discussants had not met in person and had no interest in buying the item yet they felt free to "comment" publicly on the sale; no one revealed his status or expertise (can you tell which person is the professor or which message is completely inaccurate?); situational norms were ambiguous (as in the conflict over where the discussion "belonged" and whether it was serious or a joke); disagreement resulted both in "flaming" (use of aggressive language, sarcasm, etc.) and in attempts at social control. Equally unlikely exchanges can be found in network communications of professionals, scientists, managers, and engineers.

Because most network-based communication systems have some mechanism for saving messages, the researcher can easily capture a long stream of communications in a computer forum for later analysis. John Walsh, for example, collected all the postings to a computer bulletin board whose function was to facilitate the coordination of a fantasy baseball league. Some of the messages had an instrumental function, but many of the messages were just sociable. Message traffic began to develop a common format, and users developed on-line personae. During the life of the bulletin board (a period of several months), the board developed into an on-line community, with many similarities to what anthropologists have called "third places"—places such as taverns and corner stores, which serve as an outlet for nondiscursive interaction.

Finholt and Sproull (1990) studied culture in electronic groups at a Fortune 500 firm by examining all incoming and outgoing messages saved by a sample of employees over a 3-day period (the computer could have automatically saved all of these messages, but the researchers wanted to give respondents the opportunity to delete any personal messages from the data set before the researchers saw it). Approximately 60% of respondents' computer mail was group mail sent to all people who were on a particular distribution list such as ComputerScience-Group or Cinema. Some of these groups were mandatory, some voluntary, some work related, and some extracurricular. They found that these electronic groups shared many characteristics with other types of social groups, despite the fact that members were geographically dispersed and the communication was asynchronous.

One way electronic groups differed from other types of groups was that

Person A's Message to UserFeatureForum:

I cannot imagine a pathname standard that does not
reserve * as a wildcard.   It's much more than PHC
we're dealing with here — I think most other major
operating systems use the same conventions: TOPS-
20, RSX-11W... Users of these systems are exactly
the few hundred thousand people who are most likely
to be our first customers — people who'll be
talking to these other operating systems via TTY
emulation.

Person A's Message to Cinema:

an'I likes Joe Bob.   Shucks, I though tall the
humorless prigs had already migrated to Review.
If'n ya dun lak it, y'all kin CLICK DELETE once a
week on any msg with "Joe Bob" in the header.   AH
HAS SPOKEN!   I suggest directing your brickbats,
kudos, etc. to me rather than subjecting the whole
list to any further meta-discussion.

Figure 3. Changing personas in electronic messages. From Finholt & Sproull, 1990.

whereas they were often large, some having more than 100 members, they did
not exhibit the formality and structure that is usually associated with increasing
group size. Because the size of the group was largely invisible to group members, they may have perceived it as smaller, which may in turn have encouraged
informal participation. The flexibility of the network system (which made it
relatively easy for people to generate a new distribution list) also meant that
employees could create new electronic groups as they liked, providing a dynamic
vehicle for addressing new interests, problems, and opportunities as they arose.
New groups developed different styles of interacting and cultures, and members
adapted to these differences. Figure 3 illustrates how one person changed his
persona when interacting with two different electronic groups.

Using a similar methodology, Eklundh (1986) analyzed the "dialogues" in message traffic of a Swedish network to study the nature of language in a computer medium. She concluded that computer communication is somewhere between "speech" and "writing," and her results challenge some of the assumptions of communications research about the inherent differences between written and oral communication (that spoken language is more informal and context bound than written language). Computer mail communication had some properties that differed from both other forms of communication. For example, there were fewer "face" aspects such as the greetings and pleasantries that often introduce a telephone call, face-to-face conversation, and letters.

In capturing on-line communication, researchers can observe naturally occurring organizational phenomena over time. Danowski and Edison-Swift (1985), for example, analyzed the communications patterns and content of an organizational crisis as they were reflected in interactions on a computer mail network of a midwestern state extension agency. This agency went through a budget crisis and reorganization in October of 1981. The researchers analyzed network traffic for 5 months before and after the crisis. During the crisis the number of messages increased dramatically, as did the number of people sending messages, but messages got shorter. In a social network analysis of the message traffic during the crisis, individuals' social networks became less interlocking, and the social network coalesced into one group of about 85 people (out of a total of 300 users over the year of data collection). In a content analysis of the messages sent, the researchers found that during the crisis the messages tended to focus more on the organization qua organization, rather than on the work of the organization. After the crisis, communication behavior reverted to its precrisis characteristics.

Finally, researchers can create electronic groups or otherwise intervene in computer interactions to carry out experiments or to guide data collection. Myers (1987) created a focus group bulletin board on a public-access system in New Orleans where respondents discussed their feelings and attitudes toward computer mail use. In capturing all of the message traffic, Myers attempted to understand important themes that underlie bulletin board behavior, such as a desire to have personal interaction yet remain anonymous. At present much more of this type of research is taking place than is reflected in the academic literature. Several market research firms routinely use on-line focus groups to study consumer behavior and attitudes and to evaluate products.

Studies Using Computer Data Bases and Archives

As organizations put more information and data into computer data bases, that same information becomes more accessible to researchers with network connections to them. For instance, performance measures, employee survey data, personnel background data, and organizational charts that used to reside in people's heads, memoranda, scattered file cabinets, or personal computers now may be accessible on networks to researchers. Organizations also have begun digitally archiving information they never stored before. One of the most interesting types is archives of informal information exchanges. For example, "does anybody know . . . ?" is a common phrase in organizations—typically heard in informal encounters in office hallways, before meetings begin, at the water cooler, coffeepot, and in lunchrooms. Now it is possible not only to ask and reply to such questions on-line, but also these exchanges can be saved in an archive on the network so others can use them.

Archives and data bases containing informal communications are very unlike archives and data bases containing formal communications and numerical data. Usually the information was elicited because a person was seeking a piece of current or arcane information not easily found in official documents or numerical data bases. The audience for such questions usually is sympathetic or at least tolerant because the behavior is conventional, the questions are not onerous, and answerers themselves may one day need to ask a question. In the conventional world, if an asker's acquaintances cannot provide an answer, the asker is stymied. He or she must seek an acknowledged expert, or perhaps will hold the question until an auspicious meeting, convention, or visit away from the office. But on a computer network, the asker has access to a much broader pool of information sources.

For example, an oceanographer broadcast a message to a computer network of oceanographers: "Is it safe and reasonable to clamp equipment onto a [particular type of insulating] wire?" The official instructions said, "Do not clamp." Right away the sender got several messages from other places saying, "Yes, we do it all the time, but you have to use the following type of clamp." The oceanographer did not know the scientists who responded and would never have encountered them in a face-to-face setting or in a paper memorandum, but through computer communication, he benefited from their knowledge and experience. He did not have to know in advance who would have helpful information, nor did they have to know in advance that their advice would be wanted. Organizations can create on-line archives of these questions and all the answers they receive. Then before asking a does-anybody-know question on the network, a person can check the archive for recent replies to similar questions. In this way people can share knowledge across time as well as across space. In contrast to standard data base systems that contain only answers, the archives of reply files contain questions as well as answers and thus provide information on what people want to know as well as to what they do know.

Tom Finholt is studying an archive of this form that is used at a high-tech firm and comparing it to an archive that stores more formal exchanges between

---

Question:

We have a prospect that is considering using Einzig as part of a multi-million dollar network. They already have several miles of fiber-optic cable in their facilities to be utilized as the LAN.

I need to know where Einzig is interfacing to or utilizing fiber optics (with the exception of FOX!). Any details that can be provided as to what, where, how, etc would be of great benefit.

Replies will be stored in \LB.$DATA.RALPH.FIBER and secured for netview access.

Thanks,

Ralph Kinzey

A few of the 8 replies from 3 countries that Ralph received:

From: Mazerilski_Bill @ CASG

There's a company (in Mass. I think) which sells fiber obtics modems, multi-plexors, etc. I can't recall the name. We were using the equipment at Memorex to provide electronical isolation from some test stands. We were interfacing using a standard async port. The person at Memorex who would know is Tom Silver. You'd probably better check with the sales person before calling him though.

From: BLASE_STEVE @ THAMES

I have come across a couple of fibre optic systems connected to the Einzig for terminal networks. In one case a customer uses them because they are secure (a govt customer) the other is an in house use. In both cases they are connected to the async controller and are invisible (!) to the Einzig. I can only give you the in house use which is at \thames where we use a fibre optic mux SPL lightplex 6001 with 16 ports for rs232 terminal connections. (this is being entered using it).

Hope this helps, Steve

From: MADDIN_BILL

Hi Ralphie

One of my accounts here on the planet of Riverside is using a fiber optic network and it works great. Of course the optics is totally transparent to any of the Einzig products. They just think they are talking to a modem or some EIA interface. The real brains in that network is the muliplexor that serves as the interface to the fiber optic link. In other words if the personnel in charge of the fiber optic network set you up a port on the mux, what ever your using now, I.e., Exchange, AM6520, TERMPROCESSS, etc. . will probably continue to work.

Hope this helps. Bill

Figure 4. Sample network messages from the "Einzig Computers" archive of "does anybody know?" questions and answers.

employees and designated experts. One could imagine that the network does-anybody-know procedure could generate a data base full of questions and no answers (or poor answers), thereby completely defeating its purpose. Theories and studies of this problem suggest that people will not supply as many answers, or as many good answers, as might be most beneficial to the organization as a whole (Marwell & Ames 1979; Messick & Brewer 1983; Thorn & Connolly 1987). Yet in the network and archive Finholt is studying, both the informal information-sharing procedure and the archive seem to work reasonably well, and are faster and more popular than the "ask-the-designated expert" procedure and archive. Enough people voluntarily answer the does-anybody-know questions that people find it worthwhile to ask them. These procedures are available to all employees but are used most often by sales and service representatives. A sales representative might describe a potential customer's situation and ask if any other sales representatives had dealt with similar situations. Or a service representative might ask if anyone had encountered a technical configuration similar to one he or she was trying to debug (Figure 4 displays a sample question and reply from the firm's network). Employees broadcast about six questions a day eliciting about eight replies apiece. About half of the question askers create reply files that can be read by all of the firm's other employees. The archive of reply files is accessed over 1,000 times a month.

One of Finholt's and our research aims is to understand how and under what conditions employees, and network procedures and policies, elicit the goodwill of people who are willing to provide answers voluntarily when they see questions they can answer. Also we want to learn who benefits most from this behavior and how the behavior might change social relations in the firm. These questions are related to more general theoretical questions about altruism, information exchange, and organizational citizenship, all of which have proved exceedingly difficult to observe and measure in the field. With discretionary information-sharing behavior captured in an archive, these questions are more open to systematic study.

Action Research

A traditional form of applied social research is "action research" involving systematic attempts both to study and improve social systems. A few examples of action research on networks exist in realms such as education (Salomon, in press), community participation and service (Dutton & Guthrie, 1990), and therapy. One example in the latter domain is a smoking cessation program developed for CompuServe, a commercial communications network (Schneider, Walter, & O'Donnell, 1990). Schneider et al. argue that computer communication may be a particularly useful medium for bringing smokers into behavioral treatment. Patients can access an individualized program anytime they wish without traveling to a treatment site. Also, they can begin treatment privately, without announcing that they have done so. A program evaluation indicated that of those who got the full treatment and stayed with the program, about 23% had abstained from smoking 6 months after beginning treatment. Abstinence rates were significantly higher among those patients who received the full treatment (which included an expert system to control interactions) than among a comparison group that received a simplified version of the program that did not include any personalized interactions. Schneider et al. estimate that with a small amount of expense and effort they reached about 1% of the population of smokers on CompuServe, which has a population equal to that of a medium-sized city. This suggests that network-based clinical systems have some potential for making clinical help available to a larger audience. At the same time, since the computer can be used to record the exact pattern and content of interactions during therapy, we expand the possibilities for research comparing different counseling strategies.

Networks as an Intervention in the Social World

Network-based data collection techniques such as the computer interview can help us study more people, different groups, remote respondents, and phenomena that have been difficult to study. If networks only made these data more accessible they might lead to some new insights. Yet networks have another, less direct but perhaps just as important, impact on data collection and research: they change the very environment or setting—the "field"—of our field research. Some of the studies described above, such as those of "electronic groups" and discretionary information-sharing archives, examine behavior or social arrangements that do not exist outside of a networked environment. In these cases, the network is not simply a means for passively collecting data but represents a kind of social intervention or social change. For answering some research questions, such intervention poses a source of error or bias to be avoided or minimized. Alternatively, it offers a new arena for evaluating theories and hypotheses that were developed from observations in more traditional social settings. In some cases, the intervention may be worthy of study in its own right, as an example of social change.

Studies of network communities reveal many interesting ways that network technology can be said to intervene in and alter the social world. For example:

- Communications among people who have never met in person can be frequent and close (with the result, for instance, that we can disentangle variables such as frequency of contact and self-selection that contribute to proximity effects in field research).
- Information access to organizational data that were previously centralized

and controlled by a few can be decentralized; control can be decoupled from organizational position.

* Reference groups can develop in the absence of social similarity.
* Direct participation by large numbers of employees can take place. This participation may be passive (employees gain access to information), active (employees have a voice), or both.
* People can "belong" to tens or even hundreds of electronic groups, creating the potential for dynamic and complex "linking-pin" roles and for information sharing on a scale heretofore unimaginable.
* Much of the social and contextual information that helps regulate behavior, makes for social distinctions, and defines social situations and decision frameworks is not inherently available in a network. Thus, behavioral regulation and social inequalities tend to break down, at least temporarily.

Researchers have examined each of these phenomena in studies of social and organizational processes such as coordination, distributed decision making, and control (Carley, 1988; Eveland & Bikson, 1988; Kraut & Streeter, 1990; Rule & Brantley, 1990). A different issue is whether these phenomena represent potentially significant social changes. When new technologies are introduced in organizations or society, social scientists are interested in whether the changes are temporary or not, and if they are permanent, whether the average efficiency or quality of life improves, as well as how different groups are affected by the change. A hypothesis that many people entertain about computer communication is that it will democratize communication patterns (Hiltz & Turoff, 1978). If geographical distance and time zones are less of a barrier to participation, those people who are far from the centers of activity or power will have more access to information. If social information is reduced, then social distinctions will be less of a barrier to information access. We have argued that network technology in organizations potentially benefits remote or low-status employees more than it does central, nearby, or high-status persons who already have good access to information and other people. Thus, whereas communication outcomes may improve across all groups, they should improve most among "peripheral" people. We have used both paper and computer surveys, as well as experiments, to study this hypothesis.

A survey of oceanographers' use of SCIENCEnet was one vehicle we used to study the relative impact of computer communication technology on "central" and "peripheral" people (Hesse et al., in press). We were interested in whether oceanographers who use the network and who are relatively peripheral to their discipline (e.g., those who are younger, or work at inland institutions) gain more access to resources and benefits than are gained by central scientists who use the network (Merton, 1968; Merton & Zuckerman, 1973). In addition to an overall positive relationship between using computer mail and scientific outcomes, we found that under some conditions scientists' use of the network interacted with measures of peripherality. For example, a scientist's use of computer mail was positively associated with his or her receiving professional recognition such as awards or appointment to national committees. That is, scientists who were heavier users of computer mail were more likely to receive professional recognition than scientists who were light computer mail users. But additionally, the difference between younger scientists who did and did not use computer mail heavily was significantly larger than the difference between older scientists who did and did not use it.

Because the data from our oceanographers' survey are cross-sectional, we do not know whether or not using the network played any causal role in scientists' professional recognition, but the pattern of results is consistent with such a view and also fits with the results of laboratory experiments (Dubrovsky, Kiesler, & Sethna, 1991). They are intriguing because they suggest that networks could change the structure of communication in groups and organizations by increasing the participation of previously isolated or ignored employees. Data from another study we conducted suggest, however, that the nature of this participation will be important. In that study (Huff, Sproull, & Kiesler, 1989), we examined the relationship between using computer mail and feelings of organizational commitment. The overall relationship was significant, especially for shift workers (a peripheral group compared with day workers). However, when we compared how much computer mail people received with how much they sent we found that only sending computer mail was related to commitment. These results suggest that new communication technology will have a more significant impact through changes in the participation of peripheral employees when that participation gives people a voice.

Conclusion

The populations for network-based field research will be communities and organizations with access to and familiarity with computer networks. These groups will tend to be well educated, young, and technologically sophisticated. Within these limits of feasibility, and assuming that investigators take active responsibility for ensuring privacy and informed consent, computer surveys and other network-based data collection methods offer some advantages for data collection. Our research has shown that when used in lieu of paper questionnaires or interviews, computer surveys and interviews elicit similar or "better" data (Kiesler & Sproull, 1986; Sproull, 1986). Because computer surveys and interviews can be standardized and controlled (as through counterbalancing of items), and customized for individuals, subgroups, and types of responses, they can reduce effort for both researchers and respondents, increase response rates, and improve the technical quality of data. Ease of use, interactivity, and an absence of social information (such as cues associated with presence of others) encourage respondents to disclose more information, especially personal or sensitive information. Although these advantages may induce some researchers to try computer field research, we have found that networks are interesting in their own right. Measuring the natural behavior of people in computer networks offers a glimpse of how people behave in a new communication environment. During the past decade some of our colleagues have argued that research on networks is uninteresting because the results are not generalizable to "real life." We believe that as computer networks and other computer-based technologies become ubiquitous in society, network-based field research will be increasingly useful for studying behavior in a relatively new yet "real" real-life communication environment.

References

Bailey, L., Moore, T., & Bailar, B. (1978). An interviewer variance study for the eight impact cities of the National Crime Survey. *Journal of the American Statistical Association, 73,* 16–23.

Beniger, J. R. (1986). *The control revolution.* Cambridge, MA: Harvard University Press.

Binik, Y. M., Westbury, C. F., & Servan-Schreiber, D. (1989). Case histories and shorter communications. *Behavioral Research Therapy, 27,* 303–306.

Bradburn, N. (1983). Response effects. In P. H. Rossi, J. D. Wright, & A. B. Anderson (Eds.), *Handbook of survey research* (pp. 289–328). New York: Academic Press.

Bradburn, N. M., & Sudman, S. (1988). *Polls and surveys.* San Francisco: Jossey-Bass.

Carley, K. (1988). Formalizing the social expert's knowledge. *Sociological Methods and Research, 17,* 165–232.

Collier, J., Jr. (1967). *Visual anthropology: Photography as a research method.* New York: Holt, Rinehart & Winston.

Danowski, J. A., & Edison-Swift, P. (1985). Crisis effects on intraorganizational computer-based communication. *Communication Research, 12,* 251–270.

Dawes, R. M. (1988). *Rational choice in an uncertain world.* San Diego: Harcourt Brace Jovanovich.

Dubrovsky, V., Kiesler, S., & Sethna, B. (1991). The equalization phenomenon: Status effects in computer-mediated and face-to-face decision making groups. *Human Computer Interaction, 6,* 119–146.

Dutton, W., & Guthrie, K. (1990). *Santa Monica's public electronic network: The political ecology of a teledemocracy project.* Unpublished manuscript, Annenberg School for Communication, University of Southern California, Los Angeles.

Eklundh, K. (1986). *Dialogue processes in computer-mediated communication.* Linköping, Sweden: Linköping University.

Erdman, H. P., Klein, M. H., & Greist, J. H. (1985). Direct patient computer interviewing. *Journal of Counseling and Clinical Psychology, 53,* 760–773.

Eveland, J. D., & Bikson, T. K. (1988). Work group structures and computer support: A field experiment. *Transactions on Office Information Systems, 6,* 354–379.

Ferrara, R., & Nolan, R. L. (1974). New look at computer data entry. In W. C. House (Ed.), *Data base management* (pp. 25–46). New York: Petrocelli Books.

Fienberg, S. E., Martin, M. E., & Straf, M. L. (Eds.) (1985). *Sharing research data.* Washington, DC: National Academy Press.

Finholt, T., & Sproull, L. S. (1990). Electronic groups at work. *Organization Science, 1,* 41–64.

Goyder, J. (1987). *The silent minority.* Boulder, CO: Westview.

Groves, R. M., & Kahn R. L. (1979). *Survey by telephone: A national comparison with personal interviews.* New York: Academic Press.

Groves, R. M., & Mathiowetz, N. A. (1984). Computer assisted telephone interviewing: Effects on interviewers and respondents. *Public Opinion Quarterly, 48,* 356–359.

Hagstrom, W. O. (1965). *The scientific community.* Carbondale, IL: Southern Illinois University Press.

Hannaway, J. (1989). *Signals and signalling: The workings of an administrative system.* Fair Lawn, NJ: Oxford University Press.

Hargens, L. L. (1975). *Patterns of scientific research.* Washington, DC: American Sociological Association.

Hesse, B. W., Sproull, L., Kiesler, S., & Walsh, J. P. (in press). *Returns to science: Network and scientific research in oceanography. Communications of the ACM,* 265. Working paper, Carnegie Mellon University.

Hiltz, S. R., & Turoff, M. (1978). *The network nation: Human communication via computer.* New York: Addison-Wesley.

Huff, C., Sproull, L., & Kiesler, S. (1989). Computer communication and organizational commitment: Tracing the relationship in a city government. *Journal of Applied Social Psychology, 19,* 1371–1391.

Karweit, N., & Meyers, E. D., Jr. (1983). Computers in survey research. In P. H. Rossi, J. D. Wright, & A. B. Anderson (Eds.), *Handbook of survey research* (pp. 379–414). New York: Academic Press.

Katz, J. E. (1988). U.S. telecommunications privacy policy: Socio-political responses to technological advances. *Telecommunications Policy, 12,* 353–368.

Kiesler, S., & Sproull, L. S. (1986). Response effects in the electronic survey. *Public Opinion Quarterly, 50,* 402–413.

Kraut, R. E., & Streeter, L. A. (1990). *Satisfying the need to know: Interpersonal information access.* Unpublished manuscript, Bell Communications Research, Morristown, NJ.

Larson, R. F., & Catton, W. R., Jr. (1959). Can the mail-back bias contribute to a study's validity. *American Sociological Review, 24,* 243–245.

Lederberg, J. (1978). Digital communications and the conduct of science: The new literacy. *IEEE Proceedings, 66,* 1314–1319.

Licklider, J. C. R., & Vezza, A. (1978). Applications of information networks. *Proceedings of the IEEE, 66,* 1330–1346.

Martin, C. L., & Nagao, D. H. (1989). Some effects of computerized interviewing on job applicant responses. *Journal of Applied Psychology, 74,* 72–80.

Marwell, G., & Ames, R. (1979). Experiments on the provision of public goods. I. Resources, interest, group size and the free-rider problem. *American Journal of Sociology, 84,* 1335–1360.

Merton, R. K. (1968). The Matthew effect in science. *Science, 159,* 56–63.

Merton, R. K. & Zuckerman, H. (1973). Age, aging and age structure in science. In N. W. Storer (Ed.), *The sociology of science* (pp. 497–559). Chicago: University of Chicago Press.

Messick, D. M., & Brewer, M. B. (1983). Solving social dilemmas: A review. In L. Wheeler & P. Shaver (Eds.), *Review of personality and social psychology* (pp. 11–44). Beverly Hills, CA: Sage.

Myers, D. (1987). Anonymity is part of the magic: Individual manipulation of computer-mediated communication contexts. *Qualitative Sociology, 10,* 251–266.

National Research Council, Panel on Information Technology and the Conduct of Research, Committee on Science, Engineering, and Public Policy. (1989). *Information technology and the conduct of research: The user's view.* Washington, DC: National Academy Press.

Plutchik, R., & Karasu, T. B. (1991). Computers in psychotherapy: An overview. *Computers in Human Behavior, 7,* 33–44.

Rugg, W. D. (1941). Experiments in wording questions II. *Public Opinion Quarterly, 5,* 91–92.

Rule, J., & Brantley, P. (1990). *Surveillance in the workplace: A new meaning to "personal" computing.* Unpublished manuscript, State University of New York, Stony Brook.

Salancik, G. R. (1983). Field simulations for organizational behavior research. In J. Van Maanen (Ed.), *Qualitative Methodology* (pp. 191–208). Newbury Park, CA: Sage.

Salomon, G. (in press). Studying the flute and the orchestra: Controlled experimentation vs. whole classroom research on computers. *International Journal of Educational Research, 14,* 37–47.

Schneider, S. J., Walter, R., & O'Donnell, R. (1990). Computerized communication as a medium for behavioral smoking cessation treatment: Controlled evaluation. *Computers in Human Behavior, 6,* 141–151.

Schuman, H., & Presser, S. (1981). *Questions and answers in attitude surveys: Experiments in question form, wording, and context.* New York: Academic Press.

Servan-Schreiber, D., & Binik, Y. M. (1989). Extending the intelligent tutoring system paradigm: Sex therapy as intelligent tutoring. *Computers in Human Behavior, 5,* 241–259.

Sproull, L. S. (1986). Using electronic mail for data collection in organizational research. *Academy of Management Journal, 29,* 159–169.

Sproull, L. S., & Kiesler, S. (1986). Reducing social context cues: Electronic mail in organizational communication. *Management Science, 32,* 1492–1512.

Sproull, L. S., & Kiesler, S. (1991). *Connections: New ways of working in the networked organization.* Cambridge, MA: MIT Press.

Steeh, C. G. (1981). Trends in nonresponse rates, 1952–1979. *Public Opinion Quarterly, 45,* 40–57.

Synodinos, N. E., & Brennan, J. M. (1988). Computer interactive interviewing in survey research. *Psychology and Marketing, 5,* 117–137.

Tallent, N., & Reiss, W. J. (1959). A note on the unusually high rate of returns for a mail questionnaire. *Public Opinion Quarterly, 23,* 579–581.

Thomsen, A., & Siring, E. (1980). On the causes and effects of non-response: Norwegian experiences. *Artikler. Fra Statistisk Sentralbyrå,* Nr. 121.

Thorn, B. K., & Connolly, T. (1987). Discretionary data bases: A theory and some experimental findings. *Communication Research, 14,* 512–528.

Turner, C., Dubnoff, S., & Kiesler, S. (1987). *Research plan for studies of electronic interviews in health surveys.* Unpublished manuscript, Carnegie Mellon University.

Turner, C., & Martin, E. (Eds.). (1984). *Surveying subjective phenomena* (two volumes). New York: Russell Sage Foundation and Basic Books.

U.S. Bureau of the Census (1968). 1960 census of population and housing, evaluation and research program (Series ER-60, No. 7). *Effects of interviewers and crew leaders.* Washington, DC: Author.

U.S. Bureau of the Census (1979). 1970 census of population and housing, evaluation and research program (Series PHC(E)-13). *Enumerator variance in the 1970 census.* Washington, DC: U.S. Government Printing Office.

U.S. Bureau of the Census (1971). *Current Population Reports,* P-20, No 217. Washington, DC: Author.

Waller, N. G., & Reise, S. P. (1989). Computerized adaptive personality assessment: An illustration with the absorption scale. *Journal of Personality and Social Psychology, 57,* 1051–1058.

Walsh, J. P., Kiesler, S., Sproull, L. S., & Hesse, B. (in press). Self-selected and randomly-selected respondents in a computer network survey. *Public Opinion Quarterly*. Working paper, Carnegie Mellon University.

Waterton, J. J., & Duffy, J. C. (1984). A comparison of computer interviewing techniques and traditional methods in the collection of self-report alcohol consumption data in a field study. *International Statistical Review, 52*, 173–182.

Whyte, W. F. (1984). *Learning from the field*. Newbury Park, CA: Sage.

13

Communicating Applied Social Psychology to Users

A Challenge and an Art

Emil J. Posavac

Reporting applied social psychology research to people whose lives might be actually changed by our findings is a serious endeavor, not an undertaking for the fainthearted. To do so means stepping into a real-life attitude change experiment in which the "subjects" are professionals in their own right, not introductory psychology students. They can argue with us rather than silently leaving the lab with their extra credit form properly signed. Moreover, the "subjects" in these attitude change experiments often possess more organizational power than the applied social psychologist recommending changes. Few of us were trained for this.

Before recommending that someone act on the basis of our work, we need to ask ourselves if our findings are worth using. However, even when we are sure of the worth of our work, developing insights and recommendations will remain futile exercises unless managers, consumers, practitioners, and leaders pay attention to the work, understand how to use it, and apply it. Unfortunately, the process of communication is anything but straightforward, especially when the social psychologist and the potential research-user audience spend most of their professional lives in quite different settings with vastly different values and accepted modes of communication.

Emil J. Posavac • Department of Psychology, Loyola University of Chicago, Chicago, Illinois 60626.

Methodological Issues in Applied Psychology, edited by Bryant et al. Plenum Press, New York, 1992.

This chapter includes some suggestions for bridging those differences. The chapter is directed to faculty teaching future applied social psychologists and to individuals about to embark on an applied research or policy-related career.

An assumption underlying this chapter is that the communication of findings is an essential phase of the methodology of applied social psychology. As social psychologists have worked with people outside academe, we have learned much about research methods as the previous chapters illustrate. In addition, we have learned better ways of communicating our findings both in regard to the format of our message and the content of what we say. In order to discuss some of those lessons, I first begin by describing two types of applied social psychologists and the roles they fill.

Communication and Applied Social Psychologists

Who Is an Applied Social Psychologist?

There are many possibilities, but for the purposes of this chapter, I will list only two types of applied social psychologists. Some applied social psychologists, called Type I in this chapter, hold academic positions, conduct research on social problems, and comment in journals on how social psychology theory can help us to understand social problems and to alleviate them. Type I social psychologists can be thought of as applied social psychologists; however, they do not take an active role in seeing that their work is applied in field settings. A second type of applied social psychologist, Type II, studies the same sort of problems as the first one, but does so with the intention of helping non-researchers who seek to reduce the effects of social problems or who seek to improve the effectiveness of their organizations. Although some university faculty members direct their research toward this goal, most Type II applied social psychologists work for large organizations, governmental and private. They may work in planning departments, training centers, evaluation or quality assurance programs, or independent consultant firms with job titles such as program analyst, social system analyst, or planner, among others. A major part of their jobs involves showing how social science can be used in applied settings. This chapter will focus on the communication challenges facing Type II applied social psychologists.

It is not easy to communicate social research findings and applications to human service professionals or business managers. Unfortunately, there is little in standard methods books to assist students to learn how to communicate with nonacademic users of social research. Books on writing will assist in the essential task of making prose clear and precise, but even excellent books (e.g., Becker, 1986) are not written to address the need to translate the work of applied social researchers into the language of people whose jobs may be affected by the research. It is essential that we remember that new information may not be recognized as innovative, understood as intended, or even welcomed when offered (Argyris, 1985). Since our communications to nonresearchers need to be planned as persuasive messages if they are to have an effect, reminding ourselves about the literature on attitude change may be helpful at this point.

Attitude Change Processes and the Communication of Applied Social Psychology

If applied social psychologists intend for their research to be used, then it is necessary that our research findings be presented in a manner that will change people's attitudes toward their work or toward the social problem they are trying to alleviate and, consequently, lead to behaviors that are more effective and healthy. Placing applied social psychology research reports in an attitude change framework may sensitize researchers to the necessity of exercising care in developing communication strategies. Concern about changing people would not be important if our goal was simply to carry out the research without an intention that it be used outside of the lab. Most likely, telling clients that we are out to change their attitudes and behaviors during our first contact with them may not be a good idea, but it is crucial that plans for the research and communication include such an intention.

McGuire (1985) has described attitude change by isolating four aspects of communications: the source, the message, the receiver, and the channel. Since most readers are familiar with McGuire's approach, I will only sketch the essentials of these aspects to highlight the need for special concerns in communicating with nonresearchers. As will be clear, these foci of research on attitude change cannot be treated individually; for example, the relationship between the source and the audience will affect the channel and even the message, and the identity of the audience will be a major factor in the channel chosen.

Source. Social psychologists are trained in very different ways than most human service practitioners or business managers. Since a large portion of such people see our concerns and style as pedantic, ivory tower, and seldom relevant to their concerns, we start as rather noncredible sources. As we approach the task of communicating social psychology, we need to remember that we belong to a distinct minority group; few people in business and other organizations talk as we do or think as we do. What is easy to communicate in a faculty or graduate seminar may be next to impossible in a boardroom. This is not a matter of intelligence; lots of very bright people have not studied what we have studied and do not worry about what we worry about as we design our research.

Message. Since the substance of what applied social psychologists seek to communicate is data based and far more complicated than the message used in the typical attitude change experiment, many of the principles studied systematically do not apply. The important lesson that effective applied researchers draw from the literature concerns the often-replicated finding that various ways of phrasing and ordering the message will make a difference in how the audience responds to it.

Audience. Many of the individual difference variables explored in attitude change research cannot help us to communicate the meaning of applied research, since we approach a variety of audiences containing many different people. What is important as we consider the audience is a consideration of how clients will feel about the potential impact of our recommendations on their lives. Since it is hard to imagine a role that we do not play, it might be useful to imagine someone recommending that we make changes in how we carry out our own roles. For example, college faculty members might recall how they reacted to Sykes's (1988) charges in *ProfScam*. Sykes made a number of sensationalistic attacks on college teachers that might be easily dismissed. However, some of his points are being debated seriously by people in the media and state governments as well as within higher education circles. Acceptance of these points would require major changes in the work of many university faculty members: research and publication would be de-emphasized, and undergraduate instruction would be emphasized while raising teaching loads. If university-based applied social psychologists develop recommendations for changes in the work of others, it would be wise to reflect on the reactions faculty members had when they first heard about Sykes's recommended changes for their role. Most university faculty members with whom I talked felt insulted, misunderstood, and angry. We do not want to affect our audiences that way.

Channel. The experiences of applied researchers and the findings of basic research converge on the importance of face-to-face oral presentations as a channel for changing attitudes. McGuire (1985) suggests that compared to written communications, face-to-face presentations have a number of strengths: the audience can be more active (a point to be mentioned again later), common courtesy leads people to pay attention, and the message can be adjusted depending on the reaction of the audience. The research literature is clear on the point that a written report alone cannot lead to the most effective communication in applied settings.

Problems in Communicating with People Who Might Apply Social Psychology

Regardless of the type of communication attempted, communication is a challenge. The following sections contain descriptions of five communication problems. The first three problems are related to assumptions made by university-based scholars that contrast with the views of people outside academe. Graduate students adopting academic-style communication patterns will experience difficulties when they attempt to work in applied settings. The last two communication problems are ones that we all display at one time or another.

Credibility Is Broader than Being Smart and Well Read

Social scientists receive training in a setting in which intelligence and being well informed are highly valued. When scholars communicate with others, we expect to be treated as highly credible sources when we know the appropriate research literature. Being seen as credible by journal editors is not equivalent to being seen as credible by students, by practitioners, or, even, by scholars outside our own disciplines. It is not unknown for a scholar to treat topics in a learned fashion, but yet present recommendations which will not work when practitioners try the principles in the field. As we take up the task of communicating applied social psychology to those outside the circles of journal editors and readers, and outside our classes, we may discover that we need far more knowledge than we have of "life in the trenches." Different organizations, even in the same field, develop cultures of their own (Shein, 1990) with different communication patterns.

Journal Article Style Offers Little Help in Designing Policy or in Developing Interventions

The communication style described in APA's *Publication Manual* would be expected of Type I applied social psychologists, that is, those whose interests in applications do not go beyond the Discussion sections of their papers. They will find this chapter largely irrelevant to their personal writing. However, if they teach students who intend to become Type II applied social psychologists, then the points raised and strategies suggested may be of help. Those readers who plan to work in applied settings, those who plan to communicate with people who worry more about threats to program funding than threats to internal validity or whose livelihood depends on producing products that consumers will buy should find the issues addressed to be of interest as they prepare their presentations.

Differences between journal style and a style appropriate to applied settings are significant and extensive. In addition, the nature of the audiences is quite different. Journal writers hope that some readers will be affected by their work, but there is no necessity for any particular person or group to find the material compelling. Those psychologists working in an applied setting, however, must be concerned that specific people in a particular organization will take the findings seriously, and apply them appropriately.

Psychology graduate students are seldom trained to communicate research to anyone other than similarly trained psychologists; that is a problem for those who intend to apply psychological research outside of colleges and universities. Journal style doesn't communicate with nursing managers, production engineers, or directors of training. Nonacademic readers expect less documentation of where ideas came from but more help to apply the ideas to the client's setting. Offerman and Growing (1990) describe an industrial psychologist who asks job applicants to explain their dissertations in 5 minutes to a lay audience. Those who can are more likely to do well in communicating with business audiences.

In addition to problems with how we present our information, journal articles often emphasize aspects of research that are not helpful for practitioners while providing minimal coverage of material that is essential to the person looking for ways to apply the work. Reading research reports for the purpose of learning whether a theory has been supported differs markedly from reading with a view to applying the ideas presented. Normally, we emphasize the theory, the quality of the research design, and measurement issues related to the dependent variable. If those points satisfy us, then we feel we can trust the data regardless of what the independent variable is.

Applied readers want to be assured that the research design and analyses were sound, but their primary interest centers on the independent variable. They want to know what was done to get the positive consumer reaction, the high level of patient compliance with medical care, or the enthusiastic employee reaction to a reorganized work environment. Unfortunately, few journal articles contain the kind of information that would permit one to make practical use of the ideas because so little space is devoted to the independent variable. This seems to be a common practice in psychology (see "The Trouble with Dependent Variables," 1990); however, the independent variable represents a prototype of an intervention, a teaching technique, or a policy that people might try to apply.

An article on cognitive understanding of pain (Bandura, O'Leary, Taylor, Gauthier, & Gossard, 1987) illustrates this point. While teaching a course on health and social psychology, I searched for journal articles containing ideas that could be turned into social psychologically based interventions applicable in medical care settings. Bandura's exploration into the effect of different cognitive interpretations of pain on the level of pain reported and the length of time the pain could be endured seemed quite appropriate for my course. Although I am not a medical professional and was not really going to apply this work, I read the article differently from the way I would have as a social psychologist because I wanted to use the findings as the basis for an illustrative patient training program that nurses might teach patients to apply. When I read it in that way, it became clear that our standard manner of describing research does not provide sufficient information to enable one to plan interventions as I was trying to do for my class presentation. This article is not an exception. A reason why so little basic psychological research is used by clinical psychologists (see Cohen, Sargent, & Sechrest, 1986; Kanfer, 1990; Morrow-Bradley & Elliott, 1986) may be that they cannot develop innovative interventions on the basis of information in journal articles.

Finally, the writer of a journal article cares relatively little about helping the non-research-trained reader to understand the material; those who want to read it must maintain their own motivation. Since the expected audience consists of a small group of people studying the same or similar research topics, journal writers do not need to worry much about the readers' emotional reactions. Most authors care little if people not conducting research in the same area read the work. In marked contrast, people working in a market research firm, for example, will soon be looking for different jobs if their reporting practices so disappoint their clients that applied research is misunderstood, consistently ignored, or rejected.

Standard Descriptions of Statistical Findings Are Misunderstood

When research-trained people try to communicate, one discovers that standard, widely accepted terms simply give a different impression than is intended. Table 1 summarizes some of the problems that have appeared in the literature or that I have discovered while attempting to share research with nonacademic groups. Some of these points escape a few academic psychologists as well (e.g., Sedlmeier & Gigerenzer, 1989). For example, many psychologists do not understand that a t could be statistically significant even though the raw scores of the two groups overlap to a considerable degree (Posavac & Sinacore, 1984). When Lipsey (1990) reviewed 186 meta-analyses, he learned that the mean posttreatment difference between treatment and control groups was .45 standard deviation units. This means that 67% of the treated people were better off after treatment than the typical untreated person. An effect size of .45 also means that one-third of the treated group was *less* well off than the typical untreated person. With

**Table 1. Misinterpretations of Standard Reporting Terminology
of Statistical Analyses**

Standard reporting practice	Communication problem observed
Using a numerical mean from a scale	A client question was: "Is 5.5 out of 7 good or bad?
Using a numerical mean	Information users forget that the actual values are not all essentially equal to the mean; variance is a hard concept.
Reporting two group means	Clients vastly underestimate the overlap in the scores from two groups.
Reporting the amount of overlap between experimental and control groups, or any two groups	Since most clients don't understand variance, they overestimate the degree that their services will lead people to change.
Reporting statistical significance	Information users confuse significant with meaningful or important findings.
Noting that a comparison is not statistical significant	Many clients think that a nonsignificant finding means that there are no differences between groups.

moderate-sized samples, an effect size of .45 standard deviation units is statistically reliable.

An effect size of .45 translates into 4.8% of the variance. Some psychologists have been disappointed after converting the effect of interventions into percentage of variance accounted for (e.g., Rimland, 1979). Such an effect is actually quite large relative to the impact of interventions when carried out very competently (Light & Pillemer, 1984; Lipsey, 1990; Rosenthal, 1990). There are many influences on behavior; any given influence will not be large. It is important to note that 4.8% of the variance is the same as saying that the means of two groups differ by almost one half a standard deviation. Differences between racial or ethnic groups this large in achievement, rate of unemployment, or income would have enormous social implications. Likewise two advertising campaigns whose effects differed by one half of a standard deviation on an important variable such as brand recognition or sales would be seen as decidedly different.

Expect Audiences to Be Defensive

Since our applied research could have an important impact on the audience's personal or work life, people fear the worst when they receive information or recommendations from applied social psychologists. The defensiveness appears reactions is a pressure to mold the research reports in ways that researchers find neither valid nor ethical. Some audiences of program evaluations and policy analyses intensely examine the reports for hints about how the recommended changes would affect their employment security, benefits, quality of life, or professional recognition. Organization development research frequently has an impact on established work practices and status hierarchies. The findings of market analyses may not support the hunches of some influential people in the client's organization. Even if a service deliverer or organization executive commissioned the research, one cannot assume that people will accept research that differs from cherished preconceptions.

Some Want to Dictate the Report

Most experienced applied researchers have discovered that some sponsors of their work know just what they wanted the researcher to conclude regardless of what the data actually said. I carried out a project for a person who managed a small firm which set up workshops for children and parents regarding drug abuse. He wanted an evaluation that showed that his workshops had a high benefit/cost ratio. He kept talking about how professor so-and-so from a well-known university had carried out a cost–benefit study for him and concluded that the benefits of the workshops exceeded the costs. I could not imagine how anyone could do a cost–benefit analysis on a workshop consisting of four 90-minute sessions with whatever junior high students and their parents showed up. The "cost–benefit study" turned out to have been based on the self-reported changes in drug use that the students listed after the workshop series ended. Clearly, demand characteristics could account for these changes. Nevertheless, on the basis of these reported changes, the author projected the amount of future drug abuse that would not occur due to the workshop series. The report author and workshop developer expected the state funding agency and school district administrators to read only the conclusions of the report, not to examine the basis for the conclusions. My client wanted to be sure the administrators of the state funds believed that he did effective work; he was not interested in learning anything from the research.

Applied social psychologists with even a minimal level of personal security avoid writing reports that fit the demands of a sponsor and most surely avoid carrying out a second study for people who want to dictate the results before any data are gathered.

Some Want a Report to Hide behind

Since managers are expected to be rational, there are many times when a piece of applied research is commissioned simply to provide a rational facade for delay, for a decision already made, or for support of standard procedures (Mc-Clintock, 1984). One hospital administrator was sent an initial draft of an applied social research project and was asked for comments. The researcher had worked hard at writing a succinct report with clear recommendations. The administrator's comments did not deal with the substance of the report but could be summed up in one question that he asked the author—"Where's the bull[. . . .]?" What he appeared to want was a lengthy, jargon-packed report that no one would read with understanding but which he could waive during a Board of Trustees meeting to show how seriously he takes his work. Peck and Rubin (1983) found a similar theme in a review of the role of program evaluation in a federal agency. They concluded that a bulky, but attractively packaged, report was very important. If one suspects that the project sponsor simply wants an impressive-looking final product, the social researcher will probably want to consider the ethical ramifications of carrying out the project. Accepting the assignment may require extra effort at educating the administrator, which some argue is a central role for the applied social psychologist (see Cronbach, 1980). If, on the other hand, one discovers that the project sponsor actually is interested in an applied social psychological perspective that can improve the effectiveness of the organization, one should treasure the experience. Of course, there is nothing wrong with presenting a report in an attractive format; in fact, the report should be attractive and accessible. The point is: ethical applied social psychologists do not perform research to obscure the motives of a sponsor.

Two Frequently Observed Cognitive Biases Leading to Misinterpretations

Beyond problems created by an academic communication style and beyond the difficulty of a defensive client, there are cognitive biases that will confuse communication. One bias is the tendency for people to see what they expect to see. Such a distortion can negate our efforts even when we have carefully avoided jargon and have an open and curious audience. Ornstein (1972) comments that "seeing is believing" is probably less true than the reverse, "believing is seeing." Applied social psychologists are not surprised when a client doesn't see what we see in our data, especially when the data conflict with the client's expectations. Assuming that we are dealing with people who want to know, unlike my workshop-designer client, it is quite possible that expectations will so color the reception of the message that the message will be misunderstood to fit into preconceptions. People seem to add to the message or to overlook those aspects of the message that do not fit. There is a long history of research on this topic in social (e.g., Allport, 1958) and clinical psychology (e.g., Kayne & Alloy, 1988;

Lockard & Paulhus, 1988). But even eminent scientists are susceptible, as Gould (1989) has illustrated in his review of research on some of the very earliest forms of animal life.

The reverse of the bias just discussed has also created a problem when communicating applied social research. Sometimes people hear a report of a social science finding and, without a conscious decision, incorporate the findings into their beliefs concluding that they "knew it all the time." Fischoff (1980) called this a "hindsight" bias. Controlled experimental research (Wood, 1978) shows that subjects sincerely believe that the incorporated material was already known. Unless something is done to call people's attention to what they really did believe *before* seeing the new information, assimilation can be automatic. Hawkins and Hastie (1990) point out that hindsight bias hampers adaptive learning. It is important that readers recognize that hindsight bias has been observed not only among research subjects and clients, but also among professionals. Even applied social psychologists might be affected.

Hindsight bias—incorporating new information into one's existing belief structure—has a convenient implication. If one did "know it all the time" one could reasonably believe that the information has already played a part in determining how one manages an office, serves clients, or teaches students. Thus, even though the potential user of the findings seems to accept the research and its conclusions, the user fails to recognize that the material provides suggestions about how changing one's practices could improve professional effectiveness.

Thus far, the importance of carefully crafting a report has been discussed and common barriers to interpreting applied social psychology research have been illustrated. The chapter now moves on to suggesting approaches to improved communication.

Improving the Chances of Being Listened to and Understood

Traditional training in social psychological research methods focuses on internal and construct validity rather than methods of communication. The communication of findings cannot be an afterthought; successful communication depends as much on careful planning as does the development of a valid research design. A social psychologist needs to worry about being a credible source communicating an understandable message. The channels carrying the communication will be adapted to the style of the audience, not the convenience of the researcher. In addition, we do better work when we think through the forces influencing the audience rather than assuming the potential users of the research will be motivated by purely scientific goals. Last, the researcher does better when the audience becomes actively involved rather than passively observing.

Begin with a Communication Plan

Brinkerhoff, Brethower, Hluckyji, and Nowakowski (1983) describe a "report plan" as one of the essential steps in planning a program evaluation or policy analysis. They say that along with all the issues we work with in the standard research design and policy evaluation courses, it is crucial to plan explicitly the schedule of reporting, the selection of the audiences to receive reports, and the topics to be covered in each report.

The first step in developing a plan for communication requires one to *identify the important group* who might have an interest in the work. Writers in program evaluation (e.g., Posavac & Carey, 1989) have come to call these people or groups *stakeholders*. The stakeholders involved will vary depending on the nature of the organization which might apply the findings. For example, in a market research firm the key stakeholders would be the client organization, the research team, the administrator responsible for the team, and other groups within the firm whose work will be affected by the findings of the research team. When research is done for a community agency, the stakeholders might include the research team, the staff of the agency that might adopt recommendations, the director of the staff, the people served by the agency, those responsible for funding, members of the community, and planning agencies in the area. Usually, panels of representatives of such large groups are involved, not every member.

Listing the specific content of the material that is to be communicated to each group is the second step in creating a communication plan. The lists will differ because different groups have different concerns. A client of a market research firm does not want to know anything about the data-gathering problems that the research staff must be aware of. Representatives of the community will not be able to understand the fine points of research design.

The *format, timing, and setting for the communication* would be chosen next. Much more will be said later about the format of communication; at this point, I want to stress that the communication of material can be done in memos, oral one-on-one briefings, public presentations, formal written reports, informal written reports such an illustrated brochure, or video programs among other modes of communication. Since many projects take quite a long time to complete, progress reports may be part of the plan. A schedule of reporting, unlike many academic projects, needs to be coordinated with crucial events in the organization such as the budget cycle or regular times of staff changes dependent on elections, the academic year, fiscal years, and so forth.

Table 2 was adapted from Brinkerhoff et al. (1983) to illustrate a communication plan for a project that might assist a college office employing undergraduates who provide tutoring to students. The communication process does not begin when one sits down to write the report; it begins at the very start of the project planning process. Note that the plan is based on the academic calendar to

Table 2. Illustrative Communication Plan for a Consultation Project with an Arts and Sciences College-Based Program for Underprepared Students

Key group	What they need to know	Format of the communication	Schedule	Setting
Research team	Progress to date; next step of project	Memos; research team meetings	Once a month	Team meetings
	Problems in carrying out research	Special meetings	As needed	Team and one-on-one meetings
Director of tutors	Progress updates	Oral presentations with one-page memos for the official record	Once a month	Meetings of director and lead researcher
	Final Report of recommendations	Oral presentation and written Final Report	March 15	Meeting
Advisory group of student tutors	Information to be gathered and tentative recommendations	Oral presentation and discussions	Every two weeks during planning and recommendation development	Group meetings
Advisory group of tutored students	Tentative recommendations	Oral presentations and discussions	Once or twice during development of the recommendations	Group meetings
Dean of the college	Progress updates	Copies of one-page memos sent to the Director	Once a month	Interoffice mail
	Final Report of recommendations	Oral presentation with the Director and written Final Report	April 2	Meeting

decide when to present information. Also note that the researchers believed that their work would be better if they received feedback on both the design of the research and the tentative recommendations from the current tutors. Also, note that before finalizing the recommendations, they tested out their recommendations with representatives of the people who received tutoring from the center.

In a rather similar vein, Majchrzak (1984) argues that policy researchers need to communicate "throughout the study" and to communicate with "different study users." She emphasizes that timing is critical when one works with legislators. As a matter of fact, many applied researchers must work on schedules that are set by others. There will be a time during which a study's findings may be useful; later, the study will be useless because a budget deadline has passed, legislators have already acted, or interest in the topic has waned. Majchrzak describes a study that had not been completed but which seemed relevant to a policy under consideration in Congress. Those conducting the research decided to present their incomplete results. Majchrzak believes that the researchers made the right decision; unfortunately, the incomplete study could not withstand criticisms and its findings were dismissed. If the researchers had waited, they would have had a better study to report, but it would have then been too late to have influenced the debate.

Work in a Way to Increase Credibility

The communication plan in Table 2 was based on some of the strategies that applied researchers can use to increase their credibility with potential users. It is essential (1) that those who are going to be affected view the communicator as a person or team that knows what their needs are and (2) that the researcher has taken care to tailor recommendations to the actual setting (see Argyris, 1985). Zaltman and Moreman (1988) describe the importance of personal trust between clients and researchers in advertising. One way to increase trust is to work as a team with those likely to be affected. Clients will have intimate knowledge of the setting and the people who work or receive services there. No matter how well intentioned the researchers are, they are outsiders with respect to the actual service delivery or the mission of the organization. Observations and data collection instruments will provide a great deal of information, but the people working in or receiving service from an organization can see issues and implications that external researchers will easily miss. Thus, getting feedback on the project and draft recommendations could assist the researchers in proposing effective ideas. It would be politically and practically wise to be sure that clients know that draft recommendations are going to be discussed with them before final recommendations are formed. It may be that some recommendations, if adopted, would have ramifications of which the researchers are unaware.

Although the suggestion of taking research conclusions to the possible users is quite different from the typical mode of reporting basic research, some writers argue for a more collaborative relationship between researcher and subject even in basic research. Methodologists who criticize positivism and support a more qualitative, understanding-based approach to studying behavior would not find it at all radical to suggest that applied researchers encourage participation in forming research designs and drawing conclusions (e.g., Lincoln & Guba, 1985; Patton, 1978, Polkinghorne, 1983). To reiterate, such feedback is sought to aid in fitting the research to the setting as well as possible; careful researchers will resist the intrusion of self-serving biases from all parties.

Present an Understandable Message

Successful communicators tailor their messages to the audience and present material in such a way that the audience is most likely to understand it. Applicants to the Program Evaluation and Methodology Division of the U.S. General Accounting Office (GAO) are asked to write a one-page essay describing their skills in presenting technical information in ways that are "meaningful to those in policy-making." There are some basic points that need to be addressed that are independent of the substance of the actual messages and how they are phrased. The sequence in which the following points are discussed does not imply a temporal order.

Be Clear on Why Applied Social Psychology Input Was Sought

The substantive contributions that applied social psychologists might make to an organization include the following activities: developing ideas for new programs or activities that have been useful elsewhere; supporting the work of a planning committee; redirecting the focus of an activity of the organization; developing a social psychological, conceptual basis for policy development; improving the operation of the organization; verifying that certain activities occurred or services were provided; and deciding that an activity is no longer needed or is ineffective. Projects designed for one of these purposes will differ markedly from projects serving a different one. Kennedy (1983) found that various boards of education expected quite different services from program evaluators. For example, some school boards wanted an evaluator to provide feedback to individual teachers seeking to improve their remedial tutoring, while others expected input on whether an after-school tutoring program was really needed. Of course, one can attempt to expand the client's view of the value of applied research. But it is important to begin knowing what is expected.

Be Clear on Why a Recommendation Might Work

A second general issue related to producing an understandable message involves working through the process or mechanism whereby the recommendations are believed to lead to the desired improved level of effectiveness. Backing up recommendations with a flow chart showing the processes through which the suggested actions lead to improved results is a way to do this.

A particularly instructive example of the presentation of hypothesized mechanisms to support a recommendation was developed by Cook and Devine (1982). A nontechnical approach to reducing the complications after surgery consists of helping patients to avoid lung congestion by breathing deeply, coughing, stretching and contracting one's legs, and turning from side to back and then to the other side. Since patients do not know that breathing deeply affects their recovery and since moving after surgery is painful, patients seldom do these things without encouragement or even nagging from nurses. A review of the literature using a novel approach to meta-analysis strongly suggested that this set of behaviors would help, but it is not obvious why. In making their recommendation that nurses be given the time to work with patients, Cook and Devine presented seven mechanisms to explain the connection between what they called the "stir-up regimen" and lowered levels of pain, reduced number of complications, and reduced number of days of hospitalization after surgery. Figure 1 is adapted from their presentation of their first Control Model and their Physiologic Model. The flow chart shows several ways in which physical movement is related to biochemical and behavioral variables and progress in recovery. Cook and Devine included additional flow charts by which they showed how the regimen reduced lung congestion and how that reduced complications. The presentation of the detailed models of the mechanisms makes it possible to discuss what is essential in implementing the intervention and to identify the intermediate variables to track if one wants to conduct an evaluation of the intervention after incorporating it into postsurgery care.

Assuming that the communicator has been clear on the purpose of doing the project and that the message has been refined to the point that its substance will make sense to the intended audience, let us turn to some specific aspects of producing an understandable message.

Make Communications Specific and Concrete

A concrete message is more likely to be understood than an abstract message given in theoretical terminology supported by tests of statistical significance. This point is not to imply that in order to communicate effectively one must put aside the quantitative tools that are so necessary in our work. The researcher uses all the quantitative tools that help in the analysis of the observa-

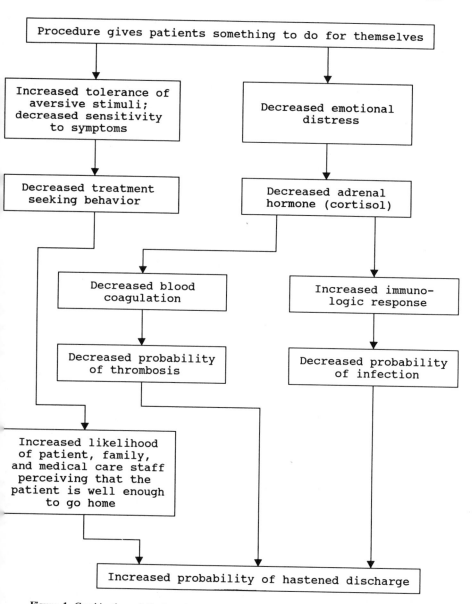

Figure 1. Combination of Cook and Devine's Control Model I and Physiologic Model used to explain how the "stir-up" psychoeducational intervention helps postsurgery patients to get better sooner. Adapted from Cook & Devine, 1982.

tions, but does not depend on the stakeholders to learn the language of statistics in order to interpret the message. As mentioned earlier, the basic research writer assumes that the burden for assimilation falls on the reader; in contrast, the applied researcher must assume as much of the burden as possible. Green (1988) suggests that brief scenarios illustrating action plans accompany each recommendation. Such scenarios would include the timing of changes, implementation steps, estimated resources needed, expected outcomes of the changes, possible negative side effects, and so forth. Rook (1987) showed that health information presented as a case history was more effective than the equivalent information presented in an abstract form in leading patients to change their attitudes and behavioral intentions.

Assuming the burden of making the communication concrete and understandable would be especially important when the audience would rather not hear the message or would find it hard to believe. For instance, Patton (1980) found that the best way to convince a school board to consider abandoning a badly flawed teacher appraisal system was not to depend on statistical analyses summarizing teacher attitudes, but to present all the written responses to two open-ended questions. It was easy for the school board to dismiss the abstract, statistical summary because such information is not closely tied to specific people and situations. Once the school board examined loose-leaf notebooks containing all the word-for-word teacher responses, they could visualize the problems with their performance appraisal system.

Although providing undigested written answers if often not appropriate, in the context of Patton's consultation it became clear that the most important message to communicate was the overall level of dissatisfaction, not the precise emphases or trends in the written comments. Type II applied social psychologists will, like Patton, be flexible in structuring their communication, not insisting on some standard mode of communication but fitting the message to the specific situation encountered. Perhaps it should go without saying that one must guard against selecting comments simply to fit client or researcher expectations; illustrative verbatim comments usually supplement, not replace, statistical analyses.

Use Multiple Channels

Basic research is largely communicated through written articles. One might be tempted to use this same channel for applied research. Since the applied researcher is often working in a specific setting, producing material that can be read elsewhere is seldom important. Applied researchers have used a variety of channels including oral briefings, short memos, press releases, chart summaries, even a cartoon summary (Kelly, 1961), as well as a formal written report.

It is likely that nearly all projects will be described in a formal *written report* since it is often necessary to document that a project was carried out. A major difference between a journal article and a report of an applied research project is the inclusion of an executive summary that can stand alone. A summary is longer than an abstract and, unlike an abstract, actually contains findings and recommendations. Posavac and Carey (1989) have discussed what to include in a written program evaluation. However, a written report cannot be depended upon to carry the full burden of communicating the findings and recommendations of applied research.

Applied researchers expect to be asked to give an *oral report* to the major stakeholders interested in the project; if not asked, the researcher may want to propose giving an oral report. The importance of the oral report probably goes beyond simple communication of information. In spite of our technological progress, personal contact remains important, even essential, in communicating applied research. The researcher should be prepared to present material concisely and clearly and answer whatever questions are posed. As mentioned above, the person-to-person setting helps the client to focus on the substance of the report and permits the researcher to match the presentation to the client's needs for explanation.

Frequently, *handouts or other visual aids* accompany oral briefings. Haensly, Lupkowski, and McNamara (1987) describe the use of self-contained charts as part of the briefing process. Each chart contains one major point with supporting data. Figure 2 contains a chart that could have been used in a briefing regarding a recommendation that might be part of the planning of a local community mental health center. The chart poses the research question raised and gives the recommendation and the essence of the data that prompted that recommendation. Note that the chart is easy to read and contains a lot of white space; the goal is to make communication easy, not to cram as much as possible onto the page as one might if it were to be published in a journal. The charts could be presented on transparencies to use with an overhead projector; the use of transparencies helps to keep the attention of the audience on the presentation.

Hint on Reporting Statistics: Keep It Simple

After carrying out a complicated and, perhaps, insightful statistical analysis, most researchers would like to describe it to potential users of the work. Researchers usually feel that readers should be permitted to evaluate the analysis for themselves. Except for baseball fans, only researchers learn very much by examining column after column of numbers. Few policymakers and practitioners want to look at many numbers, and even fewer are able to draw appropriate conclusions from them. This section suggests a few practices that, if followed,

Project Question 6. Given their problems, are adolescent boys under-served by the Community Mental Health Center?

Rationale: The Center's mission is to provide needed service to all sectors of the community; however, few adolescent boys are served compared to girls.

Core Observations:

o School District 58 reports that the drop-out rate for boys is triple that for girls.

o There are relatively few part-time employment opportunities for boys; 39% of those with part-time jobs travel outside the catchment area to work.

o 45% of catchment families include only one parent (usually the mother) according to the 1990 census.

o Compared to two years ago, police report a 52% increase in calls related to school activities (for example, fights in school parking lots or at games, suspected drug use during school).

o The "Today's Women" Program for adolescent girls staffed by community mothers and directed by the CMHC has been well-received.

Recommendation: Form after-school and weekend sports leagues and develop a tutoring service sponsored by local businesses with male leaders and directed by the CMHC.

Figure 2. An illustrative chart that might be used as a handout at an oral briefing.

will keep descriptions of statistical analyses from overwhelming our readers and listeners.

No Equations. Stephen Hawking reports that as he was writing *A Brief History of Time,* his editor told him that each equation he included would cut the sales of the book by 50%. Verdier (1984), writing to economists who prepare materials for congressional staffs, simplified the same caution into these words: ". . . [N]ever use an equation." Although regression analyzes with dummy variables, transformed variables, and interaction terms provide insight into a multivariate and nonlinear world, Type II applied social psychologists translate those insights into the language of the listeners and readers who hope to understand the report. Verdier points out that policymakers have to justify their actions to others: since they cannot understand the equations themselves, they certainly cannot use the equations when talking with their constituents.

Select a Few Striking Numbers. A few dramatic numbers can be helpful in the oral presentation or the main body of the written report. Verdier (1984) reports that in the late 1960s a major tax reform proposal received considerable impetus when a study revealed that 155 taxpayers with incomes over $200,000, including 21 with incomes over $1 million, paid no income taxes.

The dramatic numbers chosen could be percentages since most educated professionals can understand them. Complicated analyses can sometimes be simplified in creative ways to form percentages that validly represent trends, but are still easily understood. Figure 2 illustrates the type of percentages that could be used in many settings. The details of how the data were gathered and the complete tables can be placed in appendices. My experience suggests that duplicating the tables on paper that is a different color from that of the pages of the text itself will help to keep the report from appearing oppressively long.

Use a Metric Familiar to the Readers. The way that quantitative findings are coded can make a big difference in how easily they are understood (Cook, Leviton, & Shadish, 1985). Telling a school board that the improvement in reading due to introduction of a new curriculum will be approximately 15 points will fail to interest them since 15 points means different things depending on the test used. Changing the message to an 8% improvement may also not help. But saying that similar school districts adopting the curriculum found an improvement in achievement equal to one-half a grade level will be understood. This is a metric that school boards can understand.

Use Graphical Aids Whenever Possible. As personal computers have grown in power and as programs have become more flexible and friendly, graphs are increasingly easy to produce. Instead of needing a draftsperson, one can produce graphs in minutes, even color graphs with somewhat more expensive equipment. Some valuable guides to the construction of graphs have recently been published (e.g., Cleveland, 1985; Tufte, 1983).

It's best to keep graphs as simple as possible. However, even the most beautifully constructed, straightforward graph does not excuse the researcher from explaining the finding in words. Never say or write "as you see in figure X" and depend on the reader to "see." As one of my graduate instructors insisted, you must take the reader "by the hand" and go through the graph or else the reader will not see.

Involve the Audience in the Presentation

Teachers know that students who are more successful at learning, remembering, and using classroom material are more likely to be those who participate actively in classes rather than those who passively observe the instructor lecturing or demonstrating a principle. In the same way, it is crucial that audiences for applied research findings be active participants in the communication. When applied research is presented for planning or evaluation purposes, the audience may be more attentive than most college students because the client's work life could be affected. Unfortunately, this attention might be devoted to unproductive ends, disputing the material, incorporating their expectations into the results, or incorporating the results into their expectations. To counteract these tendencies it is important to get the audiences to recognize what their expectations are and to contrast the expectations with the results so that the audience will see what the new information is. In this way, they have a better chance to see that the research does have implications that go beyond what they already knew. It is no surprise that one needs to be tactful about how this is carried out. Adult education specialists know that most adults hate to be wrong in public, especially so in work settings.

In feedback sessions, one organizational consultant gives managers copies of the surveys that employees filled out and graphs without data. Individually and privately, the managers fill out their graphs the way that they think the employees in their own areas answered. Although one cannot expect the managers to estimate correctly the absolute level of the responses, managers in touch with their employees might be expected to know the relative strengths and weaknesses of their work units. By having the managers work with the variables, the consultant leads them to pay close attention to the material being presented. Only after filling out the graph with their expectations do the managers receive the actual graphs summarizing the reactions of their employees. Since the contrast between their expectations and the findings are right in front of them and since they have been paying attention to the variables, it is (1) harder for them to conclude that "we knew it all the time" and (2) less likely that they will overlook some of the findings and, thus, maintain misunderstandings.[1] Techniques such as this one cannot guarantee successful communication, but ignoring these well-documented cognitive biases only increases the probability of failed communication.

Keep Recommendations within the Psychological Reach of the Client

In trying to increase the effectiveness of an organization, improvement, not perfection, directs the recommendations for change. An old term in the attitude change literature was "latitude of acceptance" (Sherif & Hovland, 1961). It referred to a region on an attitude dimension that could be considered by the subject. An attitude statement that was too extreme to be considered would not have a meaningful impact on the individual's attitude. The applied researcher, thus, is most effective in helping an organization change or in getting a policy adopted if the position does not require a degree of change that would be rejected without serious consideration. Organizational consultants can find some things that are working well even in most ineffective organizations; these positive findings are applauded. This recognition shows the members of the organization that the consultant has listened to them and has not simply adopted a hostile approach. Then, while avoiding the recommendation of unrealistic goals, the Type II applied social psychologist can seek to assist them to improve some aspects of the organization. A troubled organization may tempt a consultant to list all the ways in which it can be improved. Such a list might show how hard the consultant worked and how much he or she knows, but listing all the problems and potential changes will demoralize the people in the organization. The consultant remembers: Improvement, not perfection.

Conversely, some areas needing improvement can be found in even the most effective organization. Although a very effective organization may well be more successful than many other similar organizations, the social consultant will provide clues for further improvement. One consultant asked rhetorically: "If I don't suggest something for even the best organization, why should they pay me?" To think of this another way: the applied researcher is not giving a final grade to an organization, but seeks to help all client organizations to improve whether an organization currently performs at the F or the B+ level.

---

[1] This procedure was developed by Raymond G. Carey of Parkside Associates, Park Ridge, Illinois. Dr. Carey reports that after the procedure was implemented, managers stopped denying that survey results provided new information.

Remember the Limitations of and the Pressures on the Audience

If we want to influence those who get our reports, we need to be aware of the limitations on their freedom to follow good recommendations. It is probably true, for example, that most college administrators would find that their students could use more tutoring than is provided. Thus, a recommendation to increase the budget of a tutoring center could probably be supported as being a good thing. However, a college dean may not have enough funds to support more than a token expansion of tutoring. An applied researcher whose recommendation is simply "expand tutoring" will not have helped the clients even if that recommendation is based on validly estimated needs and would help students. The researcher might have served better if the recommendations included specific suggestions for using the current resources more effectively, or for obtaining more resources. In this case the researcher goes beyond simply gathering data and making a recommendation about resolving problems, by taking the additional step to begin an intervention which could have a major influence on the site.

Social psychologists wanting to move from Type I to Type II interactions with potential users of applied social psychology can improve the effectiveness of the communication of their work. This is not to say that effective communication is easy or that perfection is near at hand. If this chapter helps Type II applied social psychologists to work more effectively with members of community organizations or with people in business firms, I will be pleased; perfection is an elusive quarry.

ACKNOWLEDGMENTS. The author thanks R. Scott Tindale, Raymond G. Carey, and several anonymous reviewers for valuable comments to earlier drafts of this chapter.

References

Allport, G. (1958). *The nature of prejudice*. Garden City, NY: Doubleday Anchor.
American Psychological Association. (1983). *Publication manual of the American Psychological Association* (3rd ed.). Washington, DC: Author.
Argyris, C. (1985). *Strategy, change and defensive routines*. Boston: Pitman.
Bandura, A., O'Leary, A., Taylor, C. B., Gauthier, J., & Gossard, D. (1987). Perceived self-efficacy and pain control: Opioid and nonopioid mechanisms. *Journal of Personality and Social Psychology, 53*, 563–571.
Becker, H. S. (1986). *Writing for social scientists*. Chicago: University of Chicago Press.
Brinkerhoff, R. O., Brethower, D. M., Hluckyji, T., & Nowakowski, J. R. (1983). *Design manual: A practitioner's guide for trainers and educators*. Boston: Kluwer-Nijhoff.

Cleveland, W. S. (1985). *The elements of graphing data.* Monterey, CA: Wadsworth.

Cohen, L. H., Sargent, M. M., & Sechrest, L. B. (1986). Use of psychotherapy research by professional psychologists. *American Psychologist, 41,* 198–206.

Cook, T. D., & Devine, E. C. (1982, March). *Trying to discover explanatory processes through meta-analysis.* Paper presented at the National Meeting of the American Educational Research Association, New York.

Cook, T. D., Leviton, L. C., & Shadish, W. R. (1985). Program evaluation. In G. Lindzey & E. Aronson (Eds.), *Handbook of social psychology* (Vol. 2, 3rd ed., pp. 699–777). New York: Random House.

Cronbach, L. J. (1980). *Toward reform in program evaluation.* San Francisco: Jossey-Bass.

Fischoff, B. (1980). For those condemned to study the past: Reflections on historical judgment. In R. A. Shweder & D. W. Fiske (Eds.), *New directions for methodology of behavioral science: Fallible judgment in behavior research.* San Francisco: Jossey-Bass.

Gould, S. J. (1989). *Wonderful life.* New York: Norton.

Green, J. C. (1988). Communication of results and utilization in participatory program evaluation. *Evaluation and Program Planning, 11,* 341–351.

Haensly, P. A., Lupkowski, A. E., & McNamara, J. F. (1987). The Chart Essay: A strategy for communicating research findings to policymakers and practitioners. *Educational Evaluation and Policy Analysis, 9,* 63–75.

Hawking, S. W. (1988). *A brief history of time: From the big bang to black holes.* New York: Bantam.

Hawkins, S. A., & Hastie, R. (1990). Hindsight; Biased judgments of past events after outcomes are known. *Psychological Bulletin, 107,* 311–327.

Kanfer, F. H. (1990). The scientist–practitioner connection: A bridge in need of constant attention. *Professional Psychology: Research and Practice, 21,* 264–270.

Kayne, N. T., & Alloy, L. B. (1988). Clinician and patient as aberrant actuaries: Expectation-based distortions in assessment of covariation. In L. Y. Abramson (Ed.), *Social cognition and clinical psychology: A synthesis* (pp. 295–365). New York: Guilford Press.

Kelly, W. (1961). *Pogo primer for parents (TV division).* Washington, DC: U.S. Department of Health, Education, and Welfare.

Kennedy, M. K. (1983). The role of the in-house evaluator. *Evaluation Review, 7,* 519–541.

Light, R. J., & Pillemer, D. B. (1984). *Summing up: The science of reviewing research.* Cambridge, MA: Harvard University Press.

Lincoln, Y. S., & Guba, E. G. (1985). *Naturalistic inquiry.* Beverly Hills, CA: Sage.

Lipsey, M. W. (1990). *Design sensitivity: Statistical power in experimental research.* Newbury Park, CA: Sage.

Lockard, J. S., & Paulhus, D. L. (1988). *Self-deception: An adaptive mechanism?* Englewood Cliffs, NJ: Prentice Hall.

Majchrzak, A. (1984). *Methods for policy research.* Beverly Hills, CA: Sage.

McClintock, C. (1984). Toward a theory of formative program evaluation. In D. Deshler (Ed.), *Evaluation for program improvement* (pp. 77–95). New Directions for Continuing Education, no. 24. San Francisco: Jossey-Bass.

McGuire, W. (1985). Attitudes and attitude change. In G. Lindzey & E. Aronson (Eds.), *Handbook of social psychology* (Vol. 2, 3rd ed., pp. 233–346). New York: Random House.

Morrow-Bradley, C., & Elliott, R. (1986). Utilization of psychotherapy research by practicing psychotherapists. *American Psychologist, 41,* 188–197.

Offerman, L. R., and Growing, M. K. (1990). Organizations of the future: Changes and challenges. *American Psychologist 45,* 95–108.

Ornstein, R. (1972). *The psychology of consciousness.* New York: Penguin Books.

Patton, M. Q. (1980). *Qualitative evaluation.* Beverly Hills, CA: Sage.

Peck, D. L., & Rubin, H. J. (1983). Bureaucratic needs and evaluation research: A case study of the Department of Housing and Urban Development. *Evaluation Review, 7,* 685–703.

Polkinghorne, D. (1983). *Methodology for the human sciences: Systems of inquiry.* Albany, NY: SUNY Press.

Posavac, E. J., & Carey, R. G. (1989). *Program evaluation: Methods and case studies* (3rd ed.). Englewood Cliffs, NJ: Prentice Hall.

Posavac, E. J., & Sinacore, J. M. (1984). Reporting effect size in order to improve the understanding of statistical significance. *Knowledge: Creation, Diffusion, Utilization, 5,* 503–508.

Rimland, B. (1979). Death knell for psychotherapy? *American Psychologist, 34,* 192.

Rook, K. S. (1987). Effects of case history versus abstract information on health attitudes and behavior. *Journal of Applied Social Psychology, 17,* 533–553.

Rosenthal, R. (1990). How are we doing in soft psychology? *American Psychologist, 45,* 775–777.

Schein, E. H. (1990). Organizational culture. *American Psychologist, 45,* 109–119.

Sedlmeier, P., & Gigerenzer, G. (1989). Do studies of statistical power have an effect on the power of studies? *Psychological Bulletin, 105,* 309–316.

Sherif, M., & Hovland, C. I. (1961). *Social judgment.* New Haven, CT: Yale University Press.

Sykes, C. J. (1988). *Profscam: Professors and the demise of higher education.* New York: Regnery Gateway.

The trouble with dependent variables. (1990, Spring). *Dialogue: Society for Personality and Social Psychology,* p. 9.

Tufte, E. R. (1983). *The visual display of quantitative information.* Cheshire, CT: Graphics Press.

Verdier, J. M. (1984). Advising congressional decision-makers. In D. S. Cordray & Mark W. Lipsey (Eds.), *Evaluation studies review annual* (Vol. 11, pp. 235–252). Newbury Park, CA: Sage.

Wood, G. (1978). The knew-it-all-along effect. *Journal of Experimental Psychology: Human Perception and Performance, 4,* 345–353.

Zaltman, G., & Moorman, C. (1988, October/November). The importance of personal trust in the use of research. *Journal of Advertising Research,* pp. 16–24.

Index

Qualitative data, 203–205
Quasi-experiments, meta-analysis of, 65–81
  bias estimation, 72–76, 79
  in randomized experiments, 74–76, 79
  coder reliability, 77–78
  coronary artery bypass effectiveness study,
    67–69, 72, 75–77
  effect size, 65–66
    insufficient statistical information for, 70–
      71
  pretest adjustment, 72–74
  of randomized studies, 76
  generalizability, 76–77
  inclusion/exclusion criteria, 67–71
    construct validity, 69
    external validity, 69–70, 76–77
    internal validity, 70
    statistical conclusion validity, 70–71
    validity, 68–69
  limitations, 66, 79–80
  in nonrandomized studies, 67–68
  in randomized studies, 66, 74–76, 79
  replicability, 66, 76–78
Questionnaires, on-line administration of, 242,
    243
  for sensitive data collection, 246–247

Random assignment, in community-based re-
    search, 52–53
Randomized experiment
  deception in, 53
  implementation problems, 7
Random sample survey, voluntary participation
    in, 251–252
Reactivity, 93
Recall error, 90–92
Recency effect, 99
Record-keeping system, for secondary data
    analysis, 8–9
Regression analysis, reporting results of, 289
Report(s)
  format, 278
  oral, 288
  written, 286
    executive summary, 14, 288
    versus face-to-face presentation, 272
Report plan, 280
Research and development, human services
    model of, 26
Research and Training Center on Independent
    Living, University of Kansas, 33–34

Research assistants
  drug abusers as, 57, 58
  skills of, 16
  teachers as, 209–212, 213–215
Research design. *See also* specific types of re-
    search designs
  valid, 45, 60
Researchers
  bias of, 201–202
  competence of, 45, 60–61
  ethic background of, 30
  participation in social change, 202. *See also*
    Qualitative activist research
Research staff. *See* Personnel
Resource planning, for applied social research
  data analysis, 8–9, 13
  data collection, 2–8, 13
    authorization for, 3–5
    logistics of, 7
    participants' recruitment, 5–7
    process of, 5–8
    research site selection, 2–3
  financial resources (budget), 19–23
    budget reduction methods, 22
    overhead costs, 21–22
    personnel, 19, 21
    special costs, 21
    travel costs, 21
  personnel, 1, 15–19
    budget, 19, 21
    Gantt chart for, 18–19
    person-loading table for, 16–18
    skills budget, 15–16
  project implementation monitoring, 23
  time factors, 1, 9–15
    calendar time, 9–11, 18–19
    clock time, 9, 10, 11
    Gantt chart of, 18–19
    tasks and, 11–15
    time budget, 10–12
    trade-offs in, 22–23
Respect for persons, as research value, 45, 60
Risk-benefit assessment, in ethical research,
    45, 61

Salary, of research staff, 19, 21
Sample size, adequacy of, 5–7
Sampling procedure, generalizability and, 12–
    13
San Francisco General Hospital, Substance
    Abuse Services, 50, 51, 53

ACT 7856